THE CONUNDRUM OF CLASS

The Conundrum of Class

PUBLIC DISCOURSE ON THE SOCIAL ORDER IN AMERICA

Martin J. Burke

THE UNIVERSITY OF CHICAGO PRESS
CHICAGO AND LONDON

Martin J. Burke is currently lecturing in American history at University College, Galway.

The University of Chicago Press, Chicago 60637
The University of Chicago Press, Ltd., London

Printed in the United States of America
04 03 02 01 00 99 98 97 96 95 1 2 3 4 5

ISBN: 0-226-08080-3 (cloth)
0-226-08081-1 (paper)

Library of Congress Cataloging-in-Publication Data

Burke, Martin J.
The conundrum of class : public discourse on the social order in America / Martin J. Burke.
p. cm.
Includes bibliographical references (p. –) and index.
1. Discourse analysis—Social aspects—United States—History—19th century. 2. Discourse analysis—Political aspects—United States—History—19th century. 3. Social classes—United States. 4. United States—Social conditions. I. Title.
P302.84.B87 1995
306.4′4—dc20 95-7081
CIP

∞ The paper used in this publication meets the minimum requirements of the American National Standard for Information Sciences—Permanence of Paper for Printed Library Materials, ANSI Z39.48-1984.

CONTENTS

ACKNOWLEDGMENTS

Research for this project was funded in part by the Rackham Graduate School, the Program in American Culture, and the Department of History, all of the University of Michigan. Additional time and resources were made available by the Mellon Post-Doctoral Lectureship Program and the Social Science Collegiate Division at the University of Chicago. For their generous assistance my thanks are due to the staffs of several libraries: the Hatcher Graduate Library of the University of Michigan, especially the divisions of Special Collections and Microforms; the New York Public Library; the Biblioteca Nazionale Centrale of Florence; and the Regenstein Library of the University of Chicago.

This book began as a dissertation in American Studies at Michigan. Helpful advice and assistance were offered by Gene Berkhofer, David Hollinger, John Owen King, Leo McNamara, J. Mills Thornton, James Turner, Martin Pernick, and Maris Vinovskis. My largest intellectual debt is to my advisor, Robert F. Berkhofer. During a Mellon appointment in the College of the University of Chicago, helpful commentaries and critiques came from Ted Cook, Kathleen Conzen, Margot Finn, Jim Grossman, Linda Kerber, Ralph Lerner, John MacAloon, Daniel Wolk, and the late Roger Weiss. John Boyer, Ralph Nicholas, and Diane New provided an intellectually stimulating and supportive environment for research and writing. In revising and preparing this study for publication I have been greatly aided by critical readings from Burton Bledstein and Kenneth Cmiel. Doug Mitchell of the University of Chicago Press has been an encouraging editor and guide. My greatest thanks go to Ann Moyer for her steadfast personal and professional support.

INTRODUCTION

When in 1883 William Graham Sumner, the professor of political and social science at Yale College, wished to explain to his fellow citizens "What Social Classes Owe to Each Other," he had to address an apparent paradox in the contemporary discussions of that issue. "It is commonly asserted," he observed, "that there are in the United States no classes, and any allusion to classes is resented." Yet he also noted that such terms as 'the poor' and 'the laborers' were regularly used in ways that suggested that their definitions were both "exact" and "well-understood." The existence of social classes was very often "assumed as a simple fact," especially in discussions of the alleged misfortunes of certain groups. Sumner thus found in a great deal of "public speaking and writing" on political and societal matters an "elementary contradiction": that there were classes and that there were not classes. It was a contradiction that heretofore had produced "confusion" and "absurdity," and no doubt would do so again.[1]

Were there classes in the United States? If, as Sumner argued, there were privileged groups that could make claims on the labor and "self-denial" of others, and corresponding groups that were liable to such claims, then there were classes—"classes of the oldest and most vicious type." American arrangements, as Sumner understood them, did not meet these conditions, and the political order's trajectory was away from the "old vices of class government." Political equality had, so far, precluded the formation of political classes. Should the plans for economic equality of the self-professed friends of the "working classes" be realized, however, legal demands and obligations would be placed on other men. The irony of reform was that in the name of abolishing all classes it would foster a most "vicious" classification.

"We cannot say that there are no classes when we speak politically," he maintained, "and then say that there are classes when we are telling A what is his duty to do for B."[2]

Much of the misunderstanding in this public language of classification was caused by the conflation of 'classes' as a term for both political and socioeconomic entities. While in this first sense 'classes' was not appropriate for describing the American situation, in the second sense Sumner felt that it was. Within the "industrial organization of society" he recognized such occupational/source-of-income classes as capitalists, landlords, merchants, professional men, farmers, and—with careful qualification—laborers. This latter class, in particular, had been the subject of "ambiguous definitions"; and with the term 'laborer' he wished to designate only those individuals who now possessed neither capital nor land. But given the openness and opportunity of American society, he would not accept the identification of this class as a "proletariat." 'Labor', like such designations as 'working class' and 'poor man', was an "elastic" term—one "under which any number of social fallacies may be hidden." Sumner did not doubt the utility of many of the class distinctions made in both "loosely popular" and "strictly technical" language, as long as those distinctions were made with respect to the actual efforts and activities of men and women, and as long as the terms did not transmit dubious moral or political messages. A classification of society based on the division of labor did correspond to the American context. Hence, there were not in the United States (legally mandated) classes, but there were (economically generated) classes. What troubled Sumner was not the presence of 'class' in the public lexicon, but its particular political encoding.[3]

This argument recapitulates one of the most extensively disseminated, most consistently asserted, and most tenacious of the nineteenth-century American traditions for explaining the divisions of society. And if (legally mandated) 'classes' are replaced with the term 'orders' or its synonyms, that tradition can be found in the late eighteenth century as well. As Sumner recognized, practices of classification were deeply embedded in the formal and ordinary discourse of and on politics, society, and the economy. What Americans disagreed about was the suitability of certain classifications, the implicit and explicit analyses that these terms entailed, and the consequences of classification. The societal contrasts made by many Americans from the 1780s through the 1880s—and beyond—were between "artificial" schemes of classification and "natural" ones. Or to use the more pointed juxtaposition made by Sumner's contemporary the Reverend Samuel Johnson, between "republican" and "anti-republican" usages of 'class'.[4]

The following study is a history of these conceptions of and contestations over class in American public discourse from the late eighteenth through the late nineteenth century; it focuses on a number of the ways that Americans have represented and interpreted the organization and the operation of society. It first considers the eighteenth-century transition from a "socioconstitutional" language of 'orders' to a "socioeconomic" language of 'classes'. It then examines the elaboration during the nineteenth century of models of class cooperation (of a "harmony of interests") and of class antagonism (of "a war between capital and labor"). Each of these models retained its rhetorical popularity and its explanatory power during that century, albeit among different groups. In American public discourse the proper usage of concepts of class was a problem admitting of no satisfactory solution: it was a conundrum.

While this history is concerned with representations of, theses about, and prognoses for classes in the late eighteenth and the nineteenth centuries, the conundrum of class has figured in the public discourse of twentieth-century Americans as well.[5] The discovery—or rediscovery—and the denial of class distinctions and class conflict have been recurring features in the speeches of politicians, writings of social commentators, rhetoric of radicals and reformers, and scholarship in the social sciences and humanities. Within the realm of professional historiography, a conflictual model of American class relations was central to the research program of the Progressive historians through the first half of this century. After the demise of that school, it was the advocates of a "new" social interpretation of American history who argued that 'class'—as a category, a causal agent, or both—should play a key, perhaps the central, role in the analysis of the past. Yet while there has been in the last two decades a rather high level of agreement on the importance of class, there has been little agreement on such issues as how classes are to be defined, what is or has been the nature of their respective relationships, and how precisely such an abstraction as 'class' can be used to explain the economic, social, cultural, or political behavior of Americans.[6] In spite of assertions that a proper understanding of class can be of great value, there has been, in effect, little accord on its proper application in historical research. Even proponents of a neo-Progressive interpretation of American history continue to disagree over its relative salience in their analytic triumvirate of race, class, and gender, or in their master narrative of oppression, resistance, and emancipation.[7]

Much of this methodological disagreement among historians can be traced to the employment of a number of conceptions of class drawn both from ordinary discourse and from the work of sociologists and social theorists. In depicting American society at various stages of development, scholars have relied on a number of classificatory schemes: tripartite divisions of upper, middle, and lower or working classes; a variety of Marxian approaches to class structure and relations; William Lloyd Warner's five-class model of upper, upper-middle, lower-middle, upper-lower, and lower classes; the neo-Weberian divisions of class, status, and power; the familiar distinctions between blue-collar and white-collar workers; and so forth. And depending upon the model chosen, the resulting studies may vary widely in their findings and present contradictory interpretations of similar phenomena. Although class has promised to be a useful analytic device, its usage by professional students of the American past has remained problematic.[8]

While it is tempting to announce herein that during the course of researching and writing this work I arrived at the solution to this problem—that is to say, that I established through analysis and critique a model of class that was most appropriate for a historical understanding of American society and politics—this is a temptation to which I will not fall prey. Instead I will suggest that the difficulties involved in historians' employments of class do not derive solely from their misunderstandings or misapplications, but are indicative of larger problems that have been characteristic of uses of conceptions of class since the eighteenth century. Class has been a mobile and unstable social category.[9]

'Class' can be considered one of the cluster of concepts that such philosophers as William Gallie and Alasdair MacIntyre have described as "essentially contested," or that such political theorists as Michael Shapiro and Terrence Ball have identified as "contestable."[10] Contested concepts can be found in both ordinary and technical language, have been open to a number of divergent interpretations, and have been at the center of continued controversy. Nor are these merely semantic disagreements; they are involved in substantive political matters as well.[11] Concepts such as 'justice', 'freedom', 'democracy', and 'power' have been employed in a range of public debates. Their uses have provoked chronic disputes—logical, rhetorical, and ideological—in the arenas of public discourse.[12] These are constitutive concepts that have helped to give shape to the culturally and the politically possible in civil societies.[13] When class is so considered, the disagreements found in the contemporary scholarly discourse—and by extension in the discourses of previous eras—are to be expected, rather than explained away as instances of Americans' methodological or political naïveté. These are matters for historical analysis, not for cultural apologetics.[14]

Rather than offering an answer to the possibly unanswerable question of what is the correct concept of class with which to interpret the American past, this study examines how Americans have conceptualized and contested it. The interpretive positions that I have taken in the course of this study are historicist and contextualist.[15] Instead of positing a fixed conception of class and then seeing to what degree it was approached or apprehended, I have preferred to let the actors define classes and describe class relations as they may, no matter how contradictory or confused these definitions and descriptions might at times seem to be.[16] When did Americans begin to describe their society in terms of class? Where and how did these terms come into regular use? Of what classes did Americans speak or write? What were the articulated or the assumed relations between these classes? What were the institutional and ideological contexts of such practices? What were the consequences of such arguments over or agreements about classifications in the arenas of public discourse?[17] If classes and other social and political entities are partially constituted through language, we should ask who is doing the constituting and to what ends are they so doing.[18]

'Public discourse' as employed in this research is a term adopted from students of political rhetoric, social theory, and sociolinguistics. In contradistinction to other uses of 'discourse', its use here assumes that it refers to collections of real individuals in the social world, or worlds, external to the particular text. It is discourse about something other than discourse, and the classes considered are more than the effects or events of discursive practices.[19] Those actively engaged in the production and dissemination of this public discourse were, in general, educated and literate Americans who had both the opportunity and the cultural power to speak and write on economic, political, and social questions, and who were engaged in debating a wide range of issues, from the merits of independence to the significance of the great railway strike of 1877. Included in this grouping are politicians, ministers, professors of moral philosophy and political economy, editors of and contributors to nationally circulated periodicals, and social critics active in labor and other reform movements. Though they were usually not involved in formal inquiries on class and class relations, in the process of shaping their respective arguments they had of necessity to make generalizations about and descriptions of society, and to divide their various representations of that entity into its component parts. In short, they both classified and questioned other classifications.[20] Hence it is from their writings and speeches on classes as the subjects and objects of action and analysis that the terms of public discourse on social taxonomies (which classes constituted society and by what principles they were organized) and on social relations (how the classes interacted and how they should interact) can be reconstructed.[21]

The writers and speakers concentrated on here were not, of course, chosen at random but were members of specific communities of discourse within which the languages of class were articulated and class boundaries were contested. Wherever there was extensive public debate carried on over classifications and class relations, for example, the arguments from the late 1820s onward over who was or was not a member of the 'working class', I have tried to ensure that the disputants used as exemplars were cognizant not only of their opponents, but of the opposing rhetorical and intellectual tradition(s) as well; the connections posited in this research are both interpersonal and intertextual.

In the process of gathering sources for this study, I carried out an extensive survey of a number of genres: political tracts and pamphlets, printed speeches and addresses, books and treatises, and essays and articles in newspapers and periodicals directed at a large number of readerships. These texts, by and large, were designed to address popular audiences, and as such can be considered the political primers and lexicons of American public discourse. They were produced within a variety of institutional contexts and circulated within a variety of locales; they are indicative of the many voices engaged in and viewpoints expressed in the American languages of class. For the eighteenth century over one hundred pamphlets, tracts, and other publications drawn from Charles Evans's *Early American Imprints* were consulted in original editions or in microform, along with dozens of items from edited compilations such as those of Jonathan Elliot, Paul

Ford, Bernard Bailyn, Herbert J. Storing, John Kaminski, Charles S. Hyneman, and Ellis Sandoz. The Evans selections were taken from the political science, political economy, and social science headings in the subject index. In addition I examined the full runs of thirteen magazines and periodicals drawn from the annotated bibliography in Jean Hoornstra's and Trudy Heath's guide *American Periodicals: 1741–1900.* Both the journals chosen and the selections read featured political, social, or economic analysis and commentary. Hoornstra and Heath was again the chief source for the forty-six nineteenth-century periodicals of which I examined the full runs with the abovementioned criteria. I read eleven other periodicals selectively, with the articles and essays drawn from *Poole's Index.* As to the pamphlets, speeches, books, treatises, dictionaries, debates, and government hearings from the nineteenth century, over 250 sources and collections were consulted, once again on subjects of politics, political economy, social science, and reform. The bibliography lists all the materials consulted for this study.[22]

What the relationships were between these various printed sources and the wider patterns of language use in the eighteenth and nineteenth centuries, or between class as herein examined and as conceived of and spoken or written about by the broader populace, is an open question. These connections have been investigated in the twentieth century by sociologists, social psychologists, and sociolinguists who have carried on their work by means of survey research, interviews, and participant observation. Since these means are not available for the eighteenth and nineteenth centuries, such questions can be explored by historians through the study of the opinions, beliefs, and understandings of various groups over time. In general the participants in the discourses examined herein presumed the presence of wide reading and listening publics, and carried on their debates in ordinary, not technical, language. They assumed that the conventions about which they disagreed were widely used, and that their attempts at sanctioning certain classifying practices would be effective. Often they referred to the common usage of the time; those instances where differences between ordinary and technical senses of 'class' were raised are included in either the body of the text or in the notes.[23] While the scope of this study precluded the examination of every extant eighteenth- and nineteenth-century record in which the signifier 'class' might be located, I chose sources in which socioeconomic classes were regularly and publicly written and spoken of, and in which questions of class relations were open to sustained, if not always systematic, analysis.[24] The results of this research are, I believe, applicable to the conventions to be found in both larger and more particular sites and sources from the years under consideration.[25]

The general methods used in this study are those of a cultural and intellectual history informed by scholarship in a number of disciplines concerned with the relations between the word and the world. Developments in such fields as Anglo-American philosophy of language and Continental hermeneutics, discourse analysis, sociolinguistics, and the wider fields of interpretive sociology and political science, have contributed to an approach to historical analysis sometimes referred to as the "linguistic turn." Each of these disciplines has focused on the power of language in actively constituting rather than simply reflecting social and political realities.[26]

More specifically, this study employs methods drawn from a number of ongoing projects in the history of social and political thought. One is the "critical conceptual history" proposed by Terrence Ball and Melvin Richter. They emphasize the constitutive and constraining aspects of economic, social, and political discourse. I approach the concepts articulated in the language of American politics and society as contested rather than fixed, and recognize the asymmetries of power involved in actors' uses of language.[27]

Critical conceptual history in turn has been built upon the practice of *Begriffsgeschichte*—the history of concepts—as advocated by Reinhart Koselleck. The present study also follows several of Koselleck's recommendations. It assumes that correlating semantic changes with other social, political, and economic developments is a necessary part of historical analysis, yet the assignment of ultimate cause is not a simple matter. It recognizes that the investigation of changes in semantic meaning requires the examination of a broad sample of formal texts and other sources over extended periods of time. The concepts located in these sources are more than simple reflections of other, more basic transformations. These concepts both registered historical change and gave shape to its outcomes.[28]

Finally, this research follows lines suggested by J. G. A. Pocock, Anthony Pagden, and Quentin Skinner for the historical analysis of political language and thought. Members of this "Cambridge School" have argued that the reconstruction of the conventions and the consequences of social and political ideologies requires systematic attention to the works of both major and minor writers. Like them, I focus on specific texts with intending authors and intended audiences, rather than states of consciousness or *mentalités*. Although the research programs of Ball, Koselleck, Pocock, and Pagden vary in their emphases on the relations between the speaker/writer and the language, none of them suppresses the former's communicative agency or denies the delimiting power of cultural and political traditions. Language and other social phenomena are approached as interdependent, interpenetrating systems.[29]

Thus to study the speech acts of articulate Americans from the eighteenth and nineteenth centuries is not to work in a disembodied realm of ideas, unit or otherwise, which then must be correlated to an ultimately determining reality.[30] Rather, it is to study the categories and contexts through which they understood—or misunderstood—and constructed their societies: the social classifications and social practices embodied in their language. In granting primacy in this study to actors' conceptions of class, I do not wish to reduce complex social processes and political events to the actors' versions of them. Neither do I assume that any group, be they eighteenth-century moral philosophers or nineteenth-century workingmen's advocates, had a privileged understanding of social reality. Nor do I wish to imply that these particular printed sources were the only sites of and for the inscription of social or economic difference. But I do want to suggest that the analysis of this public discourse can enhance our historical understanding of the complex and contested heritage of American political culture regarding questions of classification and class relations.[31]

ONE

The Social Taxonomies of Revolutionary America

The series of confrontations between Great Britain and its North American colonies in the years 1765 to 1783, from the Stamp Act crisis to the Treaty of Paris, generated a large volume of controversial literature. In scores of essays, sermons, and pamphlets, Americans argued over the merits of nonimportation; the relations among the crown, the colonies, and Parliament; and the possibilities of establishing republican governments.[1] These "handbills, newspapers, party pamphlets" were in the judgment of Jonathan Boucher of Virginia "the shallow and turbid sources from which they derive their notions of government"—with 'they' in this case referring to the majority of men unable or unwilling to deduce the proper laws of politics.[2] Despite the Reverend Boucher's Loyalist disdain for these texts, their readers, and their writers, such sources do provide a record of the language used to describe the composition of society and to express opinions on political and social matters. That is to say, these texts contain the social taxonomies familiar to the disputants and the audiences of revolutionary America.[3]

To designate certain topics as "political" and others as "social" or "economic" is to treat these texts in a somewhat anachronistic manner. Through much of the eighteenth century Anglo-Americans made no clear or consistent distinctions between such fields. While the "economic" was emerging by midcentury as a mode of inquiry that sought to explain the workings of "commercial" society, the "social" was not to gain full autonomy until the late nineteenth century. In colonial America, social matters were often subsumed within the discourse of politics; prosperity or misery could depend upon the proper organization and operation of the state. The controversial literature of the revolutionary era, then, with its arguments about and analyses of civil society, examined questions with political, social, and economic dimensions and implications.[4]

The language—or languages—of this eighteenth-century controversial literature was shared on both sides of the Atlantic.[5] As a political language it drew its imagery and metaphors from a variety of traditional and contemporary sources: the Hebrew and Christian scriptures; treatises by Aristotle, Livy, and other classical commentators and historians; the Renaissance political theories of Guicciardini and Machiavelli; the natural law treatises of Hugo Grotius and Samuel von Pufendorf; John Locke and the "commonwealth" tradition of James Harrington, Thomas Gordon, and John Trenchard; and the nascent sciences of man of Montesquieu and the contributors to the *Encyclopédie,* and their Scottish counterparts Francis Hutcheson and David Hume.[6] Although it provided the bases for a common lexicon and grammar, this language was by no means monolithic. Nor were its speakers and writers always bound by fixed conceptual or definitional standards. Eighteenth-century Anglo-Americans were both conservative and creative when waging their rhetorical battles.[7]

As was the case for the better part of that century, the terminology employed when referring to the divisions of society was one of 'ranks', 'sorts', and 'orders'. 'Class', though not as often used, could be substituted for any of them. Typical in this tendency was John Dickinson, who, in attacking the inequities of the Townsend Acts, asked, "How will our merchants and the lower ranks of people, on which the force of the regulations will first fall, and with the greatest violence, bear this additional load? . . . These last are to be considered in a very different light from the same class in Great Britain." The Townsend duties were not the only matter that displeased this Philadelphia gentleman. He complained as well that in America "the lower ranks of people are frequently engaged in lawsuits" because of their habit of making written contracts, a luxury not available to their equivalent "class" in Great Britain.[8] Whatever the merits of Dickinson's economic and political arguments, his choice of words was more than an example of a stage in the evolution from a premodern lexicon of 'ranks' to a modern one of 'class'.[9] Dickinson and his contemporaries wrote in a language in which 'class' and 'rank' were still synonymous, not mutually exclusive, categories. Theirs was a language of politics with a range of terms that could be drawn upon to identify the members of civil society.[10]

Despite the variety of conventions applied and the wealth of authorities appealed to in this political language, the number of patterns used in their conceptual divisions of society was quite small. Two distinct taxonomies, organized on different principles, can be abstracted from these Anglo-American sources. I will refer to one as a 'socioconstitutional' taxonomy, the other as 'socioeconomic'. Together the semantic fields of these taxonomies include the common terms for representing and understanding the organization and operation of society.[11]

Of the two the socioconstitutional taxonomy was the most regularly used in the political language of North Americans, as it had been in the language of Englishmen for hundreds of years. Within its bounds the polity served as the root metaphor for society, as if social organization mirrored the constitution of the state.[12] "In the constitution of England, the three principal forces of government, monarchy, aristocracy, and democracy, are blended together in certain proportions; but each of these orders, in the exercise of legislative authority, hath its particular department from which the others are excluded."[13] Although these remarks of Daniel Dulany, Jr., of Maryland were addressed specifically to the questions of representation for and taxation of the colonies, his Whiggish and Aristotelian sketch of the composition of government was a commonplace in colonial political discourse, as was its extension to the social world. Just as the realm had its identifiable "orders," so too did society. In considering the effects of the 1774 closure of the port of Boston, Charles Chauncy was convinced that Parliament intended to force Americans to submit to its "sovereign pleasure." This notion, Chauncy argued, was "the universal sentiment of all ranks, orders, and conditions of men from one end of the continent to the other." For Chauncy, Dulany, and their contemporaries, such imagery remained conventional throughout the revolutionary period as America continued to be spoken and written of as a society of "orders."[14]

The semantic field of this socioconstitutional schema included 'order', 'rank', 'degree', 'station', and 'estate'. When referring to specific groups, the first four terms were often modified by adjectives that denoted relative positions on a vertical axis. There were 'upper', 'middle', and 'lower' orders of mankind; there were persons of 'elevated rank' or in the 'lower ranks' and there were those in a 'more exalted station' in life. Since the locations of England's 'estates'—royalty, nobility, commonality—were self-evident, they usually required no spatial modifiers.[15] And while the first and second estates had not been established in colonial society, this imagery remained in extensive, and uncontroversial, use. Concern for a precise correlation between social lexicons and social institutions appears to be more of a problem for twentieth-century scholarship than for eighteenth-century practice.[16]

Parallel to these axes, with terms synonymous for 'order', 'rank', and 'station' were terms that made explicit connections between social position and prestige. On these scales of status—to use the modern, sociological concept—men were grouped among the 'highborn' and 'lowborn' or were identified with the 'better', 'middling', and 'meaner sorts'. This last cluster of 'sorts' was widely used in the languages both of political debate and of everyday life.[17]

A third cluster of terms in this field centered on 'class'. In its general sense of group, or coupled with modifiers of space or status—'upper', 'better', 'middling', 'lower'—'class' could serve in place of 'order', 'sort', and so on in renderings of society along socioconstitutional lines. Richard Price, a prominent English supporter of the colonial Whig cause, compared the "communities forming an empire and the particular bodies or classes of men forming different parts of a kingdom" in his pamphlet of 1776, *Observations on the Nature of Civil Liberty*.[18] In his analysis the former had no necessarily reciprocal interests, while "the different classes of men within a kingdom are all placed on the same ground. Their concerns and interests are the same; and what is done to one part must affect all." Here Price's choice of 'class' in lieu of 'order' and his use of mutual dependency and reciprocity, the ideal state of social relations posited in traditional socioconstitutional schemes, does not necessarily indicate a newly emergent social sensibility. It is, rather, an instance of the substitution of readily exchangeable categories; it is a case of synonymity.[19]

The changes of meaning that resulted in this equivalence of 'class', 'rank', and 'order' were part of the transformation of the vocabulary of early modern English, one that historians such as Penelope Corfield, Keith Wrightson, and Steven Wallech have correlated with the larger transformation of English politics and society from the sixteenth through the eighteenth century.[20] Although the details of these sociopolitical and sociolinguistic shifts are beyond the boundaries of this study, an examination of English dictionaries and lexicons of that period suggests, at the least, those patterns of language use that were in the process of legitimation and routinization. As such these texts are useful for indications of changes in the terms of public discourse, albeit indications sometimes made after the fact.[21]

In the public languages of educated sixteenth-century Englishmen—Latin, French, and English—the word 'classis' had moved away from an original sociopolitical meaning that derived from Servius Tullius's division of Rome's population into six "classes." These were based on wealth and military service; and hence 'classis' became a common term in Latin for the "orders" of society.[22] Thomas Elyot, in his Latin-to-English dictionary of 1538, defined 'classis' as a "name of shyppes," and then as "companyes or sortes of people, ordered in a citie after the value of their substaunce," and as "degrees or formes in scholes." 'Ordo' was translated as "order, the dewe place, the astate of men."[23] Elyot's was the first Latin/English dictionary compiled according to humanist philological principles. Its sources were in classical, not medieval, Latin; and there 'classis' did have naval and educational meanings, as well as social ones. In Thomas Cooper's *Thesaurus Linguae Romanae & Britannicae* of 1565 the first rendering of 'classis' is also "a navie of shipps: a shippe," and all the examples given relate to nautical matters. His second definition for 'classis' is "an order of fourmes or seates, where men sette according to their degrees. Sometimes a companie of those men." For 'ordo' his translation is "a state or order, a degree." But for Cooper 'ordo' did not equal 'classis'.[24]

Something akin to the original Latin sense of the term appeared in 1583, in Sir Thomas Smith's *De Republica Anglorum.* In the course of his descriptions of the "divisions of the parts and persons of the Common Wealth," he referred to all those who had no "voice or authorite" in that body as the "fourth sorte or class amongest us . . . which the old Romans called capite centii proletarii operae." Smith included in this class day laborers, artificers, and merchants and farmers without free lands; these "proletarii" were placed below the burgesses and yeomen in the scale of estimation and "preheminence." Although the criteria distinguishing the "foure sortes" included wealth, what was important to Smith was wealth in land as it related to political power; his fourth sort of men were those "who do not rule."[25]

Smith's return to a social, specifically a socioconstitutional, use of 'class' or 'classe' was in keeping with the practice of other English and French writers in the late sixteenth and early seventeenth centuries, but this practice was not acknowledged by all those who compiled the period's dictionaries. While John Florio's *Worlde of Words* of 1598 defined 'classe' as "a degree or form in a school, a companie. Also a navie or a fleete at sea," neither John Bullokar's *English Expositor* nor Henry Cockeram's *English Dictionarie* had entries for 'classe'.[26] An equivalence between 'classe', 'order', and 'rank' was codified in 1611 by Randle Cotgrave, however. His *Dictionaire of the French and English Tongues* described 'classe' as "a ranke, order, or distribution of people according to their severall degrees" and also notes that "in schooles (wherein the word is most used) a forme, or lecture restrained unto a certain companie of schollers, or auditors."[27]

'Classe' retained these senses—primarily educational or nautical, and only secondarily sociopolitical—in the public discourse of seventeenth- and early-eighteenth-century England. In the *Glossographia* of 1656, Thomas Blount first provided the standard interpretations, and then followed Cotgrave by noting that it is in schools where "the word is most used."[28] John Kersey's 1708 *Dictionarium Anglo-Britannicum* has for its entry "class or classis . . . a form in school; also a rank or order." In Kersey's dictionary the word appeared without a final *e*.[29] Evidence for the further extension of the semantic field of class can be found in Nathan Bailey's *Dictionarium Britannicum,* published in 1736. Bailey retains, of course, the educational usage and then proceeds to a definition of 'class' as "an order or rank; also a distribution of persons and things according to their several degrees and natures."[30] This expansion was made legitimate by Samuel Johnson in *A Dictionary of the English Language* of 1765, the lexicon most familiar to the colonial controversialists. Dr. Johnson first defines the neuter singular noun 'class' as "a rank or order of persons"; he next gives the educational definitions; and he last describes 'class' as a "set of beings or things, a number arranged in distribution, under some common nomination." He gives as well a definition for the active verb 'to class': "to range according to some stated method of distribution; to range according to different ranks."[31]

It is from this third sense as an encompassing term for any grouping that 'class' derived the semantic power and the flexibility that made it popular in both the ordinary and learned discourses of the eighteenth century. Penelope Corfield has argued that by midcentury class was becoming a "stock term and concept" in Great Britain; and while extant colonial records of linguistic change are sparse when compared to imperial ones, there is little to suggest that Americans did not as easily adopt the term as did the English. For all the controversy that references to class would provoke in nineteenth- and twentieth-century public discourse, its gradual arrival and adoption in America were uneventful.[32]

In the realms of learned discourse, Enlightenment writers made use of this expanded sense of the term to class their world anew; classification was at the center of their project for a universal science of nature and of man.[33] Through their analyses of emerging patterns of human relations, the philosophes began to develop the models for and the vocabularies of that second social taxonomy to be found in the political language of revolutionary America, the taxonomy organized around socioeconomic meanings of 'class'.[34]

If the constitution of the state was the analog for social organization in that first taxonomy, here the functional division of economic life was the root metaphor; society now mirrored the division of labor. Men could be placed in "upper," "middling," and "lower" classes on vertical axes of wealth and prestige; or they could be arranged by occupations. The asymmetries of power and privilege that were implied but not always expressed in these latter groupings were obvious to citizens of a still-deferential society; some callings appeared to be naturally higher than others. As was the case within the socioconstitutional taxonomy, 'class' could still be exchanged for 'order', 'rank', and 'estate'. The most common among the newer synonyms was 'interest'. The difference in the two schemes is to be found less in their lexicons than in the newer one's reliance upon primarily economic criteria for social discrimination. Classes and interests in this sense were part of a social idiom that developed during the eighteenth century and would eventually supplant its predecessors. It was a new means of imposing conceptual forms on social and political activities.[35]

Writing in 1774, the New York Loyalist Thomas B. Chandler attacked the advocates of nonimportation, since such policies disproportionately affected "our sailors . . . our shipbuilders . . . their smiths, carmen . . . pilots and boatmen . . . our shopkeepers and merchants . . . Now all these classes of people, and many others which I have not enumerated, must have a support, and but a few of them will be able to support themselves." If the colonial Whigs continued along the path to rebellion, the consequences for society were horribly clear. Leading men would be executed, property would be forfeit, and "the most to be expected is that the lives of those belonging to the lower classes will be spared."[36] Such uses of socioeconomic class imagery were not limited to Tory tracts. In John Dickinson's celebrated *Letters from a Farmer in Pennsylvania,* he stated his occupation as a farmer, albeit one with a few servants, a library, and "a little money at interest," who has "acquired . . . a greater knowledge in history, and the laws and constitution of my country, than is generally maintained by men of my class." Dickinson's expertise obliged him to elucidate these matters for those lower on the social scale, "such of you, whose employments in life may have prevented you attending to the consideration of some points that are of great and public importance." While most of Dickinson's fellow citizens were farmers, clearly not all farmers were the same.[37]

Perhaps the clearest exposition of a socioeconomic taxonomy in the extant eighteenth-century colonial literature can be found in John Day's *Remarks on American Affairs* of 1774. Day, a merchant of Halifax and sometime resident of Philadelphia, wished to explain to his London readers the reasons for the present political disturbances in the colonies. For Day that turbulence was caused in part by the desire of some men to establish an actual socioconstitutional system, rather than a nominal one.[38]

Day began his text by acknowledging that since "in communities there are several orders or degrees of men, each influenced by its particular station, view, or prospects, I shall therefore class out and arrange the inhabitants of North America into their several orders." His first order was those "who possess the greatest share of property, unconnected with commerce." Day argued that it is this "class" that wished to abolish the popularly elected assemblies in the various colonies, and replace them with governments controlled by a new North American nobility. Such nobles as might be required would be drawn from among their number, and would form a proper social order. The next "order in point of consequence" was commercial men, followed by a third class, the "practitioners of the law, and other officers of the courts of judicature." To this secular colonial hierarchy he added "the reverend clergy, of every sect," who made up his "fourth class." Many of the colonies' political ills were attributable to "the above four classes, or orders of men," who "have views each for their own aggrandizement, which were, however, incompatible with peace, happiness, and consequence of the great community." These upper classes were not motivated in their political behavior by the civic virtue that Day expected of them, but were driven instead by self-interest.[39]

North America's "fifth class of men . . . are the yeomanry and peasantry." It was from "the better sort of this class" that "the members of assembly . . . are chiefly chose [*sic*]." They were the largest class and provided a necessary counterbalance to the political designs of their betters. The "last order" of men were "very inconsiderable in point of property, number, consequence, or virtue to the whole community." Here were grouped "sailors, porters, fishermen, and other appendages to the large commercial towns." The inhabitants of this class were politically dangerous since they, "without fear of consequence, are ready to commit any acts of desperation or madness which may present." They were, potentially if not actually, the members of the mob, and as such they deserved to be watched and to be feared.[40]

Day's pamphlet is suggestive of the eclectic patterns of social classification that had been coming into Anglo-American usage during the course of the century. Rather than the more familiar bipartite and tripartite divisions of later eras, his was a six-class model. Day arranged a presumably male population along a vertical axis of wealth, occupation, and civic reliability—from large landholders, merchants, and professionals to yeomen and unpropertied laborers—and assessed their relative size and political power. Within each group there were implied gradations between the "better sort" and the rest that corresponded to his larger criteria. And as he made these distinctions, he moved easily between the terms of 'orders', 'degrees', and 'classes'.[41]

If Day's elaboration of a six-class model was still a relative novelty in the political language of the 1770s, his evaluation of social relationships was more in keeping with well-established conventions. In Day's rendition—one in the republican tradition of the "country" Whigs—the "yeomanry and peasantry" occupied a contested middle ground between the pretensions of a would-be aristocracy and the mindless depredations of the mob. Political stability and civic virtue were to be found in this middle class. As long as their representatives retained political power, an otherwise precarious balance would be maintained. If the "classes" were to be drawn into conflict, it would be because of a disturbance of this balance, a disruption of the regular processes of government and of the normal patterns of social deference.

In this Anglo-American Whig understanding of political and social relations, the possibility of conflict among the 'ranks', 'orders', and 'classes' was certainly recognized, but the main impetus for such conflict would come not from the clash of diametrically opposed economic interests, but from the subversion of the political system. Placing those with the most property in the first class was not in itself a problem for Day; rather it was the obvious classification to choose. He was not troubled by their wealth as such, but by their political ambitions. Like the members of the lowest order, those in the uppermost class were not to be trusted.

Implicit in this form of social and political analysis was a tension between a natural social hierarchy of occupations and an artificial hierarchy of birth and patronage; it was a tension between the structures of subordination that were naturalized within the socioeconomic and socioconstitutional taxonomic schemes. While Day assumed the desirability of the former and warned against the consequences of the latter, his brief *Remarks* did not explore the degree to which conditions in the colonies corresponded to one or the other. As apparent as this tension was to many Americans during this period, it was not to become the subject of extended consideration until after 1783, when the outcomes of the Revolution made problematic the socioconstitutional imagery of 'orders'. In these changed circumstances this tension would surface in the course of debates over the proper organization of the new republic.

To the degree that John Day and his contemporaries joined this emergent lexicon with older Anglo-American assumptions about the inevitability of sociopolitical strife, they can be said to have had an understanding of classes in conflict. That understanding was not, however, predicated upon a hostility to existing socioeconomic arrangements; theirs was a late-eighteenth-century, not a late-nineteenth-century, sensibility. Nor did the employment of the term 'class' by merchants like Day or Thomas Chandler indicate a preference for a particular political persuasion; one was a Whig, the other a Loyalist. The presumption that the use of a political language of classes and conflict should signify a commitment to some variant of radical politics is an artifact of twentieth-century scholarship.[42]

The presence, then, of a socioeconomic taxonomy in the writings of Day, Dickinson, Chandler, and their contemporaries is an index of important changes in the lexical practices of Americans, but direct connections between these changes and the political or social events of the Revolution are rather difficult to establish. The emergence of 'class' in the language of eighteenth-century Anglo-Americans preceded the political crises of the 1760s and 1770s. The gradual adoption of new forms of analysis appears to be coterminous with, but not easily correlated to, the events of the Revolution.

It is easier to connect conceptual changes in the public discourse of these Anglo-Americans to the broader intellectual changes at work in the eighteenth century. While the sources from which Americans adopted the term 'class' were many, its power and its utility were most fully developed in the Enlightenment's sciences of man. The works of both the French Physiocrats and the Scottish moral scientists, with their efforts at discovering the natural laws and narrating the natural history of society, were familiar to members of the revolutionary generation; and these texts and treatises added imagery and methods of interpretation to American political debate.

Models of classes and class relations most clearly emerged as the subjects of sustained analysis and the objects of social knowledge in the context of eighteenth-century studies of politics and political economy.[43] For François Quesnay and his disciples and successors in the physiocratic school—Mirabeau, du Pont de Nemours, Turgot—an understanding of civil society depended upon the examination of the economy. With their writings on the natural cycles of production and exchange, the Physiocrats sought to provide the governors of France with scientifically established programs that would ensure national happiness and prosperity. The political economy of the Physiocrats was both a descriptive and a prescriptive science, and as such suggested new terms and policies to its Anglo-American readerships.[44]

Quesnay, in the *Tableau économique* of 1766, divided a hypothesized French society into three classes, with each distinguished by its role in the creation and distribution of the "net product," or disposable surplus. There was a "productive" class, engaged in tilling the soil, who alone produced this surplus; a "proprietary" class of royalty, clergy, and landowners who received most of the net product in the form of rents; and a "sterile" or "unproductive" class, composed of those engaged in manufactures or commerce, who received their share of the surplus from the expenditures of the other classes.[45] This unproductive class included both wage earners and entrepreneurs. In making these distinctions, Quesnay did not intend to question the social or political primacy of the proprietary class; he presumed their place in "natural," hierarchical order. Nor did he deny the necessity of the labor of the sterile class to the system as a whole. But he did deny their ability to "produce" a surplus greater than the combined cost of their upkeep and the materials of their trades.[46] Since only the land could yield the net product upon which the revenues of state depended, Quesnay urged that government policies be shifted away from bounties on exports and manufactures and toward the promotion of a vigorous commercial agriculture.[47]

Once the central role played by the productive class was acknowledged and encouraged by the state, Quesnay assumed that relations among the three classes would be harmonious. The proprietors were not exploiting the producers; they were merely receiving their due portion of the net product. Nor did the sterile class take unfair advantage of the producers' labor; theirs was an exchange of disposable income for desired service. These physiocratic classifications served as the grounds for a political economy of class cooperation that would ensure economic growth and social stability.[48]

Quesnay's evaluative categories were a departure both from the usual description of French society in terms of 'estates' and from conventional notions about the productive roles of merchants and craftsmen.[49] In the "Dialogue on the Work of Artisans" of 1766, Quesnay answered those who objected to the novelty of his classifications by insisting on their correspondence with actual conditions. A Monsieur H., an informed representative of his critics, found the term 'sterile' to be too encompassing, "I cannot visualize any general designation which would be strictly common to them all. . . . I find difficulty in accepting your division and names which you have applied to it."[50] Monsieur N., Quesnay's physiocratic persona, rejected such appeals to the "vague expressions used in ordinary language" and argued instead for the scientific basis of his scheme: "it is not for the natural order to conform to a language which expresses only confused and ambiguous ideas; it is for the expressions to conform to the exact understanding of the natural order, in distinctions which are rigorously regulated by reality." The position of Monsieur H. could be maintained, Monsieur N. replied, "only thanks to a vague and inexact language, in which the most different ideas are expressed in the same words."[51] His science of society would replace the confusions inherent in ordinary discourse with a reliable lexicon of precisely defined classes.

The political economy of Quesnay, then, claimed to discover the natural relations among men in civil society and to describe them within an empirically verifiable taxonomy.[52] Yet with his variations on the commonplace notions of 'productive' and 'sterile', Quesnay opened himself to refutation by his critics and modification by his successors. Despite the certainty with which Monsieur N. defined his classes, neither Quesnay nor the other Physiocrats were successful in establishing a social terminology free from challenge. Definitions of classes, from their very inception in this learned discourse, provoked debates about their moral and political implications—debates that would, in time, be carried on by citizens of the American republic.

A significant alteration of this tripartite class scheme was made by Anne-Robert-Jacques Turgot. Unhappy with the connotations of 'sterile', Turgot introduced a less pejorative term. He referred to them instead as the "stipendiary" class, since they "receive their stipends from the produce of the land."[53] Turgot also observed that among certain members of this class the process of accumulating capital had produced other significant distinctions. In *Reflections on the Formation and the Distribution of Riches* of 1770, he noted that "wants of society with the vast variety of industrial products finds itself, so to speak, subdivided into two orders: that of the undertakers, manufacturers, employers, all possessors of large capitals which they make profit by from setting men at work, by means of their advance; and the second order, which is composed of simple artisans who have no other property but their arms, who advance only their daily labour, and receive no profit but their wages."[54] Similar circumstances were transforming the productive class: "The class of cultivators divides itself, like that of the manufacturers, into two orders of men, that of the undertakers or capitalists who make all the advances, and that of the mere wage-earning workmen."[55]

In Turgot's analysis the differences that were developing between wage earners and capitalists were as analytically and politically important as those among the productive, the stipendiary, and the proprietary classes. As did Quesnay, he assumed that relations among these classes would be stable and harmonious, and that prudent action by the state would ensure the progress and well-being of all.[56] And in his adherence to the doctrine of the sole productivity of agriculture, Turgot remained within the physiocratic tradition. But with its introduction of the wage earner–entrepreneur distinction, and its attempt to remove the negative connotations attached to manufacturing and to commerce, Turgot's science of society moved closer to the ones being formulated in the environs of Edinburgh and Glasgow.[57]

As did their physiocratic colleagues, the moral philosophers and political economists of the Scottish Enlightenment—David Hume, Adam Ferguson, Sir James Steuart, and Adam Smith—emphasized the interdependence of social, economic, and political circumstances. In their studies of the progress of civil society—from hunting, to pastoral, to agricultural, to commercial—they considered first the "means of subsistence" and related these means to particular social and political arrangements. The point of departure for their analyses was not the individual in a presocial "state of nature," but men in their naturally social condition. To their American audiences, the Scots introduced a science of man with a fully articulated socioeconomic taxonomy with which to explain the workings of "commercial" society.[58]

The most renowned and often-cited of the Scottish moral philosophers was David Hume.[59] Although wary of the application of general categories, he did assume that the descriptions of social and economic activities in his "science of man" bore a strong resemblance to reality.[60] In the essay "On Commerce," one of the *Political Discourses* of 1752, Hume classified men as he considered the beneficial effects of the division of labor on the progress of civil society: "The bulk of every state may be divided into husbandmen and manufacturers. . . . As soon as men quit their savage state, where they live chiefly by hunting and fishing, they must fall into these two classes."[61] Over time, improvements in agriculture will allow the support of "superfluous hands" who, in a state concerned with the happiness of its subjects, will join the ranks of tradesmen and manufacturers engaged in the "arts of luxury"; or who, in a state dedicated to the aggrandizement of the sovereign's power, will be siphoned off to the "fleets and armies." Stable polities, Hume argued, should encourage economic growth, the diffusion of property, and the expansion of the "middling ranks." Commerce, for Hume, did not threaten political liberty but promoted it.[62]

Hume also considered the civilizing influences of the expansion of the manufacturing and commercial classes—or "interests"—in the essay "Of Interest." In the course of a historical survey he proceeded from the "infancy of society," where there was but a "landed interest," to the present "useful" division of labor among farmers, artisans, and merchants. Since the welfare of each of these classes depended on the prosperity of the others, Hume believed that their interests were identical. The causes of social conflict were not to be found in the "progress of opulence," but in the patterns of economic inequality and injustice that this progress would ameliorate. Commercial republics were not fated to repeat the histories of their classical predecessors.[63]

Hume's notion of 'useful' was not applicable to all classes, however.

It included only those who "beget industry": "Lawyers and physicians beget no industry; and it is even at the expense of others that they beget their riches; so that they are sure to diminish the possessions of some of their fellow citizens, as fast as they increase their own."[64] Hume was not suggesting that society do without physicians, although a decrease in the ranks of lawyers would cause little harm. But the presence of a criterion of socioeconomic utility is worthy of note. As it was to physiocracy, the issue of what classes did or did not "beget riches" was important to the program of Scottish political economy.[65] Hume's distinction between the productive classes may have differed from that of his French colleagues, but he shared their concern with the politics of class formation. "Natural" hierarchies, as envisioned by Hume, would be grounded in economic, not legal, differences. The social order of a commercial republic should be a continuum from large landowners, through useful professionals, merchants and manufacturers, farmers and artisans, to simple laborers.[66]

While Hume's prominence during his lifetime derived chiefly from the popularity of his *History of England* and the notoriety of his religious skepticism, his comparative historical methods provided directions for subsequent research conducted by his fellow Scots.[67] One of the best-known of these studies among Americans was Adam Ferguson's *Essay on the History of Civil Society*, first published in 1766.[68] Ferguson, the professor of moral philosophy and pneumatics at the University of Edinburgh, charted the progress of man from "savagery" through "barbarism" to "polished society." At every stage he remarked on "the multiplicity of forms" of societies and the "classes into which they distribute their members." In each of these cases Ferguson was interested in the sources of cohesion and dissension; and from these examinations he offered advice to contemporaries on how to deal with the competition and conflict that marked the emergence of "polished" society.[69]

Central to Ferguson's analysis was the matter of inequality, especially in property. As did Hume, Ferguson assumed that political orders were based on institutions of private property. To promote social and political stability in the course of economic growth, he suggested that the public be made aware of the necessity of certain kinds of inequality. Those in the lower classes should understand that "[i]t is a common observation, that mankind were originally equal. They have indeed by nature equal rights to their preservation, and to the use of their talents; but they are fitted for different stations; and when they are classed by a rule taken from this circumstance, they suffer no injustice on the side of their natural rights."[70] The "stations" of commercial societies in which men were "classed according to their abilities" were predicated upon differences in strength, intelligence, and ability. In these contexts an equality of rights did not preclude an inequality of fortunes.[71] Once all citizens came to understand how natural such forms of subordination were, they could enjoy the rewards of their labors under the protection of the law. Rather than challenging the existing order, they could challenge each other in the production of additional wealth.[72]

The study of history demonstrated to Ferguson that classifications based on the division of labor were in accord with the natural principles of societal development. Yet he was less sanguine than Hume about the political outcomes of economic progress. Instincts of conflict were fundamental to human nature, and he doubted that polished societies would be free from the problems of partisan strife. Nor did he agree with Hume that the interests of the various propertied classes were in accord.[73] The powers of luxury and corruption, if left to flourish, could do to modern states what they had done to the Greeks and the Romans.[74]

Ferguson sought solutions to the threat posed by the growth of commerce to the preservation of liberty in the experience of the classical city-states. While the institutions of antiquity could not and should not be revived, their spirits could be imitated.[75] To counter the decline of civic virtues, Ferguson prescribed a regimen of political activity for the citizenry. Participation in elections, admiration for the law, and service in the militia would promote a common political identity that could transcend tendencies toward faction. Although class subordination was inevitable in commercial republics, classical conflicts were not. Antagonisms between classes could be contained and private property protected within the framework of an active polity.[76]

How to coordinate the advance of commerce with the advantages of liberty was a key element in the political and moral essays of this Scottish "historical school." The first systematic treatise on political economy produced by one of its number was Sir James Steuart's *Inquiry into the Principles of Political Economy* of 1767. Steuart, like his friend David Hume, proceeded along historical and comparative lines as he examined the genesis and the happiness of commercial states. And as did Hume, he assumed that "[t]here is no governing a state in perfection, and consequently no executing the plan for a right distribution of the inhabitants, without exactly knowing their situation as to numbers, their employment, the gains upon every species of industry, the numbers produced from each class."[77] Precise and reliable knowledge of the socioeconomic class structure was a prerequisite for the "statesman"—Steuart's shorthand for the legislators and executives charged with the enhancement of wealth and security.[78] Scientific investigations such as his own would allow the "political economy of government" to be "brought to perfection" when "every class in general, and every individual in particular, is made to be adding and assisting to the community, in proportion to the assistance he receives from it. This conveys my idea of a free and perfect society."[79] For Steuart, comprehensive state participation in the economy would be the guarantor of social harmony.

Steuart made his primary class divisions in terms of property: between men in possession of a revenue—"those who do not labour"—and men who must earn a revenue—"those who do." The first class included landlords and entrepreneurs; the second, "lower" class was composed of husbandmen, manufacturers, and "free hands." He also referred to this latter grouping as "the working class" since "whoever does or gives anything for money, I consider as a worker." Steuart's use of this term was one of the earliest in eighteenth-century treatises on politics and economics. This was an expansive sense of the 'working class' which would become a matter of some controversy in the discourse of nineteenth-century American liberalism.[80]

Between these groups Steuart posited a condition of reciprocity, albeit one in which the "subordination of classes" was presumed to be a necessity: "The desires of the rich, and the means of gratifying them, make them call for the services of the poor; the necessities of the poor, make them cheerfully answer the summons; . . . This permutation between the two classes is what we call circulation."[81] If the statesman pursued enlightened polices with "a tender affection for the whole society, and an exact and impartial regard for the interests of every class," circulation would increase and the mutual dependence of the classes would be ensured; if not, there would be wasteful conflict between the classes over limited resources. Steuart's proposals for an integrated political economy included a system of cartels and licensed monopolies, public works, protection for domestic industries, a public debt, and state-controlled central banking. Although this extensive program for commercial expansion received only limited endorsement from his Scottish contemporaries, Steuart's *Principles of Political Economy* were to gain an American admirer in Alexander Hamilton.[82]

While Steuart's socioeconomic categories and his stress on stability were in keeping with those of the his fellow Scots, his advocacy of a substantial role for the state placed him at odds with that most influential member of the group, Adam Smith.[83] In *An Inquiry into the Nature and Causes of the Wealth of Nations,* first published in 1776, Smith, too, made the assumption that the relations among the classes, or "orders of men," should be cooperative. But for Smith, it was primarily the workings of the market—and only in a limited if critical way the participation of the state—that served as the means of social stability. Despite the daily conflict of interests in the marketplace, the establishment and maintenance of a "natural system of liberty" could ensure harmony among all the contending groups in a commercial society.[84]

Smith's criteria for his classification of these groups were similar to those of Quesnay. He divided society into its "constituent orders" on the basis of their part in the production and distribution of "the whole annual produce of the land and labour of every country." The annual product "naturally divides itself . . . into three parts: the rent of land, the wages of labour, and the profit of stock." From each of these came the form of revenue with which Smith made his distinctions among "those who live by rent," "those who live by wages," and "those who live by profit." Considered as a whole, these were "the three great, original, and constituent orders of every civilized society, from whose revenue that of every other order is ultimately derived."[85] These other "orders" arose as a result of the ongoing division of labor into the different "classes" of employment, which for Smith marked the progress of nations from simple hunter-gatherer to complex commercial societies. In keeping with the conventions of the period, Smith used 'order' and 'class' as synonyms, although 'orders' tends to refer to rather large groupings, as above, while 'classes' generally refers to particular occupations, trades, and livelihoods. He also used 'rank' as a synonym for 'order'.[86]

In evaluating the relative worth of the "three great orders" to the well-being of society, Smith assigned economic and political primacy to the proprietors of land: "The interest of the first of those three great orders . . . is strictly and inseparably connected with the general interest of the society. Whatever either promotes or obstructs the one, necessarily promotes or obstructs the other" (p. 265). By "interest" Smith was referring to the increase of the annual produce, as well as any legislation that would effect it. This symmetry of interests was a result of the superior productivity of agriculture, and the benefits that accrued to the proprietors from economic growth (pp. 264–65).[87] In considering the position of the "second order," Smith made a similar argument: "The interest of . . . those who live by wages, is as strictly connected with the interest of the society as that of the first" (p. 266). Since the "labourers'" wages depended on demand, their happiness depended on the increase of the "real wealth of society," that is to say, on the growth of the annual produce.

Although Smith equated the interests of both the proprietor and the wage-earning classes with those of society in general, he made one crucial distinction. The former could gain, if they were so inclined, a "tolerable knowledge" of their own interest, and, by extension, that of society's. The wage earner could not: "he is incapable either of comprehending that interest, or of understanding its connection to his own. His condition leaves him no time to receive the necessary information, and his education and habits are commonly such as to render him unfit to judge even though he was fully informed" (p. 266). Hence, in the public arena, "his voice is little heard and less regarded." Smith's analysis of the political subordination of the wage-earning class was a recasting, in the terms of the new science of political economy, of the eighteenth-century Anglo-American argument for limiting the franchise to the owners of property. When the voice of the wage earner was raised, Smith suspected that it was the interest of the employers that was being communicated (p. 266).[88]

In considering the position of the third order, those who lived by profit, Smith found not a reciprocity but an asymmetry of interests. Since the rate of profit "is always highest in countries which are going fastest to ruin," Smith was wary of the goals of the "merchants and master manufacturers," those "two classes of people who commonly employ the largest capitals." They were members of "an order of men, whose interest is never exactly the same with that of the public, who have generally an interest to deceive and even to oppress the publick, and who accordingly have, upon many occasions, both deceived and oppressed it" (p. 267). Unlike the landowning and the wage-earning classes, who in acting in their own interest also acted—albeit inadvertently—in the interest of all, the behavior of the class of employers needed to be carefully watched by the other two. Despite

Smith's arguments elsewhere in the *Wealth of Nations* for a "natural" harmony among the classes, here such stability could only be insured by the political vigilance of the proprietors. The mercantile and manufacturing classes had promoted in Parliament bounties, monopolies, and restrictions of trade that enriched them at the expense of the other orders. For Smith, one of the central lessons to be learned from mercantilism was to distrust the "disinterested" economic policies recommended by merchants (p. 267).[89]

While Smith's classifications resembled at points those of the Physiocrats, he rejected their distinctions between "productive" and "sterile" labor: "The capital error of this system . . . seems to lie in its representing the class of artificers, manufacturers and merchants, as altogether barren and unproductive" (p. 674).[90] He argued instead that the criterion for productive labor was that which "adds to the value of the subject upon which it is bestowed." This addition came about by the earning of wages plus the creation of a profit. Since artisans and merchants made such additions, they must be considered members of the productive classes; since servants did not, they should be classed among the unproductive (pp. 330–31).[91]

Expanding upon Hume's distinctions, Smith placed in this latter class "some of the most respectable orders in the society," including the sovereign, all government officials, the military, churchmen, lawyers, physicians, and "men of letters of all kinds." To these Smith added the rather less respectable classes of actors, buffoons, musicians, singers, and dancers. Although he did not deny the utility of many of these classes, their work "produces nothing which could afterwards purchase or procure an equal quantity of labour." As for those with considerable capital who need not labor, but whose "capitals" were invested in productive activities, Smith argued that, despite their states of leisure, they were, in fact, "productive labourers." Hence the capitalist and the wage worker were, from this perspective, members of the same great socioeconomic order (pp. 330–31, 362).[92]

Smith's concern with the distinction between productive and unproductive laborers was far more than a question of scholarly nomenclature. This was a matter of politics and public morality concerning the consequences of class formation. For Smith the ratio of these classes to each other would have a direct effect on the rate of economic growth. The activities of the former classes produced value; those of the latter only consumed it. To the extent that public and private expenditures promoted the welfare and development of the productive classes, they enhanced the wealth of the nation. Tax monies spent by the government on courtiers and cannons, however, would not. Nor would the employment of domestic servants or entertainers. For Smith both the state and the citizen-as-consumer had important parts to play, albeit indirect ones, in fostering and preserving the classes that constituted society.[93]

With the *Wealth of Nations* Smith presented an integrated examination of civil society that claimed to be both true to empirical fact and judicious in its assessment of the interests of the various orders. The ends of this political economy were the expansion of economic liberties, private property, and social stability for all "ranks and conditions." A "system of natural liberty" would result in a more equitable distribution of increasing income and a more "natural" distribution of men in occupational classes. Eliminating mercantilist policies such as monopolies and excessive duties, and feudal institutions such as primogeniture and statutes of apprenticeship would promote justice. Opulence and liberty were partners, not rivals, in the progress of commercial societies.[94]

As did the writings of Ferguson and Hume, the analyses and arguments of Smith's "science of the legislator" won considerable acceptance in the Anglo-American world. These investigations of commerce and these naturalizations of subordination appeared to have more relevance and explanatory power than the political economy of the Physiocrats. But as was the case for Quesnay and the French, the social taxonomy developed by Smith and the Scots continued to provoke disagreement. Such issues as how many classes there were, which ones were or were not productive, and what the moral and political consequences of these categories might be, continued to spur debate among those engaged in the study of politics and political economy, and those makers of policy influenced by these emerging conceptual schemes.[95] And among those who turned to this new language of commerce and classes were Americans who, in the development of their own analyses, would bring the learning and the lexicons of the philosophes to bear on the political and economic conditions of their new commercial republic.[96]

TWO

A Republican Distribution of Citizens

A socioeconomic language of class made its appearance in the political discourse of the Revolution, yet the correspondence between these linguistic and political events was temporal, not causal. North Americans may have fought over the meaning of such concepts as 'liberty', 'loyalty', 'representation', and the 'rights of Englishmen', but they did not argue over 'ranks', 'orders', 'sorts', or 'classes'. The emergence of this new social idiom in their everyday and learned languages received scant attention. Unlike the political and conceptual contests waged over social categorization during the Revolution in France, the changes that occurred in those categories during the Revolution in America inspired little in the way of public controversy. However much neo-Progressive historians might wish to emphasize the degree of class conflict at work in the latter, Anglo-Americans did not engage in a conflict over 'class'.[1]

The outcomes of the American Revolution, however, did lead to a significant conceptual change. As the focus of public debate shifted from the feasibility of independence to the proper organization and operation of republican government in the years after 1783, the terminology of 'classes' began to eclipse the older socioconstitutional language of 'orders'. With no titled nobility or other legal distinctions made among men—that is to say, among white, property-holding men—socioeconomic categories came to be more useful to Americans in the emerging republican discourse on politics and society. These were to become the "natural" categories with which to speak and write about the workings of a presumedly "natural" society. Instead of claiming that theirs was a classless society, as would many of their nineteenth- and twentieth-century successors, Americans in the late eighteenth century often chose to represent their republic in terms of class.[2]

The most pressing issue in the public discourse of the new nation was the constitutional. Which arrangements of the polity were best suited for a republic was a question of more than theoretical interest to those Americans who debated it first at the state level, and then at the national level. While the members of the revolutionary generation continued to conduct their inquiries within the broad tradition of Anglo-American republicanism—or what Gordon Wood has referred to as the "Whig science of politics"—the limits of that tradition were soon apparent. Since it assumed that the 'orders' of civil societies should be balanced in their constitutions, what should be done when, as David Ramsay remarked, "no artificial distinction of ranks has been suffered to take place among us?"[3] The argument that the Revolution had removed the "invidious establishment of different orders" was a common one in the last decades of the century. What distinctions among men were natural, and how could these be best represented in the state? What might, in a political and social world seemingly made anew, the outlines of a "republican" civil society be?[4]

An early answer to these questions was offered by the Free Republican in a series of contributions to the *Boston Magazine* in 1784. He observed that there were but two "general divisions" of men in all societies: those who "depend on their bodily labours for subsistence and support" and those whose subsistence was derived "principally from the labour of others." In this "latter class" he placed not only men who "are supported by the income of their accumulated fortunes," but also merchants, physicians, lawyers, and divines. These divisions were "universally distinguished in the common language of men," and in the United States were "described by the gentlemen, and the common people."[5] To the Free Republican the natural lines of social distinction were income and occupation.

Since history demonstrated that political strife was endemic between these groups if their interests were not "balanced," the Free Republican called for the "men of property" to be formally represented in an upper house. He proposed that membership in this chamber be made proportional to property and, as an example, suggested Servius Tullius's division of Roman society into six wealth-based classes. Not all commentators on matters political were as convinced as the Free Republican of the essentially dichotomous division of society, however. The November 1785 number of the same journal carried an anonymous piece entitled "A Letter supposed to have been written by a Gentleman in this State, to his Friend in England," in which the writer pointed out that the "grand division" between the rich and poor had not yet occurred in America. In his tripartite division the "middle class of people" held the political office to which the "multitude" have chosen them. While not yet in widespread use, the term 'middle class' was in circulation by the mid-1780s.[6]

Such combinations of terminology from the moral sciences with more traditional Anglo-American prescriptions for stability were to become rhetorical and analytical conventions in the debates over the structures of republican government in the 1780s. With the "one" no longer a factor, the "few" and the "many" who composed civil society came to be described in terms of property and occupationally based 'interests' and 'classes'. Classes, then, began to emerge as subjects in and objects of American political discourse. Most writers and speakers continued to assume that relations among these groupings were antagonistic. If concord were to prevail among the contending classes, that concord would depend on the proper ordering of the state. The political economists' thesis about the natural harmony of interests found only a few advocates among American political writers during these years.[7]

The most extensive debates over the representation of the "classes" of American society came in the wake of the Philadelphia convention of 1787. To the advocates of the new Constitution, the two chambers it proposed would more than adequately represent the various "classes," "orders," and "interests" in the republic. To its opponents, the new plan was seriously flawed by the overrepresentation of the "propertied" interest at the expense of the rest of society.[8]

The Anti-Federalists presumed, as did many of their Anglo-American contemporaries, that a stable polity would be impossible to maintain in the absence of a properly designed constitution. The natural state of relations between the classes was one of conflict, as their readings of the fates of earlier republics demonstrated. In his "Essays by a Farmer" John Mercer of Maryland pointed to this tendency of the few and the many toward enmity: "between these two powers, the aristocracy and the democracy, that is the rich and the poor, there is constant warfare." Only a socially balanced government could hope to avoid such hostility.[9]

This Anti-Federalist position on the social basis of representation was elaborated by the author of "Letters from the Federal Farmer to the Republican": "If the representation be so formed as to give one or more of the natural classes of men in society an undue ascendancy over others, it is imperfect; the former will gradually become masters, and the latter slaves. It is first of all among the political balances, to preserve in its proper station each of these classes."[10] Before efforts at achieving this balance be undertaken, the Federal Farmer pointed to the need for an adequate analysis of society. "We must form some general ideas and descriptions of the different classes of men as they may be divided by occupation and politically." The two classes he discovered were the "natural" aristocracy and the "natural" democracy, "the line between whom" was "in some degree arbitrary." The first, whose size he estimated at four to five thousand, consisted of men of wealth, leading officials, and the most successful professionals. The second included the yeomanry, minor officials, fishermen, mechanics, and "many merchants and professionals."[11]

In the Federal Farmer's judgment the proposed constitution should not be ratified, since it failed to recreate at the political level those natural divisions of men found at the social level. Neither the House of Representatives nor the Senate could truly represent the various interests of the nation: "the partition between the two branches will be merely those of the building in which they sit; there will not be found in them any of those genuine balances and checks, among the real different interests, and efforts of the several classes of men in the community we aim at."[12] If the new plan of government were to be implemented, the result would ultimately be the dominion by men "of elevated classes" over the "middle and lower classes." And for the Farmer, this was not a politically desirable alternative. In accordance with the prevalent conventions, the Farmer used 'class' and 'order' synonymously when referring to specific occupations and to groups: "every order of men in the community professional men, merchants, traders, farmers, mechanics"; "several orders of men"; and "all orders of men in the community."[13]

The Federal Farmer's critique of the imbalances of classes and orders in the constitution was in keeping with those made by his fellow Anti-Federalist, Brutus of New York.[14] In his "Essays" Brutus argued that the proposed legislature could not effectively represent the majority of men. Since the "natural aristocracy" created and controlled "a great number of dependents," they would insure that only "men of their own rank" would fill the elective offices. Such a legislature, peopled only by "the well born," would exclude "the great body of yeomen of the country."[15] These Anti-Federalist arguments on representation presupposed not only a conflict of political interests between the classes, but also a social division of political knowledge. "The well born, and the highest orders in life, as they term themselves, will be ignorant of the sentiments of the middling class of citizens." Brutus's "natural aristocracy" did not understand the other classes, and thus could not legislate for them (p. 381).

In lieu of the Philadelphia proposals, Brutus insisted on a national legislature whose organization would mirror that of the society at large. It would recognize and incorporate the "natural" divisions of occupational classes: "This extensive continent is made up of a number of different classes of people; and to have a proper representation of them, each class ought to have an opportunity of choosing their best informed men for the purpose. . . . In this assembly, the farmer, merchant, mechanic, and other various orders of people ought to be represented according to their respective weights and numbers" (p. 380). Short of this alternative of proportional representation by class-as-occupation, Brutus preferred the status quo of the confederation to the inevitable tyranny of the rich that would arise from the implementation of the Federalists' schemes.[16]

Samuel Chase of Maryland raised a corresponding set of objections to the limits of the federal legislators' knowledge: "It is impossible for a few men to be acquainted with the sentiments and interests of the United States, which contains many different classes or orders of men—merchants & farmers, planters & mechanics and gentry or wealthy men."[17] Chase, like Brutus, objected to the political domination of a wealthy class ignorant not only of the views of the "middling" class, but of the "lower class of citizens" as well.[18] His concern with the political role of the "middling" class was characteristic of the Anti-Federalists. In their adaptation of classical republican and Whig arguments for balance, this class served as both the repository of virtue and the guarantor of stability. Since "every society naturally divides itself into classes," it was necessary, to "receive the middling class of people into your government," or so Melancton Smith argued to the ratification convention of New York.[19]

Only the members of Smith's middling class, composed chiefly of "the respectable yeomanry," were prepared to maintain liberty and property: "Those in the middling circumstances have less temptation; they are inclined by habit, and the company with whom they associate, to set bounds to their passions and appetites" (p. 394). Their connections with the classes both above and below them guaranteed that whatever benefited them would benefit all: "Whenever the interest of this part of the community is pursued, the public good is pursued, because the body of every nation consists of this class, and because the interest of both the rich and poor are involved in that of the middling class. . . . When, therefore, this class in society pursue their own interest, they promote that of the public" (p. 386). Since the lower house proposed by the Philadelphia convention would be dominated by the "natural aristocracy," Smith urged that the constitution be rejected. To insure that this politically unique middling class be sufficiently represented, Smith argued that the number of seats in the legislature be significantly increased (p. 183).[20]

The addresses of Smith and the essays of his Anti-Federalist colleagues were tracts written to influence the political behavior of their fellow citizens; that is to say, they were rhetorical. Unlike the works of the Scottish Enlightenment, these were not learned treatises on politics, economics, or civil society. To inquire as to the "class theory" or "class consciousness" of the Anti-Federalists on the basis of these or other textual sources is, perhaps, to ask of them more than should be expected.[21] Yet the Anti-Federalists did communicate to their audiences with a consistently applied set of conventions for analyzing what Brutus identified as "the foundation of the social system."[22] Their orders and classes were both "natural" economic groupings based on criteria of wealth and occupation, and political groupings based on membership in a "natural" democracy or aristocracy. These classes were gathered into groups of two (the "few" and the "many") or three (the "upper," "middling," and "lower") or in lists of employments of various lengths. Relations between, or among, these classes tended naturally toward conflict, but conflict that could be avoided by a balance of interests within a revised constitution or a revived confederation. The locus of class antagonism and amelioration was primarily political. It was not the presence of an oppressive "propertied interest," but the potential for artificial alliances of property and power, that endangered republican liberties.[23]

The patterns of classification employed by supporters of the proposed constitution were generally similar to those of its critics. In both Federalist and Anti-Federalist speeches and writings the "natural" units of civil society were arrayed in terms of occupation and partisan persuasion. The uncontroversial usage of this eighteenth-century lexicon—of what Brutus called "words in their common acception"—by the Anti-Federalists and their rivals is notable.[24] While neither party was class-conscious in Marxian terms, both were conscious, or cognizant, of classes. The difference lay in the Federalists' diagnoses of and prognoses for class relations in the political institutions of the new republic, most especially in the federal legislature.[25]

In the "Federalist No. 35" Alexander Hamilton addressed the "impracticable" and "unnecessary" objections made by Brutus and the Federal Farmer about the social bases of representation in the lower house: "The idea of an actual representation of all classes of the people, by persons of each class, is altogether visionary. Unless it were expressly provided in the Constitution, that each different occupation should send one or more members, the thing would never take place in practice."[26] What would occur instead, he surmised, would be the choice of "natural representatives" by the respective classes. Due to their positions of leadership in the political and economic activities of the community, these legislators would have a shared interest with and a sympathy for the classes they were to represent.

In developing this argument in favor of "natural" rather than proportional representation, Hamilton turned first to the political psychology of the artisans and manufacturers. They would, he suggested, "always be inclined to give their votes to merchants, in preference to persons of their own professions and trades," since their interests and those of the commercial class were closely linked. They would also recognize that their "habits of life" had not fitted them for participation in a deliberative assembly, whereas those of the merchant, "their natural patron and friend," had. He submitted that on the grounds of this identity of interests, "we must consider merchants as the natural representatives of all these classes of the community" (p. 270).

Hamilton's next set of "natural representatives" were members of the learned professions. Since they "truly form no distinct interest in society," Hamilton assumed that they would enjoy the "confidence" of their fellow citizens. The third and final set of legislators would be drawn from the "landed interest." Hamilton again posited a "bond of sympathy" among all members of this class, from "the proprietor of millions of acres" to one "of a single acre." Any landholder could represent the interests of them all (p. 271).

The social bases of Hamilton's legislature, then, were the two large "interests": the landed, and the combined artisanal and commercial classes. Adjoined were the dis-interested class of professionals. He dismissed the Anti-Federalist demand that "all classes of citizens have some of their own number in the representative body" by asserting that these three groups effectively encompassed all of society. These representatives would act in the collective interest of all by acting on their class's behalf. The Anti-Federalist concern about antagonism between the rich and the poor within these classes—artisans versus merchants, great landlords versus smallholders—was removed by his discovery of a "bond of sympathy" among members of the large "interests." Hamilton did not avoid the question of a social distribution of political knowledge, but assumed that the natural representatives would "understand" the concerns of all of their constituents. As to the Anti-Federalist insistence on balance in the legislature, he presumed that the "learned professions" would "prove to be an impartial arbiter" between the great interests. At many places in this essay Hamilton employed the terms and concepts of the Scottish moral scientists (pp. 271–72).[27]

In contrast to Hamilton's efforts at changing the premises of the debate over the representation of and balance among the elements of society, James Madison's *Federalist* essays continued along more traditional lines. And where Hamilton was willing to posit an identity of interests within the marketplace and the legislature, Madison was still engaged with the problem of class antagonism and the potential for oppression. In the "Federalist No. 51" he remarked that "[i]t is of great importance in a republic not only to guard the society against the oppression of its rulers, but to guard one part of society against the injustice of the other part. Differing interests necessarily exist in different classes of citizens."[28] Such protection could be provided only by a "will in the community independent of the majority," that is to say, by a monarch or tyrant, or by "comprehending in the society so many separate descriptions of citizens" as to make their "combination" impossible. Madison preferred the second option in which "society itself will be broken into so many parts, interests and classes of citizens" that oppressive "combinations" would be difficult if not impossible to form. With a regional, not an occupational, basis for representation, Madison's republic might avoid the depredations of the "few" against the "many," or of the majority against minorities. Distance and diversity could check the inherent conflict of factions and interests.[29]

Madison pursued a similar line of reasoning in the "Federalist No. 10," as he explored the question of safeguards against faction. In this most often cited passage on classes written by an eighteenth-century American, he examined the role of property in the origin of conflicting interests in civil society.

> [T]he most common and durable source of factions has been the various and unequal distribution of property. Those who hold and those who are without property have ever formed distinct interests in society. Those who are creditors, and those who are debtors, fall under a like discrimination. A landed interest, a manufacturing interest, a mercantile interest, a monied interest, with many lesser interests, grow up of necessity in civilized nations, and divide themselves into different classes, actuated by different sentiments and views.[30]

Here Madison was following the outlines of a Scottish history of the progress of commercial society, with its natural distinctions generated by sources of income, its triumvirate of the three great classes, and its assumption of differing interests on the part of each. Madison's "principal task of modern legislation" was a question of politics and political economy: "the regulation of these various and interfering interests."[31]

As in the "Federalist No. 51," Madison prescribed a regional basis of representation as a remedy for the political ills of class antagonism. To the Anti-Federalist charge that only small republics could hope to be stable, he replied that the very size and diversity of the new republic would mitigate the clash of economic interests. Thanks to geography, political and social stability could be maintained in spite of the grim lessons of republican history. While the sources of faction could not be eliminated, their effects could be controlled.[32]

Madison's criteria for classification were comparable to Hamilton's and to those of his opponents. The classes of "civilized societies," as he explained to Thomas Jefferson, resulted from men's "unequal faculties" for acquiring property. They could be "subdivided according to the different productions of different situations & soils, & according to different branches of commerce, and of manufactures." These classes and interests were not, however, the creations of the political order. Yet to the extent that "free Government" protected the results of inequalities of talent and property, these "natural distinctions" were within the purview of the "Statesman." As he had in the "Federalist No. 10," Madison again noted that "[t]here will be rich and poor; creditors and debtors; a landed interest, a monied interest, a mercantile interest, a manufacturing interest." Here again the connections between Madison and the analytic categories of the Scots were strong.[33] When Publius disagreed with the Federal Farmer and Brutus, it was over the degree to which class conflict was inevitable in the political arena, and how far class distinctions should be incorporated in the framework of the state. Neither the Federalists nor the Anti-Federalists denied the existence of classes in the United States, or questioned the salience of these socioeconomic distinctions in republican political discourse.[34]

If the presence of natural class distinctions was not a problem in the process of drafting, debating, and ratifying the Constitution, the possibility that artificial schemes of "ranks" would reemerge in the federal system was. Although Americans were well aware that "we have no legal titles or hereditary distinctions," as Melancton Smith described them at New York's ratification convention, Anti-Federalists were equally aware of the wealth and power of the "natural aristocracy." Among their litany of charges were those leveled against the aristocratic character of the upper house. Its small numbers, its considerable power, its manner of selection, and its distance from the citizenry would make it a forum for conspiracies against liberty and a home to a new senatorial order. In answering these accusations, Federalists such as Hamilton and Charles Pinckney denied that such establishments or nomenclatures had any relevance to the political and social conditions in the United States. Hamilton, in responding to Smith, dismissed any references to aristocrats: "I hardly know the meaning of the word, as it is applied." The "image" of an American aristocracy, Hamilton argued, was a "phantom."[35] Pinckney, during the course of the South Carolina convention, insisted that only one kind of demarcation was relevant in the new republic. "If we examine the reasons which have given rise to the distinction of rank that at present prevails in Europe," he explained, "we shall find none of them do, or in all probability ever will, exist in the Union." The sole form of "distinction" that might arise was that of "wealth," but differences in the sizes or sources of income did not entail differences of interests.[36] Pinckney went on to "class" the citizenry into "commercial men," "professional men," the "mechanical" class, and the "landed interest." Among these classes that "compose the people of the Union," he found "mutual dependence" and a general "mediocrity of fortune." While Pinckney emphasized the "mediocrity of fortune" in the "national character," however, he did not reject the phenomena of economic inequality or social hierarchy. Rather he refused, as did

Hamilton, to interpret these asymmetries of property and prestige as evidence of the emergence of permanent orders within the state. "A mild and equal government," Pinckney maintained, "knows no distinctions but those of merit or talents."[37]

In the political rhetoric of these Federalists the "ranks" and "orders" of more artificial types of civil society stood in contrast to the "natural distinctions" of class. Their usage suggests that the socioeconomic convention was in the process of replacing the socioconstitutional.[38] The rate of this replacement varied, of course, among respective speakers and writers. As was the case for the emergence of 'class' in the Anglo-American political lexicon, the eclipse of a socioconstitutional terminology was in general gradual, not rapid.[39] Political vocabularies do not always change at the same rate as political realities, as Bryan Magee has observed. American political institutions changed far more quickly in these years than did American political language.

Yet the changes wrought by the formation and articulation of the new state and federal constitutions did serve to remove the political and legal referents of the older taxonomic scheme; these republican constitutions did not reconstitute orders, ranks, or estates. Even though the events of 1787 and 1788 did not cause a dramatic epistemic or paradigmatic break in the social and political discourse of Americans, they did enhance the semantic and conceptual shifts already under way. The delegitimation of one mode of differentiation was accompanied by the legitimation of another.[40]

The outlines of a republican society, then, could be drawn with wealth and occupation in mind. Bereft of artificial ranks and orders, the new nation did have, in their stead, natural classes. This position was advanced by James Madison in 1792 in Philip Freneau's *National Gazette* and Mathew Carey's *American Museum.* In a piece entitled "A Republican Distribution of Citizens" he suggested that "[a] perfect theory on this subject would be useful, not because it could be reduced in practice by any plan of legislation, or ought to be attempted by violence on the will or property of individuals: but because it would be a monition against empirical experiments by power; and a model to which the free choice of occupations by the people might gradually approximate the order of society."[41] Here Madison presumed that, at least in the realm of theory, the organizing principles that underlie a republican society are those of the division of labor. Social positions would not be determined by birth or legislation—especially Hamiltonian plans of legislation—but by the "free choice of occupations."[42] While no such "perfect theory" was uniformly accepted in the years after the ratification of the new Constitution, a number of significant attempts were made at such a definition, as the naturalization of socio-economic differences of Enlightenment moral sciences was transposed into the discourse of American politics.

One of the first extended considerations of such a distribution of citizens was published in 1791 by the newly appointed secretary of the treasury, Alexander Hamilton. His *Report on Manufactures* served as more than a brief for his plans for national development by way of the encouragement of manufactures. It presented an examination of the organization and operation of American society, conducted along the lines of the new sciences of politics. As were the French and the Scots, Hamilton was concerned with both the semantic and the social dimensions of classification. In the *Report* he countered the arguments made in favor of a predominantly agrarian republic by American admirers of physiocratic ideas such as Thomas Jefferson and George Logan—arguments that assumed the moral and the productive superiority of the agricultural classes—with proposals for a more economically diverse commercial society. Through protective tariffs, bounties, and a stable system of public finance, each of the three great interests delineated in Scottish political economy—agriculture, manufactures, and commerce—might be united in the "one great common cause" of economic independence. Hamilton's plans for class formation and cooperation were to be guided by both the visible hand of Sir James Steuart's "statesman" and the invisible hand of Adam Smith.[43]

Following along the lines of Smith and Steuart, Hamilton denied that the "classes of artificers or manufacturers" should be categorized as "unproductive": "That, inasmuch as it is acknowledged that manufacturing labor reproduces a value equal to that which is expended or consumed in carrying it on and continues in existence the original stock or capital employed it ought, on that account alone, to escape being considered as wholly unproductive" (pp. 119–20). Since both these groups and the class of "husbandmen and cultivators" recreated the wealth necessary for their support and added to the number and value of goods in the marketplace, he judged the labor of the artificers and manufacturers to be as productive as that of the farmers. Hamilton continued with his refutation of physiocratic terminology and policy by questioning the utility of categories based on the production of an agricultural surplus: "Another, and that which seems to be the principal argument offered for the superior productiveness of agricultural labor, turns upon the allegation, that labour employed in manufactures yields nothing equivalent to the rent of land, or that nett surplus, as it is called, which accrues to the proprietor of the soil" (p. 122). Hamilton considered this point of physiocratic doctrine to be untenable since "this distinction, important as it has been deemed, appears rather verbal than substantial." Like Adam Smith, Hamilton found Quesnay's categories of 'productive' and 'sterile' were neither useful for the study of social and economic life nor, more importantly, useful in the formation of policy. The role to be played by the state in fostering development should not be limited due to faulty reasoning or inadequate nomenclature. American agriculture might well be predominant, but it should not be conceptually privileged (pp. 122–24).

In the *Report* Hamilton sought to replace the physiocratic terms that he found to be invidious with more satisfactory ones, and to challenge those among his contemporaries who depicted relations between manufactures and farming—and by extension those states that were or would be primarily involved in these activities—as antagonistic. "The northern and southern regions are sometimes represented as having adverse interests," wrote Hamilton. "Those are called manufacturing, these agricultural states, and a species of opposition is imagined to subsist between the manufacturing and agricultural interests." Once again Hamilton made use of the harmonious-relations model of the moral sciences as he denied the existence of interest and regional conflict: "This idea of an opposition between those two interests is the common error of the early periods of every country; but experience gradually dissipates it" (p. 163). The maxims of political science and political economy and the realities of America's advantageous circumstances suggested to Hamilton that, to the contrary, a "perfect harmony of all the parts" of the new republic might be achieved (p. 164).

As in his contributions to the *Federalist,* Hamilton explored in the *Report on Manufactures* the possibility that the strife that had destroyed earlier republics could be avoided. In his *Federalist* essays the social profile of the legislature served as the means for circumventing factional and interest-based conflict. In the *Report* the power of the national government to promote economic growth served as the guarantor of social and regional tranquility. Hamilton's interests and classes cooperated for their own and the common benefit instead of conspiring to enrich themselves at the other's expense. Although this line of reasoning failed to persuade many of his political rivals, it gave his allies and nineteenth-century disciples such as Hezekiah Niles and Henry C. Carey the intellectual grounds for a systematic interpretation of republican commercial society in which class antagonism had been eliminated. Hamilton's adaptation of Scottish political economy to the shaping of American political policy would prove to be a powerful analytic and rhetorical device in subsequent debates over the nature of the American social order.[44]

A corresponding set of proposals was made by Hamilton's colleague in the Treasury Department, Tench Coxe. Like Hamilton, Coxe saw the encouragement of domestic industry and the state's active promotion of commerce as the surest means for social and political stability. In 1794 Coxe published a collection of his addresses and essays under the title *A View of the United States of America.* These writings and other occasional pieces are of interest not only as political tracts in favor of the Hamiltonian position, but as examples of the classificatory schemes used by Coxe and other early students of the American social and economic systems. Like Hamilton, Coxe employed the convention of the three great classes or interests of agriculture, commerce, and manufactures when dividing society into units for analysis. These great classes were composed, in turn, by the "several different descriptions of citizens . . . the learned professions, planters, farmers, merchants . . . manufacturers, mechanics . . . the persons immediately employed by them." Each of these groupings could be labeled as an "interest" or "class," and the reason for its inclusion within one of the larger categories was self-evident. The only exceptions to this pattern of classifying were the "learned professions." Coxe kept lawyers and clergymen outside of the bounds of the great interests, as Hamilton had done in the *Federalist.*[45] Where exactly to locate and how to evaluate the productive role of such apparently unproductive classes were issues Coxe did not pursue, but they served as points of controversy for his contemporaries and for subsequent generations of commentators and critics alike.

In addition to this horizontal division of society into occupational classes, Coxe also used a vertical wealth-and-property-based taxonomy of upper, middle, and lower classes, or its equivalent of 'rich', 'middling', and 'poor'. In his *Observations of the Agriculture, Manufactures, and Commerce of the United States,* first published in 1789, Coxe observed that in general the inhabitants of most countries were, with respect to property, divided into three classes: "the rich, the middling, and the poor." This asymmetry in wealth was not necessarily a detriment, since "the rich, are not a useless unimportant class of citizens." Through their business activities they provided needed employment for the poor, who were "wholly dependent" on them in this regard. Coxe's next class on the scale of wealth was "the middling class of people, those who have some small property. . . . this class of people are the most numerous, and promote the wealth and strength of a nation." The middling class also benefited from the endeavors of the rich, since the latter were the primary source of the state's revenues: "If this be a just representation, the rich are to be applied to by government for money, if not to the exoneration of the other classes of people."[46] Here the three classes of society were drawn together in a system of mutual interdependence that paralleled the interdependence of Coxe's three great interests. In both cases, economic development would promote class cooperation and preclude factional strife. While Coxe was not naively optimistic about the human condition or the future of the republic, his study of the principles of political economy and his advocacy of their application gave him reason to believe—as Hamilton believed—that accord, not enmity, could be the rule in a commercial society.

This emphasis on social harmony and the indispensability of the wealthy had both intellectual and ideological implications. Coxe, Hamilton, and other members of the emerging Federalist party used it to defend their visions of a nation in which the rich played central economic, social, and political roles.[47] Their arguments for the voluntary subordination of the "many" to the "few" were justified by appeals to the "true principles of the social order" based mainly on economic criteria, instead of the "artificial" principles of the European aristocracies. The *Essay on Political Society* by Samuel Whittlesey Dana, a Federalist congressman from Connecticut, applied these "true principles," gleaned from the study of history and the natural sciences of society, to the arrangement of men in the state: "It is evident, that, in society, different degrees of wealth and of ascendant, result from the difference of industry and of talent. With relation to property, the most general distribution of humankind is into the classes of the rich and the poor."[48] Although Dana's premier class constituted the "least numerous portion of society," their possession of talent, learning, and wealth served to make them the "ruling part." In effect, he argued, "the rich," "the few," and "the rulers" were synonyms, as were the correlative terms "the poor," "the many," and "the ruled." Such a division of rewards and power was both "natural" and just, Dana remarked, since "these two classes are the same with those to which the members of society are distributed by the primordial principles of justice" (p. 34).

Dana found among the transformations of the "political society" of the day—especially in the American republican experiment—a tendency toward the replication of this "constitution of nature" not only in theory but also in practice: "A view of the obvious course of affairs of that natural order of events which we see in fact taking place, thus leads to recognize the agreement between abstract principle and actual experience. In the present case, they both lead to the same general induction; both presenting, to the observing eye, the same general classification of humankind" (p. 35). That is to say, the development of states in which men were distinguished and governed in light of "natural" socioeconomic classes was positive, reflecting the "abstract" demands of social justice. It was a process far preferable to the "evils" that resulted from the "exclusive privilege in different orders or castes" which had been typical in earlier political societies. If Americans could avoid the temptations of creating such privileges, Dana was confident that the relationship between these two "natural classes," which he equated with the two "interests" in the state, the aristocratic and the democratic, would be amicable (pp. 35–37).

The specter of social hostility had not been banished in Dana's hypothesized republican social order as it had been in Hamilton's writings, but it was relegated to a minor role. This Anglo-American commonplace of animosity between the rich and the poor—a convention that informed both Federalists and Anti-Federalists—was joined in the 1790s by a convention that depicted classes as "harmoniously associated by the constitution" (p. 56).[49] While a rhetoric of class antagonism was by no means absent from the writings of the Federalists of the late eighteenth and early nineteenth centuries—as we shall see below—an argument for "harmony" was central in many of their descriptions of and prescriptions for the republic. Through the adoption of this explanatory device, writers such as Dana not only broadened the political discourse of their era, but endowed their conservative successors in the nineteenth century with a variety of arguments for the "natural" justice of the American distributive system.[50]

The economic programs that Hamilton and Coxe developed in accordance with the new sciences were not the only ones advanced in the 1790s; nor were their readings of the political economists the only ones that contended for recognition in the arena of public discourse. Although indebted to the Scots for a social nomenclature and an emphasis on harmony, Hamilton's plans for protective tariffs, bounties, and subsidies ran counter to the policies advocated by Adam Smith. His *Reports* on manufactures, a national bank, and commerce placed him at odds as well with his former ally James Madison, who preferred a "system of natural liberty" to one of state supervision. Hamilton and Coxe found a more vociferous opponent in George Logan of Pennsylvania, who, under the name of A Farmer, published in 1792 a critique on the Hamiltonian project, entitled "Five Letters Addressed to the Yeomanry of the United States." As were Hamilton and Coxe, Logan was conversant with the Enlightenment sciences of government and society: "Happy for mankind, the present enquiry in the philosophical world is not the mechanism of the universe, or the composition of its elements, but the principles of civil society."[51] But Logan's studies of natural and moral philosophy, as well as his grounding in the Anglo-American tradition of politics, led him to quite different conclusions regarding the efficacy of the secretary of the treasury's ideas.[52]

In the second of his letters, A Farmer attacked the *Report on Manufactures* in general and Hamilton's New Jersey Society for Establishing Useful Manufactures in particular. The corporate charter that had been granted to this group for a manufactory in Paterson symbolized to Logan all that was wrong with the state's participation in the promotion of domestic industries: "Is it just that a numerous class of citizens, whose knowledge in mechanics and manufactures, not less necessary for the support of their families, than useful to their country, should be sacrificed to a wealthy few, who have no other object in view than to add to their ill-gotten and enormous wealth?" (p. 165). Here Logan distinguished between those useful artisans and mechanics who prospered without the benefits of a corporate charter, and those investors who styled themselves "manufacturers" but were in fact members of an unproductive class. This latter group, the only real beneficiaries of public support for manufactures, were engaged in subverting the republican principle of equality while they claimed to be acting for the common good.

As he weighed the social and political consequences of granting the New Jersey charter, Logan asked: "Whether it establishes a class of citizens with distinct interests from their fellow citizens? Will it not, by fostering an inequality of fortune, provide the destruction of the equality of rights, and tend strongly to aristocracy?" (p. 165). Instead of the social concord that Hamilton and Coxe forecast in their writings, Logan expected an increase in animosity to be the result of such interference in the progress of commerce.

Although himself a gentleman farmer of considerable wealth and social standing in his native Philadelphia, Logan criticized the antirepublican sentiments of the rich. "The wealthy are formed into bodies by their professions, their different degrees of opulence, called ranks, their knowledge, and their small numbers," he explained. As such they actively sought "honourary and political distinctions." While these proclivities came as little surprise to such a student of history as Logan, it was the audacity of Hamilton's projects that alarmed him. "Not content with the inevitable tendency of the wealthy to combine, they have embodied them as classes." These classes could be expected to behave as malicious, self-interested entities intent on establishing an aristocracy. Any public measures that encouraged this illicit method of class formation—corporate charters, bounties, and other "special privileges"—needed to be strenuously and decisively opposed. The very presence of such classes demonstrated to Logan the tenuous nature of the republic's political arrangements (pp. 165–66).

The distribution of citizens in Hamilton's or Coxe's America would be far from Logan's understanding of "republican," a description predicated upon the continued primacy of the agricultural interest. He was not opposed to the growth of the manufacturing or commercial classes, as long as this was the result of forces in the market, not factions in the legislature. His American "yeomanry" welcomed the collaboration of honest mechanics and merchants, but not the machinations of stock jobbers and speculators. Where Hamilton expected that commercial expansion would promote the "harmony of interests," Logan feared that the price of such development included the growth of a would-be "aristocracy" of unearned and undeserved wealth. A Farmer's mapping of the political landscape was one in which class hostility remained an important feature (pp. 165–66).

George Logan was among the first spokesmen for those groups of politically engaged Americans who gathered in opposition to the treasury secretary's projects and found their leader in the secretary of state, Thomas Jefferson. The political rhetoric of Logan and of his "Jeffersonian" colleagues was in the broad tradition of eighteenth-century Anglo-American Whigs, though adapted to new circumstances. An "aristocracy," based not on blood but on "paper" wealth, now threatened the rights of the "people," and true republicans needed to remain vigilant. The interests of these "aristocrats"—as Hamilton, John Jay, John Adams, and others in the Federalist party were labeled—were at odds with those of the "democracy." Although the Revolution had dismantled the system of colonial domination, Hamilton and company were intent on reestablishing a framework of unwarranted privilege in its place. Liberty and property, if not life, were once again at stake.

In an essay addressed to "Aristocrats in General," James Lyon, editor of the *National Magazine* of Richmond, discussed the social composition of this dangerous political "faction": "Any person who pays a moment's attention to the subject, will discover that the aristocratic faction, which is growing into influence in the United States, is built by various classes of citizens, as opposite in their interests, as their designs are to honesty, or light to darkness."[53] These "classes" were the "rich and designing" and "those who are forced by poverty or duped by fraud to range themselves under the banners of an aspiring despotism." Between the wealthy and their "unfortunate and misguided" clients Lyon placed that class whose interests represented those of the nation as a whole, the "enlightened and independent yeomanry." Although Lyon deplored this alliance between the rich and the dependent poor, and would have preferred cooperation among the three classes, he expected continued antipathy in the political arena as long as the rich pursued their self-aggrandizing goals. In contrast to Hamilton's dismissal of class or interest-based rivalries, Lyon's understanding of class relations, like Logan's, was still informed by fear of tyranny and anticipation of antagonism.[54]

This Jeffersonian interpretation of American class relations was systematized in the controversial works of Thomas Cooper. An English chemist, colleague of Joseph Priestley, and "radical" political refugee, Cooper brought his studies in the new sciences of society to bear in such pieces as the *Political Arithmetic* of 1798. His criticisms of the Washington and Adams administrations included an objection to their preference for taxing the productive classes to benefit the "unproductive," the distinction between which he made with his usual degree of scientific precision. Within the first category he included "the farmer, the wood-cutter, the miner (and perhaps) the manufacturer"; each of these "employs his capital and labour in producing real riches," or "some commodity of value." The conditional place of the "manufacturers" among the productive classes was based, he noted, on a disagreement to be found in the works of the French "Economistes" and Adam Smith. To the unproductive classes Cooper consigned "the merchant, the agent, the factor, the retailer, the clerk, the captain, the seaman," that is to say, "those employed in arranging, as sorting, transporting, dividing, what has already been produced by the capital and labour of others." These class distinctions were made with both partisan and learned criteria in mind.[55]

The locus for antagonism that Cooper discovered was one between the "interest" of the merchants, who "form a small class," and that of the "consumers," who "form the nation." In Cooper's political lexicon the terms 'consumer' and 'producer' could be interchanged. Measures such as expenditures for a large navy to protect commerce appeared to him typical of the designs that the Federalists and their New England mercantile supporters had on the wealth of the "back country farmer." In Cooper's analysis it was axiomatic that these unproductive classes would seek to turn government to their own ends. *Political Arithmetic*—which Jefferson ordered distributed as campaign literature for the election of 1800—was a call to the productive classes to protect themselves against all such threats to their rights.[56] In making this call Cooper combined a rhetoric of class and interest conflict with a technical analysis of social relations to expose the goals of the Federalist party. For Cooper, who had been jailed for violating the Sedition Act, classification was an exercise of intellectual and political power.

A rhetoric of social and political conflict was not the exclusive province of the Jeffersonian republicans, however. Their evocations of class animosity elicited from Federalist sympathizers countercharges of demagoguery that cast the champions of the "democracy" in the offending role. Public pronouncements made by Cooper and other prominent Democratic Republicans in favor of the Revolution in France were sufficient to convince Joseph Dennie, the owner and editor of the *Port Folio,* that a class-based suppression—in this instance of the "middling class" by the "rabble"—was more than a chimera. In the October 1802 issue of his journal Dennie reprinted an unsigned essay from the Frankfort, Kentucky, *Palladium,* entitled "Lessons from History," in which the author observed that "it is of the very nature and essence of despotism to make use of the rabble, and to depress the middling class of citizens."[57] The likely despots in the United States were those Jeffersonians-cum-Jacobins who wished to transport the terrors and upheavals of France to American shores. It was their conspiracy, not that of the Federalists, that needed to be exposed: "Let the real people, the householders and possessors of small property, rest assured . . . that the revolutionists of this country, the avowed admirers of the French Revolution, are no friends of the people: they may, indeed, form a league with the vicious and destitute of our cities, but they try to deceive and certainly will betray, oppress and enslave the middling class."[58] The comments of this author are worthy of note for more than their vitriolic prose. His "middling class" of smallholders was as endangered by a conjunction of a self-serving upper class and an impoverished lower class as were the "yeomanry" of James Lyon. Both this anonymous Federalist, along with his publicist Dennie, and the Jeffersonian Lyon had recourse to an image of a middle class threatened from above and below, despite their markedly different understandings of who exactly posed the threat. The device of the "virtuous middle" that they both incorporated was well-established in the tradition of Anglo-American political discourse; and their uses of it for mutually exclusive partisan ends indicates the appeal that a rhetoric of social antagonism had for Federalist and Democratic Republican polemicists alike.[59]

The variant of a republican social order most favored by Oliver Oldschool—Dennie's pen name—and the contributors to the *Port Folio* differed from Hamilton's model of the three cooperating "great classes," and from Cooper's and Lyon's insistence on the primacy of the middling yeomanry. Dennie and his compatriots preferred instead a conservative social hierarchy emphasizing a "reverence for rank" and the "correct ideas of subordination."[60] They continued to admire the balances of English civil society and drew much inspiration from defenders of that "constitution" such as Edmund Burke. Dennie agreed with Burke about the dangerous implications of the "levelling" principles of the Jacobins, and used the pages of his journal as a platform for attacking potential American levelers among the Jeffersonians and the "lower classes of our motley vulgar."[61]

In the February 1807 number of the *Port Folio,* Dennie featured an essay, "Classification of Citizens" from Edmund Burke's *Maxims,* that had appeared originally in 1791 as part of *Reflections on the Revolution in France.* Among the changes that Burke had taken to task in those passages were the National Assembly's elimination of the patchwork of counties, duchies, and provinces in favor of symmetrical departments, and its imposition of a uniform system of revenue. When it reappeared in the rather different context of Dennie's journal, it became the first piece published in the United States on the theoretical and practical questions of how best to "class" men in a state.[62]

As he compared the security of tradition with the perils of innovation, Burke reviewed the work of those "ancient legislators" who "thought themselves obliged to dispose their citizens into such classes, and to place them in such situations as their peculiar habits might qualify them to fill."[63] The results of these classifications were stable polities, well-designed to contain "the conflict caused by the diversity of interests." To these ancient achievements he contrasted the speculative social philosophers of his own day, especially the French revolutionists, who had failed miserably in their projects of classification. Through their attempts "to confound all sorts of citizens . . . into one homogeneous mass," these "metaphysical and alchemistical legislators" had denigrated the true worth of the citizenry. "They reduce men to loose counters, merely for the sake of simple telling, and not to figures whose power is to arise from their place at the table" (p. 136).

Burke regarded the detachment of men from fixed social standings in the name of "equality" as an error. By their presumptuous applications of unfounded Enlightenment notions, the French had "levelled and crushed together all the orders which they found, even under the coarse unartificial arrangement of the monarchy, in which mode of government the classing of the citizen is not of so much importance as in a republick. It is true, however, that every such classification, if properly ordered, is good in all forms of government" (p. 136). Burke did not desire to defend all the institutions or practices of the "ancien régime" from judicious reform. Nor did he wish to explain precisely what classification of citizens in a "republick" should entail, even though he was a friend of Adam Smith and an admirer of the *Wealth of Nations*. He did intend, however, to warn his British audience about the dangers inherent in speculative appeals to "equality," and to underline the benefits of a constitutional monarchy in which men had been "properly ordered" (p. 136).

Burke's critique of "metaphysical and alchemistical legislators" could be redirected by the American conservative Dennie and his Federalist readers at their Jeffersonian enemies, with their Jacobin sympathies. Burke and Thomas Cooper had clashed before over the significance of events in France and Britain. Burke's advocacy of a classificatory scheme based on "peculiar habits" and one's "place at the table" could reinforce Federalist arguments for a deferential, hierarchical society rather than the elusive "equality" championed by enlightened visionaries.[64] But where Burke could rely on the British constitution to ensure that society was "properly ordered," Dennie's Federalists did not have a parallel set of institutional arrangements or historical precedents to appeal to. Who in the new nation was responsible for the "classing of the citizen"? The legislators or theorists whom Burke ridiculed? The "vulgar" whom Dennie despised? The market in which Hamilton placed his faith? There was no Lycurgus or Servius Tullius to assign places and positions in this republic. Nor was there an American Linnaeus who could classify the social world as incontrovertibly as the natural. This question of authority was an issue for disputants in Dennie's era and for subsequent generations who disagreed over the appropriate methods, theories, and terms for classification. Not only did it generate widely divergent interpretations of the composition of American society, but it enabled those who wished to deny the very existence of social classes in the United States to challenge the "arbitrary" results of any suggested scheme.

In a July 1812 issue of the *Port Folio,* edited by Dennie's successor Nicholas Biddle, the Observer commented on the problems raised by the apparent lack of an agreed-upon social nomenclature among his contemporaries: "It is an easy thing to classify men. Thousands have done it in many different ways, and thousands may still do it, without copying one another and without exhausting the subject. In this view, the great community of mankind appears a vast field, which every intellectual surveyor divides at will, and yet with some approach to rectitude in the result. It is indeed approximation only."[65] The open-ended nature of the classificatory process and the multiplicity of classes thereby proposed did not trouble the Observer, since the "classes" were primarily heuristic devices. These classes existed, to be sure, but as theoretical constructs. They were templates created by men through which to view society; they were not the independent, empirically verifiable units of Quesnay and company.

An absence of consensus regarding the social world came as no surprise to the Observer, then, given the diversity of men who undertook the task and the "different distributions" that they applied. To engage in debate over correct social schemata was to misunderstand the contingent nature of these categories: "The real gradations of character in society consist of undistinguishable degrees; which consequently set every sort of description at defiance. . . . Classification is designed less to settle or denote the exact merits of what it comprehends than to aid the mind in the prosecution of other purposes."[66] In assessing the value of these classifications, the Observer was more concerned with their efficacy than with their accuracy. While he did not desire to banish 'classes' from the realm of social analysis, he did suggest that all such terms were of limited usefulness. This rather interesting excursion into philosophic nominalism or methodological individualism was the first contribution to a nineteenth-century American discussion on the social order in which writers who pursued lines of reasoning similar to that of the Observer moved toward a rejection of the term and a denial of the phenomenon of 'classes' in American society. But in 1812 the Observer's doubts about the utility and universality of classes placed him at a remove from a majority of his fellow "intellectual surveyors," who preferred a rhetoric of precision to one of "approximation only." For them the classes of American society were natural and real, rather than artificial or arbitrary.[67]

The Observer was not alone in his assessment of the difficulties inherent in delineating, much less agreeing upon, a classification of the citizenry of the young republic. Writing from a decidedly different political position from the federalism of Dennie's or Biddle's *Port Folio,* John Taylor of Caroline was also dissatisfied with the social nomenclature used by his contemporaries, as he was with the vagueness of much American political discourse. "Political words of all others are the most indefinite," he complained in *Construction Construed, and Constitutions Vindicated,* "by account of the constant struggle of power to enlarge itself, by selecting terms not likely to alarm, but yet capable of being tortured by construction to produce events generally execrated."[68] Taylor's own campaign to expose and defeat that "power"—here identified with the Bank of the United States and other such Hamiltonian innovations—included an effort to bring more precision to the vocabulary of American politics, in particular to its political economy. The Virginian was conversant with the writers of the Scottish school, especially with Smith and Steuart, and with the linguistic theories of Locke and Horne Tooke, and drew upon them to formulate a Jeffersonian critique of the policies proposed and the terminology employed by his Federalist adversaries.[69] While his agreement with the empirically minded British that "the moral world, like the physical world, is subject to system and regularity" enabled Taylor to write on social arrangements with far more confidence than the nominalist Observer, he too recognized the problems of authority and accuracy that might beset any classificatory schema proposed by American analysts.[70]

Taylor developed his analysis of what constituted a suitable model for republican social relations in a series of essays that attacked both the theoretical bases and the practical implications of Federalist politics, especially the work and the words of John Adams and Alexander Hamilton. Their commitments to what Taylor saw as a hierarchical model of a society arranged by "orders," and their attempts at augmenting the wealth of the uppermost of these by means of banking and tariff legislation, convinced Taylor of the threats posed by the Federalists to American liberties. In *An Inquiry into the Principles and Policies of the Government of the United States,* first published in 1814 but composed prior to 1811, Taylor used the three volumes of Adams's *Defence of the Constitutions of Government of the United States of America* as evidence of complicity in "the artifice of compounding a society of orders, and not of individuals." In Taylor's judgment, Adams's insistence on the necessity of balancing the "natural" orders of society—the rich and the poor, or the natural aristocracy and democracy—and his exposition of that balance as manifest in the constitutions of ancient and modern states were based on an untenable theory of government and society. The orders that Adams thought occurred naturally in the histories of republics were, in fact, the unnatural results of the violations of the laws of political economy by way of unwarranted taxation, legislative patronage, and "paper systems." Adams's "theory of ranks or orders" was of little value in explaining the constitution of the American polity since, as Taylor argued, "no balance of specifick property among confederated orders can exist in communion with the present state of knowledge, commerce, and alienation." Taylor's use of "alienation" here was in reference to the legal process of the alienation of real property and the social and political consequences that ensued. In Taylor's republican context, the more alienation, the better.[71]

If the establishment of distinct orders was not a necessary condition for political stability according to Taylor, neither was the related assumption that a state of hostility among social groupings was "natural." In both cases Adams was in error. "The system of balance of orders is bottomed upon the idea of some natural or political enmity, between the one, the few and the many," Taylor noted, and despite Adams's exhaustive recounting of the internal conflicts that had destroyed earlier republics, Taylor remained unconvinced of its applicability to American circumstances (p. 203). "Election does not yet engage two orders of rich and poor in perpetual hostilities in the United States, but all ranks vote individually, interwoven and comixed." Were conflict to arise among these ranks, it would be provoked by such political intrigues as the Bank of the United States. For Taylor the nexus of republican conflict was not between the orders of rich and poor, but between the partisans of liberty and those of tyranny. Neither wealth nor poverty alone were reliable indicators of political behavior (pp. 130–31).[72]

Taylor rejected the premises of what he considered to be Adams's social and political theory, save in those instances where it corresponded to the "laws of nature": "the only use which the theory of ranks or orders has been pleased to make of the laws of nature, is drawn from the existing inequality among the talents and qualities of men" (p. 351). This "inequality" in turn did not correspond to the conventional division of the one, the few, and the many: "the magick contained in the number three is the magick of habit, not of nature. Human qualities are infinitely more divisible" (p. 351). But his recognition of the potential for infinite divisions among men did not lead him to the same conclusions as the Observer.

Taylor, the student of natural and moral philosophy, argued instead that an intellectually adequate system of classification was possible, though he confessed that he was not attempting such a task: "The possibility of effecting a classification of the beings or individuals of the moral world, and of assigning to each his proper class, by way of an impartial and careful investigation of phenomena, with a degree of accuracy, exceeding even the classification of the vegetable kingdom, is not incomprehensible" (p. 349). He addressed here the problem of authority by positing among the human faculties an ability to classify: "And its importance seems to have been suggested by divine intelligence, in having implanted in every breast, an auxiliary to the head in the prosecution of this science, of acute discernment, and instinctive integrity" (p. 349). The physical location of this auxiliary in the breast suggests a correspondence to the "moral sense" and "sentiments" that Francis Hutcheson and Adam Smith had explicated in their systems of moral philosophy. Taylor relied on this combination of reason and sentiment in the *Inquiry into the Principles* to "arrange a few of those moral beings, called political, by the test of fact"—a test that Adams's theory did not withstand—and not to present a comprehensive classificatory scheme. Yet it was is clear that such a "philosophically" reliable description could be drawn in conformity to the "laws of nature" (p. 349).

John Adams replied to these "strictures" against his work in a series of letters to John Taylor written in 1814. He acknowledged that *A Defence of the Constitutions*—"a book that has been misunderstood, misrepresented, and abused"—had been a source of controversy ever since its publication in 1787, but he remained adamant about his use of the term 'aristocracy'.[73] Taylor had failed, as had many other critics of that text, to appreciate the discrimination between artificial and natural forms of civil inequality made in *A Defence*. The former were "created and established" by law; the latter were the product of "superiorities" of virtue and talent. Among Americans, Adams maintained, only natural distinctions prevailed: all were "born to equal rights, but to very different fortunes." Since Taylor's sensitivity to the misuse of political words was so clearly informed by Locke's chapter "The Abuse of Words" in *Essay concerning Human Understanding,* Adams wondered why his own sense of 'aristocracy' was so readily misconstrued.[74]

Adams reflected as well on the effects of political change on the linguistic habits of Americans: "Some years ago, more than forty, a writer unfortunately made use of the term better sort. Instantly, a popular clamor was raised, and an odium excited, which remains to this day, that no man dares to employ that expression in conversation, in a newspaper, or pamphlet, nor in the pulpit."[75] What had happened to 'better sort' was now happening to 'natural aristocracy', no matter how helpful the concept still might be. The partisans of a "democratical" republic were again eliminating objectionable items from the national lexicon. Even such a long-standing phrase as 'the ranks of society' was now suspect. If Taylor were "shocked" by the connotations of 'rank,' Adams suggested that he use 'class' instead. For Adams the conceptual cost of linguistic vigilance could be high. Words had been used before to "signify anything, everything, and nothing." Taylor especially should be careful that ambiguities in his own party's language did not conceal instances of "fraud and injustice." Adams had great respect for Taylor as a patriot, but strong reservations about him as a republican theoretician.[76]

Adams's response notwithstanding, Taylor returned to the subject of classification and the political implications of "artificial distinctions" in *Construction Construed, and Constitutions Vindicated,* published in 1820. Here the particular target was the Federalists' advocacy of "protecting duties and bounties" for manufacturers, policies that placed the government in the position of assigning citizens to occupational categories "as a means for making some men subservient to the avarice of others." The "exclusive privileges" proposed by Hamilton in his *Report on Manufactures* presumed a utility of distinctions that Taylor questioned: "We have been led into this error by the abundance and vagueness of words. The words 'agriculture, manufacture, commerce, profession and science' have produced artificial distinctions; which have obscured the reach of the inclusive word 'labour'."[77] Since the natural faculty of "labour" made of all men who exercised it "manufacturers," Hamilton's bounties for only a select few were the ploys of a charlatan involved in "making the plenty of words change the nature of things" (p. 208).

In his investigation of this "natural faculty" Taylor did not doubt that actual distinctions existed among the agricultural, mercantile, or scientific "classes"; but he did object to the inequitable results of the divisions enforced in Hamilton's political economy. He faulted his adversary for failing to understand that "labour is in fact the only manufacturer," and therefore "workers upon the land, or upon the ocean, who give things new form or new places, are all manufacturers." As such, they should expect equal treatment, not "exclusive privileges" from their government. Only the "inclusive" term of 'labour' should enter into the political calculus: "If man were classed by the colour of their hair, yet the generick term 'man' would include them all. Classed by their occupations, all are also included by the generick term 'labour'. They all have the same rights, whatever might be the outlines of their physical or moral qualities" (p. 207). Hamilton's preferment of the manufacturers and investors amounted to a "confiscation" of the labor of farmers and sailors for the "comfort" of others. He made "artificial distinctions" among the occupational classes when only natural ones should be allowed. Despite Hamilton's claims to be informed by the principles of science, he violated the natural laws of civil society, and like Adams championed a bankrupt social theory. Each of these Federalists sought to recreate unnatural, unrepublican social and political orders.

The distinctions that Taylor recognized as "natural" in *Construction Construed* were those generated by the inequality of talents and abilities. "Society may be divided into the classes of rich and poor," he observed, and of these two "the poor class is by far the most numerous." Each of these large classes was composed in turn of occupational groups, with "employers," or "capitalists," prominent in the former, while seamen and the "agricultural occupation" were heavily represented in the latter. As long as this distribution into classes of wealth and occupation was not the creation of the state but of "natural" forces, Taylor was satisfied. Nor did he challenge the "productive" status of many among the capitalists as did his fellow Democratic Republicans Logan and Cooper: "I freely admit, that capitalists, whether agricultural, commercial, or manufacturing, constitute useful and productive classes in society, and by no means design, in the use of the term, to insinuate that it contains an odious illusion" (p. 234). Taylor reiterated his sole criterion of "fair and honest industry" in assessing the worth of the "capitalists," and rejected only those whose wealth was a creation of "legal coercions." Here Taylor followed Adam Smith in arguing for the productivity of employers and capitalists who subscribed to the principles of a "natural system of liberty."

Despite Taylor's often scathing attacks on "capitalists," they were not as a class culpable. Only those owners of capital who stood to benefit from Federalist economic programs did he presume to be a part of the politically suspect unproductive classes. Taylor's analysis was often anticapitalist—given his expansive use of that term—but was not opposed to what would later come to be known as liberal capitalism. To find in Taylor or in other Jeffersonians some variant of a nascent or essential American republican hostility to capitalism is to push these sources past the bounds of late-eighteenth- and early-nineteenth-century socioeconomic understanding and terminological usage. It was not the development of a commercial republic or the flourishing of "manufacturing" capitalists that troubled Taylor, but the political subversion of the marketplace.[78]

Taylor turned once more to the topic of productive and unproductive classes—an issue that had divided the French from the Scots and would continue to provoke debate among Americans through the nineteenth century—in his *Tyranny Unmasked,* published in 1822. The "tyranny" referred to was again the result of the "false political economy" of protective tariffs, monopolies, and similar instances of "exclusive privilege." Each of these transferred property from the "labouring classes" of society—that is to say, the "agricultural" and "mechanical classes"—to the "capitalists," and each was the result of the "pernicious mental labours" that he fought to expose. Since the "common appellation" of "unproductive labour" did not aid him in this task, Taylor introduced his own set of terms.[79] "I am not satisfied with the usual division of productive and unproductive labour," he complained. "It comprises in one class all bodily, and in the other, all mental labours; and seems eminently defective as to the latter class." Taylor instead subdivided the "mental" category into "moral and immoral labour." That, in turn, enabled him to classify philosophers, authors, lawyers, physicians, and tutors—all those who "produce knowledge, justice, health, and instruction"—as producers. Merchants, too, were classed as productive, since their "moral labour" tended to "excite and satisfy wants" to the benefit of all. To maintain the "correspondence between natural and social laws" that he presumed was necessary for a scientific classification of men, he relegated to the unproductive category all those involved in creating "social mischief": speculators, bankers, capitalists, and other potential aristocrats. As for those occupied in the business of governing, he judged the morality of their labors in light of their support for true or false systems of political economy. Although politicians, as a class, were neither productive nor unproductive, the "moral" status of Hamilton, Coxe, and their Federalist friends was not a matter of doubt.[80]

These revisions of the criteria of productivity allowed Taylor to delineate a distribution of the citizenry in which more occupations were included within the productive, and hence more politically reliable, classes than in the schema of George Logan or Thomas Cooper. It provided him with a rhetorical device with which he could posit a state of peaceful mutual dependence among the great majority of American "producers," who were following the natural dictates of the market, while still warning of impending class antagonism. If Taylor's producers remained on guard against the stratagems of the unproductive class, their republican liberties would be preserved. Without that vigilance, the American social order would eventually resemble that of Great Britain, with its "tribes of tenants, labourers, and mechanics panting for a revolution, and breaking out in frequent seditions."[81] That system was the one most cherished by Hamilton et alia, and its conditions foreshadowed the results of their politics. Taylor presumed neither a necessary harmony of all the interests nor an inevitable antagonism between the many and the few. He placed his productive and unproductive classes in a theoretical setting in which there was the potential for social stability or incessant strife.

As in his other essays, Taylor in *Tyranny Unmasked* based his version of a republican social order on a combination of the principles of moral philosophy and political economy—Adam Smith's in particular—and the conventions of Whig and Jeffersonian rhetoric. His "labouring classes" were naturally arranged by occupation and wealth, but that arrangement was easily unsettled. The political ambitions of unprincipled men were often, regrettably, at odds with the maxims of political science. Although Taylor, like his political and intellectual adversaries, did not intend to develop a fully articulated conceptual system in these pieces, but rather to apply his writings to the immediate issues of American political life, his synthesis, like Hamilton's, provided both his allies and his successors with a persuasive interpretation of the structure and dynamics of American civil society.

Where Hamilton's inheritors would attempt to banish class conflict from the realms of American political and learned debate, Taylor's Jacksonian legatees would rely on it as an important explanatory device, while arguing that their policies could keep it in check. And where authors in the tradition of the Observer wished to deny the existence of social classes, or at least to reduce them to heuristic labels, Taylor's successors in the sciences of politics in the United States would respond with arguments for an empirically grounded descriptive system drawn in conformity to the canons of Anglo-American natural and moral philosophy. While Taylor may not have solved the dilemma of imprecision in American political language, his contributions to this discourse on the social order aided the following generation, especially the Jacksonians, in the formation of their versions of a republican distribution of citizens.

For Taylor, as for many of the participants in the public discourse of the late eighteenth and early nineteenth centuries, neither the reality of socioeconomic classes nor the utility of a language of class was at issue. "Nothing is more evident than that, as we advance in knowledge of new things, and of new combinations of old ones, we must have new words to express them," as Thomas Jefferson observed in 1817.[82] When collections of citizens of this commercial republic were categorized, they were regularly and uncontentiously referred to as 'classes'.[83] America was not a classless but a naturally classed society. The points of contention were where exactly the divisions should be drawn, who had the authority to make them, how these classes related to each other, and what the political consequences of classification were. Each of these issues—the taxonomic, the relational, and the ideological—continued to generate debate among politicians, reformers, and scholars through the nineteenth century, as changes in American society engendered changes in its analysis.[84]

THREE

The Poetics and Politics of Productive Labor

During the closing years of the eighteenth century and the opening years of the nineteenth, Americans incorporated the categories of Enlightenment social science into their lexicons of public affairs. They commonly and uncontentiously used classifications of occupation, wealth, and prestige in everyday and learned discourse. These classes became "natural"—or naturalized—modes of social differentiation. Their interpretations of class relations were more controversial. Whether the various interests in a commercial society tended toward hostility or harmony was an open question in the rhetoric of republican politics.

Americans continued to employ a language of 'classes' and 'interests' throughout the middle decades of the nineteenth century, especially in discussions about and debates over the contours and consequences of economic growth. That the United States was a "rich and rising community," as the *North American Review* reminded its readers in 1827, was not a matter of doubt.[1] That all classes would benefit from an ever-expanding market was at issue, however; so too was the role that the state should take in promoting development. Within these ideological contexts 'class' went from being a relatively neutral to a rather contested term, and the definitions of eighteenth-century science became salient distinctions in nineteenth-century politics and culture.[2]

Among the Americans who regularly classed the citizenry—and frequently challenged other classifications—were those who applied the sciences of man in society to the analysis of conditions in the United States. In their treatises, textbooks, addresses, and essays, these exponents of the principles of moral philosophy and the sciences of politics constructed a model of social relations that classified individuals in terms of employment and income, and emphasized the mutual dependency of the respective classes. Despite important differences over technical points and national policies—the protective tariff and public finance in particular—these political economists and theorists agreed that in a "natural" social order like their own a "harmony of interests" could and should be the rule.[3]

In making their arguments these "intellectual surveyors" were joined by politicians and commentators, often of a conservative bent, who relied on the doctrine of harmony to refute charges of injustice and oppression leveled by a variety of social critics. Together these professionals and publicists created a durable convention in public discourse that represented the United States as a society formed by classes, but freed from class conflict, a conceptual mapping of the social order in which classes were naturalized and with which class relations were domesticated.[4]

These antebellum Americans identified themselves with and participated in the larger currents of international learning and literature—as had their predecessors—especially by way of the various transatlantic reviews.[5] Though they elaborated influential models of American social and economic exceptionalism, they were not intellectual isolationists. But the settings in which they worked and the positions that they occupied in the cultural division of labor often differed from those of their British and Continental counterparts. American men of affairs and moral philosophers such as Mathew Carey and John McVickar, for example, had no central gathering place akin to the Political Economy Club of London. Nor was their influence on public matters as direct as that of David Ricardo or other members of Parliament.[6] Nonetheless, they did make up a self-aware—if widely dispersed—community of discourse, one linked less by institutional than by textual ties and connected to the broader public by way of lecture circuits, voluntary associations, and the periodical press. "Here in America, the class of professed philosophical writers cannot be said to exist," as Edward Everett explained in the *North American Review,* "and the duty of directing the opinions of their fellow-citizens necessarily devolves on some class of professional or practical men."[7]

Although the Americans who constructed the model of the harmony of interests acknowledged the central role of Adam Smith and his fellow Scots in the formation of their sciences, they stressed as well the work of Smith's French follower Jean-Baptiste Say and of the English political economists Thomas Malthus and David Ricardo. Since they conceived their task to be the application of the universal principles of moral philosophy to the particularities of American conditions—rather than the production of "new" knowledge—they were prepared to disagree with the established authorities if it appeared that reality was at variance with theory. They were less concerned with creativity as such than with clarification and commentary.[8]

An important example of the distance between European principles and American practices can be found in the distinction between productive and unproductive labor. As Helen Boss has demonstrated, this apparently simple but chronically contested dichotomy has served as a shorthand for a cluster of controversial issues involving the creation and the distribution of wealth and power from the eighteenth century through the twentieth.[9] To antebellum political economists, the physiocratic and Smithian uses of these terms seemed to class a number of eminent and obviously productive callings among the morally suspect "consumers." This usage had opened a conceptual space that could serve as the site of erroneous, and potentially dangerous, social and political speculation, and required revision or replacement.

In lieu of Adam Smith's category of 'productivity', a number of Americans preferred Jean-Baptiste Say's more generous one of 'utility'. In both his *Traité d'économie politique* of 1803—translated into English and published in 1821—and his shorter *Catechism of Political Economy,* Say argued that members of the learned professions, officials, entertainers, and domestic servants were all "producers" of "immaterial products." These products consisted of utilities created and subsequently exchanged for fees, and they provided Say with grounds for arguing that "almost everybody produces." Say's *Catechism* was often adopted for use in secondary schools during the antebellum era, while the *Traité* was widely used as a textbook in colleges and universities. Through Say's modifications of Smith and through their own analyses, American moral scientists could move away from the conceptual dilemmas implicit in Smith's dichotomy toward a classificatory scheme that they deemed more appropriate to their circumstances.[10]

Daniel Raymond, an attorney from Baltimore, was one of the first Americans interested in the new sciences of politics and political economy to address the issues and implications of classification in detail. In *Thoughts on Political Economy,* published in 1820, he took exception to the "strange doctrine of productive and unproductive labour" expounded by Quesnay and Adam Smith, and to the classifications deduced from it. The book went through four editions and was widely known and cited by supporters and critics; among his admirers was John Adams. Raymond argued that these categories related to neither the "real nature of things" nor to the "true meaning of words." Though he did not completely abandon the terms 'productive' and 'unproductive', he did attempt to apply them to actual, not hypothetical, divisions in American society.[11]

Much of the disagreement about these terms, he maintained, was attributable to the careless treatment of language. "Almost every word in our language has a literal and a figurative meaning, and an indiscriminate use of words in their literal and figurative sense . . . cannot fail to produce ambiguity and confusion." His concern about the ambiguity of words was neither idiosyncratic nor idealist; this position was consistent with early-nineteenth-century American assumptions about the workings of the English language. In order to avoid any further "confusion" he conducted his analysis with expressions that were familiar and relevant to his readers (pp. 67–68).[12]

Raymond suggested that the greater portion of American occupations should be considered productive since "all labour is productive, which causes any of the necessaries or comforts of life." This expansive definition enabled him to rectify the "gross abuse of language" and the "unpardonable denigration" that classed authors as unproductive. These men of letters—with Raymond among them—had devoted their "intellectual power" to the "promotion of human happiness." To the now-diminished category of nonproducers, he relegated gamblers, "swindlers," and their allies, the speculators and stock jobbers. He was certain that the labor of all of these classes was "wholly useless" (pp. 207–8, 205).

Yet Raymond expressed some uncertainty about the worth of other professions that Adam Smith and the "Oeconomists" had judged as unproductive. If the labor of stage players, poets, painters, and musicians promoted the spread of "vices," they should be consigned to that class; if not, they should be grouped with the majority. He applied a similar test to legislators, judges, lawyers, clergymen, teachers, and physicians. Despite his defense of these intellectual laborers, he confessed that their efforts were sometimes "injurious." Raymond's assessment in each case was a moral one, but he was sufficiently familiar with the attitudes of his contemporaries to recognize the difficulty of generalization. Moral philosophers and political theorists were not the only ones to differ about the social utility of actors or attorneys. These were matters of controversy among ordinary citizens as well. For Raymond the evaluative classifications of a science of society should correspond to socially accepted standards. While he was not an advocate of what some historians have identified as a "moral economy," he was in favor of a political economy predicated upon a common morality (pp. 204–6).[13]

Raymond admitted the difficulty of making meaningful distinctions between the classes in light of the variety of public sentiments. "It is impossible to class the different occupations . . . ," he observed, "and say this is a productive, and that an unproductive occupation, because different people have different notions of what is useful, innocent, and moral" (p. 206). He did not intend to abandon political economy's claim to scientific status by pursuing this line of reasoning to any skeptical conclusions, however. In Raymond's estimation the source of this dilemma was to be found in the citizenry, not in the science. "The difficulty of classification . . . does not arise from the imperfection of the definitions and distinctions, but from the diversity of opinion as to the character of certain actions" (p. 206). But he did not propose a solution to this problem save in those instances where the "definitions" did correspond to community opinions, as in the case of speculators.

Although he raised an issue that he could not—or would not—resolve, Raymond's difficulties with classifications and moral evaluations underline a recurring point of contention in antebellum political economy and theory. If there was an inconsistency between technical definitions and commonplace distinctions, how might it be corrected? In the case of the terms 'productive' and 'unproductive', the general tendency was to do as Raymond had done and to argue that almost all employments were productive.

Raymond took less exception to Scottish interpretations of social relations than he did to their classifications. He emphasized the "dependence of one class of society upon another," as had Smith and Hume, under a system of "equal laws." Were the "natural equality" of citizens violated, however, he presumed that wealth and power would accrue to only one class. Such was the case in England, where the "artificial" practices of primogeniture, entails, and exclusive privileges had perpetuated an "unnatural" division of property. This had led in turn to "starvation among the ranks of the labouring classes," the very groups who "support the whole superstructure of civil society." Raymond had no desire to see a repeat of these conditions in the United States. Thus he found little merit in the writings of Thomas Malthus and others who deduced supposedly universal economic principles from the decidedly unnatural institutions of English society (pp. 315–16, 216, 273–74).[14]

Raymond also rejected the "chimerical theories" of William Godwin and the Marquis de Condorcet, which promised a "perfect equality" among men by way of a periodic redistribution of property. Their envisioned equalities of wealth and power also would be artificial, since nature distributed talents and strengths among individuals unevenly. Although Raymond acknowledged a "natural" right of men to ownership of the earth, this "undefined" right did not take precedence over the rights of private property guaranteed by civil society. "An agrarian law," he submitted, "or any other forcible equalization of property is unnatural." This interpretation of "natural equality" entailed an equality of civil rights and accepted an inequality of property, though it did not endorse the "curse" of chattel slavery. Raymond had called on Congress to prohibit the extension of slavery in an 1819 essay, *The Missouri Question.* The presence of slaves in Missouri would threaten the labor of the "middling classes."[15] But he had no quarrel with a social and economic hierarchy, as there was in New England, as long as its class structure was the result of personal effort and equitable legislation (pp. 228–30, 46).[16]

To ensure this "natural equality" and to enhance class harmony within the United States, Raymond advocated a series of legislative measures. He recommended strict regulations on banking and on the issuance of corporate charters in order to prevent the unwarranted growth of "private monopolies." He supported a protective tariff and publicly underwritten monopolies such as canals and railways to foster national economic development. These latter proposals brought him into favor with the partisans of Henry Clay, for whom Raymond anonymously wrote a campaign pamphlet on the American System in 1826.

Through his writings Raymond came to play a significant role in the intellectual life of the Whig party. He argued that the federal government should take an active part in both preserving and promoting the interests of the producing classes. While at a theoretical level he granted that there was a "natural" harmony of interests, at the practical level he contended that public policies and legal protections were needed to maintain the mutual "dependence" of the classes. His faith in the efficacy of the state placed him at odds with the doctrines and the disciples of Adam Smith and David Ricardo; but it won him the esteem of Americans of a "nationalist" persuasion, the self-professed followers of Alexander Hamilton.[17]

Mathew Carey, the emigrant Irish publisher and pamphleteer, was a leading figure among these nationalists during the 1820s. The *Thoughts on Political Economy* had so impressed Carey that he nominated Daniel Raymond for a professorship at the University of Maryland, a chair in political economy that he offered to fund. The necessary agreements could not be reached, however, and Raymond remained in Baltimore as a member of the bar. But Carey was not to be dissuaded from his campaign to disseminate the truths of protectionist economics and "nationalist" politics. From his press in Philadelphia he issued the *Political Economist,* a journal that featured a mixture of scholarly analysis, partisan commentary, and "extracts" from the proceedings of a number of local and state agricultural, manufacturing, and commercial associations.[18] One such piece was taken from an address by Isaac C. Bates, a Massachusetts lawyer and legislator, to the Hampshire, Franklin, and Hampden Agricultural Society of Northampton in October 1823. As a presentation in a regional setting of the principles and classifications that Carey and Raymond were promoting on the national scale, it is both a conventional piece and a significant text.[19]

During the course of a routine disquisition in favor of a protective tariff, Bates, an amateur of political economy, paused to comment on the structure of American society. "The classification of men in society is not arbitrary," he observed, "but grows out of the nature of things." This derivation from human nature protected the social and occupational hierarchy from the meddling of self-serving politicians or ill-informed theoreticians. As manifested in the United States, this natural class system was immutable: "[The] diversity of occupations forms classes, all governed by the same motive, and posting, with what ability they have, to the same results. Were you to take the fabric of the social state to pieces . . . it would make itself up again in the same general form" (p. 61). And as long as these social distinctions were governed by the rules of "ability," they would be just.

Though Bates was not specifically concerned with the nuances of the debate over productive and unproductive labor, he did respond to allegations made about the usefulness of his class, the attorneys. In defending his profession Bates appealed to a common standard of morality. "As in every character, so in every class, there are blemishes and defects," he admitted. Yet the presence of a few unscrupulous barristers did not warrant the label of unproductive for all members of this class. "There are lawyers who are the ornaments of their profession," he explained, and "others who are the disgrace of it" (p. 61). His apologia for lawyers is significant for more than its admission of lapses in professional conduct. Of interest, too, are the references to the "nature of things" in his analysis of American social arrangements. Bates's rhetorical position assumed that his audience was acquainted with both the charges leveled against lawyers and—more importantly—the argument that any particular system of classification was "arbitrary." Though an occasional piece, Bates's address suggests that the issues that Raymond and others were debating in treatises and learned reviews were also open to question in more popular arenas; it also suggests that Carey's subscribers and readers were familiar with the terms of these discussions. Mathew Carey's popularizations of protectionist economics included the diffusion of arguments that the United States was a 'natural' social order disposed toward stability and class harmony. This was to become an important line of reasoning for subsequent writers and spokesmen in both the protariff and the Whig ranks.[20]

The members of the protectionist camp were not alone in their portrayals of American society as 'natural'. Similar descriptions of the United States—albeit with different political prescriptions—were made by many who espoused the free-trade principles of classical political economy. The problems of definition inherited from Adam Smith remained as points of contention among them, but John McVickar, Thomas Cooper, and others tended to subscribe to expansive, not exclusive, conceptions of the American producing classes and to the related doctrine of class cooperation. If "the language of political economy is the language of reason and enlarged experience," as the Reverend McVickar suggested, then its use would help banish the "early and natural prejudice" that the rich exploited the poor, or that the "interests" of both were opposed. To advocate such "prejudice" was to ignore the maxims of empirical science and common sense, the very subjects that McVickar lectured on at Columbia College as the professor of moral philosophy, rhetoric, and political economy.[21]

While moral philosophers in the United States turned mainly to the subject of ethics in the closing decades of the nineteenth century, they were still concerned during the middle decades with larger questions in the moral, or social, sciences. Through their teaching, writing, and speaking they endeavored to "instruct the conscience" of the citizens on issues of politics, law, psychology, and public finance. Antebellum moral philosophers defined their roles in American culture as the expositors of practical truths and the defenders of social order. Like their eighteenth-century Scottish precursors, they were "professors of virtue." They expounded a secularized Protestant ethos of production for an expanding commercial society.[22]

In accord with his public and pedagogic duties as cleric and as professor, John McVickar published *Outlines of Political Economy* in 1825. That work consisted of a reprint of John Ramsay McCulloch's article "Political Economy" from the 1824 supplement to the *Encyclopaedia Britannica,* plus McVickar's extensive explanatory notes and commentary. He composed it for use as both a college text and a resource for the interested reader. McCulloch, in turn, had written the *Britannica* article to summarize and popularize the political economy of David Ricardo. McVickar's text, then, was the first introduction to the "liberal system" of British political economy prepared for a general American audience. The text received considerable attention at the time of its publication; the work was complimented by Thomas Jefferson and Chancellor James Kent, among others. McVickar supplemented *Outlines* in 1835 with his *First Lessons in Political Economy,* a text written for the common schools; with a series of public lectures on the same subject; and with a constant stream of articles and pamphlets.[23]

McVickar hoped that his readers, by following *Outlines,* would come to understand what McCulloch had described as the "various general laws which regulate and connect the apparently clashing, but really harmonious, interests of every different order in society."[24] McCulloch's contrast between "apparently clashing" and "really harmonious" interests was critical. As T. W. Hutchison has so forcefully and cogently argued, neither David Ricardo nor his orthodox followers presumed that class relations in a commercial society were necessarily antagonistic. Social harmony was a "self-evident" conclusion of the science of political economy as Ricardo understood it. The connections between Ricardian theories of rent, profit, and wages, and systematic conflict among the "three classes of the community" were made instead in the works of his intellectual critics (such as Henry Carey) and his heterodox successors (such as Karl Marx). Although

McCulloch's and McVickar's deduction of an axiomatic class harmony out of the terms of Ricardian political economy might seem to be wrong-headed, if not perverse, to later audiences who assume that this tradition contains a class-conflict analysis, recent revisionist scholarship suggests that such conclusions were in keeping with those of Ricardo and his supporters. Hutchison, especially, has argued that Ricardo "expounded doctrines of the harmony of class interests, between labourers and capitalists, in more extreme terms than any subsequent, important, bourgeois 'apologist.'" Hutchison sees the development of a class antagonism position from Ricardo as part of Marx's position and a Marxist reinterpretation of his predecessor's work.[25]

In *Outlines of Political Economy* McVickar assigned part of the responsibility for this apparent antagonism to Adam Smith. He complained about the "invidious distinctions" made in the *Wealth of Nations* "between the various classes of the community." Instead of Smith's "narrow and imperfect" categories of 'productive' and 'unproductive' labor, McVickar made a threefold division along the lines recommended by Ricardo, Malthus, and Say. He distinguished every class by its source of income, not by its supposed productivity. The labor of all, save for beggars and thieves, was assumed to be productive. The three main classes were "holders of land," capitalists, and an "industrious" class that was subdivided into "labourers" and those "who increase the power of the above." McVickar placed in this last category the formerly 'unproductive' workers in government, education, and the sciences. This move enabled him to avoid the "unjust conclusion" of Adam Smith that would have condemned "Watt, Whitney, and Fulton" to the ignominy of the unproductive classes. McVickar preferred the generosity of the Ricardian distinction between 'directly' and 'indirectly' productive labor to the moral dilemmas of the Smithian dichotomy.[26]

Even these improved criteria should be used carefully in the course of social and political analyses, McVickar warned. As a rhetorician he was quite sensitive to the power of words. The separate categories of 'direct' and 'indirect' labor did not imply the separation of interests: "This classification is convenient for reference but dangerous for reasoning, as tending to lead the economist to the false inference of divided or opposite interests among the different classes of the community."[27] By dismissing as "prejudice" any evaluation of social relations predicated on an opposition of interests, McVickar turned the assumption of class harmony into an axiom. As such it involved no proof, but it could direct colleagues, students, and the general public away from any "false inference" about the workings of commercial society. By separating the task of "reasoning" about class relations from the referential function of classification, McVickar contributed to the formation of a durable interpretation of American society in which occupational classes abounded, while class antagonism was absent. His rejection of class conflict was less an exercise in "bourgeois" apologetics than a consistent application of the principles of Ricardian social science. *Outlines* was one of the elementary texts in the nineteenth-century liberal discourse of American social exceptionalism.[28]

McVickar's derivation of public policies from the "natural laws" of political economy was in line with the "liberal system" of Ricardo and Smith. The most effective way to promote economic growth and societal happiness was to minimize the interference of the state; therefore all bounties, privileges, monopolies, and other instances of preferential legislation should be abolished. Chief among these offenses was the tariff, and McVickar was firmly opposed to protectionism in its political and intellectual manifestations. He was also a strong advocate of structural reforms of the financial system; his *Hints on Banking* was an influential text with the free banking movement in the state of New York. McVickar's proposals for banking reform had a major impact on the shaping of New York's Free Banking Act of 1838 and the federal National Banking Act of 1863.[29] His exposition of the ethical and practical advantages of the "liberal system" put him in good standing with New York financiers and men of commerce; he was an important source of scientific validation and moral ratification of their particular economic positions. To them, McVickar's *Outlines* demonstrated the happy correspondence between a free, open market and a free, natural society.[30]

The president of the College of South Carolina, Thomas Cooper, found a similarly propitious relationship between the policy of free trade and the interests of Southern planters and merchants. By the time of the publication of his *Lectures on the Elements of Political Economy* in 1826, he had undertaken a number of changes of profession and place of residence. During the first two decades of the nineteenth century Cooper had been a federal magistrate, an editor of the *Emporium of Arts and Sciences,* and a teacher of chemistry at Dickinson College in Pennsylvania. In 1819 Thomas Jefferson tried to secure for his old ally the chair in chemistry at the new University of Virginia.

But Cooper's public attacks on Calvinism and his espoused philosophical materialism led to serious opposition to the appointment on the part of Virginian Presbyterians. He accepted instead a professorship in chemistry at South Carolina, where in 1821 he was elected president; in 1825 he began to offer formal instruction in political economy. To best explain that "science of fact, not of conjecture," to his students, Cooper assigned them McVickar's *Outlines* until his own lecture notes could be printed. Due to its hasty and unsystematic composition, Cooper's text contained a number of contradictions, but it did present the arguments of one of the most active intellectual champions of the "liberal system" in the South.[31]

Along with his occupation Cooper had changed his opinion on a number of issues in politics and political economy. Once an enemy of slavery, he was by 1826 a small slaveholder and a defender of unfree labor on the grounds of states' rights, though not on the basis of economic efficiency. Cooper's political and constitutional justification of slavery was characteristic of many of his fellow Jeffersonians. His analysis of slave labor in terms of political economy was in keeping with that of Adam Smith and the British liberal tradition. Slave labor was less efficient and produced less wealth than did free labor, since it was involuntary. Thanks to the writings of David Ricardo, Cooper had become a firm opponent of the tariff, despite some previously expressed sympathy for protective duties. He had also moved away from the positions on productive labor and class antagonism that had appeared in 1798 in his *Political Arithmetic.*[32]

Cooper returned in *Lectures* to the topics of classification and class relations in a chapter on definitions. There he took exception to the "defective" categories of Quesnay that classed merchants and manufacturers among the unproductive; this was a distinction that was no longer as salient as it once had been. He now included these two callings among the producers, where they were joined by men of science and men of letters. "He is a producer of no mean consideration," Cooper explained, "who contrives to give value and utility to that which had none before." Only those individuals who avoided all work (like sinecure holders) or whose "labour may well be dispensed with" (like entertainers) were assigned to the "unproductive class." Cooper here followed the example of McVickar by replacing a troublesome set of distinctions with an expansive definition of the producing classes.[33]

But in a subsequent section of *Lectures,* "Productive and Unproductive Labour," Cooper indicated to his readers that this eighteenth-century dichotomy still had much to recommend it. He followed Adam Smith by assuming that the ratio between these two great classes was a central factor in explaining economic growth, stagnation, and decline, and by using the direct creation of wealth as the decisive discriminatory criterion. Thus Cooper classed not only obvious drones as nonproducers, but the professionals whom he just had placed in the productive column. To avoid the unfavorable connotations of 'unproductive', Cooper employed Smith's notion of the social usefulness of certain types of labor: "to say that any member of society is not of the productive class does not amount to denying his utility." He was able, therefore, to advise his fellow philosophers and scientists to find comfort in their classification as "unproductive, but useful" laborers. "Political economy," Cooper observed, "teaches us to hold in reverence any of the classes described by the Poet as 'fruges consumere nati.' "[34]

Cooper did not reconcile his inconsistent use of these categories in *Lectures,* but he did clarify his arguments in the second edition of the text and in a subsequent abridgment published in 1833 under the title *A Manual of Political Economy.* By the beginning of that decade the question of who constituted the productive and unproductive classes had moved from the technical discourse of college professors to the wider arena of political debate. The activities of the men and women involved in the workingmen's parties and other related movements for reform had politicized the term 'producing class'. In their calls for the increased influence of the 'workingman' in public affairs, they sought to exclude from that category owners of factories and heads of large commercial concerns, among others. They were engaged in a project of political mobilization and conceptual closure. Cooper, an eighteenth-century Anglo-American radical, was vehemently opposed to the politics and the rhetoric of these nineteenth-century radicals. Yet he welcomed the chance to examine their platforms and proposals. The workingmen's advocates needed to be corrected, not silenced. Through *Lectures* and *A Manual of Political Economy* he could make clear to the public the elements of an established science and could expose the errors of the "mechanic political economists."[35]

Cooper noted that "it has been agitated whether the manufacturer and the merchant have a right to be counted among the producing classes," a question he emphatically answered in the affirmative. He placed them in the same category as farmers, sailors, and "operatives in manufacture." When deciding the standing of other occupations, he proceeded along Smithian lines. "That most useful class of literary and scientific men" were "non-productive" as were bankers, brokers, and shopkeepers. Cooper continued to emphasize the utility of these classes to society as a whole; though they were not "working men," their "labour of the brain" did contribute to the common good. Only those who would not work or were engaged in detrimental pursuits should be held up for scorn as "non-producing" consumers.[36]

It was Cooper's judgment that the proliferation of faulty schemes of classification among the operatives could lead to disastrous political results. The mechanic economists had misunderstood the productive role of the landowners and manufacturers; they imagined that the "labouring classes" could do without the classes of capital. Thomas Skidmore and Frances Wright had concluded that only radical reconstruction of the laws of inheritance and reformation of popular education could resolve the American dilemma of unequal distribution of wealth and property. But these proposals, Cooper argued, were little more than demands for equality of fortunes. These measures would produce "artificial equality" in violation of the laws of Smithian and Ricardian political economy. Were the mechanic economists to have their way, the government would once more be in the business of compelling the "labouring" class to support the "drones." In order to alleviate the supposed sufferings of a misconstrued laboring class, the "natural liberties" of the producing majority might be destroyed.[37]

The distance that Cooper placed between himself and the champions of the workingmen is indicative of the differences between the idioms of Anglo-American radicalism in the late eighteenth century and those of the mid–nineteenth century. His radicalism was grounded in the Enlightenment politics of Adam Smith and company—in a "bourgeois radicalism," as Isaac Kramnick has called it—while the radicalism of William Heighton and Langton Byllesby was intended, in part, as a critique of classical political economy. Though Cooper approved of trade unions, favored free public education, and called for tax relief for the poor, he did not assume that American arrangements were inherently unfair or unjust. Within the liberal system, as Cooper explained it, "superior industry" was rewarded with "superior advantages." While he remained as suspicious of the acquisitive instincts of mercantile and commercial men in the 1830s as he had been in the 1790s, he did not endorse a politics of essential class antagonism. Like his fellow Jeffersonian John Taylor of Caroline, Cooper could severely criticize capitalists without calling into question the fundamental premises of capitalism.[38]

Despite Cooper's dismissal of the radical reformers, some elements in his analysis of American class relations are similar to theirs. In *Political Arithmetic* of 1798 he had presumed that the productive and unproductive classes were antagonists in the political realm, a conflict that was still implied in *Lectures.* "All the unproductive class must be maintained by the labouring, the working classes," he argued. "Those who produce nothing, must live upon the earnings of those who produce something." If the instruments of that maintenance were monopolies, privileges, or "incorporated companies," the minority of "consumers" would exploit the productive majority.[39] Cooper reiterated this position in *A Manual of Political Economy,* where he identified the tariff as the most obvious engine of class oppression. Protective duties amounted to public subsidies of one class at the expense of the others. More than McVickar and other exponents of free trade, he emphasized the dangers of the unnatural factors at work in an otherwise natural American economy.

Cooper discovered another potential source for class antagonism in the factory system so favored by northern protectionists. He worried that the lives of America's urban poor would come to resemble those of Britain's working classes. In a review of Jean Simonde de Sismondi's *Nouveaux principes d'économie politique* for the *Southern Review* of 1829, he paused to warn of the parallels between the situations of "operatives" in Britain and the United States: "It may well become the labouring classes in our country, who are yet free and intelligent, to consider these circumstances, and before they give an additional impulse to this system, to examine its ultimate results" (p. 270).

To avoid the miserable conditions of their British counterparts, Cooper suggested that the members of the American "labouring classes" should carefully calculate their political and social interests in the light of economic science, in particular its injunctions against the tariff. While such a proposal was rather modest in comparison to the projects of the mechanic economists, Cooper's pessimistic forecast of the fate of the "operatives" was closer to the rhetorical stance of the radicals than it was to the optimism of McVickar and later exponents of liberal political economy.

The American republic, in Cooper's estimation, was still liable to the depredations of monopolists and "non-productive" capitalists, and to the degradation of the "working classes" in manufactories. These practices remained potential—though not inevitable—sources of class hostility. His study of Ricardo had convinced him of the explanatory power and the efficacy of liberal economics, but it had not led him to abandon a rhetoric of conflicting interests. The sciences of politics and political economy did provide the outlines of a "natural," cooperative social order, but they did not guarantee that class antagonism or class distinctions would disappear.

It was to these distinctions and their implications that another contributor to the *Southern Review* took exception. In an unsigned piece on Cooper's *Lectures,* the reviewer found such questions as "whether . . . the artist is to be classed with the artizan, and the magistrate with the merchant, under some common denomination" to be little more than "metaphysical speculation." Although he did not object to the elucidation of the "principles of economic science" by Cooper and his peers, the reviewer did wonder about their debates over the distinctions between the productive and the unproductive classes: "We consider many of the recent discussions in regard to definitions, as embracing questions of arrangement too refined to be useful, and as involving the propriety of classifications, meant merely as aids to investigation, and never urged as differences found in the nature of things."[40] Since these "aids" had evidently become a hindrance in Cooper's investigations, the reviewer recommended that they be dispensed with. His dissatisfaction with these terms led him to conclude that these classifications were at best heuristic devices, and that a terminology inherited from the Physiocrats and Adam Smith was of little relevance to the "nature of things" in the America of 1826. "The complete accuracy of our classifications," he submitted, "may be a subject of speculative curiosity."[41] The extent of such curiosity notwithstanding, neither the conceptual boundary disputes over who was or was not a producer nor the assumption that such classifications did or did not correspond to the natural order could be so simply removed from the arenas of American public discourse.

While the principles of free trade, protection, and—after the election of Andrew Jackson in 1828—banking were at the center of debate among politicians and political economists, it was the unexpected appearance of the self-styled workingmen's parties that engendered the most concern over usages of 'class'. If the criticisms made by Robert Dale Owen or George Henry Evans were to be seriously entertained, the issue of who was or was not a "producer" must be more than a matter of "metaphysical speculation"; definitions were themselves political actions. And if the radicals' analyses of an apparently "natural" social and economic order had any merit, the interpretations of American class relations that were predicated upon class cooperation were open to question. The mechanic economists and the workingmen's parties posed a series of political and conceptual challenges that needed to be addressed.[42]

The rhetorical strategy most favored by the opponents of the workingmen's movements was, first, to deny any exclusive claims to the title of 'working' or 'producing' class(es); then, in turn, to dismiss any appeals to the conflicting interests of producers and consumers. Since almost all citizens were "workers" in an expansive sense, how could there be any fundamental differences of interest among them? This line of argument was pursued by Edward Everett of Boston in *A Lecture on the Working Men's Party*. In response to his own query about who should belong to such a party, Everett replied, "[A]ll who do the work." Among the "working men" he numbered the supposedly unproductive classes of merchants, poets, lawyers, teachers, painters, and architects. "All these pursuits are in reality connected with the ordinary work of society," Everett contended, "as directly as mechanical trades, by which it is carried on." Thus only "bad men" who defied the law or the moral sensibility of the community should be excluded from a party of the "working men." Only their labors were truly unproductive. The appropriation of the title of "workers" by the mechanics was a categorical error that might lead to a false inference of enmity among the classes. "There is a close and cordial union between the various pursuits and occupations," Everett insisted, since it was obvious that "all are parts of one whole."[43]

James T. Austin offered a similar, if more detailed, assessment of social relations in an essay, "Classes of American Society," for the *Christian Examiner*. Austin, a Massachusetts politician and sometime attorney general, denounced the efforts to organize Americans into "hostile parties" and to promote the idea of "opposition among different classes." These projects were ill-conceived and ill-advised. They posed a threat to the system of "popular government," which rested upon the "mutual affection and esteem" of the classes for each other. Austin was resigned to parties organized around differing "principles," but he was unsure if the political order could tolerate parties based on class affiliation.[44]

To expose the errors of the Workingmen's parties, Austin turned to an examination of the class structure of American society, and to the claims that the rich and poor were antagonists: "Before parties can be formed with the design to divide the rich from the poor, or the working man from the idle, it should be ascertained whether any classes properly so distinguished, do in fact exist in our community" (p. 253). In Austin's estimation they did not. Since legislation had eliminated the practices of primogeniture and entail, and thus effectively mandated equal inheritance, there was no "prescriptively affluent class" in the nation, nor could one arise. By changing his definition of 'class' from one of occupation and wealth to one of legal condition, Austin was able to claim that, while individuals might be rich, "here we have no class of rich men." Bereft of a "monied aristocracy," American society had neither the elements necessary for any real antagonism between the rich and poor, nor the "excuse for any controversy . . . founded on the distinctions of wealth" (pp. 254–57).

As for the poor, the absence of legal discriminations and the unlimited opportunities for "acquiring property" in the United States prevented them from becoming a proper "class." And having disposed of these two erroneous categories, Austin proceed to dismiss the relevance of the term "working classes . . . as the phrase is beginning to be used here." With its meaning limited to "operatives" in factories, the phrase was of little use in describing the American social order. "However exact the term may be in European nations, or elsewhere in the world," he maintained, "the distinction intended to be conveyed by it, is perfectly arbitrary and according to our notion, absurd" (p. 264). The arbitrary character of the term stemmed from the exclusion of so many workers from the "working classes." Like Everett, Austin preferred a more encompassing notion of who was a worker: "Every man, or almost every man, is a working man, unless he has grown old in labour." He recognized only the tiny minority who "contribute nothing" as a nonproducing class; every other calling was included within the "working class." Hence the coterie of workingmen's advocates caused confusion when they criticized as useless the members of the professional and commercial classes (pp. 264–68).

In Austin's estimation this divisive rhetoric encouraged the dissemination of irrelevant ideas about social relations. Despite the cries of class oppression, in the United States there was a "happy coincidence" of class interests. "The suggestion of a contrary interest in the different classes of society," he noted, "may be suspected to be the fruits of an evil design" (p. 268). To represent class relations in terms of conflict was to engage in more than a series of categorical errors. To do so was an indication of the "unfair designs" that the radicals had on the property of the true working class; it was evidence that their failings were moral as well as intellectual. In his attack on the workingmen's parties, Austin sought to deny them any claim to ethical or political legitimacy, and to force their interpretations of American society from the realm of respectable discourse.

Emory Washburn, Austin's colleague in the legislature and a professor of law at Harvard, shared this concern about the claims made in the name of the "working class." The "outcry" over the "rights" of the workingmen prompted Washburn to compose an article, "The Laboring Classes of Europe," for the *North American Review*.[45] There he objected to the analogies made between the condition of the "laboring classes" in Europe, particularly in Britain, and the circumstances of the same classes in America. To describe the actual sufferings of the English workers and then to call on American mechanics and laborers to defend themselves "as if there were some real analogy" between the two situations was to "mislead the public sentiment." Washburn rejected these comparisons and their consequences. The "arbitrary and artificial" gradations of European societies, he submitted, were created by legal restrictions on the accumulation and use of property. But in the United States the law ensured free access to property and equitable distribution of the "rewards of industry." The classes that had developed in American society were produced by natural economic forces and were protected by a fair system of laws.

In some cases Washburn accepted, and in others he rejected, the applicability of the term 'laboring classes' to American social arrangements. If that phrase appeared in a political rhetoric that evoked images of the "starved mechanic" or the "oppressed manufacturer," its use was invalid. In his rendering of the republic's social order there were no institutions to "grind down the laboring classes to the dust." But if the term was merely a shorthand for artisans and laborers who enjoyed equal privileges with all other callings, then the "laboring classes" did indeed exist. Hence the appeals of the workingmen's and trade union movements were based on a serious misinterpretation of the class structure of their own society, and their programs were little more than attempts to "subvert the laws" that actually promoted their true interests. Washburn, like Austin, sought to deny the legitimacy of analyses predicated on class antagonism. And as did Austin, he emphasized the political and legal differences between the class systems of Europe and America. Only the Europeans had fixed social hierarchies; only they, in this juridical sense, had a class system that was real.

By shifting the criteria for what constituted the 'laboring' and the other classes, Austin and Washburn could delineate an American social order in which classes were at times real and at other times illusory. This rhetorical device of rendering problematic the very subject under consideration was also employed by the New York journalist James H. Lanman in a contribution to the *American Monthly Magazine* on the problem of "Social Disorganization."[46] Lanman's topic was the recent national speaking tour of Frances Wright, whom he accused of appealing to the "jealousies" of the "working men" when urging their political independence. Lanman restricted his sense of "working men" to "individuals who acquire their daily subsistence by manual labor," but he rejected the proposition that "the rich are encroaching upon their rights." Different sources of income did not necessarily lead to different interests, he insisted. There were no grounds for attacks upon the "now wealthy class" by any other class. To propose a politics of class confrontation with a language of class antagonism, as did Frances Wright, was to misunderstand and misrepresent the nature of American institutions: "It may be made plain to everybody that there is no natural ground of hatred by the poor toward the rich, because there are no classes recognized by the constitution. In the eyes of the government, all men stand on the same level."[47]

Legal equality, then, precluded the formation of the very entities that Wright sought to mobilize. Lanman, like Washburn, used a hypothesized legal definition of social classes, a category he then found absent in the American context. This absence in turn permitted him to reduce the classes that he wrote about to linguistic conventions of common usage. Thus he could easily employ the term, while denying the existence of that for which the term stood when he was confronted with a rhetoric of class conflict. This strategy allowed Lanman to dismiss Wright's critique of American social relations as a collection of mistruths, just as it allowed Austin and Washburn to counter the claims of the workingmen's parties. In each instance the ability to refer to 'classes' was the prerogative of those who insisted that the social order was natural; it was not the right of those who criticized American conditions. Use of the term 'class' was not in itself, therefore, a commitment to radical politics. It was the rhetorical context of usage that transformed 'class' from a neutral to a controversial term. These arguments about appropriate classifications were not simple assertions that America was a "classless" society but attempts at limiting the rhetorical and the analytical uses of 'class' in the public arena.

How to refute the "peculiarly destructive" ideas of the workingmen's movement was also a subject for discussion in the pages of Condy Raguet's free-trade journal, the *Banner of the Constitution*. In an editorial that appeared in the 2 March 1831 edition, Raguet described the "spirit of inquiry" then current among the "working men." These inquiries had resulted in the propagation of a number of truths and falsehoods concerning the American economy. Among the most offensive errors was the argument, "so strongly urged of late," that the laborer was denied his proper share of the wealth "as society is organized."[48] Raguet assumed that this attack on the owners of capital and on the principles of distributive justice would have serious social and political implications: "If this sentiment should become widely diffused, it will lay the foundation for the bitterest animosities and jealousies between those who are designed, by the natural order of things, to be the best friends of each other" (p. 111). He was convinced these "false doctrines" were so powerful that, if the "working classes" subscribed to them, the stability of an otherwise harmonious social order would be threatened. Although the class antagonism preached by the radicals was contrary to the "natural order of things," American society was vulnerable to these incorrect ideas, especially when they were translated into political activities.

To protect the public from these "destructive" notions, Raguet urged that the "correct" principles of political economy be better communicated by more lectures on the subject, and by familiarizing more editors with the maxims of that science. He recognized that many of his readers felt that the discipline had little to offer in "reference to the general interests of society," save on the issues of the tariff and public works. But had the working classes been taught that in the market system there was of necessity an equitable exchange between employer and laborer, they could have recognized the errors of the Workingmen. There would be little talk about conflicting interests if the population knew what political economy had demonstrated, that "the interests of the two are so fairly and advantageously blended, that the workingman could not do without the capitalists, nor the capitalist without the workingman" (p. 112). The appeals of the radicals, therefore, were best met by a wider dissemination of this axiom of mutual dependence. Their criticisms of American society had no grounding in the "nature of things."

The popularity of dangerous premises among the "producing classes" also drew the attention of William Duane of the *Aurora,* a Philadelphia journal favorable to Andrew Jackson. In a piece addressed "To the Working Men," Duane criticized their habit of identifying themselves as a "separate" interest and class, as well as their charge that political institutions favored the rich. "The idea is too loose for argument," he noted, "and does not arrive at the conclusion it surmises." A careful study of American conditions had demonstrated to him that the various "pursuits" were bound together by ties of "mutual support," and that political power was already in the hands of the "most numerous": the "producing classes." If the producers desired a "redress of grievances," they did not have to pursue mistaken theories; the "remedy" for their problems was to be found in the political system. The "producing classes," Duane explained, should support the true party of the "working men," the party of Andrew Jackson.[49]

Duane's political message in the *Aurora* underscores the decidedly partisan dimension of these assessments of, and appeals to, the 'working' or 'producing' classes—however widely or narrowly defined. While the workingmen's parties tended to support Andrew Jackson at the national level, on the local scene they were rather more independent and challenged the already established parties for power. William Duane was a Jacksonian Democrat from Philadelphia; Condy Raguet was an ex-Federalist, sometimes anti-Jackson publisher with Washington and Baltimore interests; and Everett, Austin, and Washburn held elective office in Massachusetts as members of the Whig party. They wrote pieces in opposition to the Workingmen with immediate political goals—not detailed social and conceptual analyses—as their purpose.

Yet their resistance to the appropriation of the phrase 'working class' when used in a limited and confrontational sense, and their consistent reference to a natural harmony of interests are worthy of note. Edward Everett and William Duane recognized the appeal of the radicals' rhetoric and the necessity of contesting it. They were aware of the cultural power wielded by their opponents, as well as their own. Their assertions that the terms of classification had been misunderstood assumed that a proper understanding could be agreed upon in the civic arena. As distant as they were from their opponents, they inhabited a common world of printed public discourse.

Despite the clear differences in the party affiliation and preferred policies, Duane, Austin, et alia made use of the same conventions in rebutting the claims of the Workingmen. The demise of that movement had more to do with its internal dynamics than with the criticisms of either Whigs or Democrats, but the results of its brief appearance included a politicization of the American lexicon of class. Members of the two major parties developed rhetorical strategies with which they could claim to represent the real working class or could deny, if need be, that class's existence. They could elaborate a model American society that was indebted to works of the moral philosophers and political economists, one composed of mutually cooperating occupational classes with little need for either the rhetoric or the remedies of the Workingmen.[50] Though the presence of classes or the question of class relations was never as systematically denied as were many dimensions of slavery in antebellum political discourse, those who insisted on the importance of class antagonism in America could expect to be met by these writers with countercharges of demagoguery and deception.[51]

The classifications made by Austin and company were attempts at enforcing conceptual closure, but they were only partially successful at best. They hoped, as did Thomas Cooper, to constrain the terms of debate and to deny legitimacy to some specific uses of 'class'. But in this era public discourse on classification and class relations was pluralistic, not monolithic. Americans did not uniformly subscribe to some generalized "producers' ethic" that bound them together in a creed of one great productive class. Nor did they simply espouse a liberal ideology of classlessness that denied the presence of actual socioeconomic divisions, or the possibility of class hostility. Instead, they disagreed with each other over class nomenclature and class relations. Their disagreements came not in the course of an endless, groundless contest of classifications, but in contexts of substantive debates over political and economic choices. "If facts are still doubtful, and principles unsettled," as Alexander H. Everett observed in the *North American Review,* "the same words must, in the nature of things, be used by different writers in different senses."[52] By the middle decades of the nineteenth century, 'class' had become one of those words.

FOUR

The Rhetoric of Reconcilable Class Conflict

The imagery and arguments about class harmony promoted by the moral philosophers and political economists enjoyed considerable currency in antebellum public discourse. But theirs was not the only mode for interpreting economic conditions or inscribing social arrangements in the United States. While the economists were examining and celebrating the beneficial processes of growth and diversification, others were far less satisfied when they considered the changes so engendered. To many Americans developments such as a more complex system of commercial and financial institutions, an increasing distinction in urban centers between master mechanics and journeymen, and the appearance of British-styled manufactories with their classes of dependent wage earners—developments later colligated by historians with the terms 'industrial' or 'market' revolutions—were not read as signs of progress. Nor could many contemporaries account for the often disturbing results of these processes by appeals to the principles of political economy. No matter how revolutionary the 'market revolution' might have been in economic terms, these changes provoked intense debate over the consequences of commercial capitalism.[1] Rather than accepting these transformations as the necessary outcomes of natural laws, a large, if disparate, collection of social critics, politicians, journalists, trade unionists, and self-styled radicals and reformers developed their own explanations of the workings of American social and economic life.[2]

In so doing, the participants in this tradition of public discourse were indebted less to the works of Adam Smith, David Ricardo, and their successors, than to those sciences of society that had arisen in response to the problems created by the often dramatic patterns of social and economic change in contemporary Europe. From the works of critics such as Robert Owen and Charles Fourier, their American counterparts adopted the position that modern society was constructed "radically wrong" and was in need of substantial reformation.[3] To these arguments they joined those well-established conventions of Anglo-American republican discourse that emphasized the rapacity of the aristocracy and the perpetual enmity between the rich and the poor. Although not usually presented in the context of formal treatises, a set of alternative models with which to analyze the structure and dynamics of a commercial capitalist society were elaborated in their speeches and writings. Within this counterdiscourse on class they emphasized conflict, albeit a resoluble conflict; and through it they sought to assert cultural control over the categories of 'laborer', 'producer', and 'worker'. Thus in antebellum America, contests between the classes entailed contests over classification.[4]

William Maclure—Robert Owen's partner in his New Harmony, Indiana, experiment—was one of the first observers-cum-reformers to suggest what the findings of a science of society would be when applied to American circumstances. Already renowned as a geologist and as president of Philadelphia's Academy of Natural Sciences, Maclure established a School of Industry at New Harmony in 1826 to advance the twin causes of educational and social reform.[5] To that community's *Disseminator of Useful Knowledge* and *New Harmony Gazette,* he contributed essays on these and related topics, which he collected and published in 1831 as *Opinions on Various Subjects: Dedicated to the Industrious Producers.* As this last title indicates, the discrimination between types of 'producers' had not lost its categorical efficacy in Maclure's scientific analysis of society.[6]

Before proceeding in this task, Maclure noted, one needed to have recourse to first principles: the division of all societies between the "two natural classes of producers and consumers, the industrious laborers and those who live on the fruits of their labor," and the contradictory interests that of necessity arose between the two. These distinctions and assumptions, he maintained, were central to an adequate explanation of the seriously flawed organization of contemporary economic, political, and social affairs. Although Adam Smith had introduced such a schema in the *Wealth of Nations,* it had since disappeared into the "labyrinth of words" constructed by his successors. The ability to make substantive and pejorative distinctions between the classes—an ability that for Maclure was central to any plans for social and political renovation—had been lost within the conceptual maze of classical political economy. Rather than promoting the "intricate and mysterious science" of Ricardo, Malthus, et alia—the "artificial and complicated systems" that supported the unnatural state of the nonproducers—Maclure called for a new political economy, one designed to meet the pressing needs of the industrious producers in the working classes.[7]

While Maclure acknowledged the importance of the Smithian dichotomy, he defined 'productive' and 'nonproductive' labor along more restrictive lines. To the first he admitted only those who "labour with their hands, and produce," the farmers, artisans, and perhaps the merchants; while in latter he classed all others who had "acquired a sufficiency to live without labour." Here Maclure decisively excluded from the ranks of producers the bankers and possessors of capital—whether derived from "the accumulation of industry, hereditary power, or pillage"—who were championed in Anglo-American political economy.[8] Nor did he accept the arguments of Jean-Baptiste Say and others in favor of the productive activities of members of the three professions; doctors, lawyers, and clergymen produced "only air, modified by the throat and mouth into sounds called words." Maclure, like Owen and many of his fellow reformers, was hostile toward organized religion. Fortunately not all learned callings were as suspect, and Maclure was able to place his fellow teachers of "exact science" in the ranks of the industrious.[9]

This "broad" line of demarcation was, for Maclure, far more than the arbitrary analytic device that it might appear to be to later readers. Distinctions between the productive classes and their opposites, with the resultant clash of interests, were to be found at the center of every society and polity. This classification was not a "partial or casual" one dependent on local circumstances, Maclure insisted; it represented a fundamental division of interests whose origins were to be discovered in the very nature and organization of mankind. From the perspective of Maclure's political anthropology, the consumers had "in every stage of civilization" aggregated to themselves property and power at the expense of the workers. Even in the American republic—where in a population that he estimated at thirteen million, only five hundred thousand were among the nonproductive—Maclure found that effective governance and control over the distribution of wealth had passed into the hands of those who lived without labor. Later he increased this favorable ratio of producers to consumers to that of "at least one hundred to one." Here the precise numbers seem of less importance than his insistence on the overwhelming superiority of the "working producing classes" in the American populace.[10]

Although Maclure acknowledged that the modern institutions of representative government had been developed to rectify the asymmetries between the two great classes, he was not convinced that they always did so. These political arrangements could work, he argued, only in nations where all men were enabled to vote. While this was the case for the half of the United States without property qualifications, in the remainder the interests of the nonproducers were certain to prevail. In these areas where only the propertied were represented, political conditions were already, or soon would be, akin to those in Britain and France.[11]

Unlike many of his contemporaries, however, Maclure was unwilling to find all European governments wanting when compared to that of the United States. Rather than celebrating the benefits of the federal Constitution, he suggested that a legislative reconstitution along class lines could better serve the needs of the productive majority. As an example he pointed to Sweden, with its four houses of peasants, burgesses, clergy, and nobility. "By this arrangement," he maintained, "the industrious and productive classes have full possession of one-half of the elective power of the nation."[12] Maclure's preference for representation by class—for a system of equivalence between political and socioeconomic structures—is reminiscent of the proposals of many Anti-Federalists. Though such arguments had been made some forty years earlier in a quite different context, they had also questioned the simple correspondence between the American legislative system and the class interests of all citizens.

In order to recover their lost rights, Maclure recommended that the "working classes" of the American republic exercise their political and economic power. Through such alliances as the workingmen's parties and the "trades' unions lately combined," the producers could assert their numerical preponderance in both the market and the polling place. By so doing they could increase their share of the "fruits of their toil and labor" and abolish the monopolies, charters, and "exclusive privileges" arrogated by the consuming classes. In addition to the repeal of special charters, particularly those for banks and monopolies, Maclure argued for a reform of the legal code and a direct tax on property. Each of these steps would help lessen the power of the "already rich." Though Maclure shared with supporters of Andrew Jackson a common rhetorical stance in opposition to a "monied aristocracy," he doubted that the prevalent parties could protect the interests of the productive majority. Since the consumers would "legislate for the interest of their own class," the producers should support only candidates drawn from their own numbers.[13]

In evaluating the progress of the workingmen's movement in Philadelphia, Maclure emphasized the influence of the writings of his fellow Owenite John Gray. Gray's *Lecture on Human Happiness*—first published in London in 1825 and reprinted in Philadelphia in 1828—had explained to the "mechanics and working classes" the implications of society's division between producers and nonproducers. Even though Adam Smith had first presented this argument in the *Wealth of Nations,* Maclure considered that text to be "too voluminous and abstract to reach the comprehension of millions." Due to the social division of social knowledge, Smith was "read and understood only by those of the consuming classes." Gray's *Lecture* was not a refutation of the truths in the *Wealth of Nations,* but a popularization of them. William Maclure, like a number of his British radical contemporaries, did not find in Smith's work an apology for the standing order, but an advocacy of substantial social change.[14]

Even if the workingmen's parties and trade unions did succeed in alleviating the proximate causes of the producers' distress, Maclure maintained that a more lasting remedy was to be found through a reform of American education. If one assumed, as did Maclure, that "knowledge is power" in all political societies, in America the institutions needed to appropriate that power were not yet available to the productive citizenry. To provide better access to that scientific learning upon which a social and political reformation would be predicated, Maclure proposed the establishment of free public schools and suggested a variety of pedagogic and curricular innovations.[15] He expected that, through schooling, the producing classes would become fully cognizant of the conditions of their oppression. Only then would they assert their relinquished powers and seek to restore a natural division of property—"more or less into equal parts"—in the republic.[16] For Maclure, public schools were not to serve the consuming class as instruments of social control, but were to be arenas for developing the producing classes' self-awareness.

Though Maclure anticipated the formulation of a political economy in the service of the "working classes," his *Opinions on Various Subjects* was neither a formal treatise on, nor a sustained examination of, the topics of such a study. Yet the outlines of Maclure's positions on society's ordering and operation are presented therein, as are the rhetorical strategies characteristic of Owenites and labor reformers in the late 1820s and 1830s. With its two "great" classes ranged in opposition and with the majority economically and politically subservient to the nonproductive few, he judged that America's present dispensation was at odds with the dictates of reason and of liberty. For the industrious classes of the United States, at least, the institutional means necessary to effect a restorative change—schools and suffrage—were available within the present, "unnatural" order. What was lacking was the knowledge, and the power, that a science of society could bring. Through his writings and educational experiments Maclure sought, as did his collaborators in the American Owenite venture, to enlighten the producing classes and to exhort these potential agents of change to undertake measures to ensure that a new class harmony would replace the prevalent "opposition of interests." Were such a transformation to come to fruition, Maclure expected a society of small, self-contained communities of producers joined in a loose federation.[17]

Frances Wright, Maclure's correspondent and colleague at New Harmony, also subscribed to this assessment of the "artificial state" of American society. After her Owen-inspired experiment at Nashoba, Tennessee, had failed to provide a practical formula for the abolition of slavery, Wright removed in 1828 to New Harmony. There she joined in the editing of the *New Harmony Gazette;* she purchased the journal in the following year, transferred it to New York City, and retitled it the *Free Enquirer.* In conjunction with Robert Dale Owen—son of the philanthropist—Wright used the journal and her skills as an orator to forward the cause of "radical reform," a phrase that in her lexicon encompassed the issues of deistic free thought, public education, the rights of women, the plight of the "industrious class," and the ultimate renovation of the "frame of existing society."[18]

When examining the framework of American society, Wright observed with regret that it had been divided into competing units: "We are partitioned off into classes, and arrayed against each other, in despite even of our own will, by the habits of our youth, and the contrasted and conflicting interests of our after years."[19] Among the factors responsible for this situation were such "defective arrangements" as exclusive and frivolous schooling and such false ideas as excessive competition. These ideas and institutions had been engaged—at the expense of the laboring class—in the service of a "professional aristocracy" of priests, lawyers, and legislators, and their colleagues in banking and speculation. America was composed of "heterogeneous fragments," and the largest fragment, the industrious class, was in jeopardy. She found that "practical equality" was a commonplace in republican rhetoric but not in reality.[20]

Wright argued that the "novel and excessive impetus" of economic change was as great a threat to America's industrious "mass" as it was to their peers in Europe. The speed of development and the cupidity of the new aristocracy had precipitated a crisis that could result in the "destruction" of the laboring class's liberty. Yet her concern with the baleful effects of economic transformation was not limited to the industrious class; she assumed that the "ruin of all small capitalists" would also ensue. Should the laboring class, however, in concert with honest men from all other classes, exert political power in the cause of "gradual, but radical reform," they could prevent their "enslavement." It was this ability of the American industrious classes to express their wills through such mechanisms as the legislatures that distinguished them from their European counterparts. For Wright the political culture of the United States could prevent the forthcoming "revolution" from reaching a violent culmination.[21]

To emphasize the severity of the current situation, Wright had recourse to particularly martial imagery: "What distinguishes the present from every other struggle in which the human race has been engaged, is that the present is, evidently, openly and acknowledgedly, a war of class, and this war is universal."[22] Since the belligerents involved here were the aristocrats (the "booted and spurred riders") and the people (the "ridden"), Wright's evocation of the specter of social conflict was more characteristic of the broader conventions of late-eighteenth- and early-nineteenth-century British radicalism than it was of specifically American Owenite rhetoric. Though the extent of her contemporaries' recognition of this belligerency in 1830 is open to question, Wright was among the first analysts of nineteenth-century America society to describe its social relations in terms of an evident "war of class." Within the bounds of American public discourse, her use of such language prefigured the employment of a lexicon of belligerent class conflict by subsequent generations of social critics.[23]

Although Wright was prepared on at least one occasion to depict relations between the classes as entailing a "struggle" or "war," she did not maintain this position consistently. In the course of a subsequent address to the young mechanics of New York, delivered at her New York Hall of Science, she argued that, while attempting to excite the industrious class to political action, she did not seek to promote interclass discord: "And if ever my words have provoked a feeling of hostility in man towards man, or in class towards class, I have sinned against my intentions." As these remarks were made in the wake of internecine disputes among the groups composing the Workingmen's party of that city, her proximate intentions, in this instance at least, were to distance and distinguish herself from the faction led by Thomas Skidmore. Wright also expressed reservations about the usage of the term 'workingmen' by some of her colleagues: "To the title of Working Men as the distinctive epithet of reformers, I object. All men and women ought to be workers, but at the present time, when operative and intellectual labor is unhappily separated, the title sounds unfairly exclusive and our object being union, exclusion, even in sound, should be avoided." At a more general level, her reliance upon an imagery of social strife is characteristic of a political rhetoric concerned less with the triumph of the industrious class than with the restoration of that class to a once-enjoyed condition of equality.[24]

As the most efficient means to that egalitarian end, Wright favored reforming the organization and the curriculum of American schools, rather than changing the present distribution of wealth. Instead of the private academies that inculcated the children of the rich with the habits and tastes of aristocracy and the desire for exclusive privilege, republican schools should be free, mandatory for all, and concerned with the teaching of practical skills. She based this "national" and "rational" plan of education on a series of state-sponsored boarding schools in which the principles and practices of equality would be imparted. Once this system was established, she expected that a thoroughly republican generation of Americans would emerge—one quite different from its parents, who were "reared . . . in the distinctions of class." These institutional and ideological innovations would over time produce in American society one class—an all-inclusive class of industrious women and men.

Wright's faith in the efficacy of educational reform paralleled that of William Maclure's; it is indicative of the emphasis that Owenites placed on the power of institutions in the formation of individual character, and by extension the character of an entire people or nation. Class formation was for them as important an issue in the classroom as it was in the workplace. To rid the republic of aristocrats, the American industrious should remove the aristocratic tendencies still embodied in their educational system. If the schools now served to promote an invidious "distinction of class," they could be used instead to eradicate "unnatural" class and gender divisions. Rational education would re-form all citizens into members of the great producing class.[25]

In her assessments of the American republic, Wright pointed to the discrepancies between its discursive promises and its social practices. "We speak of equality," she observed, "and we are divided into classes." From the perspective of the "science of human life" that she wished to foster, the presence of these contentious classes was symptomatic of the ills that beset all modern states; it was a division that she found neither in accord with reason nor compatible with a truly republican polity. For Wright, as for Maclure and others associated with Owen, her proposed reforms aimed to eliminate social discord and replace it with the new harmony of a transfigured society of the "industrious producers" alone.[26]

Langton Byllesby of Philadelphia—the sometime editor, inventor, and printer—shared with Frances Wright and William Maclure a deep dissatisfaction about conditions in the American republic. In his *Observations on the Sources and Effects of Unequal Wealth,* published in 1826, Byllesby drew upon the writings of Owen and of his exponents William Thompson and John Gray, to form his own critique of "existing systems." Social and economic changes, he observed, had generated an "excessive inequality" of wealth for the nonproductive few. Were the majority to enjoy the equal rights intended by nature and explicated by Thomas Jefferson—rights that entailed the possession and enjoyment of wealth—American class relations needed to be transformed. To abet that transformation, Byllesby proposed to examine the principles of the "social economy" that were now in practice in the United States.[27]

Byllesby explained that a number of elements had combined to give rise to an "oppressive" disparity in wealth among Americans: "fixed property" in land, in particular the custom of inheritance and "perpetual ownership"; the lending of money at interest and the correlative institution of banking; the derivation of unwarranted profits through "trafficking and commerce"; and the baneful effects of laborsaving machinery and competition. Together these conditions had worked to the benefit of the consumers, most especially the "traffickers"—that is to say, the merchants and capitalists—and to the decided detriment of the mechanics and farmers in the productive classes.[28]

In distinguishing between the classes of producers and consumers, Byllesby employed the dichotomy that the American political economists had found to be so unsatisfactory; and as was the case for Maclure, Byllesby's choice of classifications was more than a matter of theoretical speculation. Both were efforts at exercising conceptual closure. Hence from the class of producers Byllesby excluded merchants, bankers, insurers, lawyers, their respective clerks, and all "whose occupation is not the production of something directly or indirectly for the subsistence or enjoyment of mankind." His use of the criterion of indirect productivity, however, permitted him to include doctors, teachers, and men of science among the producers. There would even be room within this indirectly productive class for the now suspect "traffickers," if only their commercial and financial transactions were carried on with the "equitable" principles of cooperation, not competition, in mind. These were the very principles, Byllesby suggested, with which a forthcoming system would "supplant" one of unequal wealth and "individual privation." When established—it seems—the new social economy would preclude the necessity of the producer-consumer distinction since the "trading classes" would be joined with the "labouring, and all other classes" under the rubric of "productive." By emphasizing current class boundaries, Byllesby wished to hasten their dissolution.[29]

Byllesby was unclear as to how, exactly, the shift from the old social economy of competition to the new one of cooperation was to came about, and on what the "precise features" of the resultant system would be. Rather than suggesting specific means of change such as political action or educational reform as did Maclure or Wright, he referred instead to a number of institutions and situations where such transitions were already under way. These "practical illustrations" included George Rapp's religious community at Harmony, Robert Owen's cotton mill at New Lanark in Scotland, and the Co-operative Society of London. Although Byllesby expressed reservations about certain facets of each, together they indicated the general direction that affairs should and would take. Yet while he declined to prescribe specific societal remedies, he did recommend that his fellow mechanics establish cooperative ventures—an "Association of Mutual Advantage"—along the lines of joint-stock companies. There they might free themselves from dependency on "traffickers" and ensure an "equitable" return for their endeavors. In such a fashion at least some members of the productive majority could move toward a social order based on the "correct idea of the relations of man to man."[30]

Byllesby expected that, once the movement for reform had begun, it would derive "correct" ideas not from the "political economics" of the day, but rather from "experiment" informed by the theories of Robert Owen and other "philanthropists." Although uncomfortable with Owen's religious heterodoxy, Byllesby approved of Owen's attempt to bring reason to bear in a reappraisal of the workings of society. Like the American Owenites, he assumed that the results of such endeavors would be a renewed social order with both political and economic equality for the productive classes of the citizenry.[31]

In this rendering of American society—one that incorporates many of the prescriptive and descriptive elements common to the discourse of antebellum radical and labor reform—Byllesby posited a once-extant condition in which the productive class had enjoyed, or at least had the potential to enjoy, equal access to wealth and to control over the results of their labors. Notwithstanding the presence of a few consumers, it was, in effect, a one-class society. But thanks to the machinations of the nonproducers—Byllesby's greedy merchants and usurious bankers—where there once had been but one class, there now were two. To check this unwelcome and unnatural inclination toward an oppressive social bifurcation, Byllesby recommended positive, if less than detailed, action to the class of producers. The future of an unreformed American social order would be one of division and strife, whereas in a reformed setting unity and tranquility would prevail.

Byllesby, Wright, and Maclure bisected society along the productive-nonproductive axis, divisions in which the position of certain occupations was open to constant debate. Their contemporary, and Wright's adversary, Thomas Skidmore preferred to base his distinctions on the criterion of property. With the publication of his *Rights of Man to Property!* in 1829, Skidmore, an inventor, machinist, and leader in New York's Workingmen's party, joined in the censure of the prevailing order and proposed a plan for "pulling down the present edifice of society." Its replacement would be a reconstructed republic featuring not only political equality, but an equality of property as well; it, too, would be a society with room for only one class.[32]

As he surveyed a social order that he characterized as marred by the oppression of the many by the few, Skidmore emphasized the existence of a fundamental partition along the lines of property holding: "Whoever looks at the world as it now is, will see it divided into two distinct classes; proprietors and non-proprietors; those who own the world and those who own no part of it. If we take a closer view of these two classes, we shall find that a very great proportion even of the proprietors, are only nominally so; they possess so little, that in strict regard to truth, they ought to be classed among the non-proprietors" (p. 125). Since there was an "enormously unequal" distribution of property in the United States, he was not persuaded by the claim that it was widely dispersed among the populace. Though in a nation inhabited primarily by artisans and agriculturalists almost all could be construed as "proprietors," it was not simply the ownership of property that was at issue, but the amount owned. Thus in America, as in "all countries and all ages," the elementary class distinctions lay between those propertied and not, or between the rich and the poor (pp. 3–5).

In setting the bounds of this division, Skidmore moved from conventional tripartite schemes of classification to a bipartite one. He joined together the "poor and middling classes" who comprised "ninety-nine parts in every hundred of the whole population of every country," into one of the two great "parties" and these he set in opposition to the remaining one-hundredth, the rich (p. 17). Even if Americans used a three-class imagery in their everyday language, Skidmore found that a division of society by two was analytically and politically more salient (p. 368).

If, as Skidmore contended, the maldistribution of wealth was the primary cause of the "oppressions" and "destitution" that the poor and middle classes faced, the means for correcting these conditions were at hand. Through the exercise of their political rights, the class of nonproprietors could reassert their rights to property. He called upon the nonproprietary majority in his own state of New York to summon a convention for the purposes of drafting a new constitution, one in which the republican dilemma of an inequality in property could be resolved. That document would abolish all standing debts, lay claim to all the property that New Yorkers held within the state, and arrange for its regular redistribution on an equal basis to all citizens, male and female, over eighteen years of age. Everyone was to have a sufficiency of property by way of a share or dividend; no one could bequeath their share to descendants. If in the years between maturity and death some citizens prospered due to talent and diligence while others did not, there was little need for concern, since the resulting inequalities were both legitimate and temporary. Though the electorate could mandate the parity of resources, it could not undo economic distinctions among men and women intended by nature (pp. 131–45).[33]

The purpose of Skidmore's deliberately radical and provocative plan was less the permanent equalization of individual fortunes, than the elimination of those objectionable elements that had fostered the separation of the "two distinct" classes. In addition to providing an equal share of the common patrimony to all adults, he recommended that the new constitution enfranchise women, blacks, and Indians; prohibit banks; repeal charters; and sell off the property of the churches. Upon the successful implementation of these policies, Skidmore was confident that economic and social relations among the citizens of the state—and by extension among all Americans, since New York was to be the exemplar—would at last be grounded in a true, not a nominal, equality. Hence should society be "organized upon principles . . . such that every man must live by his own industry," the lines between the poor, middling, and rich would disappear, and with them would go the logic and the locus of class oppression.[34]

Although Skidmore maintained that his work "has no example"—and when comparing the scope and potential effects of his redistributive policy to the proposals of other Americans in the radical camp, he was quite correct—he noted as precedent the agrarian laws of the Roman republic; and it was with the epithet 'agrarian' that he and his program were labeled by hostile commentators such as Thomas Cooper. In considering the possibility of a modern variant of agrarian legislation, Skidmore first presented and then refuted Daniel Raymond's arguments against the possibility of an equal division of property. As the title of his text indicates, Skidmore was indebted to Thomas Paine, though he criticized Paine's support for civil protection of private property. He did cite with favor Byllesby's *Observations on the Sources and Effects of Unequal Wealth,* in particular the latter's reservations about Robert Owen; but he was less impressed with the notions of those "reformers," that is to say, Wright and Robert Dale Owen, who insisted that changes in the system of education were a sufficient remedy for society's ills. While provision would be made under Skidmore's new social order for general and equal schooling, he insisted that the division of property must be given precedence; and from that fundamental reform all other requisite changes would follow.[35]

Notwithstanding Skidmore's self-distancing from Wright and the Owens, his assumption that "all human society . . . is constructed radically wrong," and the rhetorical strategies that he used to deconstruct and then reconstruct its "present edifice" were similar to those of his partisan rivals. So, too, was his judgment that a now segmented American society might soon be made anew through the political efforts of the majority, in this case the nonproprietary class. Skidmore, as one of the organizers in the spring of 1829 of the Workingmen's party in New York City, believed in the efficacy of both electoral and rhetorical action.[36] In emphasizing the persuasive power of the "printing press" as a vehicle for the mobilization of the voting public, he argued that in the state of New York only one-twentieth of the population was unable to read: "Whoever, therefore, comes before an American community, with a printed proposition, presented in a clear and plain language . . . cannot fail to be well received" (pp. 9–10). With *The Rights of Man to Property!* Skidmore helped give shape to a political language in which class divisions were accentuated, and by which "artificial" class formations might be abolished.

The medium of that message in the late 1820s and 1830s was not limited to the books of Skidmore and Byllesby or to Wright's addresses, of course. Through the various newspapers of the workingmen's and trade unions movements, editors and journalists such as George Henry Evans of the *Working Man's Advocate* of New York and William Heighton of the *Mechanic's Free Press* of Philadelphia also warned that the "working" or "laboring" classes had lost, or were losing, their rightful position of equality thanks to the "anti-republican, oppressive, and unjust," contrivances of their opposites, and that steps toward rectifying these predicaments must be taken.[37] Although a variety of reforms were suggested—including free public education, mechanics' libraries, the abolition of imprisonment for debt, the equal taxation of property, and an end to monopolies and exclusive privileges—Evans, Heighton, and company insisted that change depended on the victory at the polls of representatives of the "working classes." The politicization of the "productive labourers" in turn required their recognition of common "rights and interests." In William Heighton's adaptation of Francis Bacon's celebrated phrase, class awareness was predicated upon the "power of knowledge."[38]

How then did Evans, Heighton, and company describe the "sectional divisions" of American society into classes? In order to "call things by their right names"—as Seth Luther put it—they regularly employed a number of conventions drawn from everyday language, from the traditions of American political rhetoric, and from the contemporary "sciences" of reform: the familiar dichotomy between those who composed the "industrious and productive classes" and the "idle and non-productive"; a parallel moral discrimination between occupations that were or were not "useful," with bankers and the like most decidedly in the latter group; the vertical grading of classes as lower, middling, and higher; the standard juxtapositions of the rich or aristocrats and the poor; and construals of the laboring or working classes broad enough to include those who "manufacture the choicest fabrics, and whose labor brings forth the choicest specimens of art," while restrictive enough to exclude lawyers, brokers, and owners of commercial real estate. These classifications involved both moral appraisal and political evaluation.[39]

And how did Evans, Heighton and their associates explain the "relation that exists between these classes and the working classes"? With the classes arrayed against each other in a contest over equal rights—the understanding of which, in general, excluded Skidmore's equality of property—their representations of American social relations stressed conflict. This was a conflict between the classes, however, that had been generated by republican political and economic arrangements and could be resolved by them as well. These workingmen's advocates presumed the superiority of representative democracy and private property. But since, as they observed, the apparatus of the "parties of the day" were controlled by the "aristocracy," the producing classes had little recourse but to rely on their own efforts. "We desire," as Evans explained in response to the criticisms of Thomas Cooper, "simply to find and to elect legislators who, when the interests of different classes appear to clash, will prefer that of a large majority to a small minority." While Evans recognized the division between the producers and their opposites, he rejected Cooper's contention that it was the divisive appeal of the workingmen's parties that was exacerbating social tensions: "We want nothing exclusive . . . no combination of the poor against the rich, of the laborer against the landholder, nor even of the non-privileged against the privileged." The goal of the movement was, Evans maintained, equal treatment for the "interests" of all, including those of the often scorned banker and lawyer.[40]

In the pages of the workingmen's and trade union journals of the late 1820s, 1830s, and 1840s, there developed the vocabulary and grammar for an analysis of American society that was predicated on conflict. Evans and company described and evaluated a political and social system that had once accorded with the imperatives of republican equality, but now was at variance with it. They subscribed as well to the position that, in implementing the necessary correctives, the agents of restorative change would be the members of the productive majority as represented either by trade unions or by legislators and parties favorable to the needs and requests of the workingmen. Through the exercise of the franchise, that crucial device that distinguished them from their counterparts in Europe, they could expect that in resulting social arrangements the pretensions of a resurgent "aristocracy" would be kept in check. The distinctions by class that occurred among the inhabitants would be those generated by the dictates of nature and an equitable marketplace, not by those of artifice or avarice. Although it often lacked a thorough exposition, theirs was a model of social and economic relations marked by conflict, but conflict that could be contained within the bounds of the political order. Theirs was a rhetoric of a reconcilable class conflict.[41]

Stephen Simpson of Philadelphia presented a more formal rendering of these complaints against "the existing unjust relations of man to man" in *The Working Man's Manual: A New Theory of Political Economy*, published in 1831. Simpson, who had run for Congress in the previous year as a candidate of both the Workingmen's and the National Republican parties, sought to explicate the general principles of that movement for the "working classes," and to introduce them to his understanding of "an American theory on that interesting subject." It was a theory, he contended, that differed from those of such "deceivers of the populace" as Adam Smith, and such "fanaticks" and "demagogues" as Thomas Skidmore. The Scottish economist wished to convince the producing classes of the justice of the present, inequitable "distributive system," and the American radical hoped to enforce an equality of wealth or a "community of property," according to Simpson. He preferred to base his own political economy on an equality of rights—especially the right of the producing classes to enjoy that wealth that only they could produce.[42]

Although Simpson referred to Smith and his successors as "apologists of tyranny," he was not prepared to dismiss all the findings of their "science." Despite their collective failure to apply the principles of justice to the systems that they examined, Simpson maintained that they did provide a precise description of the processes by which "capital extorts from industry": paper currency, funded debts, and corporations. And since a thorough comprehension of these institutions was essential to ameliorative political activity, Simpson and his intended audience were, ironically, in the political economists' debt. Simpson was highly critical of the political economy of Adam Smith et alia, in particular the advocacy of free trade and the acceptance of the current distributions of rewards as natural. He was willing to make some exception for Say and Sismondi, who expressed concern for the "principles of natural justice"; and he held in great esteem and recommended the works of John Taylor of Caroline. In matters relating to charters, monopolies, and so forth, Taylor was a "conclusive authority." Simpson also admired and approved of the work of Taylor's ideological nemesis, Alexander Hamilton.[43]

Simpson acknowledged that the moral philosophers had been "very scientific" when making their "distinctions and classifications of the elements of society." Thanks to their careful attention, he was better able to draw the lines between a constituency gathered from the class of producers, that is to say, the farmers, manufacturers, and mechanics, and their nonproductive opposites. He rejected attempts to designate as "productive" such occupations as stockbrokering that supposedly created a demand for labor; only those who actively created real wealth should be regarded as producers. In evaluating the often uncertain place of the merchant, Simpson noted that "science compels me to maintain a principle, that throws him out of the productive and labouring class, which creates the wealth of the nation." The efforts of the class of merchants could be assessed as "useful," nonetheless, assuming that they were not also members in the class of the "idle"; but neither they nor any of the other nonproducers should expect any more than their due portion of rewards. Although Simpson found little merit in the prescriptive aspects of established political economy, some of its descriptive features could be turned to the advantage of the scientists of the working classes. For them, at least, the technical dichotomy that troubled the economists might still have rhetorical value.[44]

In offering solutions to the dilemmas that now faced the class of working men—as broadly but not too broadly construed— Simpson supported the general range of measures to enhance "equality"; he especially favored the movement to curb the power of the large capitalists, those who "live and grow rich by the labour of others." Even though he assumed, as did many involved in that movement, that capital and labor were "opposing interests," it was not the mere existence of the class of capitalists that created a political problem for Simpson, but that class's collective will to excessive power: "we propose no wrong to capital and capitalists, but that they shall do no wrong in law and equity."[45]

Yet despite his often harsh strictures against the "privileged classes" and their institutional bases in monopolies, banks, and corporations, Simpson did favor the Bank of the United States, since only it could provide the financial stability necessary for mechanics to employ their "small capitals." He also supported the American System of Henry Clay: its protective duties and public expenditures would operate to the benefit of the producers. As a political economy that claimed to have the needs of the "working man" in mind, Simpson's "new theory" was directed less toward anticapitalist initiatives than toward the removal of accrued distortions from what was otherwise a just system. If the needed reforms were carried out, the current "social economy" of "extortion" would be replaced by one in which a measure of "harmonious dependency" among men could be realized.[46]

Simpson described, in a manner similar to that of his admired predecessor John Taylor of Caroline, a divided American society in which the producers and the capitalists were at odds; yet while undue economic power was coursing toward the idle, the "labouring" classes did retain the resources necessary to prevent their complete subjection. And though as the publisher of the *Pennsylvania Whig* he rarely agreed with Taylor's legatees in the party of Andrew Jackson, Simpson shared with the Democrats a social analysis with a decided emphasis on conflict. Simpson's *Working Man's Manual,* as a tract written by both a "workie" and a Whig, demonstrates that a rhetoric of reconcilable class conflict was not limited to the relatively marginal discourse of radical reform, but formed part of the broader political culture of the 1830s and 1840s.[47]

Simpson's partisan affiliation notwithstanding, it was contemporary members of the Democratic party who far more often used an imagery of hostility between the laboring classes and capitalists—or between the now anthropomorphized categories of 'labor' and 'capital'—when criticizing the supposedly malicious designs of their political rivals. Their "democratic principle," as John L. O'Sullivan explicated it in the first number of the *Democratic Review,* was developed to defend the agricultural, mechanical, and laboring classes against the designs of the "self-styled 'better classes'." Thus for O'Sullivan, only the continued presence of his fellow Jacksonians in positions of public power could guarantee the deserved, but threatened, equal rights of the "producing mass." Despite the minority's preference for "social distinctions," the Democracy intended to "substitute harmony and mutual respect for the jealousies and discord now subsisting between different classes of society, as the consequence of their artificial classification."[48] In this interpretation of American social relations, the Whigs were responsible for fomenting unrest, and the Democrats were the guarantors of stability and of a natural scheme of social distinction.[49]

While the structure of American society and the organization of political parties had changed profoundly since the 1790s, the contours of change in the language of politics were less dramatic. The political rhetoric of the Jacksonian Democrats recalled that of the Jeffersonian Republicans, particularly on questions of political economy. This relative continuity was less the result of an ideological spell cast by a nostalgic republicanism—or by a hegemonic liberalism—upon Americans than it was an ongoing response to the exigencies of capitalist commercial development. What the role of the state should be in the marketplace was as salient an issue for John O'Sullivan as it had been for George Logan; and what the constitutional provisions for a central bank were was as pressing a question for William Leggett as it had been for John Taylor. The politics of class formation and class relations—especially by way of finance and trade—continued to be debated in the public arena in terms such as 'artificial' and 'natural', which were transposed from eighteenth-century contexts to those of the nineteenth century.[50]

The recharter of the Bank of the United States and the provisions of the federal tariff provided the institutional and ideological settings for the Jacksonians' rhetoric of reconcilable class conflict.[51] In party organs, on campaign platforms, and in the halls of Congress, Democrats railed against what Andrew Jackson labeled the "privileged order" of paper wealth and the "artificial" class distinctions perpetuated by the "rich and powerful."[52] This "contest between capital and labor," as Congressman George McDuffie of South Carolina described it, encompassed "all sections of the union, and all classes of the community." It was not limited to the manufacturing centers of the Northeast, nor was it simply an affair of anticapitalist agrarians or protosocialist artisans.[53] Jackson and his supporters pitted a broadly defined producing majority in the agricultural, mercantile, and manufacturing classes against a consuming minority involved in banking, speculation, and commerce. At stake were the rights of the "great body" of people to be spared from the oppression of inequitable taxation—that is to say, from protective duties—and to enjoy the "fruits of their toil" through a sound, stable currency.[54] A victory for the Democracy in this contest would result in what Samuel Tilden of New York called a new "social system": one in which "the security of all classes in their property causes the most rapid growth and the most useful investment of capital, and increases the diligence and efficiency of labor."[55] The Jacksonians could attack the "great moneyed corporations" in the name of the planters and "industrial classes" while promoting their own version of laissez-faire capitalism.[56] "The claims of the honest capitalist and of the honest laborer are equally sacred," as William Gouge explained, "and rest, in fact, on the same foundation."[57]

One of the most articulate exponents of a class analysis among the Jacksonians was William Leggett, editor of the *Evening Post* and the *Plaindealer* in New York.[58] In the pages of these journals Leggett examined what he understood to be the antagonistic bases of American party politics. "The one party," he explained, "is composed in great measure of the farmers, mechanics, labourers, and other producers of the middling and lower classes, according to the common gradation by the scale of wealth." This was the party of Jackson. Their rivals, the party of the "consumers," consisted of the "rich, the proud, the privileged": those who, "if our government were converted into an aristocracy, would become our dukes, lords, marquises, and baronets." These class coalitions were engaged in an epic "struggle" over the control and the scope of the state; within this "mutual aggression," the "aristocrats" attempted to dominate government for their own benefit, while the "agrarians" tried to secure "equal protection" for all classes of people. Either a new American aristocracy or a genuine democracy would emerge in the end.[59]

In spite of the controversial connotations of the term 'agrarian' as applied in partisan exchanges, Leggett described himself as a member of an "agrarian school of politics" that endorsed equal rights, "enterprise," and "competition." His conservative critics to the contrary, though, he did not intend to "overthrow standing property rights." He identified this "agrarian school" with the tradition of Adam Smith, Jean-Baptiste Say, and John Taylor of Caroline, but not with Thomas

Skidmore.[60] Leggett and his fellow Locofocos were often considered "radical," however, since they demanded dramatic changes. To bring an end to "monopolies," Leggett proposed a general law for incorporation without state charters; and to prevent the "mixture of politics with banking," he promoted a system of unregulated "free" banking. Leggett regularly equated the principles of the Democracy with the "noble science" of Adam Smith, which was "silently and surely revolutionizing the world." The freedom championed in Leggett's "democratick" journalism was the freedom to be let alone, the freedom of "laissez nous faire."[61]

The social order envisioned by Democrats from the late 1820s through the 1850s was egalitarian, but with an antebellum American liberal pedigree. The "precise equality" they evoked was one of "equal rights and equal laws" for "freemen." Jackson and his followers did not assume that an "equality of talents . . . or of wealth" was possible; nor did they presume that women or free people of color could or should enjoy the same rights and privileges as other classes of citizens.[62] "Distinctions in society," Jackson maintained, "will always exist under every just government." But once "equal protection" and "equal benefits" were restored, the otherwise "conflicting interests" of the republic could again be harmonized. The Democracy did not propose to eliminate the "wealthy few," but to delimit this class to their "just portion of influence" in public affairs. The Democrats berated the "great capitalists" in order to promote unity among the producers and to secure political power among the "laboring classes."[63] This was to be a particularly durable Democratic tradition throughout the nineteenth and into the twentieth century.[64]

The Jacksonians' use of a political rhetoric of class conflict prompted countercharges of demagoguery from the opposition. The most vociferous of these came during the course of the presidential campaign of 1840 in reaction to Orestes Brownson's essay "The Laboring Classes"; this piece first appeared in Brownson's *Boston Quarterly Review* and was subsequently reprinted in pamphlet form by the author, and by backers of William Henry Harrison. By the time of that electoral campaign, the intellectually peripatetic Brownson, who had worked with Frances Wright and Robert Dale Owen on the *Free Enquirer* and had been active in the workingmen's groups in New York, had come to support the Democracy as the force best equipped to defend the interests of the working classes. Although Brownson's piece was not deliberately produced as an item of partisan literature, the Whigs introduced it as evidence of the dangerous "unadulterated Locofocoism" supposedly current in the ranks of Van Buren supporters.[65]

While Brownson's proposed topic in the essay was a review of Thomas Carlyle's *Chartism*—a text that Brownson found wanting both for its style and for its recommendation of education and emigration as palliatives for the distress facing the English worker—its theme was an exploration of the composition and the prospects of the "laboring classes" in Europe and the United States. To allow himself a degree of precision when using that protean category, he removed from consideration any members of the "middle class," and denominated as the "real proletarii" only those laborers bereft of any resources—land, money, houses, tools—save that of their physical labor. Brownson reckoned that one-half of the population would fall within these stringent limits; among the remaining half he distinguished that "class of proprietors who are not employers," the farmers and independent artisans, from the merchants, bankers, and the other truly "non-workingmen." In the "struggle . . . between wealth and labor" that he predicted, the former would be allied with the laboring classes while the latter would constitute the forces of opposition. Even though Brownson's social lexicon here included a middle class, or classes, his analysis of social relations tended to stress the bipolar (pp. 366–67).[66]

For Brownson it was the imminence of such a conflict that indicated the deteriorating state of present circumstances. The genesis of the "crisis" at hand could be found in the "actual condition" of the producers of wealth: "all over the world the working classes are depressed, are the low and vulgar, and virtually the slaves of the non-working classes." Hence the Chartist movement that so troubled Carlyle was for Brownson the English manifestation of an international response by workers to their ever-increasing impoverishment. Yet in that nation, regretfully, no resolution was possible save for a cataclysmic war between rich and poor. And if this were to be the fate of England, should a war of the classes be expected in the United States? While Brownson would have preferred that the "social reforms" he proposed be carried out by political means, he expected such resistance by the rich that in America, too, such a conflict was a distinct, if distasteful, possibility (pp. 364–66, 376, 395).

Brownson was highly critical of the ever-encroaching "system of wages" in the United States, a system that he compared unfavorably to chattel slavery, which, in spite of its multiplicity of evils, was able to provide a modicum of care for those unable to support themselves. He was rather skeptical about the wage system's celebrated ability to make rich men out of the industrious poor. While not denying the incidence of upward—or downward—mobility, Brownson doubted that such cases greatly affected the larger patterns of the distribution of wealth. "The relative numbers of the two classes," he observed, "remain, or may remain the same." But since in his estimation the "operative at wages" was something less than a free man, the issue that Brownson found to be most pressing was how to "emancipate the proletaries," or how to remake the laboring classes into the independent farmers and artisans they ought by rights to be (pp. 372–73).[67]

Brownson advocated, as the means of this transformation, changes in the flawed "constitution of society," particularly in the realms of religion and political economy, with priority assigned to the first. Although once a Universalist minister, Brownson called for the abolition of "sacerdotal corporations" and the professional ministry: it had been the "class of priests" who had obfuscated Christianity's message of equality and had diverted public attention from the social injustices of the day. The ministry was primarily responsible for the conditions that led to the oppression of the working classes; clergymen, even more than the capitalist and the factory owner, were the targets of Brownson's invective. Since Brownson assumed that religious reformation must precede political renovation, once the power of the "hireling clergy" was dispersed, the legislation required for the "elevation of laboring class" could be enacted (pp. 385–86, 388–89).

These "social reforms," as presented by Brownson, included standard elements of Jacksonian political economy such as attacks against monopolies, special privileges, and banks. Each of these practices and institutions—most expressly the last—had been used by the "natural enemies" of the "proletaries"; and each should be under the control of the laboring classes. But Brownson's essay did more than reiterate the Jacksonian litany. He moved well beyond the range of an accepted Democratic agenda and into the realm of radical reform by suggesting that the institution of hereditary property be eliminated. Although he provided little detail about implementation, he proposed that upon a citizen's decease, his or her property should devolve to the state, and from there be equitably distributed to members of the succeeding generation. Regarding the ownership of property, then, the economic and social configuration of the nation would be determined solely by the exertion of individuals; whatever classes of rich and poor might develop would be temporary. Brownson argued that, in order to resolve the dilemma posed by the presence of the proletaries, the conditions of their existence as a propertyless class be eliminated (pp. 392–95).[68]

Yet in a society so dedicated to the cult of private property, Brownson expected to find little support for such a simple, if audacious, proposition. Before the rich would relinquish the traditional rights of inheritance, they would resort to the "strong arm of physical force," and he did not wish to hasten class warfare. For the moment, then, he assumed that his proposal would remain speculative (pp. 394–95). But however germane his injunctions against organized Christianity, and however feasible his plans for social renovation, Brownson anticipated and received severe criticism, most pointedly from the Whigs. To them Brownson's essay served as a token of the Democrats' contempt for religion, their designs on property, and their unprincipled provocation of class jealousies within an otherwise harmonious social state. And to Democrats already engaged in a rather contentious presidential race, Brownson's assaults on established institutions caused no little embarrassment.[69]

In answer to these varied critiques, Brownson subsequently published a second essay in defense of "The Laboring Classes" in the *Boston Quarterly Review*, in which he distanced his "principles" from those of the Democratic party, and through which he sought to explicate further his propositions for the benefit of the upset and unconvinced among his "conservative friends." In addressing objections to his indictments of contemporary Christianity, he offered little respite to its apologists or its priesthood. The radical discontinuity between the preachings of Jesus and the practices of his American followers, he insisted, still needed to be resolved. This discrepancy in the realm of religion had its social equivalent in the purported and the actual conditions of the laboring classes. Regardless of the claims made by the "upper classes" that with a vote and a fair chance in the marketplace the workingman was a truly independent agent, Brownson maintained that the proletary, while in a state preferable to that of the chattel slave, experienced little in the factory or in the field that resembled freedom or equality (pp. 420–61).[70]

For Brownson the American dilemma continued to be how to eliminate the "horizontal division" of society into two classes: the owners of capital, and the performers of labor. Even though this separation ran counter to the national imperative for equality and had been less pronounced in the United States than in Europe until late, it was now becoming more distinct. From an analytic stance informed in part by his readings in the works of such "French Radicals" as St. Simon, he saw this division as characteristic of the structure of modern states, and was willing to absolve the class of capitalists of at least some of the responsibility for the "vices" of present social arrangements. The capitalists, like the laboring classes, were trapped in a "false position"; they too had been the subjects of distorted "systems and organizations." The renovation of society would bring relief not only to the proletaries but to that demiclass now arrayed against them (pp. 468, 471–72, 510).[71]

When prescribing the methods for social reconstitution, Brownson took little heed of his critics and continued to inveigh against the practice of inheritance. Although he acknowledged the utility of reforms such as free trade and universal education, he doubted that these or related reforms could provide adequate sustenance for the laboring classes. Nor were appeals to the venerated right to vote sufficient. While the workers' franchise was a positive good, "it by no means gives them that degree of political power, which theorists imagine." Without the practical equality of fortunes that the "more ultimate, more radical" step of abolishing inheritance would entail, Brownson was certain that the present separation between the classes could not be transcended (pp. 474–77).

By eliminating the "privilege" of hereditary property Brownson intended to conjoin the classes of labor and capital; the former proletaries would be capitalized, while the ex-capitalists would have to labor. All would be masters of their respective economic fates. His reformed social order bears a strong resemblance to Thomas Skidmore's one-class society of propertied proprietors, save for the mechanisms of redistribution. Brownson hoped to make these alterations through the patterns of inheritance, and not through any general policy of surrender and regrant in the present generation. Like Skidmore, Brownson recommended that a "general valuation" of present holdings be taken, but expected no need for constitutional changes. The administration of each individual's "capital" was merely a matter of accounting. And to persuade the "conservative portion of the community" of the logic and the orthodoxy of his opinions on property, Brownson cited as authorities Jefferson and the legal commentaries of Blackstone and Chancellor Kent. His detractors notwithstanding, he neither wished to hold all property in common, nor to disturb the rights of the individual holder, as long as these were circumscribed by a lifetime. For Brownson, as for Skidmore, the rights to property were fundamental American rights, and he sought to restore them to the now deprived proletaries. By so doing, there would no longer be a definable working class within the United States, yet all classes of Americans would be workers (pp. 479–84, 486–91, 495–97, 500–502).

No matter how effective his scheme might be in promoting economic equality or social justice, Brownson assumed that it would meet with fierce resistance from the conservatives, even to the point of armed conflict. Yet the aggressors in this anticipated strife between the people and their "masters" would not be the oppressed laboring classes; instead the "aristocracy" would resort to arms rather than give up their privileges. In the envisioned "war between two social elements," the people would be forced to fight in defense of their rights, as did their English and American forebears in the Civil War and the Revolution. But no matter how bellicose this imagery was, Brownson's "proletaries" were not radicalized anticapitalists or stateless sansculottes bent on overturning the existing social order. Like Skidmore's nonproprietors, they were incipient smallholders, shopkeepers, and self-employed mechanics. Nor was their "party of reform" the American Jacobins. It was, rather, the Democrats set against the barely disguised Whigs in the "party of privilege." Thus his prophesied class struggle would recapitulate the fundamental political struggle between the aristocrats and the democrats (pp. 505–9, 478–79).[72]

Whatever the efficacy of Brownson's unorthodox economic and ecclesiastical arguments or the impact of his proposals on the fate of Martin Van Buren's campaign, his essays in *The Laboring Classes* exemplify a number of the conventions with which the structure and the dynamics of American society were depicted in the public discourse of the 1830s and 1840s. In these representations the nation was bisected along lines of wealth, occupation, and property; the lower class of the poor, the laboring, the proletaries, was to be distinguished from the upper class of the rich, the employers, the capitalists; and the boundaries between those classes were becoming more fixed over time. These lines in turn were paralleled by lines of political affiliation, with the interests of the first class, as defended if not defined by the Democracy, in evident opposition to those of the second class, as served by the Whigs. There were, in addition, two middle classes in Brownson's rendering of contemporary society: those in Carlyle's England, whose oppression of the working class and hostility toward the Chartists made them the equivalents of the American upper class; and that class of independent, self-employed proprietors, who were politically aligned with the laboring class and who served as a reminder of what that class once was in the United States, and a model of what it again might be.

Brownson's depictions of an increasingly divided society, and the terms of his social lexicon—with the exception of 'proletariat'—in the "Laboring Classes" articles were common to his former associates in the workingmen's and trade union movements and to many who identified themselves with the Democracy. As a description of society's lowest, propertyless class, Brownson adopted the term 'proletaries' from the French 'prolétaires' and from the Latin 'proletarii'. It appears that the term had little extended usage when compared to the more common, if less precise, 'laboring' or 'working class(es)'.[73] Brownson and Simpson might disagree as to which was the real party of the laboring classes, however those classes might be conceived; Brownson and Wright might argue over which group or phenomenon was primarily responsible for the workers' plight. Nonetheless, Brownson shared with Simpson and Wright a political language with which they emphasized the present social conflict and advised measures to arrest it.[74]

However, when Brownson expressed doubts about the ability of the political system to deal effectively with, or even to constrain, the laboring class's mounting difficulties, he moved past the limits of the rhetoric of reconcilable class conflict and into a discursive space where American institutions required not political reform but replacement. While the "Laboring Classes" essays contained the elements for a number of renderings of the social order, his suggestion that political action would not necessarily accomplish social renovation resembled the arguments of the "French Radicals" and of the American advocates of the "social science" of Charles Fourier, whose interpretations of social and economic relations were by 1840 beginning to be known among critics of the standing order. In this admixture of Jacksonian liberal and European socialist class analyses, Brownson reached—and crossed over—the boundaries of legitimate political discourse on class.[75]

To Charles Fourier the primary cause of the "deeply seated miseries" that beset contemporary civilization was the competitive and "coercive" organization of society. It could be cured by substituting a social order based instead on the cooperative principles of "association." His leading exponent and exegete in the United States was Albert Brisbane, who adapted the terms and precepts of Fourierist "social science" to American circumstances from the large corpus of the master and his disciples. Brisbane presented these in a series of popular works: the *Social Destiny of Man,* published in 1840; *A Concise Exposition of the Doctrine of Association* of 1843; and a series of articles on "Association and Attractive Industry" for the *Democratic Review.* In each of these settings Brisbane engaged in an examination and a critique of the present "repugnant" structure of society, and offered suggestions on how it might be reordered along more reasonable lines.[76]

When examining the current social dispensation, or "civilization" in Associationist parlance, Brisbane found its "social evil" manifest everywhere: in corporate monopolies, in chattel slavery, in the "animosity and antagonism" that existed between all classes, in the "industrial prisons" of factories, and in the "industrial servitude" that had come to be the lot of the laboring classes. He construed this latter category broadly as the "hired classes" and counted all who worked for wages among them; he reckoned that they made up, on average, three-quarters of a nation's working population. Even though he recognized that all classes suffered from the effects of a distorted social order, in his recounting of these wrongs it was the working classes who figured most prominently as the victims. But while Brisbane described the progressively worsening conditions of the laboring classes, and the "augmenting" power of capital over labor, he did not assign ultimate responsibility to employers. It was not the capitalist, landlord, or factory owner who was at fault, but the "false organization" of society that was in the end to blame.[77]

Brisbane, proceeding upon lines suggested by Fourier, also distinguished between society's producers and nonproducers. Although the 'producing class' was not coterminous with the 'laboring class' in Fourierist discourse, both served similar rhetorical ends. Brisbane estimated that the number of persons "actively" involved in producing constituted only one-third of the population, with the rest dependent on their exertions. His nonproducers included the standard classes from political economy—the idle, fiscal agents, "controversialists and sophists," and so forth—as well as members of otherwise productive classes such as manufacturers engaged in unproductive activities. For Brisbane the presence and numerical preponderance of the nonproducers indicated the wastefulness of a society based on economic competition. When society was reorganized on the basis of association, a "true economy" would be realized, and the distinctions between these classes would disappear.[78]

This reordering would not be effected through political mobilization, however. In contradistinction to many of his contemporaries' solutions to the problems besetting American society, Brisbane questioned the efficacy of political action. "Political reforms operate merely on the surface of society," he observed; "they cannot go to the root of social evil." He noted that, while in the United States there was an ostensible commitment to political equality, this had been quite limited in practice, due to the absence of social equality. The American celebration of rights and liberties had been used to conceal "social bondage." Only when the "true social order" of association was established did Brisbane expect there to be meaningful social and political equality. For the Fourierists the "social system" was fundamental, and only there could systemic transformation be attained.[79]

Instead of inducing social change by way of "party agitators" or by any resort to faction and violence, Brisbane and his fellow Associationists preferred the methods of example and persuasion. To achieve the first, they worked to organize experimental communities, or "phalanxes," along lines suggested by Fourier. There the master's rather complex theories of attractive industry could be applied, and there the economic and social superiority of association would be demonstrated. The successful phalanxes could then serve as models for a general social renovation.

Brisbane argued that in the phalanx those energies otherwise wasted in "anarchical competition" would be turned toward greater productive efficiency, and would result in a higher rate of wages and profits. Thus the American problem of the presence of the "hired class" could be resolved. Increased wages would provide workers with the savings necessary to purchase shares in phalansterian cooperative undertakings, which Brisbane likened to joint-stock companies. Whereas in the "false system of industry" the working classes were effectively prevented from accumulating property, through associated industry the laborers would become "co-interested proprietors." And while the phalanx represented a community of efforts, there was to be no community of property. "The principle of private property," he insisted, "will be strictly observed." By joining together in the phalanx the classes who possessed capital and those who owned only their labor, association could eliminate the "general conflict of interests" and the arbitrary class boundaries created by the current "industrial servitude." In Brisbane's projected social order, the only classes that would arise were those formed by the voluntary choice of occupations, and each of these would of course be productive. By replacing the economy of competition with one of association, America's class antagonisms would give way to substantive social harmony.[80]

No matter how promising the social economy of association appeared to be for Brisbane and company, it was in practice extremely difficult to realize. Of the dozens of communities that were organized or planned during the 1840s, only one, the North American Phalanx of Red Bank, New Jersey, remained in existence for over two years. But however limited Association's practical applications were, at the conceptual level the achievements of the Associationists were less ephemeral. During the 1840s Brisbane's writings and those of his colleague Parke Godwin found a receptive audience among many in the ranks of the reform-minded. And by way of Horace Greeley's *New York Tribune* and Associationist publications such as the *Harbinger* and the *Phalanx,* Brisbane's and Godwin's notions were widely circulated. Whether or not the Fourierists' experiments were practicable, the social analyses of the Associationists appeared to have had at least an explanatory value for many.[81]

The American followers of Fourier, in claiming for Associationism the title of the "science of society," placed themselves in direct opposition to the established principles of orthodox political economy. The "misdirected" practitioners of that discipline, as Brisbane explained, had failed to comprehend that the now extant "system of industrial and commercial relations" was false, and that the "economical laws" of competition deduced from it were false as well. What else, Brisbane asked, would account for their "blindness" when faced with the obvious superiority of Associationist social and economic schemes? Political economy had confounded the present distribution of wealth with a rational scheme of rewards; and the political economists had praised as "natural" a set of oppressive class arrangements, which were at variance with the true dictates of nature. Neither Brisbane nor Parke Godwin were surprised that the economists could not begin to explain the rising strife between employers and workers or the "rapidly deteriorating" conditions of the majority of the population.[82]

Yet these were issues that, Godwin warned, were most certainly in need of explanation, issues that must be settled either by science or by "revolution." Associationist social science, he argued, could in fact account for American anomalies such as a permanent class of wage earners, and the "perpetual and bitter hatred and war" between the classes of capital and those of labor. These and all other social ills were manifestations of an erroneously organized social order. Associationism could supply a rational, systematic alternative to that order, one in which the now pauperized workers could expect to become proprietors, and the now conflicting interests of the respective classes could be finally reconciled. Associationism was a science that promised to its audience and adherents what political economy could only proclaim: a truly "harmonic society."[83]

But while Brisbane, Godwin, and their associates employed an imagery of harmony in their social analyses, they shared little else with the political economists, save for a continuing emphasis on the centrality of private property. To the Associationists the harmony of interests would be the end result of a professedly radical restructuring of the social order, a process that would begin with the rejection of the very premises of liberal competition. American society, as presently organized, comprised mainly the classes of nonproducers, the translation of whom into producers would entail far more than the definitional moves of the political economists. It was a social order marked by an increasing incidence of both inter- and intraclass conflict, and was as far removed from social harmony as could be imagined.

Through their dismissal of the principles of the political economists, and their unfavorable appraisal of current arrangements, the Associationists joined in the elaboration of that broader tradition of antebellum public discourse that emphasized class conflict while it advised reform. The American Fourierists had significant differences with the other groups of social critics over what forces or classes, if any, were responsible for the condition of the producers; and they had substantial tactical disagreements over the proper methods of relieving the workers' intensifying miseries. But these differences notwithstanding, the Associationists shared similar linguistic conventions, rhetorical strategies, and practical ends with the Owenites, the workingmen's advocates, and others in the ranks of radical reform.[84]

In developing this discourse—or counterdiscourse—on the American social order, these writers declined to accept as "natural" what appeared to them to be an unequal, unjust, and increasingly polarized society. They construed the 'laboring class' in exclusive, rather than expansive, terms; and they defended the utility of an eighteenth-century category of 'producer' derived from a social science whose other interpretive principles they tended to reject. They were involved—as were their political and intellectual opponents—in a contest over representations and class relations. The war between the classes invoked by Frances Wright and Orestes Brownson entailed a war over words. Though their arguments were convincing to few among the exponents of an ideology of class harmony, their pessimistic appraisals of the future of an unreformed American economic and social order continued to have explanatory and exhortatory power to a later generation of critics. Though the institutional links between antebellum and subsequent 'laboring class' movements were difficult to maintain, the rhetorical links were strong.

The analyses that these scientists of society developed and the debates in which they engaged indicate that, at the lexical level at least, the American working class was already in the process of being made during the "market revolution" and before the complete onset of industrial revolution. The concern from the mid-1820s onward lay with who would appropriate—or expropriate—the title of 'laboring class'. If these related revolutions provoked a series of contests over workers' control, they led to contests over conceptual control as well. "Words undergo variations in their meaning," as William Leggett observed, "to accommodate them to the varying usages of men."[85] While these questions may have been displaced in American public discourse by the sectional conflict of the 1850s and the national crisis of the 1860s, they were not dismissed. These antebellum contests over "who produces" and "who classifies" in a liberal capitalist republic would continue, in new contexts, in the course of the social and economic transformation of America in the years after the Civil War.

FIVE

The Harmony of Interests: An American Ideology of Social Interdependence

Both the antebellum radicals and the Jacksonians sought to circumscribe the category of the 'laboring' or 'producing' classes and to emphasize class antagonisms for political and rhetorical ends. By so doing they developed a durable tradition for representing class relations in the United States. Their rhetoric of reconcilable class conflict emerged in the middle decades of the nineteenth century in the course of ongoing contests over the connections between a capitalist economy and a democratic polity, or between the market and the state. The voices and viewpoints within this arena of public debate were many and varied, however; for every argument that stressed social discord, counterarguments about class cooperation appeared in abundance.

From the 1830s through the 1850s an intellectual community of professors, politicians, editors, and journalists continued to disseminate the doctrine of the harmony of interests, and to argue that the republic's social arrangements were in accord with the dictates of nature. These men of letters presumed that they could influence public opinion and give shape to the terms of public discourse through their commentaries and criticisms; they were concerned with the pragmatics and the political consequences of language.[1] They routinely dismissed the dire warnings about the expansion of an oppressed 'working' class as imprecise or impractical; and they regularly recast that issue by insisting that all 'laborers' were also 'capitalists', and vice versa. In their interpretations of class relations, a rhetoric of socioeconomic difference gave way to one of similarity. Classes were constantly being made and remade by the continual choices of free individuals in the marketplace, they argued. The presence of occupational classes and the premises of individualism were quite compatible within this tradition of American liberalism.[2]

One of the most prominent antebellum proponents of class harmony was the Reverend Francis Wayland, the professor of moral philosophy and president of Brown University. Wayland's two major texts, *Elements of Moral Science* of 1835 and *Elements of Political Economy* of 1837, were widely used and very influential. In *Political Economy* Wayland attempted to apply systematically the laws of moral philosophy regarding the creation and distribution of wealth, and to clarify for his students and the general public some of the issues raised in the course of this application. One of the most pressing of these questions, he observed, was the definition of 'laborer'. For Wayland every individual engaged in "human industry" was a laborer. Philosophers, lawyers, clergymen, and physicians were as much laboring men as those who worked on farms, in mines, or in factories. The exclusion of any "classes of laborers" from the laboring classes, therefore, was a violation of the principles of a science that made divisions according to "the order in which they actually appear among men."[3]

In Wayland's analysis the existence of class distinctions in commercial society was not evidence of significant differences in class interests. "All the classes of laborers," be they owners or operatives, depended on each other; it was "unreasonable" to suggest otherwise. Wayland strenuously rejected the social interpretations of the radicals and trade unionists. "The capitalist and the laborer are equally necessary to each other," he maintained. "All attempts to excite the prejudices of the poor against the rich, or of the rich against the poor, are no less injurious to the interests of both classes, than they are wicked and detestable" (p. 405). To check the spread of such "detestable" ideas among his fellow citizens, Wayland relied on the power and the precepts of the moral sciences. To those in the "lowest class," he prescribed hard work and frugality. Practicing these virtues, rather than engaging in "wicked" schemes, could lead to the "accumulation of a little capital." To those in the higher classes who had already earned their rewards, he recommended ethical conduct in the pursuits of business. Social stability, for Wayland, ultimately depended on a high degree of moral and behavioral consensus (pp. 339, 49).

Although the American social order in Wayland's estimation tended naturally toward harmony, it required the conscious and constant moral support of all the classes. The proper knowledge of society's operations, then, was of the utmost concern for both the scholar and the citizen at large. Wayland made a strong connection in his texts between the control of public knowledge and the exercise of public power, a connection that was also emphasized in the writings of many of his colleagues. Those members of society who had the ability and the duty to make classifications—the moral philosophers, publishers, and political economists—were assumed to play an extremely important social role.

The power of correct and incorrect notions of class relations was also emphasized by Henry Vethake, the professor of mathematics at the University of Pennsylvania. Vethake was the first professor of mathematics and astronomy at the University of the City of New York—later New York University—and later served as president of Washington College in Virginia. He took up the professorship at Pennsylvania in 1836, and exchanged it for the professorship of intellectual and moral philosophy in 1855. Like Francis Wayland and many other nineteenth-century academics, Vethake offered courses of study in a number of subjects, with political economy among them. He had published *An Introductory Lecture on Political Economy* in 1831, and delivered a series of lectures at the New York Young Man's Society in 1832. He published his lectures on Ricardian free-trade economics, *Principles of Political Economy,* in 1838, and included in that treatise a contribution to the antebellum debate over an adequate and appropriate social nomenclature. Since the definitions of "technical terms" had to be brought into accord with "popular acceptation" or else be "forgotten," as Vethake explained, he intended to cast his terms in conformity with "common usage" whenever possible. And from this position he went on to consider the "practical and moral advantage" of abandoning the "technical" distinctions between productive and unproductive "labourers." This would be, he suggested, a highly advisable move.[4]

After reviewing the unfortunate history of that set of classifications, Vethake followed Jean-Baptiste Say's precedent and included the possessors of capital and the producers of both material and immaterial "utility" within the category of "productive labourers." If this were done, he submitted, the perplexing "distinction in question" might "disappear altogether." And once banished from the lexicon of political economists, it could be removed, along with its divisive implications, from public discourse in general (pp. 35–37). The responsibility for correcting the conceptual and political damage done by these was the moral philosopher's.

> If he shall succeed in banishing from the *popular language* such phrases as "the productive classes" and the "unproductive classes,"

> he will have done more to prevent the "workmen" of a country from esteeming themselves to be the only useful portion of society, than he could possibly do by reminding his readers that, every time he writes the word unproductive, that his object in applying it to any individual is not to pronounce him unproductive of utility. (p. 39)[5]

This approach had led to confusion in both technical and "popular" language, and in the case of certain of the "workmen" of the United States, it had resulted in false conclusions about the workings of the marketplace.

Vethake's particular targets here were the trade unions. He argued that, in attempting to increase wages while limiting output, they were acting against the common "interests" of workers, capitalists, and consumers. Furthermore, they encouraged the dissemination of discredited theories: "A greater evil still is their tendency to propagate the notion that, so far from the natural course of things being on the whole . . . the most conducive to the interests of both rich and poor, a constant struggle of the poor against the rich is imperatively required" (p. 326). That "notion" was not only contrary to the natural laws of society, Vethake observed; as an example of the "revolutionary temper of the times" it demonstrated the damage that could be done by a misunderstanding of these laws. Despite claims to the contrary, the unions benefited neither the general public nor the "labouring class." Only the mutual "co-operation" of all the classes, he maintained, could ensure that the workman would be able to rise "in the scale of society" (pp. 405, 99).

Vethake stressed, as did Francis Wayland, the important didactic positions that the practitioners of the moral sciences occupied in American society. "By inculcating upon the rich and the poor, that their interests, properly understood, are not in opposition to each other," they contributed greatly to the maintenance of social "tranquility." This state of affairs had been disturbed by doctrines that questioned the natural justice of the distributive systems, errors that the lower classes, in particular, were "apt to imagine." It was the task of the political economist, then, to dispel such ideas and replace them with a "proper" delineation of American arrangements (p. 405).

Vethake's America, like Wayland's, was theoretically free from class conflict but vulnerable to mistaken "notions" about class relations. His task, like Wayland's, was to exercise as much control as possible over the classifications used in "popular language," and to ensure that those classifications would not be used to emphasize class antagonism. These commentaries on the terms of "popular language" were more than just the complaints of college professors, therefore. They were the expressions of writers aware of the power of language and concerned about their own ability to police the terms of public debate. In attempting to expel conceptions about class antagonism from the realm of respectable discourse, Vethake, Wayland, and their colleagues became partisans in what Pierre Bourdieu has called the "classification struggle."[6]

Vethake was confident that the maxims of the moral sciences would prevail; he was also aware that, in the wake of the panic and subsequent depression of 1837, an appeal to the harmony of interests might not convince all his fellow citizens. Where responsibility for that economic debacle should be assigned and which political party could best assure renewed growth were points of difference between Wayland and Vethake. Wayland, a free-trade Whig, faulted Andrew Jackson and his attack on the Bank of the United States. Vethake, a Democrat with Locofoco connections, placed more blame on the banking system at large. Their preferences, then, inclined them in opposite political directions. But whether the government was in the hands of the Whigs or the Democrats, they were certain that the current crisis would pass, and that the economy would return to a natural equilibrium. Hence the radical critics who had found in these hard times evidence of the permanent impoverishment of the working classes had mistaken temporary dislocations for permanent conditions. The only real sources for class conflict or oppression, in Wayland's and Vethake's estimation, were the machinations of the purported friends of the workingmen. Trade unions, strikes, and demands for a ten-hour day pitted the classes of America against each other, not the normal operations of a natural economy. If freed from the consequences of these "wild schemes," the natural cooperation among the classes would, of necessity, reassert itself.

Alonzo Potter, in *Political Economy: Its Objects, Uses, and Principles, Considered with Reference to the Conditions of the American People,* also set out to address the supposedly pressing need for explanations of the true principles governing society. Too many Americans, in his estimation, were engaged in disseminating such falsehoods as "the notion that there is an essential opposition between the rights of capitalists and labourers; that the one class can be sustained and advanced only by crippling the other." He held the trade unions, radical reformers, and, on occasion, the Democratic party responsible for circulating this insidious information. Potter, the professor of rhetoric and moral philosophy at Union College, published the text in 1841 for use in the schools and by the general public; and he hoped that a popular guide to economic science would aid his readers, in particular the mechanics, in divesting themselves of any such "prejudice." An Episcopal clergyman, Potter later served as bishop of Pennsylvania, and wrote on temperance and educational reform.[7]

In composing *Political Economy* Potter borrowed extensively from George Scrope's *Principles of Political Economy . . . as Applied to the Present State of Great Britain,* to which he added notes, commentary, and a supplementary chapter, "The Condition of Labouring Men in the United States."[8] Even though Potter was in general pleased with the findings of the Englishman's text, he was concerned that his American audiences might draw the wrong conclusions from Scrope's definition of the three "principal classes." When Scrope followed the Ricardian convention of dividing these into the classes of "labourers, landowners, and capitalists," Potter was ready to make an exception. "It is a happy thing for the American people," he noted, "that this separation, so fruitful in jealousy and strife, has not yet become prevalent among them" (pp. 202–3). But when Scrope suggested that these classes were "by no means nicely distinguishable," and that many "labourers" were also effectively "capitalists," Potter was more pleased. Any recourse to language that might imply inherent social antagonism was disturbing to him; any emphasis on the "closely entwined and enlaced" interests of the classes was reassuring (p. 228).

Potter's chief rhetorical nemesis in *Political Economy* was the movement that purported to represent "those classes in society usually, but in this country very inaptly, denominated the working classes," the trade unions. As an example of their misinterpretations of the American socioeconomic system, he cited the preamble to the constitution of the Philadelphia Trades' Unions Association, a text that stated that "those who do not labour to produce are supported by those who do." Potter objected to its definition of a "producer," one that excluded merchants, tradesmen, bankers, magistrates, lawyers, physicians, and "mere capitalists" from membership in the association, and rhetorically removed them from the working classes. But all of these men, Potter insisted, were truly "producers." By what right did a few members of the "labouring class" claim the title as their own? Potter was, in effect, indicting the trade unions for learning too well their lessons from Adam Smith, and for ignoring the subsequent improvements in political economy that had set aside this troublesome dichotomy. If the Philadelphian artisans had understood current economic "science," they would have realized that in America every man was a "working" man (pp. 233–35, 242 n, 300–301).

Potter worried that these ill-informed organizations, composed chiefly of journeymen, would come to "regard employers as a hostile class." Although almost all Americans were "producers," he acknowledged that only in the case of farmers were "capital and labour" still embodied in the same individuals. In cities and manufacturing towns the inevitable process of the "division of employments" had created the "two great classes" of capitalists and "labouring men." The members of these classes tended to be drawn from "opposite extremes" on the "social scale," and, regretfully, the normal operations of business tended to make "competitors" of the two. But, Potter maintained, the competition over wages did not justify an inference of some fundamental "struggle" between the classes in America. "It ought hardly to be assumed," he remarked, "that in such a country labouring men are already the victims of a grinding oppression" (pp. 261, 251–52, 263–64).

Rather than being victims of the marketplace, the workingmen were busily acquiring the property, or capital, that would encourage them to rise on the "social scale." Thanks to the particular "genius of American society," as Potter described it, positions on the social hierarchy of wealth were attained by "enterprise and virtue," not by "hereditary distinction" or "privilege." The notions of the journeymen to the contrary, "there is here no class of rich or poor." Yet the unfounded accusations and unreasonable demands of the trade unions could "alter" this naturally just social order by establishing "castes, privileged and unprivileged." But if mobility within the open occupational structure were limited, "servile wars" could result. The only threats to American social stability that Potter acknowledged were to be found in the rhetoric and requests of a minority among the "working" men (pp. 261, 239, 297).[9]

Potter delineated an American social order that was composed of peaceful and interdependent occupational "classes." The fluid boundaries of these groups permitted him to class the largest of them, the farmers, among the "labourers" or the "capitalists," as need be. Even in the case of the "manufacturing towns," where distinctions of employment and wealth were quite apparent, Potter presumed that no permanent class divisions would emerge. He strenuously objected to "inapt" uses of the term 'working class' in the social lexicon of

America; and he preferred to define out of existence any modes of classification that might suggest social discord. Even if the resulting categories were somewhat confusing, Potter was not troubled, as long as social concord could be inferred.

Henry C. Carey, the Philadelphia publisher, investor, and self-taught master of political economy, shared this faith in social harmony and this animus against unions. Carey was the most internationally influential political economist and social scientist produced in nineteenth-century America. In *Essay on the Rate of Wages* of 1835 and in the three volumes of his *Principles of Political Economy* of 1837–40, Carey insisted that the interests of every class—the capitalist and the laborer, the landlord and the tenant, and even the "planter and his slaves"—were joined together in a beneficial mutual dependence.[10] But Carey submitted that the rhetoric of the radicals was not the only source for the "misconception" about class relations; the principles and the proponents of Ricardian theory were just as responsible. By suggesting that wages and profits were "natural antagonists" in that an increase in one caused a decrease in the other, Ricardo and his followers had provoked the "cry of poor against the rich" and the subsequent, regrettable "rise to trades' unions." Carey argued that the majority of Anglo-American political economists were liable for the contemporary increase in class antagonism despite their assertions of the axiom of social harmony.[11]

To resolve the conceptual and the cultural problems caused by Ricardo, Carey offered his own original interpretation of the relation of wages and profits. He based his analysis on comparative historical and statistical evidence as well as on deductions from first principles. Instead of a higher rate of wages indicating a lower rate of profits, as it did in a Ricardian model, the rise of one ensured the rise of the other. The more that profits accrued to the class of capitalists, the more monies would be disbursed for wages, as employers competed for profit-producing employees. Thus an increase in wealth for one class led to the increase of rewards for the other. Carey's favored example of this fortunate tendency was the United States, where the wages and the expectations of the "labouring classes" had increased with the growth and greater profitability of the economy. "If the workmen and the labourers could be made to understand the subject," Carey observed, "they would see that the division between themselves and the capitalists, on the rate of wages, is regulated by a law immutable as are those which govern the motion of the heavenly bodies." Neither the unions with their complaints about untoward profits, nor the Ricardians with their anticipation of lower rates of return, had understood the true mechanisms that guaranteed social stability (p. 16).

When considering the relations of wages to profits, and the correlative relations of the classes that received them, Carey dismissed any notion "that the interest of the labourer and the capitalist are directly opposed to each other." And while he used the standard terms 'laboring classes' and 'capitalists' in the course of his analysis, he suspected that classifications in the actual world were less distinct than these semantic conventions might suggest. As he surveyed the operations of the American economy, he noted that the majority of men engaged in "labour," the farmers, also possessed capital in land and implements. Hence they were also "small capitalists." The same was true for men in the artisanal and mechanical classes; shoemakers, tailors, engravers, and engineers all owned "capital" in tools and skills. Only the "common labourer" remained outside of this expansive grouping of "capitalists," but experience indicated that even he could expect to be included once he had accumulated any "capital" in knowledge and skill with which to command higher wages. Carey attributed the "double capacity of labourer and capitalist" to these occupational classes; this definitional move further reduced the theoretical grounds of conflict. How could the "labouring classes" be ranged against the "capitalists" when they were likely to be coterminous (pp. 28, 22–23)?

On the question of the other potentially divisive dichotomy, the inherited categories of 'productive' and 'unproductive' labor, Carey followed the example of his English contemporary Nassau Senior and rejected Adam Smith's criteria. He preferred, instead, to consider almost all labor 'productive', since most classes were engaged in producing either commodities or services, and to let the issue be. Neither in Carey's political economy nor in his America was there room for concepts that might imply antagonistic classes or conflicting interests.[12]

Carey's prescriptions for policies to promote economic development granted priority to increasing the freedom of capitalists, especially large capitalists like himself. He called for the passage of general incorporation acts to safeguard the limited liability of investors, defended the Bank of the United States as a source of sound credit, and favored a tariff for revenue only. On this latter policy of "free-trade" he was at odds with his protariff father, Mathew Carey, and closer to the position of his Ricardian rivals. Although the younger Carey would ultimately become reconciled to the wisdom of the elder's beliefs, his attitude toward the tariff question in these years was secondary to his insistence that the government should expedite the formation and acquisition of capital. By so doing, the "interests" of every occupational class would be promoted. State-sponsored capitalist development did not cause class antagonism, as the Jacksonians claimed; rather, it ameliorated class relations.

Carey's brief for the "capitalist," of whatever size or variety, won approval in his Philadelphia business circles and in the upper echelons of the Whig party, where he came to play an important intellectual role. By continually equating the betterment of the capitalists with the betterment of the "labouring classes"—who were themselves but nascent capitalists —Carey provided rhetorical and conceptual support for opposition to trade unions and to legislation concerning the hours and conditions of factories. To infringe upon the rights of the owners was, in reality, to limit the rights of the "workmen." And in carrying the rejection of class conflict a step farther than the American Ricardians, Carey contributed to the construction of a model of American social relations in which only the "harmony of interests" had explanatory power.

The sense of urgency expressed by Carey, Potter, Vethake, and Wayland over the power and the propagation of misleading models was not limited to the realm of formal treatises in moral philosophy. Classifications and class relations were regularly explored—not ignored—in antebellum periodical literature. Questions of politics and political economy were favored topics in such journals as the *Merchant's Magazine and Commercial Review* of New York, the *Southern Quarterly Review* of Charleston, and the *North American Review* of Boston; and an ideology of interdependence similar to that of the moral scientists could be found in their pages. In an essay, "Abuses of Classification," for the January 1842 issue of the *Merchant's Magazine,* William Dolby, a New York man of letters, decried the "invidious distinctions which ignorance and cupidity have endeavored to connect with classification." The sources of those invidious distinctions were two: the "absurd charge," derived from the doctrines of Adam Smith, that merchants acted in ways contrary to the general interest; and a contemporary "outcry" that the interests of the "mercantile" class were at odds with those of the "working class." For Dolby, both the Smithian and the radical schemes of classification amounted to a series of conceptual "abuses."[13]

In their stead, Dolby offered an image of harmonious American class relations. "The classification of society," he suggested, could be compared to the "component parts" of the engine of a steam vessel, with the "progress" of the whole dependent on the "mutual relation" of each part. Dolby then turned to the conventions of classical political economy in observing that "[i]n this young and thriving country, the division of labor has contributed much towards a classification of the people; but this classification is only adopted so far as to help the general good" (p. 43). Thus a social model and a social lexicon derived from the "division of labor" could best serve the conceptual needs of Americans. Yet Dolby was concerned that, even in the case of this "natural" system of classification, faulty inferences would be drawn. "The classification of employments does not necessarily cause a classification of interests," he maintained (p. 44).

Despite his faith in the efficacy of the division of labor, Dolby was aware of the appeal that class antagonism might have for some of his fellow citizens. He accused those who employed this rhetoric, "one of the most shallow and superficial of all second-hand opinions," of demagoguery. They sought power by "dividing" and "instigating" the people against each other; and they abused the terms of public discourse in pursuit of "unwarrantable" ends. While Dolby was too polite to name names —although the trade unions and the Locofoco wing of the New York Democracy come to mind—he strongly objected to his opponents' distortions of the natural process of classification and their deception of the public. By "hiding from them the knowledge of their united and real power," the abusers had provoked "petty jealousies" and "mistaken feelings" of class animosity among the populace. Hence, for Dolby, the theoretical issues of an accurate system of classification could not be separated from the practical results. It was imperative, he explained, that Americans recognize the actual outlines of their social order (pp. 43, 46).

What those outlines might be was discussed by the Reverend George W. Burnap of Baltimore in "The Social Influences of Trade and the Dangers and Duties of the Mercantile Class" in the *Merchant's Magazine*. Burnap, an author, Unitarian minister, and amateur political economist, had first delivered the essay as an address at the Mercantile Library in Baltimore, where he depicted the "inevitable partnership" between the classes of labor and capital.[14] The guarantor of this "partnership" was the normal operation of an American economy in which the mercantile class played a central part in producing wealth. Burnap, like Dolby, described the distinctions in occupation and wealth that developed in this context as "natural." These were manifestations of "the general principle of the division of labor, which has appropriated all the different employments of life into distinct classes of individuals" (p. 417). And, as such, the interests of these classes could not be in opposition. To proclaim class antagonism, Burnap argued, was to participate in a "political cheat." If classes were the creations of primogeniture, entail, or a "hereditary aristocracy," claims about the rich oppressing the poor might have merit; but this clearly was not the case in the United States. As long as the "division of labor" produced distinctions among Americans, Burnap's audiences could be assured that their socioeconomic system was equitable, and their positions within it were natural (p. 419).

Burnap returned to these themes in "The Sources of National Wealth," written for the *Southern Quarterly Review*. Where he had previously extolled the virtues of the mercantile class, he now defended the professional classes from the hoary charge that they contributed "nothing" to the nation's wealth, that is to say, that they were a class of "unproductive consumers." This slander was, regrettably, by now part of the "common prejudice"; and it was perpetuated by certain "speculative writers" who "classed" lawyers, physicians, et alia among the unproductive.[15] Burnap argued that, on the contrary, the professional classes were just as "productive" as any other; the lawyers, for example, acted as "guardians of property" and so aided in the increase of wealth. Here Burnap followed the accepted line of reasoning among American political economists and dispensed with the niceties of the productive-unproductive dichotomy. His choice of terms is less worthy of note than is his recognition of the "tenacity" of that dichotomy in the "common prejudice." Twenty years of classifications and counterclassifications notwithstanding, Burnap had to admit that these misleading categories remained in circulation and continued to find favor in the works of "speculative" social critics.[16]

In the *Southern Quarterly Review* essay, as in his paean to the merchants, Burnap assumed that his immediate readership was cognizant of the correct principles of social organization, while a larger, potential audience was still prey to social errors. Burnap, like Dolby, admitted that there existed conceptual differences over the composition of American society, and that information and disinformation about the social order were distributed unequally. The mercantile and the professional classes had no need to be disabused of the notion that they were "unproductive"; nor did they doubt that the rich and the poor, labor and capital, were partners. It was the lower classes who needed to learn the truths of the moral sciences. They composed the audience for the rhetoric of class antagonism. Even though the Reverend Burnap never relinquished his faith in the persuasive powers of those sciences, he anticipated an American social order in which their cogency and explanatory value would be questioned by many in the less-favored classes.[17]

The rhetorical equation of social stability with general comprehension of the model of a harmony of interests, made in such occasional pieces as Dolby's and Burnap's, was more fully developed by Francis Bowen in the course of his articles on contemporary developments in politics and economics for the *North American Review*.[18] Bowen, whose appointments at Harvard in history and moral philosophy included lectures on political economy, was certain that an otherwise tranquil "social scale" would be upset if the "great truth" of these disciplines were ignored: "There is a danger, from which no civilized community is entirely free, lest the several classes of its society should nourish mutual jealousy and hatred, which may finally break out into open hostilities, under the mistaken opinion that their interests are opposite, and that one or more of them possess an undue advantage, which they are always ready to exercise by oppressing the others."[19] To Bowen, nothing could be more at variance with the principles of a moral science based on the "observation" of social interaction and the maxims of common sense. A consideration of these sources clearly demonstrated that class cooperation, not conflict, was in keeping with the nature of things. Neither the European socialists nor their American disciples had any substantive grounding for their plainly subversive analyses.

Yet Bowen did not intend to compose an apologia for the practice of political economy, or to engage in a simple dismissal of socialism. He acknowledged the theoretical accomplishments of Adam Smith and David Ricardo, but he objected to those interpretations of their works and to the writings of their followers that indicated the necessity of fixed class boundaries. If the natural tendency of wages was downward toward a "bare sufficiency for subsistence"—as the theories of the "English economists" suggested—the consequences for American society would be disastrous. For Bowen the preservation of republican political institutions and the "general consent" of the people depended on the "well-grounded hope" of all to rise on the "social scale." Should there be a "gradual depreciation" of wages and a replication of the "lamentable conditions" of Great Britain, he feared that the class of "laborers" would demand reforms that might "wreck" the "social system" of the United States. The "irretrievable penury" of the laboring class in an imagined Ricardian future would make impossible the "mobility" in which Bowen placed his faith. Within the bounds of Bowen's idealized American social order, the "class of laborers" was able to earn sums adequate both for their daily needs and for savings. This class embraced individuals destined for a higher "rank," thanks to their frugal initiative, as well as those whose talents or predilections suited them best for a life of ordinary labor. It was not, nor could it ever be, a permanent grouping of wage laborers at the mercy of an uncharitable market.[20]

Bowen elaborated his analysis of the beneficial aspects of American society in *The Principles of Political Economy* of 1856, a volume culled from his Harvard lectures, Boston public addresses, and pieces for the *North American Review*.[21] He explained that the only impediments to the accrual of wealth by the "middling" and "lower" classes were the natural, "inevitable" differences of skills and strengths. Whatever distinctions arose from a "fair rivalry" among Americans for rewards were just, he maintained, and "ours is the only community on earth of which this can be said." Unlike the "division of society" in other states, Bowen remarked "here there are no castes" (pp. 113, 122–23).

Bowen pursued this contrast between the natural scheme of division by "class" and the patently unnatural boundaries of "caste" in his evaluation of the structure of English society. There the "top and bottom" classes—the "laboring poor" and the "nobility and landed gentry"—were better conceived of as "true castes." A multitude of legal restrictions ensured the "fixedness" of their respective fortunes and "stagnation" within the social spaces they occupied. Only among the "large and influential" group in the middle did Bowen find the pattern that identified a natural set of social arrangements: "The middle class—what on the Continent would be called the bourgeoisie, the merchants, the manufacturers, the small tradesmen, the master mechanics—are about as busy as we are here in the pursuit of wealth" (pp. 124–25). This diligently acquisitive English "bourgeoisie" composed the one part of the social triumvirate in which location on the "social scale" had been earned; only this "middle class" merited the label of "class." Otherwise, the artificial barriers that entrapped the poor and sheltered the titled prevented the "mobility" of classes and perpetuated castes. "For nothing short of a miracle," Bowen proclaimed, "can elevate or depress one who is born a member of either." Such a system lent itself to the replication of, not to innovation within, existing hierarchies (pp. 124–25).

Bowen compared the system of castes in Britain to the class system of the United States. Here the modern phenomenon that he labeled the "industrial organization of society" had removed all "arbitrary" distinctions. Thus differential positions of the American laboring, middle, and upper classes were the responsibility of the members of these groups, and were not, as in Britain, the results of discriminatory legislation. "It is impossible," in this republican hierarchy of wealth and prestige, "that any class, as a class, should be duly unfavored." While Bowen admitted that in "individual cases" favoritism might prevail over the rule of "competition," at the collective level this could not occur. Competition, if "unfettered," would guarantee an equitable distribution of wealth and income to all members of society (pp. 113, 52).

Although Bowen was willing to acknowledge that the results of a constant contest for riches would inevitably be unequal, he preferred to stress the relative uniformity of conditions in the United States. "The bulk of our people, at least those who are native-born," he notes, "may be said to belong to the class of independent laborers, or small capitalists." Thanks to inheritances, loans from friends, savings, and the "ease of credit," the individual who worked for wages could also acquire the "capital" necessary to make him a self-reliant capitalist. "To be in receipt of wages is not in America, as it is generally in Europe to be entirely dependent upon wages," or so he argued. Here Bowen joined with the majority of his fellow economists in claiming that the theoretical lines between the classes of labor and capital were extremely difficult to trace in the American context, and that, on the practical level, most laboring men were incipient capitalists. Upon close examination, the three classes of the social order melded into one (pp. 199–202).

Since the majority of the citizenry in Bowen's estimation were members of this class of laborers-cum-capitalists, the supposed locus of class antagonism disappeared. "How is it possible," he asked, "that the poor should be arrayed in hostility against the rich," in a setting where the former class constantly replenished itself from the latter?

This "peculiar mobility of society" was evidence that "all classes," no matter what their present disposition, were "inseparably bound" in a "community of interest." Where the socialists expected that only an equal division of property could restore a lost tranquility, and the trade unions hoped in vain to revive the anticompetitive ethos of the "ancient guilds," Bowen looked to the blessings of an "unrestrained" drive for enrichment to ensure "cooperation and mutual dependence" among the classes. In this classical liberal analysis, economic competition precluded social conflict (pp. 123, 201, 18, 228).

Through his articles, public addresses, and *Principles of Political Economy,* Bowen intended to "explain and teach" to as large an audience as possible the "truths" of a science about which a "common prejudice" existed. Bowen felt that the "dissensions" among his colleagues were, in part, responsible for this unfortunate situation; but he was less interested in the reform of economic theory than he was in reasserting the didactic authority of the discipline. If Ricardo was mistaken on wages, or Smith on the effects of tariffs—the New Englander Bowen favored protecting his region's manufacturing concerns—these lapses were best accounted for by the particularities of the British situation. They were not sufficient grounds for the "proudly and willfully" held prejudices of certain influential Americans.[22]

Given the results of European class animosities of 1848, the taste for socialist ideas among self-styled reformers, and the insistent "cry" of the trade unions, there was an immediate need to defend the doctrine of class cooperation and to demonstrate the effects of social mobility: "The question respecting the distribution of property which has chiefly been discussed only in the abstract by politicians and political economists, has now become one of practical interest and of the gravest importance" (p. 493). Bowen hoped that his readers would bear in mind the findings of his research when facing attempts to disturb the free access to property and the accumulation of capital. It was on these "characteristic features" of the American order that its "republican institutions" and stability depended. The time for deliberate ignorance of the maxims of "social economy," Bowen submitted, was well past (pp. 17, 201, 230).

Bowen's writings were a quite self-conscious effort to defend the American distributive system from its critics, both foreign and domestic. To do so he relied on the established convention of class harmony, to which he appended the remarkable device of social mobility. The latter process was a logical extension of the confidence expressed by Bowen's predecessors and peers in the ameliorative powers of economic growth. From this optimism Bowen developed a central explanatory device for the uniquely "natural" workings of the American order—one that continually created and recreated social classes without engendering strife. Social mobility moved the worker's horizon of expectations from the present to the future; and it assessed the conditions of the lower classes in terms of circumstances that had not yet occurred. The experience of the working class in the United States was one of anticipation, not exploitation.

The phenomenon of mobility did not preclude the existence of real boundaries, however blurred, but it did encourage the lower classes to identify their interests with those of the middle and the upper groups. It did not eliminate classes, but it did prevent the crystallization of a fixed class system. In this limited sense, then, American society was classless. Since all individuals were, or one day would be, at least "small" capitalists, the appeal to social mobility allowed Bowen to remove the possibility of class conflict from his representations of social relations.

With this innovative conception of social mobility Bowen at once reinforced and significantly expanded the rhetorical and explanatory power of the American social analytics developed by the antebellum moral scientists. His successors in those disciplines, as well as subsequent celebrators of the virtues of American society, could draw if they wished upon the axiom of harmony and upon a range of practical examples of worldly success when making their arguments about class cooperation and mutual dependence. By the late 1840s this was—and through the rest of the century would continue to be—a pervasive ideology that naturalized and domesticated the social and economic divisions generated by the growth of American capitalism. The discursive practices of Bowen and company were grounded in the terms of Anglo-American liberalism, but they did not involve a categorical assertion of classlessness. A 'classless' society in the terms of this lexicon did not mean one exempt from 'natural' differences, but one without an intergenerational perpetuation of unnatural distinctions. These antebellum liberals developed their own particular *ideologia americana* of social classes without social conflict.[23]

But by closely identifying the legitimacy of the system with the probability of upward advancement, Bowen and company opened this line of analysis to question and refutation by critics not enamored of such deliberately conservative reasoning. If social mobility was not the norm for members of the laboring class, as it appeared not to be in the years after the Civil War, did this presage a stratified order on the European plan? Bowen, in an 1870 revision of *Principles of Political Economy,* replied no. Yet this remained a nagging question to which he and fellow champions of the status quo were obliged to reply.

Bowen's favorable comparison of American to European social institutions was, of course, a commonplace in nineteenth-century public discourse; the *exemplum bonum* of the new republic was contrasted to the *exemplum malum* of the old world. Calvin Colton made a similar evaluation in *Public Economy for the United States.* Colton—whose career included service as a minister, a campaign biographer for Henry Clay, a spokesman for the Whig party, and the holder of the chair in public economy at Trinity College—composed the text in 1848 as an exposition of the benefits of protectionist economics, and as an enthusiastic evaluation of the republic's social arrangements. "The plan of American society," he observed, "is to give all classes equal chances; that of European society, to maintain the distinction of classes."[24]

Colton, like Bowen, focused his attention on Great Britain, where he identified a tripartite system of the "superior," the "intermediate," and the "laboring" or "working" classes. Britain's institutional configurations were such that the first two groups lived at the expense of the third: "this superincumbent weight of society bears down on the substratum of the laboring classes." While those engaged in commerce, manufacturing, and the trades, "what are commonly called 'the middle classes,'" were able to enjoy the benefits of mobility— of "creeping upward" in Colton's imagery—the laboring classes of Britain were not. The arrogance of the privileged and their own despair held them in check. "The laboring classes are not only considered as born to that position," Colton noted, "but they consider themselves as born to it." Without a total restructuring of the social order, "the working classes" in England were "doomed" (pp. 163–64).

Social conditions in the United States, however, were quite different. Here the "laboring men" could earn high wages, accumulate capital, and easily purchase land. A pervasive "spirit of proprietorship" ensured that, "in all cases," farmers, artisans, and even common laborers could "work for themselves." Colton was careful to include within this "very comprehensive class" of independent laborers not only those involved in "manual toil" in any branch of industry, but any "laborer" engaged in meeting the various "wants of society." He bypassed the bothersome discrimination between productive and unproductive callings by arguing that the familiar litany of scholars, artists, authors, magistrates, and so forth should be "properly ranked among laborers." What were hardened lines between the working and middle classes in Britain had given way in a republican setting; a few rich men notwithstanding, Colton's America had but one class (pp. 165, 275–76).

Colton traced the origins of this exceptional social "plan" to a Revolution that "broke down the barrier of classes." In 1776 the new nation became a "community of working men." Within this original workers' republic, the "rights of labor" were protected from European-styled "usurpation," and the high wages earned by the laboring class were attributable to "political freedom." Colton's reading of those "rights" centered on the ability of the "laborers" to benefit from the free accumulation of property, a process best expedited by the "American System" of the Whig party, especially by the protective tariff. In this Whiggish interpretation of class relations, the "rights" of the laboring classes were not threatened by the "capitalists," no matter what certain Democrats might claim. Since the laborer was the "original, fundamental, most indispensable capitalist in the world," Colton could dispense with any contrary arguments. Neither in their guise as workers nor as capitalists could members of this one great American class oppose the interests that were common to all (pp. 285–89, 292–93, 273–76).

Though Colton chose to define his subject as "public" rather than "political" economy, *Public Economy* was a decidedly political text. From a rhetorical stance typical of partisan literature he objected to the "laissez-faire" tariff and to the domestic policies of the Democracy, and he equated the programs of the Whigs with the future happiness of the republic. Colton's work is worthy of note in the context of antebellum discourse on the social order as an instance of the classes-without-conflict argument, pursued here by a northern Whig. By incorporating a number of standard conventions, Colton delineated a model of American society in which a wide range of occupational classes were part of the greater class of labor, or the "working men." That class could also be addressed as the class of capitalists, if the situation so required, thanks to the open access to wealth guaranteed by the republic's political institutions. In contrast to the social structures of Europe, the American social system was predisposed to harmony and stability and required only the responsible leadership of the Whigs.[25]

Colton's evocation of an essential harmony of class interests was as characteristic a move for Whig theoreticians and politicians as appeals to class antagonism were for the Jacksonians. So too was his reliance upon an expansive—rather than exclusive—definition of the working classes. "The laborers of the United States," as Daniel Webster described them, included "all who in some way or other belong to the industrious and working classes." But both parties claimed to represent the interests of all classes of labor, and both railed against "unnatural" forms of classification. These similar partisan tactics do not necessarily indicate an ideological consensus about classification or class relations, however. Although it was generally agreed that "labor" was "the great producer of wealth," one party's producers could be classed among the other's exploiters. "To talk about rich and exclusive corporations is idle and delusive," Webster maintained. "There is not one of them into which men of moderate means may not enter."[26] Yet it is interesting to note that in a political culture where a great deal of energy was expended in campaigning against social groupings—be they Freemasons, immigrants, Catholics, or slaveholders—no party ran against the "working classes," or identified themselves with the interests of the "nonproducers." "There is a power in names," as Webster appreciated, and the rhetorical power of the category of 'producer' was recognized by the Democratic, the Whig, and subsequently the Republican parties.[27]

Colton's treatise is also of interest for its remarks about the "scientific status" of political, or public, economy. Colton recognized the recent emergence of another "science" concerned with a similar set of social and economic questions: "there is a science of the social state, or of sociology, as M. Comte calls it, which approximates to, more properly, perhaps, lies behind the science of political economy." While Colton's comments on this new science of society go no further than noting that it was not sufficiently unified, his acknowledgment of Comtean "sociology" points to the interest in the Frenchman's work expressed by a number of American writers.[28]

Among those intellectuals who found Comte's and Herbert Spencer's new terminology appealing was Henry C. Carey, the former Whig now turned Republican. When in 1858 Carey published a three-volume study, *The Principles of Social Science,* he noted a debt to Comte for the taxonomy of the sciences, even though he criticized the static, ahistorical dimensions of Comtean "sociology." For Carey the "principles" of a science more fundamental than political economy served as additional evidence of the "perfect harmony of real and true interests among the various classes of mankind" that he had demonstrated in his previous research.[29]

While Carey's invocation of "harmony" had remained a constant in his writings from 1835 onward, he had reversed his position on the tariff in 1847, and was now an ardent advocate of protection. His critique of Ricardo's ideas on wages and rents became an intellectual crusade, as Carey placed himself in opposition to the principles of the liberal system. So complete did he wish this break to be that by 1858 he had discarded the label of "political economy" in favor of one with no Ricardian connotations. "Social science and the political economy of the schools," he insisted, "are thus the precise antipodes of each other." The concept of a "politico-economic man" and the attendant distortions of the "Ricardo-Malthusian doctrine" only served to protect the English class "that lives by appropriation." It was Carey's task in *The Principles of Social Science* to expose this class before they completely established themselves in the United States.[30]

The power of the class of "appropriation"—whom Carey identified in its present incarnation with "successful bankers" and "traders"—was strong enough to reverse the natural processes of economic development in England and much of Europe. There the "gulf dividing the higher and lower classes of society," Carey noted, was an "ever widening one," increasing at the expense of the "middle classes." Lest this pattern be repeated in the United States, he urged that the "equality of condition" of Americans be defended against the designs of the domestic variant of the appropriators, the "traders" opposed to protective duties. The "real and true interests of society"—as indicated by the "laws" of social science—and the exploitations condoned by political economy could be distinguished by reference to the tariff. If adequate protective measures were enacted, the momentum of American society toward increased wealth could be sustained, especially for the class of laborers. If the Ricardian heresy professed by the Democrats continued to inform public policy, however, Carey feared that the "mass" of citizens would be oppressed by the class of traders.[31]

Even though Carey had recourse to a rhetoric of social conflict in this instance, he remained confident about the categorical necessity of class cooperation. The careful study of the laws of his improved social science could prove to the "capitalists" and the "workingmen"—who were but small capitalists in the making—that there was still a "perfect harmony of real and permanent interests" between them. Though Carey may have joined the advocates of "modern socialism" in rejecting the theories of Ricardo and company, he did so toward a different end. He did not wish to reform or replace the American economic and social system, save for the tariff, but to celebrate it. The "social science" he had learned from Comte helped him to do so. Carey continued to project his vision of a harmonious, expanding, effectively one-class American society for the next two decades, and he was joined by a "school" of disciples. The intellectual, and rhetorical, appeal of a Comtean "science of the social state" for Carey and the Careyites lay in its syncretic, universalizing tendencies, and in its reinforcement of an already established line of social reasoning. If "social science" could prove more conclusively that the American dispensation was the most "natural" of all, so much the better.[32]

The implications of Comte's ideas for the analysis of American society were also considered by Thomas Prentice Kettell in a series of essays for the *Merchant's Magazine.*[33] In his "Review, Historical and Critical, of the Different Systems of Social Philosophy," Kettell, the former editor of the *Democratic Review,* called for the creation of a "new and more comprehensive science for the investigation of social phenomena" that would embrace and supersede the established moral sciences. This new discipline of "sociology" would "analyze and reduce, to its constituent elements, the composite structure of human society." Kettell claimed to have invented the term 'sociology' independent of Comte and of his fellow American George Fitzhugh, both of whom, he noted, used the term only in a "very contracted sense." Kettell, in his more generous construal of 'sociology', emphasized historical comparison as a method for analyzing "social phenomena."[34]

In examining the "structure" of contemporary commercial societies, Kettell maintained that the "social distinctions" common to all were those created by differences in wealth. Even the castes of "Hindostan," to the degree that they were based on this economic criterion, resembled the apparently natural class divisions of the "advanced" states. "In every such society," he explained, "there exist at least these three grand divisions . . . the high, the low, and the middle, or rich, poor, and moderately circumstanced." The tripartite social hierarchies that he discovered conformed not only to observation, but to the tendency in nature toward a division by "trinities" that in turn expressed a "fundamental, organic law of creation." Here Kettell added the authority of a Comtean cosmic scheme to the well-established convention of the three "natural" classes.[35]

In assessing the relations among these "constituent elements," he contrasted the characteristic tranquility of present arrangements with those in the past: "As to the concord which generally and so happily exists between the different orders of modern society, as between the rich and poor, the capitalists and laborers, it may be remarked that we have so long been accustomed to it, that . . . we do not appreciate it."[36] In the oppression of the "great artisan or mechanical class" of ancient Greece, and in the internecine class conflict of Rome, Kettell found examples of societies unable to reconcile their members to the necessary asymmetry of rewards decreed by nature. Such a reconciliation, and the resulting class concord, had emerged in American society through an improved "moral sense" of the "true relations between labor and capital." If laborers and capitalists were cognizant of their mutual dependency, they would work to "harmonize their relations" in pursuit of the common goal of increased wealth. The sources of this knowledge were the principles of political economy and the empirical discoveries of sociology.[37]

Though his interpretations of those principles were sometimes at odds with those of the Whig moral philosophers—as a Democrat he favored free trade and preferred that government "let the people alone"—Kettell subscribed to many of their assumptions about American society. His investigations in a still-emerging "social science" reaffirmed the standard judgment that the United States was perhaps the best example of an economy and society organized in accordance with the dictates of "nature." But in surveying contemporary "systems of social philosophy" Kettell encountered a considerable number of self-styled "scientists" who denied that American society in particular, or modern society in general, was "natural." In order to promote a better understanding of the accepted truths of "sociology," he had to address the errors of socialism.

While Kettell admitted that "great inequality" and "social distress" were among the more regrettable features of all modern societies—though in such "new countries" as the United States inequality was not "very great" nor was social distress "very serious"—he rejected the notion that a complete restructuring of political and social institutions was necessary to ameliorate these conditions. The analyses of the "political school" of social philosophy—those who followed in the tradition of William Godwin—had concentrated on only one of the multitude of factors influencing social well-being. It was a serious mistake, Kettell maintained, to claim that "the social grievances of mankind are referable, mainly and fundamentally, to political causes." And as a Democrat who preferred a minimal role for government, he did not favor schemes in which the power of the state would be enhanced. He passed a similar judgment on the "schools" of social philosophy that envisioned the "perfectibility of man" as an "attainable end," or that insisted that a few "fundamental errors" were responsible for all society's ills. In answering the criticisms of the domestic advocates of Robert Owen and Charles Fourier, Kettell replied that if such "errors" did indeed exist in American society, they were yet "subtle and undiscovered."[38]

Once dismissed, the various complaints of reformers and socialists had little effect on Kettell's analysis. Like the "science" of political economy to which it was akin, "sociology" as practiced by Kettell presented an image of the United States as a society in which the causes for class "grievances" were few and the potentials for conflict were none. He found much to be concerned with in the socialists' misconceived "social philosophy," but little to dissuade him from his trust in a necessary "harmony" of all interests. In his pieces for the *Merchant's Magazine* Kettell helped contribute to a tradition of American public discourse in which the socialists served primarily as a rhetorical foil. Practicing social science was not necessarily the same as espousing socialism. For Kettell, as for Carey, the appeal to Comtean sociology reinforced the already established principle of American class cooperation.[39]

The exponents of this position had developed, from the 1820s onward, a distinctive model of the American social and economic order. As generated by the imperatives of the division of labor, it was composed of 'classes' of occupation and of wealth; as regulated by the 'principle' of competition, it ensured an equitable, if unequal, distribution of rewards to the respective classes; and as sustained by social mobility and an axiomatic class harmony, it was a system spared from the conflict endemic to other, less 'natural', forms of arrangement. Its classes—whether one, two, three, or many—could be distinguished for analytic purposes, but in practical terms the lines of demarcation were difficult to establish, and in any case were of less importance than the common categorizations of 'producer', 'laborer', 'worker', or the common stratifications of 'lower', 'middle', and 'upper'. The existence of occupational classes—those natural results of a combination of private choice and public policy—was conventional, not controversial, in the terms of this discourse. Advocates of this tradition of American liberalism did not uniformly subscribe to an ideology of classlessness, but they did deny that there were essentially conflicting classes in the marketplace and the republic. Their claims about classlessness were rhetorical devices, and not necessarily ontological commitments.

American society, as represented by this model, made manifest the blessings of an open, competitive system and was in need of no "fundamental" reforms nor open to any substantive critique. But no matter how strongly they insisted on the superfluity of such lines of criticism, the advocates of the classes-without-conflict model recognized the appeal that the "prejudice" and "errors" of their rhetorical foes had for some of the citizenry, at least for those less conversant with the true principles of social organization. If any factor could precipitate unnecessary and unwanted strife, it would be the acceptance of these competing representations of the social order. Class antagonism was as much an ideological phenomenon as it was an institutional matter. These constant reaffirmations of the doctrine of harmony indicate that class was a salient political and intellectual issue in the antebellum era, as it would be for the rest of the century. Terms of classification and interpretations of class relations continued to be contested, not ignored, in the arenas of American public opinion.

The intellectual partisans of the marketplace, as well as its critics, were well aware that there was "power in names." In contrast to the Jacksonians and the antebellum radicals, the advocates of class harmony wished to expand the category of the 'producing classes' for their own political and cultural ends. The Whigs and their Republican successors could claim to be the real party of the working classes and could offer as evidence a coherent socioeconomic policy based upon protective duties and occupational opportunities.[40] And the practitioners of the moral sciences could continue to equate the dimensions of American market society with the dictates of nature. The antebellum conjoining of mobility and harmony in the name of all classes proved to be a durable analytical and rhetorical device. It would be employed again, in new political and ideological contexts, when Americans examined their reconstructed society in the years after the Civil War.

SIX

The War between Capital and Labor

In his 1872 study of Americanisms the lawyer and linguist M. Schele De Vere noted the prominence of one topic in the nation's political language: "The question of the day, full of import here as in the old world, is that of free labor, as far as it involves the impending conflict between capital and labor." While the epithet "free" was once used in opposition to the labor of slaves, it had been adopted in the cause of the "independence of the workman as regards his employers." Where the United States had faced an "impending conflict" over slavery, it now faced the prospect of another war—a war between capital and labor.[1] Although many of his contemporaries wondered how impending or real this conflict was, De Vere's assessment of the issues that dominated popular and learned discourse was fair. The "labor question"—which included the issues of strikes and labor radicalism, the social effects of economic development and depression, and the growth of an apparently permanent laboring or working class—was "full of import" in the public discourse of the late 1860s and 1870s. "You want to make the intellect of the country discuss the question," as Wendell Phillips told his audience in Faneuil Hall in 1865. The "labor question" was one to which the exponents of the *ideologia americana* of class cooperation on the one hand and the rhetoric of reconcilable class conflict on the other replied in markedly different ways; and from that question another interpretation of American social relations was developed. The "struggle to define and to arrange the true relations of capital and labor" that Phillips described led to important changes in the ways that the "intellect of the country" used the term 'class' and represented American class relations.[2]

Few of the amateur and professional practitioners of the moral sciences expressed doubt about the axiom of societal harmony during the 1860s and 1870s. Neither the rhetorical insistence of social critics nor the practical incidence of strikes and labor violence persuaded them that relations between the respective classes should be construed as anything but cooperative. They continued to dismiss criticisms of American capitalism as misinterpretations of the fundamental laws governing society; and they considered incidents of unrest unfortunate examples of how much trouble such misunderstandings could cause. Despite the considerable structural and intellectual changes at work in late-nineteenth-century America, there was considerable continuity in the premises and terms of formal social analysis. The liberal ideology of classes without conflict was particularly durable.

There was continuity as well in the social roles played by these professors of moral philosophy and political economy. As did their antebellum counterparts, they addressed their arguments to a number of audiences: to students, colleagues, the makers of policy, and a larger general public. Social analyses that reiterated and reinforced the ideology of class harmony were to be found in the limited, if influential, medium of textbooks and formal treatises; in contributions to the more widely circulated periodicals, journals, and reviews; and in the notes on the lecturer's podium and the minister's pulpit. In an era in which changes in technology and distribution were forming a national reading public, these writers and speakers were not divided from this audience by the lines of disciplinary specialization. Even more than their professionalized successors, they exercised significant cultural power in setting the terms of public discourse. And within the bounds of that discourse, they represented the American republic in a manner similar to their predecessors: as a society composed of mutually dependent classes, and one ultimately spared from interclass strife.[3]

Yet in spite of the moral scientists' professed confidence in their social maxims, they often found it necessary to acknowledge and account for the apparent popularity of contradictory lines of reasoning—the "folly of the supposed antagonism" between capital and labor—among many Americans. The theoretical concerns expressed in the 1830s and 1840s about the political and social consequences of an estranged laboring class were becoming practical ones in the 1860s and 1870s. Amasa Walker's explanation of this problem was typical of the majority of moral scientists, those who favored the politics of laissez-faire and free trade. In his 1866 *Science of Wealth* Walker, then lecturer in public economy at Amherst College, assigned responsibility for the prevalence of such errors to a number of exigencies: to "unprincipled" politics, to a "false social and political opinion" that maintained that "hatred and retaliation" were the "normal relations" between capital and labor, and to the "misapplication of language" by certain writers on this subject. Before the science of wealth could effectively ameliorate the "exacerbation of mutual distrust" among Americans, it needed to resolve at least some of its difficulties with definitions.[4]

In Walker's estimation the central factor that promoted conceptual confusion also distinguished political economy from the other sciences: it lacked a discipline-specific technical language and had to "adopt words in common use." The issues that political economists addressed—"wealth," "value," "labor," "capital"—were themselves terms drawn from "popular language." As such they were subject to a multiplicity of meanings and to imprecise employment leading to "ceaseless entanglements" and "perplexities." Walker did not explain why political economy "has not the option of making or choosing its own terms" but rather assumed, as did many of his Anglo-American colleagues, that the terms of popular and technical discourse would tend to be the same. While Walker did not present a comprehensive lexicon to his readers, he did define such words as 'labor' and 'capital' in a manner that might preclude popular misinterpretations of their actual relations.[5]

'Labor', for Walker, was the voluntary efforts of men to produce "objects of desire"; while 'capital' was, quite simply, accumulated labor. Each term represented but a different form of the same phenomenon. The classes of laborers and capitalists, therefore, could be distinguished by the forms of labor—present and past—that were at their disposal and that they brought to the processes of creating wealth. And in all such endeavors, he argued, the elements and the classes of capital and labor necessarily relied upon each other. They were "partners." This interdependence did not, however, prevent the classes possessing the various forms of labor from constantly competing for larger shares of the wealth produced. Yet neither the frequency nor the intensity of this competition indicated to Walker the presence of actual enmity between the laboring classes and the capitalists. Economic competition was not the same as class antagonism for him. There were instances, of course, where the rights of one of the partners had been violated by the other; but he attributed these to ignorance and "evil passions." Descriptions of antagonistic relations between capital and labor were, in Walker's judgment, exercises in "false philosophy," since his science demonstrated that such antagonism did not exist. Although Walker rejected this "false philosophy," he recognized its power. He attributed the Revolution in France to the popularity of a "principle of hurt" among the two great classes.[6]

Walker's interest in the efficacy of terminology also led him to consider that "severely contested" question in political economy, the distinctions between productive and unproductive labor. Although he found that issue to be of little consequence on its own merits, it was the source of a more "grave" matter, the "sweeping condemnation" of a number of useful and important classes. Walker faulted Adam Smith for popularizing this "unfortunate" discrimination; and he praised later writers for eliminating it from the terms of learned discourse. For Walker all labor was productive, and all persons involved in stimulating production were members of productive classes. Walker granted no conceptual space to allegations about productiveness or to implications of class animosity. He was interested, however, in assuring that the contributions of the "learned and artistic" classes, his own included, were freed from the odium of the label 'unproductive'.[7]

In dismissing the theoretical possibility of class antipathy, Walker was joined by such associates as Arthur Latham Perry, professor of political economy and history at Williams College, and Albert S. Bolles, editor of the *Norwich Bulletin*. Perry, in his *Elements of Political Economy,* had explained that there was no "natural opposition" of capitalist and laborer. Instead, they were for him what they had been for Walker, mutually dependent "partners in the same concern" from which the one derived profits and the other wages. If they were so considered, there could be no reasonable grounds for either the "common jealousy" expressed by workers for employers, or the common supposition of a "deeply-seated antagonism" between the classes. As did Walker, Perry argued for an all-inclusive understanding of the productive class: "our language must be broad enough to cover all the cases."[8]

When Bolles, in his *Chapters in Political Economy,* turned to the topic of the actual dealings of laborers and capitalists, he could not discover any "real" class antagonism. "And this," he noted, "is the common language of all who have investigated the subject." Even though

Bolles did admit that members of the two classes often conceived of themselves and their interests in terms of opposition, he did not recognize any "enmity between them." Rather he emphasized, as did Walker and Perry, the essential unity underlying these relations. From the perspective of their science, then, the popularity of contradictory interpretations was indicative of cognitive failures on the part of social critics, and not of substantive problems in the social order.[9]

In insisting upon the categorical necessity of class cooperation, and in admitting that some Americans adhered to contradictory interpretations of social relations, the advocates of free trade agreed with their rivals, the supporters of protection. Henry Carey and his followers composed a large part of this second group, and they continued to stress the doctrine of harmony that Carey had discovered years before. Yet, as he observed in a pamphlet on the relation of capital and labor, the opposite often seemed to be the case: "it has more and more taken the form, as it now bears the name, of a war between capital and labor." And, as he noted with regret, both sides in this contest regularly based their arguments on erroneous premises.[10]

Carey published this pamphlet in 1873 while serving as chairman of the Committee on Industrial Interests and Labor at Pennsylvania's constitutional convention; through it he criticized attempts to incorporate measures regulating wages and hours in that document. For Carey, legislation to limit the workday to eight hours was both futile and unjust to all involved, since it proceeded on the assumption that labor and capital were "naturally hostile," when in fact those two elements and their related classes were conjoined in a "partnership." Even if, he suggested, socioeconomic conditions degenerated to the point where laborers and capitalists might "go to war," the bonds of this partnership remained "indissoluble." If members of these classes turned on each other, they would be acting in ignorance and in violation of the natural dictates of social harmony (pp. 7–10).

No matter how inevitable this struggle might appear to be, Carey explained, the laws governing "societary system" would not permit a clash between its constituent parts. The disturbances and inequalities that signified to others the worsening condition of the American laboring classes were interpreted by Carey as the results of free trade. It was the commercial policies of the "monopolistic nations"—that is to say, Great Britain—that had provoked a "revolt" of labor against capital, and had distorted market relations in the United States.

Carey's solution to this problem was, as usual, a protective tariff. Constant invocations of bellicose imagery notwithstanding, a real war between the classes of capital and labor in the United States would be impossible (pp. 10–16).

Carey's faith—despite evidences to the contrary—in an essentially cooperative social order was shared by his disciples, among whom was Robert Ellis Thompson, professor of social science at the University of Pennsylvania and editor of the *Penn Monthly.* "Social science," as Thompson described it, studied man "as existing in society"; and political economy was the "art by which this science is carried into practice." While "labor and capital in conflict" were in an "unnatural state," Thompson argued in *Social Science and the National Economy,* "harmony" was their "true relation." Nonetheless he allowed that, for the present at least, conditions appeared to be better explained in terms of social antagonism. In Europe and in the United States "grave injuries" had been done to the laboring classes in the course of an "unnatural" contest between labor and capital.[11]

When accounting for this troubling discrepancy between the laws of nature—as demonstrated by social science—and the actions of men, Thompson proceeded in a manner similar to Carey's. He interpreted the current "misery" of the working classes as a consequence of the popularity of the English economists. Capitalists, he noted, were particularly well disposed toward a political economy that justified low wages as necessary and natural, even though Carey's work had proven the benefits of higher wages. By following the principles of classical political economy, the capitalists had needlessly engendered social strife and had endangered not only the working classes, but themselves. They had exposed the "industrial state" to the criticisms of socialists and communists who had, in their stead, appreciated the oppressive logic of Ricardian economics, and who in Europe, at least, sought to "overthrow the frame-work of modern society." For Thompson the anomaly of American class animosity could be attributed to the "absence" of reliable knowledge about the workings of the "industrial state." If the various classes of society, especially the capitalists, appreciated the "essential harmony of their interests" and restored these natural relations, all contemporary, and decidedly unnecessary, social hostilities would come to an end. The proclaimed state of war between capital and labor, which in principle should not be, then in practice would not be.[12]

As did Carey and Amasa Walker, Thompson subscribed to the conventional classes-without-conflict position, yet in so doing, he acknowledged that the findings of science and the attitudes of some of his fellow citizens seemed to be at odds. Although the social scientists were certain that within the United States there was no possibility of a genuine animus between the classes, for the moment there appeared to be at least the impression of antagonism. While Thompson did not attempt to reconcile this problem, save for insisting on the certainty of class harmony, his recognition of this variance between social scientific theory and popular practice was characteristic of that of many of his peers. Or as Albert Bolles was to observe in an 1876 study, *The Conflict between Labor and Capital,* "notwithstanding this very palpable truth, anything but harmony exists between the two classes."[13]

In considering the possibility of a phenomenon that his discipline had persistently denied, Bolles, for one, arrived at the explanatory boundaries of the model of societal harmony. Despite his own stated certitude in the "truth" of class cooperation, he conceded that it was also "painfully true" that the recent relations between the two great classes had been marked by an ever-increasing "feeling of antagonism." In both the Old World and the New, he observed, the "ties" that had once drawn together the capitalists and the laborers, the employers and the employed, were now being broken; and the result of the subsequent "readjustment" was a tangible, if hopefully temporary, conflict. While these patterns of change in Great Britain and on the Continent indicated to Bolles the not unwelcome end of the European working classes' "servility," their import for the United States was another matter. Here the arrival of a "wave of discontent" among the workers and the concomitant presumption of hostility by members of both classes signified the ascent of the heresy of opposed interests. Bolles's Americans, it seems, were busily engaged in a process of confounding the basic principles of their social and economic order. Thus he accounted for the paradoxical occurrence of two contradictory truths—the imperative of class harmony and the presence of class antagonism—by maintaining the primacy of the first, and explaining away the second as the consequence of collective misconception.[14] In attempting to remove this confusion and in "toning down" extant antagonism, Bolles was prepared to recognize the actuality of the emerging "conflict between the two classes." At the same time, he wished to deny the utility of class conflict as a category for the analysis of American conditions. What others might mistakenly construe as a war of the workers against the capitalists, Bolles contended, could be better interpreted as a "contest" among various incarnations of the laboring classes. Insofar as capital was but a form of accumulated labor, he suggested—after Walker et alia—that those who possessed it might also be denominated "laborers." He further argued, along lines that by 1876 had been well established by earlier advocates of the social order, that the multitude of "gradations" from the capitalist to the laborer among Americans has made it quite difficult to "classify all persons." For Bolles these classifications "shade off almost imperceptibly," and as they disappeared one into the next, so too did the purported differences between the elusive classes. "The *true* interests of labor and capital," he reiterated, "are identical." A close examination of the conflict between labor and capital demonstrated to Bolles what he and his colleagues had previously affirmed: that there was not, nor could there be, any authentic manifestation of class antagonism in the United States.[15]

It is easy to dismiss the tangled reasoning of Bolles and his colleagues as simple—or simpleminded—exercises in economic apologetics, or as instances of collective social denial. But as attenuated as these arguments might appear to be, they do indicate the power exercised by the axiom of class harmony among these late-nineteenth-century American analysts. When faced with disjunctions between their interpretive categories and the social conditions to be interpreted, they consistently sought to support the former. Their commitments to the adequacy of their classifications were stronger than the apparent changes in American class relations. Both laissez-faire, free-trade liberals and interventionist protectionists continued to assert the ideology of American social exceptionalism through the last decades of the nineteenth century. Popular perceptions of class warfare did not displace the doctrine of class cooperation in many of the venues of American public discourse.

*N*o matter how strenuously Bolles and company questioned the ontological status of class antagonism, there were other participants in the public discourse of the 1860s and 1870s who doubted neither its existence nor its explanatory value. To those involved in the trade unions, reform associations, and political parties composing the movement for labor reform, the conflict of capital and labor served as a focal analytic and rhetorical category. Their understanding of American arrangements, in contradistinction to the harmonious partnerships posited by the moral scientists, was characterized by the seemingly inexorable spread of "wage slavery," by the constant aggression of the ever more powerful employers, and by privation and involuntary idleness among many workers in the wake of the panic of 1873. It was a social and economic order in which the depiction of class relations as a war between capital and labor was far more than a metaphorical device; to many it had every appearance of being a reality.[16]

In his capacity as president of the Iron Molders' International Union and the National Labor Union, William Sylvis was during the 1860s one of the most forceful exponents of these competing representations of the "the principles which underlie the present social structure." This subject, as he remarked to the IMIU's 1864 convention in Buffalo, had been addressed in "thousands of volumes"; but, in general, these were neither reliable nor conceptually satisfactory. What made this body of texts suspect to Sylvis was the social locations of their authors: these "economists," he observed, were members of the "privileged classes," and as such they had consistently favored the "ideas of capital" while disregarding those of labor. Therefore the economists' accepted notions of the rate of wages, of the source of wealth, and of mutually dependent class relations were self-serving and "absurd." And rather than perpetuate these absurdities, Sylvis sought to advance opinions more appropriate to the declining circumstances of the laboring classes in America.[17]

When viewed from this perspective, Sylvis found that the classes' vaunted "equal partnership" was an illusion; and he emphatically denied any intrinsic identity between capitalists and labor. Were the "luxury" of the one and the "poverty and want" of the others sufficient "evidences" of a harmony of interests? What belied such a "theory" to Sylvis was the institution of employment for wages, in which the incompatibility of interests was brought into relief as employers and "employees" vied with each other over a necessarily inequitable division of limited profits. Even if the workmen were to have the right to "place a valuation" on their own efforts—as would be expected of "co-partners"—the system of wages would, he maintained, still generate an elementary antagonism between laborers and capitalists. Society's "two distinct classes" were thus drawn by Sylvis into a "sort of irrepressible conflict," one that had "commenced with the world, and will only end with it." Inasmuch as he was delivering this address during the course of the Civil War, his evocation of an "irrepressible conflict" was not fortuitous. That phrase had been popularized by William Seward in the 1850s as a description of the impending struggle between the advocates of free and slave labor; and here Sylvis was transposing the locus of this "conflict" from the yet unresolved issue of slavery to the evidently irresoluble question of wages. In a society still racked by the events of this first struggle, Sylvis' choice of words was not trivial.[18]

Although Sylvis acknowledged that due to its emphasis on class antagonism his "new" estimation of America's social organization might be "unpopular"—especially since he was contradicting the "almost universally received opinions" on the topic of capital and labor—he continued to insist upon the actuality of class antinomies in his public speeches and writings. Like the moral philosophers whose "received opinions" he intended to displace, Sylvis recognized and emphasized the power of denomination and interpretation. During the 1865 gathering of the IMIU at Chicago, Sylvis took note of, and rejected, the charges of those who warned that he and other "advocates of union" among the workers would destroy what were still "harmonious" relations. The reverse, he suggested, was the case. A "clashing of interests," a "social revolution," was already under way within the United States, and though the "collision" had not yet turned violent, the laboring class, if required, would fight. But if "property is preserved not by policemen, but by ideas," as Sylvis assumed, the "war of classes" would be a conceptual contest—a war of classifications.[19]

For the present, then, Sylvis expected this conflict to be carried on, at one level, by the forces of labor with the rhetorical weapons of "fair argument" and honesty directed against the envy of the capitalists and the "sophistry" engaged in their service. Those sophists who needed to be met and overcome in the arena of public discourse were, not surprisingly, the acknowledged authorities on "social and political economy" from Adam Smith through Henry Carey. In a manner highly reminiscent of Stephen Simpson's *Working Man's Manual* of 1831, Sylvis derided the economists, especially Smith, as "apologists for tyranny," and criticized their studied avoidance of the principles of justice. Nonetheless he did grant that in their "classifications of society" they were quite "scientific." Such was not the case, however, for either their announcements of interdependence or their apologies for the degradation of the laboring class. On these and other concerns

Sylvis felt that his audiences had little to learn, but much to fear, from the "ideas of capital" and their proponents.[20]

In lieu of the "existing system of distribution"—as delineated and defended by Carey and the rest—Sylvis called for a variety of economic and political reforms such as eight-hour-day legislation, and a system of credit and currency more favorable to the working classes than was the prevalent "money monopoly" of the nonproducers. To bring to an end the "enslaving" effects of wages and the "false social system" they nurtured, he actively promoted the establishment of producers' cooperatives. There the now divisive differences between the classes could be first mollified and then eliminated, since in cooperatives the working men would own and exercise control over the now antagonistic elements of capital and labor. In time, due to superior efficiency, the cooperatives would force their wage-slaver competitors to adapt the new format or face ruin. Through the system of cooperation, Sylvis predicted, "we will become a nation of employers, the employers of our own labor." Once this reunion had been effected, it would "forever destroy all antagonisms." Thus Sylvis argued that cooperation, in tandem with other demands of the labor reformers such as the eight-hour day, would enable the "laboring people" of the United States to break free of the cycle of an otherwise "never-ending" class conflict.[21]

Sylvis's evaluation of the imperiled position of an exclusively construed class of producers and his delineation of the contemporary "collision" between labor and capital were regularly put forward by labor reformers during the 1860s and 1870s, although not all in the NLU or other associations would so strongly emphasize the categorical imperative of class antagonism. In its published "Address . . . to the Workingmen of the United States" an NLU committee led by Andrew C. Cameron, editor of the *Working Man's Advocate* of Chicago, noted that "[s]o far from encouraging the spirit of hostility to employers, all properly organized unions recognize an identity of interests between and confer as many benefits on the employer as the employed."[22] Achieving this "identity" depended on the employers' accepting the rights of the working classes to organize, and would be expedited by the successful implementation of the NLU's proposals; once done, the two groups could naturally cooperate. As serious as were the "existing evils," they could be effectively countered. While Cameron and the committee recognized that, at present, labor and capital's antagonism was a "self-evident proposition," they interpreted it as the product of an "iniquitous" and politically manipulated system of banking and currency; they did not presume that this state of conflict must "necessarily exist." Though they allowed that American society had but "one dividing line"—that which separated the "class that labors" from the "class that lives by others' labors"—this need not always be a line of battle.[23]

In assessing the modern social order, Cameron had recourse to that rhetoric common to his and the previous generation of workingmen's advocates and labor reformers, the rhetoric of a reconcilable class conflict. Should the "laboring classes" of the United States recognize and exercise their economic and political powers—powers created and sustained by such "republican institutions" as private property and manhood suffrage—they would be able to "remedy" the "abuses of the present industrial system." That system, when suitably reformed, would give way to one in which the "wealth producing classes" would enjoy an equitable share of what they had created, and in which the "non-producing classes"—the bankers, insurers, middlemen, and "employing capitalists"—would be obliged to "earn a living by honest industry." Through the various mechanisms of reform, the latter classes would come to resemble their opposites; the employees would become employers; and, as Ira Steward promised in *The Eight Hour Movement,* "every man will be a capitalist." Hence the "one dividing line" that currently bisected society could, in time, be diminished or even erased.[24]

Both the extent and the ease of this incipient American reformation were open to serious question, however, within the community of labor reform; so, too, were the projected contours of the renewed social order. Although many sought, as did Cameron, to restore the nation's "republican institutions" to their prelapsarian conditions, there were others, especially among those well-disposed toward the varieties of American radicalism and European socialism, who wished to consider a "thorough reconstruction" of social and economic relations. And if one were to assume, as did the Massachusetts labor reformer and one-time candidate for governor Edwin M. Chamberlin, that the ownership by one class of the "surplus wealth" produced by the other was the main cause of poverty, inequality, and crime, considerable alterations in the "customs and laws of society" were warranted.[25]

Chamberlin presented his analysis of the "dispute" between the "poorer classes" and the capitalists in an 1875 volume on the Sovereigns of Industry, a group founded in the previous year as a laboring men's equivalent to the Patrons of Husbandry. For Chamberlin the contest for "industrial freedom" was both international in scope—with the American "Labor Reform agitation" compared here to the activities of the German socialists, the English trade unions, and the Communards in France—and beyond resolution within the confines of the prevalent "unjust" system. "We can hope for no lasting reconciliation of these classes," he contended, "or rather we can hope for no enduring peace till the classes themselves disappear." The impetus for this change—one intended to "overturn the existing structure of society"—was to be found in the trade unions and the Cooperative movement.[26]

The emergence of the cooperatives, Chamberlin argued, was far more than the "momentary expression" of the producing classes' dissatisfaction with the organization of commerce and industry: it signified instead a "new disposition" of the contending "forces" of capital and labor. By means of the cooperatives—which for Chamberlin and many contemporaries encompassed both enterprises for consumers and joint-stock manufactories—the working classes would receive the "full value" of their efforts and would be freed from their "dependence" on the capitalists. These "idle and speculative" classes, in turn, could be dispensed with. Chamberlin further assumed that, once the cooperatives had been established, they could serve as examples for other, more drastic reforms. While the general population now relied upon the capitalists for work and wages—or for "whatever comfort and liberty" they might know—with the latter's eclipse the community at large would instead become the employer. Though such assets as land, communications, railroads, and mines were now in the possession of the minority, he suggested that they be taken over by the state and held in common. Hence, in order to eliminate the conditions that had reduced the working classes to a "servile position," Chamberlin was prepared to violate the sanctity of the right to property. Since cooperation's "ultimate end" was the "destruction of the profit system," its success would eventually result in the disappearance of the classes and the institutions fashioned by that system which, he predicted, "will sooner or later be swept away."[27]

As to the manner in which this "destruction" would occur and the ostensively socialist "Republic of Labor" be proclaimed, Chamberlin was not certain. Since the cooperatives were not "organizations militant," as were the unions, the dissemination and emulation of the former's messages and methods could induce the peaceful realignment of the standing order. One of the great strengths of the current configuration of capital and labor was, in Chamberlin's judgment, its pretensions to authenticity. This system "looks natural enough," and unless it was the object of skeptical inquiry, it appeared to be of "universal extent," of "remote antiquity," and—most important—"essential to the work of production." Cooperation and labor-reform "agitation" could help promote the conception and construction of an alternate "system," one truly in keeping with nature's intended equality. For Chamberlin these movements could begin the critical process of denaturalizing the institutions and delegitimating the ideology of American capitalism. But were such endeavors to be effective, they needed to be more than the textual "guerrilla attacks" of detached reformers. They required the political participation of the working classes.[28]

Yet Chamberlin also warned of an "impending danger," of a "rupture" in class relations: "it may be that the dispute between capital and labor is to end in violence and bloodshed." His producing classes had risen in a "sudden revolt" against "corporate usurpation"—that "tyranny" of banks, bondholders, and railroads imposed upon them in the course of the Civil War—and could in extreme circumstances be expected to resort to force. Although Chamberlin was most decidedly opposed to such a course, it had become for him—and in his estimation for American society—a definite possibility.[29]

Whereas for Chamberlin in 1875 the advent of a physical confrontation between the classes was still a conjectural matter—as well as an effective rhetorical device—in the wake of the railroad strike of 1877 that conflict seemed to have moved from the realm of the potential to that of the actual. For Ezra Hervey Heywood, an anarchist and former president of the New England Labor Reform League, that summer's riots along the nation's railways were events in which the "irrepressible conflict" had erupted—events proving that "between labor and capital there can be no truce, no compromise." In an essay, "The Great Strike," for the *Radical Review,* he likened the trainmen's actions to the patriots' stance against tyranny during the American Revolution and insisted that, despite the arguments of the "recognized exponents of thought," an analogous "tyranny of capital" now existed within the United States. For such self-styled "unbiased observers" as Heywood and his confederates in the "movement" for labor reform, the "artificial subjection" of the working people was all too apparent; and though he did not find the "destruction of life or property" to be a "judicious method" of advancing reform, like Chamberlin he understood the expedience of the turn toward violence.[30]

Notwithstanding his appreciation of the strikers' reactions, Heywood announced his, and the labor reformers', opposition to strikes as wasteful and unnecessarily damaging. He preferred in their stead the "peaceful methods of evolution" for attaining his goal of the "abolition of capital," a process that would involve an end to the monopoly of credit, to private property in land, and to the class that possessed them. But as objectionable as he found the "philosophy" of strikes to be, he was even more opposed to the modes by which these events were conceived of and interpreted by defenders of the extant order. "By defining strikes as essentially mutinous and revolutionary," Heywood declared, "the dictionaries conspire with the capitalists against the liberty and the natural rights of working people to property in the fruits of their labor." Rather than admitting their responsibility for the "impoverishment" of the working class, the American class of tyrants, and the "knights of the quill" in their service, had tried to define away the consequences of capitalism. In Heywood's judgment they were deliberately confounding the tactical errors of the Great Strike—serious though these were—with the underlying justice of the strikers' demands. Even if, as Heywood allowed, few of the trainmen either frequented the meetings or considered the "wide-scattered ideas" of the labor reformers, they nevertheless shared in the same "spirit." It was a spirit that was troubled by the dominant social constellation, and that would be at ease only when the producing classes were again in the ascendant.[31]

Heywood's concern with the effects of this "conspiracy of dictionaries" and the pronouncements of the system's champions underscores a recurrent theme in the discourse of the labor reformers: their cognizance of the cultural power exercised by their opponents. Like Chamberlin, Heywood recognized the significance of the capitalists' propensity to identify that which was natural with that which was to their advantage; and like Sylvis, he was aware that the reformers needed to develop a countervailing line of reasoning, one more relevant to the experience of the laborers than any stipulated state of harmony. Despite the determined conceptual resistance of the "recognized exponents of thought," the real presence of antagonistic classes needed to be fully articulated before it could be eliminated. Labor reform's challenge to the social order, then, entailed first the contesting of, then the replacement of, existing social categories.[32]

The difficulties in definition encountered in the reformer's task of asserting class antagonism were touched upon by Jesse H. Jones, a minister, Christian socialist, and organizer of Boston's Christian Labor Union. In an article for the *International Review,* entitled "The Labor Problem: A Statement of the Question from the Labor-Reform Side," the Reverend Jones admitted that "I speak of the laboring or wage classes, and this phrase is distasteful to many true-hearted Americans. With much energy they deny that there are any fixed classes in America. That is a noble feeling from which their denial springs; and I could wish the case were what they persuade themselves that it is. But I cannot make the facts; I can only declare them."[33] As presented by Jones, the facts indicated the segmentation of American society into two classes: one of "managers" who owned the land, houses, mills, raw materials, and final products; and one of "wage workers" who owned nothing, save for their ability to do labor. Inasmuch as nine-tenths of the class of "toilers" were therein trapped by economic conditions over which they had no control, he concluded that such a division was by now permanent. Incantations of equality or mobility notwithstanding, Jones declared that "a fixed, hopeless, proletariat, wage class is the very foundation of our industrial system," and that the "drive" of this system was toward the ever more rapid increase of this supposedly fictitious entity.[34]

For Jones an America so separated was not the exemplar of economic or social justice, since between the managers and wage workers—or the "czars" and the "serfs"—class relations were by their nature "tyrannous." Nor was it a republic that could sustain for long the contradictory claims of both "industrial kings" and a class who were but "one step above slaves." The "structure" of American society was in need of immediate renovation, he warned, by way of either reform or revolution. Of these alternatives he favored the first as the means for "abolishing both classes altogether."[35]

Although Jones did not greatly concern himself with the precise details of such a change, he did argue that the model for reshaping the "un-American industrial system" was already available within the nation's political institutions, specifically the New England town meeting. Industrial managers should be chosen by the managed; there should be a joint division of everything produced; and productive capital assets should be held in common. "The capitalists and the toilers," Jones reasoned, "must be one." Were industrial affairs to be conducted in this democratic and egalitarian style, the "vast proletariat" could reassert their abrogated rights to property, and regain that control over their employments now ceded to the "managing classes." By adopting a "town meeting labor system"—a procedure that he hoped could be carried out peacefully at least within the United States—the differences in power and possession between these two classes could be removed. While a decidedly "fixed" set of classes was characteristic of the "wage-labor system," in spite of the disclaimers of its beneficiaries, Jones expected the creation, or re-creation, of an American social order in which the "noble feeling" of the laborer might be realized; one in which talk of an open class structure, or even of the absence of classes, would be more than nonsense.[36]

In the "Labor Problem" essay Jones made his classifications in light of the ownership and control of the "means whereby . . . people can get a living." By doing so he was able to delineate clearly an America in which the appearance of the two contentious classes of managers and wage workers was the social result of rapid, and rapacious, economic growth and the correspondent "industrial" transformation of the republic. In his America of 1880 the "labor problem" was becoming, or had already become, the central problematic; and the ever evasive category of "producer" was no longer of sufficient discriminatory or exhortatory value. Even though the "productive" class and its definitional inverse would continue to inhabit the discourse of those involved with the question of labor during the last decades of the nineteenth century, Jones's usage in this piece is indicative of the lexical arrival of an American 'proletariat', and of a radical's rhetoric concerned less with settling upon the criterion of 'productive' than with taking possession of the means of production.[37]

However different their respective appraisals of the nation's political institutions might be, Jones shared a number of these descriptive and prescriptive elements with the proponents of the socialisms of Karl Marx and Ferdinand Lassalle. Insofar as the socialists offered their criticisms in foreign languages, especially in German, they remained on the margins of American public discourse. But by the 1870s their calls for the social emancipation of the "working classes" by a political party of that class—or classes—were being disseminated, however sporadically, in English. A "Workingmen's Party" was formed in 1876, and in the following year was renamed the Socialistic

Labor Party. The SLP was the product of a merger of three smaller Lassallean and Marxist parties. The Lassalleans insisted on the primacy of political action, while the Marxists emphasized trade union activity. As was the practice for radical movements, it explicated its positions by way of party newspapers and pamphlets such as the *Tracts of the Socialistic Labor Party,* an English-language primer in socialism composed by Joseph A. Labadie, Judson Grenell, and John Francis Bray. For them socialism meant replacing a social order predicated upon "injustice" with one organized in accordance with the findings of "scientific truth"—the truth as established by the science of Marx, not by that of Adam Smith.[38]

The America depicted by Bray and company bore a strong likeness to that of others engaged in the wider currents of labor reform. Its citizens were divided between the useless, employing nonproducers and the wage-earning, working classes; and its class relations resembled those of serfdom. Instead of a celebrated equality, access to wealth and to political influence within the United States was in fact determined by "social status," even though, as Bray noted, the Constitution did not acknowledge the "mastership of one class over another." For Bray the political rhetoric of the late eighteenth century had been overcome by the economic realities the late nineteenth. Socialism proposed an end to this oppression, not by "revolution" but by more tranquil measures, some of which, nonetheless, went beyond the accepted understanding of what was constitutional. To destroy these "class divisions," Bray and his associates recommended that the "wage class" and the farmers assert their numerical and electoral strength through the SLP, and so take over the direction of government from the "capitalistic labor pirates." Once the workers were so empowered, there could follow, "gradually and wherever practicable," the transfer of the "means of labor" from the employers to the general community. Bray maintained that socialism would not abolish property, however; nor would it attempt to impose any "unnatural equality." Yet it most certainly would do away with all obviously unnatural inequalities and artificial classifications; and in so doing it would create that "harmony between capital and labor" that the sciences of "existing society" could promise but could never deliver. If there were to be a classless and harmonious America, Bray explained, it would have to be a socialistic America.[39]

In presenting the SLP's critique of the prevailing "industrial system," Bray and company also remarked upon the contravening role played by that system's intellectual partisans. As had Heywood and Sylvis, Bray found that each time the working classes attempted to give voice to their discontents, they were met by "half a million editors, professors, lawyers, ministers, and other worthy representatives," who cautioned them to keep their "hands off" so admirable an "order of things." These "literary champions of capitalism"—or so they were called by the 1880 convention of the SLP—carried on their defenses in the pages of the *Nation,* the *North American Review,* and other "prominent publications." And though the figure of a half million was somewhat exaggerated, Bray's sense of the depth of the expressed opposition to labor reform in general, and to socialism in particular, was more accurate. The "labor question" was widely debated by Americans from the late 1860s onward, and many of the disputants remained unconvinced of either the feasibility of reformers' plans or the fixity of the class in whose name these schemes were proposed. Notwithstanding the socialists' assurance that their "remedies" were supported by "the soundest principles of socio-political economy," what exactly those principles were, and how they were to be applied to the social ordering of the United States, remained matters of considerable disagreement. In late-nineteenth-century America there was no easy or rapid conceptual change from a discourse of class cooperation to an acceptance of class antagonism. Classifications and class relations remained open to considerable controversy.[40]

*T*hese "literary champions of capitalism" were a professionally and politically diverse lot, but they did subscribe to at least one common position: with their announcements of antagonism, the radicals and labor reformers had demonstrated a "profound misunderstanding" of the actual relations between the classes. Whatever the changes in the occupation, size, and situation of the country's workforce—as brought on by economic expansion or, after 1873, by depression—there was no reason to presume the inevitability of social strife. That there were, and would be, disputes between employers and employed was obvious, yet the apparition of strikes, however intense these might be, was not necessarily the same as a declaration of war between capital and labor.[41]

The extent of this supposed antagonism among the working classes was addressed by Edwin L. Godkin in the course of an 1868 article on cooperation for the *North American Review.* To Godkin, the editor of the *Nation,* the popularity of the cooperative movement in Europe and the relative lack of interest in it displayed in the United States suggested differences in the "class feeling" of the respective groups of workers. For the Europeans the historical traditions of "class distinctions" and the more recent experience of being "massed together" in manufactories under the "regime of wages" had given rise to both a sense of "isolation" from the rest of society and a sense of identity with one another—a "veritable loyalty to their class as a class." Cooperation, which sought to supplant that regime through a "real social revolution," was, he explained, an expression of that loyalty, of class feeling.[42]

However pervasive such sentiments might be among Europe's workers, Godkin could discover very little of these feelings among Americans. Working for wages did not here imply any permanent subjection; it was instead an expected means of moving from the "employed" to the "employers." Nor was there—with the possible exception of the large cities—any certain connection between one's occupation and one's social position. In comparison with Britain or France, then, there was in this country an "absence of class distinctions." The "social degradation" that this movement intended to displace, and the antagonistic "class feelings" that were implicated, did not have fully developed counterparts in the United States. Cooperation, he observed, was not as necessary here. Godkin did find the idea of cooperation to have merit, however, and hoped for the growth of "industrial partnerships" in the United States as an answer to the manifest shortcomings of the "wages system." And though he admitted to "plenty of discontent" among the working classes, as evidenced by strikes and the other ills of the "wages system," Godkin did not anticipate the replication of European conditions in the American republic.[43]

One of the characteristics and causes of those conditions was, in Godkin's analysis, the prevailing "strength" of the idea of the "dissociation" of capital and labor. His Europeans had accepted, as a "fundamental" principle of social organization, that the owners of each must form "separate and distinct" classes; "class feeling" was the corollary to this principle. His Americans, however, had not as yet countenanced either social closure or class hostility. But, as Godkin had warned in the *Nation,* there was an emerging "labor crisis" within the United States. If, at the behest of trade unions and labor reformers, the class that had already "appropriated to their exclusive use the title of 'working-men'" completely assented to the fallacy of opposed interests, "class feeling" would become an American phenomenon as well.[44]

In an unsigned piece, "The Workingmen's Ideal Society," in the September 1869 issue of Godkin's *Nation,* the author noted that in the called-for reorganization of society there would be no place for the "existing 'middle class,' as it is called—that is, traders, bankers, capitalists, large landowners, philosophers, students, 'men of leisure,' and professional men, except, perhaps, school teachers and doctors." Although the "middle class" in this instance was an expansive—and elusive—category, its composition was not extensively debated in comparison to the question of the composition of the "laboring," "working," or "producing" class.

Simon Newcomb, astronomer, amateur of political economy, and professor of mathematics for the United States Navy, expressed similar misgivings about the conceptual influence of the "present labor movement." In addition to his career in astronomy and mathematics, Newcomb wrote extensively on economic issues for such journals as the *North American Review* and the *Nation.* In an 1870 *North American Review* essay, "The Labor Question," Newcomb took issue with those who wished to "wage war" against capitalists on behalf of the laboring classes. Not only had these "enthusiastic reformers" misread social and economic principles; they had misconstrued the very classes at issue. "The term 'laboring classes' is so vague," he argued, "that we shall be led into confusion unless we define with greater precision the class whose interests are to be considered." Though allowing that in many cases it was difficult to "draw a line" between the classes of laborers and capitalists—carpenters who owned the capital of their tools, for example, could be regarded as both—he maintained that this should not preclude an effort to distinguish them with greater clarity.[45]

In Newcomb's estimation the laboring classes embraced far more than the class of "skilled" laborers. He included in addition the "unskilled," whose occupations demanded only physical strength, and the "intellectual" laborers, among whom were members of the professions and those involved in "planning, directing, and managing." To Newcomb, all who labored with "head or hand" were members of the laboring classes. Taken together these classes accounted for nine-tenths of the American population; within a population of 36 million

Newcomb's widely defined "laboring classes" numbered some 32.4 million. Only those who lived "without exertion" on interest did he place within the "quite small" class of "capitalists proper."[46]

Where the reformers and trade unionists were mistaken, then, was in equating "a fraction of the laboring population," the mechanics, for the entirety; and if their classifications were suspect, so too were their propositions. Newcomb argued that, in attempting to increase wages by striking and by limiting their memberships, the unions were acting to the detriment more of the laboring classes—as precisely defined—than of the capitalists. It was other "laborers" who paid for the craftsmen's wages and services; it was the "neglected class" of the unskilled who were denied access to the trades; and it was the laboring classes in general who gained from the increase of capital. Farmhands were rarely in attendance at "labor conventions," he noted, nor were hod carriers usually seen in "eight-hour" processions. The reformers' calls for cooperation had more merit, but here, too, "false theories" were in vogue. Rather than replacing the capitalists, the cooperatives should take advantage of their resources and expertise by forming genuine partnerships with them. Although Newcomb acknowledged that the two elementary classes each had different and specific interests, this did not suggest to him a conflict of the same.[47]

For Newcomb the "labor question" was very often a question badly posed in public discourse. Improving the condition of the laboring classes was to him a matter of some consequence, but any improvements should be judiciously made for the benefit of the greater laboring majority; in no case should schemes for "sudden" or "universal" change be entertained. A more effective remedy for the problems of labor, he suggested, would be the introduction of the study of political economy into the public schools. Were the prospective members of the laboring classes to comprehend their real social positions and economic interests, they would not be prey to enthusiasms and errors. Newcomb, like Godkin, took seriously the heralding of a war between the classes, even though he rejected the heralds' premises. His retort, like Godkin's, was to insist on the soundness of the accepted "principles of social organization," and to deny the specificity of the title of "laboring class."[48]

The recurrent question of who was and was not a laborer and the implications of these definitions were also of concern to Horace Greeley, editor of the *New York Tribune*. Greeley, in the 1870 *Essays Designed to Elucidate the Science of Political Economy,* held that this science dealt with "facts as they are"; and one of the most important of these facts was "the existence of a very large class in this and a still larger class in most other countries, who are distinguished, however inaccurately, as the laboring class, as they live by selling their labor for wages, instead of applying it to production of their own account."[49] He deemed this distinction to be inaccurate because it disregarded the efforts of the lawyer, the doctor, and the clergyman. Since each of these worked for wages, he observed, each deserved to be classed with the other "working men." Nevertheless, the "popular conception" of the laboring class was in practice more constricted, and as a journalist Greeley felt obligated to accede to a usage that had only the recommendation of "convenience," not of accuracy. But there were, he insisted, far fewer American nonlaborers than was "vulgarly supposed."[50]

As dissatisfied as he was with the restrictions of this "popular conception" of class divisions, Greeley was even more unhappy with the vulgar imputation of social conflict. Labor and capital were neither "naturally" nor "properly" antagonistic, he declared. Yet he admitted to the presence of a "seeming if not real antagonism" and assigned responsibility for it to the inefficiencies and abuses of the "wages system." Instead of societal harmony, that set of arrangements had fomented social "hostility" between employer and employed; and due to this disturbing tendency it was in need of gradual replacement by the spirit of cooperation. While Greeley's criticism of the "vicious" wages system and his advocacy for cooperative ventures echoed his professedly radical Associationist stances of the 1840s, he did not in 1870 identify himself with those of his fellow citizens who sought to "array labor against capital." Employers were not, he insisted, "habitual oppressors"; nor was capital, when "justly acquired," anything but beneficial to the "poorer" classes. Despite his often harsh strictures against the wages system, Greeley had no wish to incite further one class against another. For Greeley there was already enough of this "seeming if not real" contention at hand.[51]

Just how "radically mischievous" the language of "labor parties and labor reform" could be was also discussed by the Reverend Samuel Johnson of Salem, Massachusetts, in a contribution to the *Radical.* Johnson, the transcendentalist author and Unitarian preacher, objected to the tone of labor reform's appeals, which, he claimed, were intended to divide American society into "definitely hostile classes." In a manner familiar to Newcomb, Godkin, and other contemporaries, he protested against the "arrogant assumption" of the "honorable" title of "working-men" by that movement, and asked by what right it had excluded all but manual laborers from the meaning of the term "laboring class." Was labor as "clearly distinguishable" from capital as their dichotomies presumed it to be? Were educators merely "drones in the industrial hive"? Were poets and philosophers not laborers, too? Such distinctions were for Johnson signs of the "arbitrariness" of labor reform's analysis of the social order, one that was derived from the traditions of neither "science" nor "freedom."[52]

However arbitrary his opponents' choice of words might be, Johnson's were not; and in connecting "science" to "freedom" he brought to bear a second source of authority to refute their arguments. The divisive rhetoric of the labor reformers, it appeared, ran counter not only to the axioms of economic science, but to the "whole sense of American civilization." That civilization, as interpreted by Johnson, provided no "basis" for the formation of a "laboring class" distinct from the producers at large; it was a "pure delusion," he argued, to assume otherwise. From those who would "rally" in the cause of this class of producers he demanded to know "where or how they will draw the line which justifies their use of this anti-republican name of 'class'." From Johnson's perspective, any attempts to define, much less to represent, an exclusive "laboring class" were in contravention of the political traditions of the United States; such activities were, as quite simply stated, antirepublican. A republican nomenclature, by comparison, would encompass all producers, both the rich and the poor; and only in this "largest sense" would the use of "laboring class" be legitimate.[53]

This indictment of labor reform's antirepublicanism was not limited to questions of terminology, however. In proclaiming that labor and capital were "natural enemies," the reformers had revealed their affinities for European socialism and for such "old world" notions as the "strife of classes." To Johnson there were troubling parallels between the calls of the International Workingmen's Association for the abolition of private property—or "mere rapine seriously proposed in the name of liberty"—and such native manifestations of labor reform as the National Labor Party's programs on the currency, credit, and the eight-hour day. Both sets of proposals involved enhancing the power and justifying the interdiction of the state. And though the Americans were still far from embracing the socialists' principle of "absolute coercion," Johnson surmised that the logic of labor reform could lead in that most antirepublican of directions.[54]

By conjoining the principles of political economy to those of the American political tradition, and by comparing labor reformers to the radical socialists of the International Workingmen's Association, Johnson sought to discredit the former's premises and conclusions. Inasmuch as they stressed the low wages and poor working conditions of manual laborers, their criticisms were not unwarranted. But their "industrial wisdom," with its emphasis on antagonisms—"actual or supposed"—and its readiness to set class against class, proved to him to be no wisdom at all. For Johnson the theoretical grounds of the reformers' analyses were of foreign derivation, and the classifications so derived had no domestic incarnations.[55]

Johnson's unfavorable comments in "Labor Parties and Labor Reform" were part of a well-established rhetorical tradition that since the late 1820s had defended expansive rather than exclusive definitions of 'laboring class', and that had rejected the application of class antagonism to American circumstances. His remarks are also suggestive of a tendency on the part of the "literary champions of capitalism" of the 1870s and later to associate a delineation of contentious classes with the advocacy of socialistic and communistic systems. Within this emerging tradition of public discourse, employing the terms 'laboring' and 'working' classes in the context of critiques of the social order would be more than a categorical error; it would be a contradiction of the "whole sense of American civilization." To so construe the classes of America was to engage in conceptually dangerous behavior—or in subversive speech acts, to use a late-twentieth-century parlance.[56]

In contrasting their scientifically informed, ontologically reliable descriptions of the state of the "laboring class" and the relations between capital and labor with the popular misconceptions at large, the analyses of Johnson, Greeley, et alia are indicative of the cultural dissension generated by the usage of that term and the interpretation of those relations in the public discourse of the 1860s and 1870s. These "literary champions of capitalism" continued to recognize, to varying degrees, a social order with an almost all-inclusive category of laborers; and in their social analytics they continued to assume the possibility of classes without conflict. Referring to an American "laboring class" in this expansive, "republican" style was perfectly acceptable behavior; it did not, in Godkin's sense, promote "class feeling." Greeley was furthermore willing to acquiesce in the restriction of the referents of that class to wage laborers, if only for the sake of "convenience," for communicative ease. But not one of the literary champions of capitalism was prepared to equate the presence of a "laboring class"—either in theory or in practice—with the presence of an essential class antagonism. To so do most certainly would provoke "class feeling" where there should be none. In those instances when such "anti-republican" usage was encountered, they preferred to challenge the accuracy of the appellation 'laboring class' and the existence of the correlative conflict.[57]

Yet it was this latter variant of the 'laboring class' that was implied, when not directly indicated, in many of the "popular conceptions" with which Greeley and company disagreed. Even though their societal classifications were recommended by their colleagues in economic science and reaffirmed in the respectable press, these had to contend with both classifications of convenience (the inevitable inaccuracies of common speech) and classifications of political expedience (the ones enunciated by the proponents of labor reform). In the 1880 supplement to Webster's *American Dictionary of the English Language,* "working man" was defined as "a laboring man, a man who earns his daily support by manual labor"; while in the 1865 edition "working class" was defined as "the class of people who are engaged in manual labor, or who are dependent upon it for support; laborers; operatives;—chiefly used in the plural." In these instances one could, after Ezra Heywood, accuse the dictionaries of conspiring in favor of the labor reformers rather than the literary champions of the capitalists.[58]

No matter how problematic the moral scientists and men of letters found the labor question to be, their definitions could not displace an expanding class of industrial wage earners, nor could their rhetorical strategies so simply bring to a halt the conflict between capital and labor. The "struggle to define and arrange" class relations that Wendell Phillips had evoked was an ongoing struggle to legitimate, or delegitimate, certain interpretations of the contours and consequences of American capitalism; and it resulted in the partial naturalization, or renaturalization, of class antagonism in the arenas of public discourse. While there may not have been an increase in class consciousness, in a Marxian sense, there certainly was increased cognizance of the problems of classification and class relations. By the 1870s 'class' was a far more controversial and politicized concept than it had been earlier in the century.[59]

EPILOGUE

The conundrum of class that William Graham Sumner described in *What Social Classes Owe to Each Other* in 1883 was not limited to the realm of academic debate. Nor was Sumner's discomfort about the use and abuse of language idiosyncratic. During the course of an 1878 investigation by the House of Representatives on the "causes of the general depression in labor and business," Sumner appeared as a witness before a select committee at the General Post Office in New York City.[1] While responding to a question by the chairman, Abram S. Hewitt of New York, about the effects of the depression and the condition of the "laboring classes," Sumner stopped to take exception to that label. "I do not like to use that term," he noted, "but I mean the non-capitalist class." He went on to object to the implication that the "classes are separate in interest." Hewitt replied that he had "only used the term 'classes' because in the evidence heretofore given, the term had been used," and many witnesses had claimed to "represent particular classes." Sumner accepted that answer, but he impressed upon the committee that he would "like to be understood as denying that you can make this distinction." The "social and industrial forces" at work, he maintained, were drawing all Americans together. "We cannot separate ourselves if we wanted to." Both the professor and the politician agreed that 'class' was often appearing in the context of erroneous or dangerous representations of American society.[2]

Given the attitudes of many of the witnesses appearing before the committee, Sumner's suspicions were well founded. Hewitt and his colleagues heard from labor reformers, members of trade unions, and representatives of the Greenback Labor and Socialistic Labor parties. The congressmen engaged in exchanges with witnesses such as Isaac

Bennett, a cigar maker and member of the SLP, and Robert W. Hume, a teacher and representative of the American Labor League, over the merits of exclusive and expansive definitions of the 'laboring', 'working', and 'producing' classes. And they listened to detailed analyses by Adolph Douai, the translator of Marx's *Capital,* about the "unnatural relation" that existed between capital and labor.[3] Yet the witnesses testifying at these hearings were not uniformly antagonistic to American capitalism. A number of them, including Joseph Bishop of Pittsburgh, an iron puddler and the former union president of the Sons of Vulcan, agreed with Congressman Hewitt and Professor Sumner about the "common interest" of employers and employed, and about the absence of any "inherent conflict" between capital and labor in the United States.[4]

The voices and viewpoints expressed at these congressional hearings are indicative of the diversity of classifications, and disagreements about class relations, in late-nineteenth-century America. That diversity and those disagreements were expressed in even greater detail during the Senate's 1883 investigation of the "Relations between Labor and Capital." These hearings were held in Washington, D.C.; New York City; Manchester, New Hampshire; Boston; Birmingham, Alabama; and Augusta and Columbus, Georgia. Dozens of witnesses, both workers and employers, gave testimony. The semantic field of 'class' and 'classes' that was mapped out during the course of the Senate investigation encompassed 'class' as an occupation (for example, the class of shoemakers), the "working class," the "educated classes," "middle class," "laboring classes," the "non-laboring classes," "class rule," "class struggle," "oppressors and the oppressed," "producers," "non-producers," the "upper class" and "lower class," "capital and the ruling classes," "privileged classes," and "permanent classes." Some of these uses rose to the level of explicit definitional and interpretive disagreements between the committee's chair, Hugh Blair of New Hampshire, and his colleagues, with witnesses such as Robert Layton, Grand Secretary of the Knights of Labor; John Campbell of Pittsburgh, a member of the Brotherhood of Telegraphers; and Charles Lenz of the SLP. Such disagreements included the meaning and application of the terms 'capitalist(s)', 'laborer(s)', 'workingman', 'employers', and 'producer', and the "lines . . . between capitalists and laborers."[5] Over eight hundred pages of testimony from these hearings demonstrate that there was not in 1883, any more than there had been in 1783, a single "language" or lexicon of class in American public discourse. There was instead a variety of terms—some of them durable, others transitory—that Americans used, and a number of interpretive frameworks in which they used them.[6]

Despite the significant institutional and ideological changes of the late nineteenth century, there was considerable terminological and rhetorical continuity in American practices of classification. Critics of the "industrial" system's alleged injustices continued to employ the rhetorics of both reconcilable and irreconcilable class antagonism well past the end of the century. The first device remained a staple among trade unions, reformers, and certain sections of the Democratic party. The second—that of irreconcilable class conflict—moved from the margins to the center of American popular discourse in the wake of the riots and social upheavals of 1886 and beyond.[7] The American 'producing class' was represented politically and symbolically by the Knights of Labor in the 1880s; and it emerged again in a final rhetorical contest against the 'nonproducers' in the campaigns of the Populists during the 1890s. By the turn of the century, however, the imagery of the 'producers' in these rhetorics—be they classified in exclusive or expansive ways—began to give way to other schemes: to the dichotomies of the 'working class' versus the 'capitalists', and to the tripartite division of 'upper', 'middle', and 'lower' classes. The ambiguities of this popular usage were no more readily clarified than those of the usage of the social critics.[8]

The axiom of social harmony continued also to be stressed among preachers, publishers, professors, and politicians.[9] For members of the Republican party especially, categorical class cooperation and an expansively defined laboring class remained central tenets of their socioeconomic theory.[10] This American ideology was—and would be well into the next century—a powerful, pervasive mode of interpretation based on the assumption that the social, political, and economic configurations of the republic were generally in keeping with the laws of nature. The tenacity of this rhetoric indicates that the conventions and the assumptions of American liberal capitalism might be more durable, and the pace of change slower, than the periodizations of historical scholarship suggest.

In his congressional testimony and in his text, Sumner found that American classifications were often mired in terminological confusion, and that questions of class relations were also prone to "unclear and contradictory theories." Although he rejected the premises and the prescriptions of the "social doctors" of reform, he was not prepared to join with the antebellum moral scientists or the literary champions of capitalism in their conventional celebrations of the harmony of interests. "To say that employers and employed are partners in an enterprise," he remarked, "is only a delusive figure of speech. It is plainly based on no facts in the industrial system." Between capitalists and laborers, the employers and employed, there was real antagonism and a "collision" over wages. But there was also a transcendent identity of class interests in the larger undertakings of the "modern industrial system." From Sumner's perspective this was a system of "great social cooperation" which nonetheless generated a constant conflict of economic interests, yet this conflict was not the same as the class struggle imagined by "enthusiastic social architects." Thus he could acknowledge the presence of class antagonism, but limit its extent and its import to contests in the labor market. This modification of the model of classes without conflict involved less the rejection than the partial displacement of the doctrine of societal harmony.[11] For Sumner, and for many who espoused this modified form of liberal analysis in the late nineteenth century and into the twentieth, the conflict over wages was fundamentally different from the conflict over the legitimacy of capitalism. Within this emerging idiom of American liberalism, 'classes' signified occupational groups and vertical distinctions of wealth, but these classes were not fixed, nor were they necessarily collective actors in social and political life.

By acknowledging in 1883 at least some degree of American class animosity, Sumner was at odds with the accepted axioms of his disciplines and the assumptions of the majority of his fellow social scientists. But he was not alone in his rejection of an inevitable, inviolable harmony of interests. His recasting of the *ideologia americana* is indicative of the generation of new forms of social analysis and new lexicons of liberalism that began to appear in the last decades of the nineteenth century.[12] Among that younger cohort of academics who worked to reformulate the professional organization and the theoretical practice of the social sciences in America during these years, there was a widely shared presumption that the "modern industrial system" did indeed engender conflicts between the classes. While political economists and sociologists such as Richard T. Ely, John Bates Clark, Henry Carter Adams, and Lester Frank Ward strongly disagreed with Sumner over the best means to deal with that conflict—they favored an enhanced role for the state instead of Sumner's laissez-faire—they did agree with him that it was the social scientist's responsibility to provide reliable answers to the labor question. "If it be incendiary to proclaim only an irrepressible conflict between capital and labor," Clark argued in the *New Englander,* "it is imbecile to reiterate that there is no possible ground of conflict between them, and that actual contests result from ignorance."[13]

Clark and company were interested in neither the conceptual obfuscations of many of their professional colleagues nor the seditions of the radicals. Before the question of labor could be answered, they argued, it needed to be reconsidered. It would not be helped by further confounding social categories or by denying class antagonism. They found it necessary, as did Sumner, to test the prevailing wisdom and to correct ambiguous definitions in the light of changing conditions. To them the analytic language and the underlying assumptions of the political economists Adam Smith, David Ricardo, and Jean-Baptiste Say were no longer applicable to the realities of American "industrial" life. For this reason, the contests over the implications of the classification systems used by classical political economy seemed of less and less importance in the disciplinary discourses of the newly "professionalized" social sciences. They continued to use classifications of occupation and wealth as standard analytic units, and recognized forms of contingent class conflict. But the emergence of the social sciences in the United States was not marked by the introduction of systematic modes of class analysis.

For Sumner, as for many other students of the social order, it was not the reality of socioeconomic distinctions that was in question, but rather their proper denomination and—most important—the correct interpretation of these groups' relations to each other. The often passionate disagreements over nomenclature in which Sumner and his contemporaries engaged were about the representation of the groups in society, not about the existence of such groups. 'Class', in their language, was both a signifier and a signified. At stake in the semantic contests of the statesmen and social scientists was who would exercise control over classification, and which issues could be legitimately articulated in the arenas of public discourse. The rhetoric of a reconcilable class conflict would regularly be challenged; articulations of irreconcilable class antagonism would constantly be denied; and the open boundaries of an all-encompassing American 'laboring class' would be firmly defended. Depending on who did the interpreting, then,

America had or did not have social classes; those classes were or were not in conflict; and that conflict might or might not be resoluble within a liberal capitalist state.

My own emphasis on "contested interpretations" in the course of this study warrants clarification. If the language used by actors partially shapes their social realms, we need to be aware not only of their lexicons, but of the assumptions they made about how language can be put to work, that is to say, their rhetorics. An important distinction must be made between social classes as the subjects and objects of interpretation in these texts on the one hand, and social classes as being nothing but interpretations on the other. Save for a handful of nominalists or skeptics—the *Port Folio*'s Observer for example—eighteenth- and nineteenth-century speakers and writers subscribed to some variant of realism. For them, debates over classifications were more than matters of definition: these arguments had clear policy implications. From John Taylor of Caroline to John Francis Bray, these Americans emphasized the critical and the political connections between the word and the world.

In examining the contradictions involved in the subjects of classification and class relations in the United States, Sumner hoped to refute the theories of the "world reformers" and to encourage a more informed, more coherent public discussion of relevant political and economic issues. "Popular use," he proposed, "should conform to correct definitions."[14] This call for terminological consistency and the desire to exercise conceptual control echo the earlier physiocratic and Scottish projects for the sciences of man. Sumner's call also anticipates the debates by later generations of social scientists over the proper models and metaphors of classification. For modern historians his counterposing of "popular use" to "correct definitions" evokes current methodological and historiographical problems regarding class, problems particularly resistant to resolution. When analyzing historical evidence of classificatory practices, which voices should be listened to and which viewpoints should be granted privilege? The questions remain at the end of the present century, as they did at the end of the last: whose usage and whose definitions?

Much of the conceptual debate carried on over class from the late eighteenth through the late nineteenth century, then, was grounded in larger interpretive endeavors that sought to naturalize or denaturalize, and legitimate or delegitimate, the terms of American public discourse. When, where, how, and why Americans wrote and spoke about classes involved institutional and ideological exercises of cultural and political power. It is not the discovery of classes or the awakening of class consciousness that best characterizes these American languages of class. Rather, there has been from the first an ongoing contestation and elaboration of classifications and class relations in the context of a political culture predicated upon equality. What forms of subordination are "natural," what the relations among the classes should be, and exactly who constitutes those classes, are cultural and political problems that have admitted no easy solutions.

The linguist Richard Grant White noted in 1883 that the confusion and dissension over class distinctions in the United States arose from the "misapprehension of the true meaning of words."[15] But as we have seen, the problem was even more fundamental than White realized. For there never had been a single true meaning of the concept of 'class' in the nation's public discourse; there was always diversity and disagreement. In the attempts of Americans to establish and enforce these diverse and even contradictory meanings, we can recognize, if not resolve, the conundrum of class in American culture.

NOTES

Abbreviations

DAB	Dictionary of American Biography
HOPE	History of Political Economy
JAH	Journal of American History
JEH	Journal of Economic History
JHI	Journal of the History of Ideas
JMH	Journal of Modern History
WMQ	William and Mary Quarterly

Introduction

1. William Graham Sumner, *What Social Classes Owe to Each Other* (1883; reprint, Caldwell, Idaho: Caxton, 1954), pp. 13, 15–16. On Sumner see Bruce Curtis, *William Graham Sumner* (Boston: Twayne, 1981). On Sumner's analyses of social classes and class relations see Charles Page, *Class and American Sociology: From Ward to Ross* (1940; reprint, New York: Octagon, 1964), pp. 73–110. Page's reading of Sumner relies heavily on later works such as *Folkways*, and at times is at variance with Sumner's arguments in *What Social Classes Owe to Each Other*.

See also Robert C. Bannister, *Sociology and Scientism: The American Quest for Objectivity, 1880–1940* (Chapel Hill: University of North Carolina Press, 1987), pp. 87–110; Bannister, "William Graham Sumner's Social Darwinism: A Reconsideration," *HOPE* 5 (1973): 89–109.

2. Sumner, *What Social Classes Owe to Each Other,* pp. 13–14, 34–35. Sumner quite forcefully reiterates this last point at the essay's close: "If we refuse to recognize any classes as existing in society when, perhaps, a claim might be set up that the wealthy, educated, and virtuous have acquired special rights and precedence, we certainly cannot recognize any classes when it is attempted to establish such distinctions for the sake of imposing burdens and duties on one group for the benefit of others" (p. 144). For Sumner the presence of such legal claims and bonds was characteristic of a "social structure" based on the principles of "status." The United States, by contrast, was

a society based on "contract" (pp. 22–24). Here Sumner employs a variant of a dichotomy that would become a commonplace in twentieth-century social science.

3. Ibid., pp. 18–20, 55–56, 69–70, 71–74, 102, 108, 111. Sumner also writes of employers as a class; he uses the terms 'higher' and 'middle' class, but without engaging in precise definition; and he castigates the class of "aristocrats" and the plutocracy (pp. 86, 89–90, 110). In carrying on standard conversation, Sumner, too, had to have recourse to the terms of 'class'.

4. On Samuel Johnson see the discussion in chapter 6.

5. The theses, prognoses, and implications involved in the use of classifications are discussed by Keith Graham, "Class: A Simple View," *Inquiry* 32 (1989): 419–36. See also R. D. Bramwell, "On Classifying," *Etc.: A General Review of Semantics* 38 (1981): 373–85.

6. Among the many articles and essays on what can and cannot be done with concepts and models of class, see the exchange of Michael A. Bernstein and Sean Wilentz, "Marketing, Commerce, and Capitalism in Rural Massachusetts," with Winifred B. Rothenburg, "Markets, Values, and Capitalism: A Discourse on Method," *JEH* 44 (1984): 171–73, 174–78. See also Donald L. Winters, "'Plain Folk' of the Old South Reexamined: Economic Democracy in Tennessee," *Journal of Southern History* 53 (1987): 565–86.

7. See, for example, the contributions of Peter Stearns on social history, Allan Bogue on political history, and David Brody on labor history in *The Past before Us,* ed. Michael Kammen (Ithaca, N.Y.: Cornell University Press, 1980). Among the strongest proponents of the centrality of class is Michael Katz. See his "Social Class in North American Urban History," *Journal of Interdisciplinary History* 11 (1981): 579–606. On the use, or misuse, of class analysis in American historiography, see Ian Tyrell, *Class Analysis and Liberal History in Twentieth Century America* (Westport, Conn.: Greenwood Press, 1986).

The salience of class and class analysis in the doing of European history is considered in Jack Amariglio and Bruce Norton, "Marxist Historians and the Question of Class in the French Revolution," *History and Theory* 30 (1991): 37–55; Harvey J. Kaye, "History and Social Theory: Notes on the Contribution of British Marxist Historiography to Our Understanding of Class," *Canadian Review of Sociology and Anthropology* 20 (1983): 167–92; Alvin Y. So and Muhammad Hikam, "'Class' in the Writings of Wallerstein and Thompson: Toward a Class Struggle Analysis," *Sociological Perspectives* 32 (1989): 453–68; Peter Burke, *History and Social Theory* (Ithaca, N.Y.: Cornell University Press, 1992), pp. 58–63. The limits of class analyses are discussed by William Reddy in "The Crisis of the Class Concept in Historical Research," in *Money and Liberty in Modern Europe: A Critique of Historical Understanding* (Cambridge: Cambridge University Press, 1987), pp. 1–33.

For a compendium of neo-Progressive scholarship see Eric Foner, ed., *The New American History* (Philadelphia: Temple University Press, 1990).

8. On methodological differences among historians see Robert J. Gough, "Class and Early American History," paper presented at the annual meeting

of the Organization of American Historians, Detroit, April 1981; Maris A. Vinovskis, "Searching for Classes in Urban North America," *Journal of Urban History* 11 (1985): 353–60; Peter Hall, "The Problem of Class," *History of Education Quarterly* 26 (1986): 569–79; "Class," in Harry Ritter, *Dictionary of Concepts in History* (New York: Greenwood, 1986), pp. 44–50. For an overview of Marxist class theory see Erik Olin Wright, "Varieties of Marxist Conceptions of Class Structure," *Politics and Society* 9 (1980): 323–70. In Katz's work the primacy of a two-class model is stressed, whereas in the work of the "new" labor historians influenced by E. P. Thompson, there is less emphasis on the formal definition of class and more on the study of class as a process. See Katz, "Social Class in North American Urban History"; Alan Dawley, *Class and Community: The Industrial Revolution in Lynn* (Cambridge: Harvard University Press, 1976); Sean Wilentz, *Chants Democratic: New York City and the Rise of the American Working Class, 1788–1850* (New York: Oxford University Press, 1984). Neo-Weberian models have influenced the study of social mobility and of American politics. See, for example, Reinhard Bendix, ed., *Class, Status, and Power* (London: Routledge and Kegan Paul, 1967). There are, of course, many other variations. In his studies of colonial Massachusetts and New Hampshire, Bruce Daniels employs a five-class model based on wealth. See Daniels, "Defining Economic Classes in Colonial New Hampshire, 1700–1770," *Historical New Hampshire* 28 (1973): 53–62; Daniels, "Defining Economic Classes in Colonial Massachusetts, 1700–1776," *Proceedings of the American Antiquarian Society* 83 (1973): 251–60. Lee Soltow uses a six-class model in "Socioeconomic Classes in South Carolina and Massachusetts in the 1790s and the Observations of John Drayton," *South Carolina Historical Magazine* 81 (1980): 283–305. For instances of how the choice of classificatory schemes affects historical explanation, for example the study of social mobility, compare Stephen Thernstrom, *The Other Bostonians: Poverty and Progress in the American Metropolis, 1880–1970* (Cambridge: Harvard University Press, 1973), to Margo A. Conk, *The United States Census and Labor Force Change: A History of Occupation Statistics, 1870–1940* (Ann Arbor: UMI Research Press, 1980). On parallel problems in British historiography see P. N. Furbank, *Unholy Pleasure; or, the Idea of Social Class* (Oxford: Oxford University Press, 1985), pp. 51–62.

9. The historical "mobility and instability" of the categories of social classes are discussed in Bernard Susser, *The Grammar of Modern Ideology* (London: Routledge, 1988), p. 20; Reinhart Koselleck, "Begriffsgeschichte and Social History," in *Futures Past: On the Semantics of Historical Time,* trans. Keith Tribe (Cambridge: MIT Press, 1985), pp. 82–83.

10. William B. Gallie, "Essentially Contested Concepts," in *The Importance of Language,* ed. Max Black (Ithaca, N.Y.: Cornell University Press, 1969), pp. 121–46. Gallie suggests that such concepts as 'work of art', 'democracy', or 'Christian doctrine' can be usefully considered contested. See also the chapter "Essentially Contested Concepts" in his *Philosophy and the Historical Understanding* (New York: Schocken, 1964), pp. 157–91. Alasdair MacIntyre, in his essay "The Essential Contestability of Some Social Concepts," *Ethics* 84 (1973): 1–9,

transposes the argument from the general to the social, a move made by practicing social scientists and theorists such as Clifford Geertz and Steven Lukes.

In *Language and Political Understanding: The Politics of Discursive Practices* (New Haven: Yale University Press, 1981), Michael J. Shapiro expresses reservations with the modifier 'essentially', but does argue that "concepts which refer to any social dimensions of persons, either explicitly or implicitly, are contestable" (p. 210). Terrence Ball, in *Transforming Political Discourse: Political Theory and Critical Conceptual History* (Oxford: Blackwell, 1988), suggests that the concepts that constitute political discourse have at least "contingently contested meanings." See also the introduction to *The Nature of Political Theory* (Oxford: Clarendon Press, 1983), pp. 1–16, by the editors David Miller and Larry Siedentop; and in the same volume John Gray, "Political Power, Social Theory, and Essential Contestability," pp. 75–101.

11. The philosophical debate over essential contestability is examined in Norman S. Care, "On Fixing Social Concepts," *Ethics* 84 (1973): 10–21; John Kekes, "Essentially Contested Concepts: A Reconsideration," *Philosophy and Rhetoric* 10 (1977): 71–89; Kai Nielsen, "On Rationality and Essentially Contested Concepts," *Communication and Cognition* 16 (1983): 269–81; Peter Ingram, "Open Concepts and Contested Concepts," *Philosophia* 15 (1985): 41–59. See also D. E. Bradshaw, "The Nature of Concepts," *Philosophical Papers* 21 (1992): 1–20.

12. On the rhetorical, political, and ideological uses of essentially contested concepts, see Eugene Garver, "Rhetoric and Essentially Contested Arguments," *Philosophy and Rhetoric* 11 (1978): 156–72; Garver, "Essentially Contested Concepts: The Ethics and Tactics of Argument," *Philosophy and Rhetoric* 23 (1990): 251–70; Christine Swanton, "On the 'Essential Contestedness' of Political Concepts," *Ethics* 95 (1985): 811–27; Andrew Mason, "On Explaining Political Disagreements: The Notion of an Essentially Contested Concept," *Inquiry* 33 (1990): 81–98. Both Swanton's distinctions between a relativist and a skeptical version of essential contestedness and Mason's suggestions about the limits of intellectual authority in political debates should be of interest to intellectual historians.

John Gray has argued that "we must recognize that intractable controversy about such terms as 'justice', 'power', and 'democracy' expresses disagreement that is at once conceptual and substantive" ("On Liberty, Liberalism, and Essential Contestability," *British Journal of Political Science* 8 [1978]: 391). Following along lines suggested by Alasdair MacIntyre, Gray notes that, "[u]nless there is some agreement about what a democracy or a just society looks like, we have no reason to characterize a conflict as a conceptual conflict" (p. 391).

13. On the "partially constitutive" dimensions of social and political concepts see MacIntyre, "Essential Contestability," p. 3; Alasdair MacIntyre, "The Indispensability of Political Theory," and David Miller, "Linguistic Philosophy and Political Theory," both in *Nature of Political Theory,* ed. Miller and Siedentop; Gray, "Liberty," pp. 393–94; Quentin Skinner, "Language and Social Change," in *The State of the Language,* ed. Leonard Michaels and Christopher Ricks (Berkeley and Los Angeles: University of California Press,

1980), pp. 562–78; John Searle, "Explanation in the Social Sciences," and Karl-Otto Apel, "Intentionality and Linguistic Meaning," both in *John Searle and His Critics,* ed. Ernest Lepore (Oxford: Blackwell, 1991).

14. On the contestability of class, Peter Calvert has suggested that class meets Gallie's criteria, and that many of the problems involved in contemporary social scientific usages of class are clarified by recognizing this condition (*The Concept of Class: An Historical Introduction* [London: Hutchinson, 1982], pp. 209–15). Philip Furbank, however, is less certain that all of Gallie's stipulations are met (*Unholy Pleasure,* pp. 67–69). Both Calvert and Furbank raise questions about the conceptual utility of class.

15. On historicism, contextualism, and the doing of American history, see Robert F. Berkhofer, *Beyond the Great Story: History as Text and Discourse* (Cambridge: Harvard University Press, 1995). As Christine Swanton has observed, arguments that certain social and political concepts are "contested" usually indicate a commitment to some form of relativism or skepticism along such lines as "[n]o such conception is the best conception of X, or at least one cannot be warranted in a claim to know that such a conception is the best" ("'Essential Contestedness' of Political Concepts," pp. 819, 814).

16. The varieties of 'class' in late-nineteenth- and twentieth-century America have been the subjects of a number of historical and sociological studies. See Margo Anderson, "The Language of Class in Twentieth Century America," *Social Science History* 12 (1988): 349–75; Arthur Marwick, *Class: Image and Reality in Britain, France, and the United States of America since 1930* (New York: Oxford University Press, 1980); Milton M. Gordon, *Social Class in American Sociology* (Durham, N.C.: Duke University Press, 1958); Page, *Class and American Sociology.* See also Paul Fussell, *Class: A Guide through the American Status System* (New York: Summit, 1983). In *The Concept of Class* Peter Calvert argues that "[t]he use of a concept of class to analyse American society was virtually unknown before the Great Depression of 1929" (p. 183). This is, I would argue, a rather difficult claim to sustain.

For studies of 'class' in English discourse see Asa Briggs, "The Language of 'Class' in Early Nineteenth Century England," in *Essays in Labour History,* ed. Asa Briggs and John Saville (London: Macmillan, 1960), pp. 43–73; Geoffrey Crossick, "Classes and Masses in Victorian England," *History Today* 37 (1987): 29–35; Penelope Corfield, "Class by Name and Number in Eighteenth Century Britain," *History* 72 (1987): 38–61; Corfield, "From Rank to Class: Innovation in Georgian England," *History Today* 37 (1987): 36–42; R. S. Neale, *Class in English History, 1680–1850* (Oxford: Blackwell, 1981); Neale, *Class and Ideology in the Nineteenth Century* (London: Routledge and Kegan Paul, 1972); Steven Wallech, "The Emergence of the Modern Concept of 'Class' in the English Language," Ph.D. diss., Claremont Graduate School, 1981; Wallech, "Class versus Rank: The Transformation of Eighteenth Century English Social Terms and Theories of Production," *JHI* 47 (1986): 409–31.

On the contestation involved in the "discourse of class" among social scientists, see Zygmunt Bauman, *Memories of Class: The Pre-history and After-Life of Class* (London: Routledge and Kegan Paul, 1983), pp. 36–38; Bauman,

"Class, Social," in *The Social Science Encyclopedia,* ed. Adam Kuper and Jessica Kuper (London: Routledge and Kegan Paul, 1985), pp. 110–13; Peter Martin, "The Concept of Class," in *Classic Disputes in Sociology,* ed. R. J. Anderson, J. A. Hughes, and W. W. Sharrock (London: Allen and Unwin, 1987), pp. 67–96; Barry Hindess, "Class Analysis as Social Theory," in *Politics and Social Theory,* ed. Peter Lassman (London: Routledge, 1989), pp. 48–61.

17. On the range of questions to be raised and examined in the course of a conceptual history, see Keith Tribe's introduction to Koselleck, *Futures Past,* p. xii; Melvin Richter, "Reconstructing the History of Political Languages: Pocock, Skinner, and the *Geschichtliche Grundbegriffe,*" *History and Theory* 39 (1990): 60–65; Rolf Reichart, "Einleitung," in *Handbuch politisch-sozialer Grundbegriffe in Frankreich, 1680–1820,* ed. Rolf Reichart and Eberhard Schmitt (Munich: Oldenbourg, 1985), pp. 39–146.

18. On the linguistic constitution of social and political entities, see Richard Harvey Brown, *Society as Text: Essays on Rhetoric, Reason, and Reality* (Chicago: University of Chicago Press, 1987); Brown, *Social Science as Civic Discourse: Essays on the Invention, Legitimation, and Uses of Social Theory* (Chicago: University of Chicago Press, 1989); Murray Edelman, *Constructing the Political Spectacle* (Chicago: University of Chicago Press, 1988).

On the interactions of symbolic and social constructions see John B. Thompson, *Ideology and Modern Culture: Critical Social Theory in the Era of Mass Communication* (Cambridge: Polity Press, 1990); Pierre Bourdieu, *Language and Symbolic Power* (Cambridge: Harvard University Press, 1991).

19. See, for example, Paul E. Corcoran, *Political Language and Rhetoric* (St. Lucia: University of Queensland Press, 1979), p. xiv. For Corcoran 'public discourse' serves as a very general term for the use of language to make purposeful statements about politics and the social order; and within the "sphere of public discourse" he locates such items as campaign speeches and letters to the editor on economic issues. See also Ronald F. Reid, "Some Thoughts about Historical Rhetoric and Criticism," in *Three Centuries of American Rhetorical Discourse: An Anthology,* ed. Ronald F. Reid (Prospect Heights, Ill.: Waveland, 1988), pp. 1–33; Joel Sherzer, "A Discourse-Centered Approach to Language and Culture," *American Anthropologist* 89 (1987): 295–309; William M. Berg and J. Michael Ross, "The Linguistic Organization of Public Controversy: A Note on the Pragmatics of Political Discourse," *Human Studies* 5 (1982): 237–48; Doris Graber, "Political Languages," in *Handbook of Political Communication,* ed. Dan D. Nimmo and Keith R. Sanders (Beverly Hills: Sage, 1981), pp. 195–225; Robert Paine, "When Saying Is Doing," in *Politically Speaking: Cross-Cultural Studies of Rhetoric,* ed. Robert Paine (Philadelphia: Institute for the Study of Humanities, 1981), pp. 9–24; Roger Fowler, *Literature as Social Discourse: The Practice of Linguistic Criticism* (Bloomington: Indiana University Press, 1981), pp. 27–28; Jonathan Culler, *Structuralist Poetics: Structuralism, Linguistics, and the Study of Literature* (Ithaca, N.Y.: Cornell University Press, 1975), pp. 132–33; Paul Ricoeur, *Interpretation Theory: Discourse and the Surplus of Meaning* (Fort Worth: Texas Christian University Press, 1976), pp. 34–37.

In her study *Theories of Discourse* (Oxford: Blackwell, 1986) Diane Mac-

Donell draws upon the work of Michel Pecheux, Louis Althusser, and Michel Foucault to emphasize the ideological struggles involved over the meaning of words. See also Hayden White, *The Content of the Form: Narrative Discourse and Historical Representation* (Baltimore: Johns Hopkins University Press, 1987). Foucault's emphasis on the relations of discourse to domination informs the work of such "new historicists" as Richard Terdiman. See Terdiman, *Discourse/Counter-Discourse: Theory and Practice of Symbolic Resistance in Nineteenth Century France* (Ithaca, N.Y.: Cornell University Press, 1985); Terdiman, "Is There Class in This Class?" in *The New Historicism,* ed. H. Aram Veeser (New York: Routledge, 1989), pp. 225–30. On postmodern understandings of discourse as action and concealment, see Ian Angus and Lenore Langsdorf, *The Critical Turn: Rhetoric and Philosophy in Postmodern Discourse* (Carbondale: Southern Illinois University Press, 1993), pp. 16, 182.

20. On the processes of classification see Bramwell, "Classifying"; Graham, "Class."

21. On the importance to historical analyses of the terms used by actors, see Gareth Stedman Jones, *Languages of Class: Studies in English Working Class History, 1832–1982* (Cambridge: Cambridge University Press, 1983), pp. 21, 23, 94. Arthur Marwick, while writing from a perspective quite different from that of Jones, also comments on the need to employ the language used by the people studied (*Class*, pp. 17–18).

The dimensions of cultural and political power involved in actors' categorizations and classifications are examined in Pierre Bourdieu, *Distinction: A Social Critique of the Judgment of Taste,* trans. Richard Nice (Cambridge: Harvard University Press, 1984), esp. pp. 466–85. Other works that consider this problem include Murray Edelman, *Political Language: Words That Succeed and Policies That Fail* (New York: Academic Press, 1977); Norman Fairclough, *Language and Power* (London: Longman, 1989); Roger Fowler, *Linguistic Criticism* (New York: Oxford University Press, 1986); Steven Mailloux, *Rhetorical Power* (Ithaca, N.Y.: Cornell University Press, 1989); John B. Thompson, *Studies in the Theory of Ideology* (Cambridge: Polity Press, 1984).

22. On printed sources as popular political primers see Michael Lienesch, *New Order of the Ages: Time, the Constitution, and the Making of Modern American Political Thought* (Princeton: Princeton University Press, 1988), p. 11; Jean Hoornstra and Trudy Heath, eds., *American Periodicals, 1741–1900* (Ann Arbor: UMI Research Press, 1979).

23. For the distinctions between ordinary and technical language, see Charles E. Caton, ed., *Philosophy and Ordinary Language* (Urbana: University of Illinois Press, 1963), pp. vi–vii. On the vocabulary of political language see Corcoran, *Political Language and Rhetoric,* p. xii; he argues that, "save for a small number of words, there is no evident shift to a special vocabulary or grammar to read or speak about politics." See also Stanley Cavell, *Must We Mean What We Say?* (New York: Scribner's, 1969); Charles Crittenden, "Ontological Commitments of Everyday Language," *Metaphilosophy* 5 (1974): 198–215.

Both ordinary and technical uses of such concepts as 'class' are discussed from a different perspective in Derek Layder, *The Realist Image in Social Science*

(New York: St. Martin's, 1990). He questions how much "slippage" there is between these uses, and cautions against the presupposition of a necessary identity between the lay and the technical (pp. 140–50).

24. The problems of what sources should be used in the analysis of socio-political concepts is discussed by Werner Conze, "Histoire des notions dans le domaine socio-politique," in *Problèmes de stratification sociale,* ed. Roland Mousnier (Paris: Presses Universitaires de France, 1968), pp. 31–36.

25. Other approaches to the conventions and the consequences of classification in America include Allan Kulikoff, *The Agrarian Origins of American Capitalism* (Charlottesville: University Press of Virginia, 1992); Fred Bailey, "Tennessee's Antebellum Society from the Bottom Up," *Southern Studies* 22 (1983): 260–73; Bailey, "Class Contrasts in Old South Tennessee," *Tennessee Historical Quarterly* 45 (1986): 273–86; Richard P. Horwitz, *Anthropology toward History: Culture and Work in a Nineteenth Century Maine Town* (Middletown, Conn.: Wesleyan University Press, 1978). The ongoing research of Burton Bledstein on letters, diaries, almanacs, and personal journals in the nineteenth century is suggestive of a range of sources, methods, and patterns of popular classification.

Among the various methods used in the analysis of semantic change, the computer-aided lexicons generated by Mark Olsen and his associates appear to offer historians a very fine degree of precision, albeit for smaller sets of sources and shorter periods of time than covered in this study. See, for example, Mark Olsen and Louis George Harvey, "Contested Methods: Daniel T. Rodger's *Contested Truths,*" *JHI* 49 (1989): 653–68.

26. For systematic explanations of these positions see Charles Taylor, "Interpretation and the Sciences of Man," *Review of Metaphysics* 25 (1971): 3–51; Michael A. K. Halliday, *Language as Social Semiotic: The Social Interpretation of Language and Meaning* (London: University Park Press, 1978); Roger Fowler, Bob Hodge, Gunther Kress, and Tony Trew, *Language and Control* (London: Routledge and Kegan Paul, 1979); John Gumperz, ed., *Language and Social Identity* (Cambridge: Cambridge University Press, 1982); James Boyd White, *When Words Lose Their Meaning: Constitutions and Reconstitutions of Language, Character, and Community* (Chicago: University of Chicago Press, 1984); Michael Mulkay, *The Word and the World: Explorations in the Form of Sociological Analysis* (London: Allen and Unwin, 1985); Michael T. Gibbons, ed., *Interpreting Politics* (New York: New York University Press, 1987); George W. Grace, *The Linguistic Construction of Reality* (London: Croom, Helm, 1987); Edelman, *Constructing the Political Spectacle;* Richard Harvey Brown, *Social Science as Civic Discourse;* Bruce Lincoln, *Discourse and the Construction of Society: Comparative Studies of Myth, Ritual, and Classification* (New York: Oxford University Press, 1989); Pierre Bourdieu, *In Other Words: Towards a Reflexive Sociology* (Stanford: Stanford University Press, 1990).

The implications of the analysis of discourse for the social sciences are considered in George V. Zito, *Systems of Discourse: Structures and Semiotics in the Cultural Sciences* (New York: Greenwood, 1985); Jack Bilmes, *Discourse and Behavior* (New York: Plenum, 1986). See also Teun A. Van Dijk, ed., *Handbook of Discourse Analysis,* vol. 1, *Disciplines of Discourse* (London: Academic Press, 1985).

On the intersections between the history of philosophy, intellectual history, and interpretation, see Paul Oskar Kristeller, "Philosophy and Its Historiography," *Journal of Philosophy* 82 (1985): 618–25; Hans-Georg Gadamer, "The History of Concepts and the Language of Philosophy," *International Studies in Philosophy* 18 (1986): 1–16; Stephen H. Daniel, "Metaphor in the Historiography of Philosophy," *Clio* 15 (1986): 191–210; Jorge J. E. Gracia, "Texts and Their Interpretation," *Review of Metaphysics* 43 (1990): 495–542; C. Behan McCullagh, "Can Our Understanding of Old Texts Be Objective?" *History and Theory* 30 (1991): 302–23.

27. Ball's outlines for and assumptions about a "critical conceptual history" are to be found in his *Transforming Political Discourse,* pp. 4–24. There Ball acknowledges the influence of contemporary German scholarship on the history of concepts, especially the work of Reinhart Koselleck. See also Terrence Ball, James Farr, and Russell Hanson, eds., *Political Innovation and Conceptual Change* (Cambridge: Cambridge University Press, 1989); Terrence Ball and J. G. A. Pocock, eds., *Conceptual Change and the Constitution* (Lawrence: University Press of Kansas, 1988).

Melvin Richter in "Conceptual History (Begriffsgeschichte) and Political Theory," *Political Theory* 14 (1986): 604–37; "Begriffsgeschichte and the History of Ideas," *JHI* 48 (1987): 247–63; and "Reconstructing the History of Political Languages," argues for a conceptual analysis of American politics and society that would complement recent scholarship on France, Germany, and Britain. The phrase "contested intellectual constructions" is his.

28. The premises and practices of *Begriffsgeschichte* are discussed in Reinhart Koselleck, ed., *Historische Semantik und Begriffsgeschichte* (Stuttgart: Klett-Cotta, 1979); Koselleck, "Time and Revolutionary Language," *Graduate Faculty Philosophy Journal* 9 (1983): 117–27; Koselleck, "Begriffsgeschichte and Social History," in *Futures Past,* pp. 159–99; Koselleck, "Linguistic Change and the History of Events," *JMH* 61 (1989): 649–66; Dietrich Busse, *Historische Semantik: Analyse eines Programme* (Stuttgart: Klett-Cotta, 1987).

See also James Sheehan, "Begriffsgeschichte: Theory and Practice," *JMH* 50 (1978): 312–19; Irmline Veit-Brause, "A Note on Begriffsgeschichte," *History and Theory* 20 (1981): 61–67; Richter, "Conceptual History"; Richter, "Begriffsgeschichte and the History of Ideas"; Richter, "Reconstructing the History of Political Languages."

On the limits and the presuppositions of this approach, see Jeremy Rayner, "On 'Begriffsgeschichte'," *Political Theory* 16 (1988): 496–501; Melvin Richter, "Understanding 'Begriffsgeschichte': A Rejoinder," *Political Theory* 17 (1989): 296–301; Rayner, "On 'Begriffsgeschichte' Again," *Political Theory* 18 (1990): 305–7.

29. Among J. G. A. Pocock's many methodological and programmatic pieces, see "The Reconstitution of Discourse: Toward the Historiography of Political Thought," *Modern Language Notes* 96 (1981): 959–80; "The Concept of a Language and the Métier d'Historien: Some Considerations on Practice,"

in *The Languages of Political Theory in Early-Modern Europe,* ed. Anthony Pagden (Cambridge: Cambridge University Press, 1987), pp. 19–38. See also Pagden's introduction, pp. 1–17, in which he distinguishes this project from Lovejoy's history of unit ideas, and from the poststructuralists' assertion that texts are not the work of conscious agents. The range of and the responses to Quentin Skinner's work are the subject of James Tully, ed., *Meaning and Context: Quentin Skinner and His Critics* (Princeton: Princeton University Press, 1989). See especially Skinner, "Language and Social Change," "On Describing and Explaining Beliefs," and "On Meaning and Speech-Acts," pp. 119–34, 235–58, 259–88.

Ball, in a paraphrase of Martin Heidegger, suggests that "we not only have these discourses but they also have us" (*Transforming Political Discourse,* p. 11). The programmatic points of comparison of the Cambridge School and *Begriffsgeschichte* are considered in Richter, "Reconstructing the History of Political Languages."

30. Interdependence and interpenetration of intellectual and social systems are discussed by Martin Hollis, "The Social Destruction of Reality," in *Rationality and Relativism,* ed. Martin Hollis and Steven Lukes (Oxford: Blackwell, 1982), pp. 67–86. There Hollis warns of the problems that are posed by "the presumption that social and intellectual systems can be separated and then related as cause and effect" (p. 70).

31. In *Languages of Class* the social historian Gareth Stedman Jones has argued that 'class' is a word situated in a language and "should be analysed in a linguistic context." He also cautions against the assumption that 'class' as a counter of social description, as an effect of theoretical discourse in economics, as a species of political self-definition, or as a "cluster of signifying practices" has one single reference point in an anterior social reality. For Jones it is problematic to talk of class, or other social categories, as existing prior to their articulation through historical actors' language (p. 7). Philip Furbank has also emphasized the linguistic dimensions of the study of class: "It is very much, from one point of view, a linguistic problem and belongs to that 'large class of cases,' in which, according to Wittgenstein, 'the meaning of the word is in its use in the language' " (*Unholy Pleasure,* p. 5).

Stedman Jones's turn to discourse is strongly criticized by Bryan Palmer in *Descent into Discourse* (Philadelphia: Temple University Press, 1990). For Palmer such moves may lead historians into idealism or nihilism, and away from the objective, critical stance of historical materialism. See also Peter Hudson, "Proletarian Experience, Class Interest, and Discourse: How Far Can Classical Marxism Still Be Defended?" *Politikon* 14 (1987): 16–35. Gregory Claeys in his call for a "social history of language" in *Citizens and Saints: Politics and Anti-Politics in Early British Socialism* (Cambridge: Cambridge University Press, 1989), pp. 17–19, is more sanguine about the prospects of conjoining the study of language, politics, and society. See also Lynn Hunt's analysis of linguistic change in *Politics, Culture, and Class in the French Revolution* (Berkeley and Los Angeles: University of California Press, 1984), pp. 19–51; and Ira Katznelson's argument that "class is discursive" in *Working-Class Formation: Nineteenth-Century Patterns in Western Europe and the United*

States, ed. Ira Katznelson and Aristide Zolberg (Princeton: Princeton University Press, 1986), p. 34.

Since this study historicizes class in the realm of American public discourse through the late nineteenth century, such debates by twentieth-century historians are significant, but of secondary import.

Chapter 1

1. The standard bibliographical guide to this controversial literature remains Charles Evans, *American Bibliography* (New York: Peter Smith, 1941), specifically volumes 3 (1751–64) through 6 (1779–85). Collections of these sources include Bernard Bailyn, ed., *Pamphlets of the American Revolution, 1750–1776* (Cambridge, Mass.: Belknap, 1965), vol. 1 (1750–65); Charles S. Hyneman and Donald Lutz, eds., *American Political Writing during the Founding Era* (Indianapolis: Liberty, 1983); Merrill Jensen, ed., *Tracts of the American Revolution: 1763–1776* (Indianapolis: Bobbs-Merrill, 1967); Edmund S. Morgan, ed., *Prologue to Revolution: Sources and Documents on the Stamp Act Crisis, 1764–1766* (Chapel Hill: University of North Carolina Press, 1959); Richard B. Morris, ed., *The American Revolution, 1763–1783* (New York: Harper and Row, 1970); Ellis Sandoz, ed., *Political Sermons of the American Founding Era, 1730–1805* (Indianapolis: Liberty, 1991).

Questions about the extent of circulation, the composition of readerships, and the effects of these writings are considered in Bernard Bailyn and John B. Hench, eds., *The Press and the American Revolution* (Boston: Northeastern University Press, 1981); Richard D. Brown, *Knowledge Is Power: The Diffusion of Information in Early America, 1700–1865* (New York: Oxford University Press, 1989); Reid, *Three Centuries of American Rhetorical Discourse.*

2. Jonathan Boucher, *A Letter from a Virginian, to the Members of Congress* (New York: n.p., 1774), pp. 4–5. More recent evaluations of the importance of these sources are found in Forrest McDonald, "A Founding Father's Library," *Literature of Liberty* 1 (1978): 4–15; Georgia Holmberg, "British-American Whig Political Rhetoric, 1765–1771," Ph.D. diss., University of Pittsburgh, 1979, p. 8.

3. The use of 'taxonomy' here is intended to evoke more than a Linnaean imagery of fixed or static arrangements, although such imagery would be a commonplace to many late-eighteenth-century North Americans. See Robert H. Wiebe, *The Opening of American Society* (New York: Knopf, 1984), pp. 8–9; Christopher Looby, "The Constitution of Nature: Taxonomy as Politics in Jefferson, Peale, and Bartram," *Early American Literature* 22 (1987): 252–74. I am using it as well in an anthropological and sociological sense. As defined by Anthony P. M. Coxon, P. M. Davies, and Charles L. Jones, "A semantic hierarchy, or taxonomy, provides a conceptual framework within which lexical items . . . can be located" (Anthony P. M. Coxon, P. M. Davies, and Charles L. Jones, *Class and Hierarchy: The Social Meaning of Occupations* [London: Macmillan, 1979], p. 56). A taxonomy in this sense incorporates both descriptive and relational elements.

4. On the dependence of the 'social' upon the 'political' see Sheldon Wolin, *Politics and Vision: Continuity and Innovation in Western Political Thought* (Bos-

ton: Little, Brown, 1960); J. R. Pole, *Political Representation in England and the Origins of the American Republic* (New York: St. Martin's, 1966). On the emergence of the 'economic' see Wolin, *Politics and Vision,* pp. 292–300; Joyce Appleby, *Economic Thought and Ideology in Seventeenth Century England* (Princeton: Princeton University Press, 1978); Keith Tribe, *Land, Labour, and Economic Discourse* (London: Routledge and Kegan Paul, 1979); Edward J. Harpham, "Class, Commerce, and the State: Economic Discourse and Lockean Liberalism in the Seventeenth Century," *Western Political Quarterly* 38 (1985): 565–82; Hiram Caton, *The Politics of Progress: The Origins and Development of the Commercial Republic, 1600–1835* (Gainesville: University of Florida Press, 1988); Gordon Wood, *The Radicalism of the American Revolution* (New York: Knopf, 1992).

On the nineteenth-century emergence of the 'social' see Tom Bottomore and Robert Nisbet, eds., *A History of Sociological Analysis* (New York: Basic Books, 1978).

5. These transatlantic dimensions are discussed in Bernard Bailyn, "Political Experience and Enlightenment Ideas in Eighteenth-Century America," *American Historical Review* 67 (1962): 343–44; Jeffrey Barnow, "American Independence: Revolution of the Republican Ideal," in *The American Revolution in Eighteenth Century Culture,* ed. Paul J. Korshin (New York: AMS Press, 1986), pp. 31–74.

6. This brief genealogy of the sources of Anglo-American political discourse is not exhaustive. In addition to J. R. Pole and Sheldon Wolin, see Bernard Bailyn, *The Ideological Origins of the American Revolution* (Cambridge, Mass.: Belknap, 1967); H. T. Dickinson, *Liberty and Property: Political Ideology in Eighteenth-Century Britain* (New York: Holmes and Meier, 1977); J. G. A. Pocock, *The Machiavellian Moment: Florentine Political Thought and the Atlantic Republican Tradition* (Princeton: Princeton University Press, 1975); Nicholas Phillipson and Quentin Skinner, eds., *Political Discourse in Early Modern Britain* (Cambridge: Cambridge University Press, 1993); John Zvesper, "The American Founders and Classical Political Thought," *History of Political Thought* 10 (1989): 700–718; Morton White, *The Philosophy of the American Revolution* (New York: Oxford University Press, 1978); Lienesch, *New Order of the Ages;* Henry Phelps Brown, *Egalitarianism and the Generation of Inequality* (Oxford: Clarendon, 1988); Peter Gay, *The Enlightenment: An Interpretation* (New York: Knopf, 1969), esp. vol. 2, *The Science of Freedom.*

See also David Berman, "Irish Philosophy and the American Enlightenment during the Eighteenth Century," *Eire—Ireland* 24 (1989): 28–39; Carl J. Richard, "A Dialogue with the Ancients: Thomas Jefferson and Classical Philosophy and History," *Journal of the Early Republic* 9 (1989): 431–55; Robert A. Rutland, "Madison's Bookish Habits," *Quarterly Journal of the Library of Congress* 37 (1980): 176–91.

7. The questions of which political traditions were the most influential and which were the master texts of Anglo-American republicanism have been the subjects of extended debate among historians and political theorists. See Joyce Appleby, "The Social Origins of American Revolutionary Ideology," *JAH* 64

(1978): 935–59; Appleby, *Liberalism and Republicanism in the Historical Imagination* (Cambridge: Harvard University Press, 1992); Robert Zaller, "The Continuity of British Radicalism in the Seventeenth and Eighteenth Centuries," *Eighteenth Century Life* 7 (1981): 17–38; James T. Kloppenberg, "The Virtues of Liberalism: Christianity, Republicanism, and Ethics in Early American Political Discourse," *JAH* 74 (1987): 9–33; J. G. A. Pocock, "Between Gog and Magog: The Republican Thesis and the Ideologia Americana," *JHI* 48 (1987): 325–46; Thomas Pangle, *The Spirit of Modern Republicanism: The Moral Vision of the American Founders and the Philosophy of Locke* (Chicago: University of Chicago Press, 1988); Stephen M. Dworetz, *The Unvarnished Doctrine: Locke, Liberalism, and the American Revolution* (Durham, N.C.: Duke University Press, 1990); Ronald Hamowy, "*Cato's Letters,* John Locke, and the Republican Paradigm," *History of Political Thought* 11 (1990): 273–94.

8. John Dickinson, *The Late Regulations respecting the British Colonies* (Philadelphia: William Bradford, 1765), in *Pamphlets,* ed. Bailyn, p. 680.

9. For this line of argument see "Class," in Raymond Williams, *Keywords: A Vocabulary of Culture and Society* (London: Oxford University Press, 1976), pp. 51–59. See also Briggs, "Language of 'Class'," pp. 5–8. Both Williams and Briggs see the shift in usage from 'orders' et alia to 'classes' as signifying the transition from a premodern to modern, or precapitalist to capitalist, understanding of society.

10. Previous analyses of eighteenth-century Americans' conceptions of society include the work of Jackson Turner Main and Robert J. Gough. In *The Social Structure of Revolutionary America* (Princeton: Princeton University Press, 1965) Main found a plethora of terms for identifying the constituent units of society and concluded that "the historian who tries to discover the Revolutionary Americans' ideas about class is confronted with a set of irreconcilable beliefs" (p. 228). A similar lack of conceptual consensus was discovered by Gough in "Towards a Theory of Class and Social Conflict," Ph.D. diss., University of Pennsylvania, 1977. Gough argues that "eighteenth century writers seemed to have disagreed among themselves on this point as much as present Americans do" (p. 603).

Other studies that consider these issues include Thomas M. Doerflinger, *A Vigorous Spirit of Enterprise: Merchants and Economic Development in Revolutionary Philadelphia* (Chapel Hill: University of North Carolina Press, 1986); Edmund S. Morgan, *Inventing the People: The Rise of Popular Sovereignty in England and America* (New York: Norton, 1988); Gary Nash, *The Urban Crucible: Social Change, Political Consciousness, and the Origins of the American Revolution* (Cambridge: Harvard University Press, 1979); Steven Rosswurm, *Arms, Country, and Class: The Philadelphia Militia and the "Lower Sort" during the American Revolution* (New Brunswick: Rutgers University Press, 1987); Ronald Schultz, "Thoughts among the People: Popular Thought, Radical Politics, and the Making of Philadelphia's Working Class, 1765–1828," Ph.D. diss., University of California, Los Angeles, 1985; Charles S. Steffen, *The Mechanics of Baltimore: Workers and Politics in the Age of Revolution, 1763–1812* (Urbana: University of Illinois Press, 1984).

11. The term 'socioconstitutional' is used by Bernard Bailyn in an essay, "Common Sense," in *Fundamental Testaments of the American Revolution* (Washington, D.C.: Library of Congress, 1973), p. 9.

Among the "patterns" that are not discussed below are the divisions along the lines of religion, race, ethnicity, and sex. Any abstraction will fail to do justice to the richness and complexity of a historical tradition; but in making this abstraction I wish to clarify, not to do violence to, the terms of Anglo-American political discourse.

12. See Stephen Foster, *Their Solitary Way: The Puritan Social Ethic in the First Century of Settlement in New England* (New Haven: Yale University Press, 1971), pp. 26–27; David Galenson, "'Middling People' or 'Common Sort'? The Social Origins of Some Early Americans Re-examined," *WMQ* 35 (1978): 499–540; Peter Laslett, *The World We Have Lost* (New York: Scribner's, 1971), pp. 23–24; Keith Wrightson, *English Society, 1580–1680* (New Brunswick: Rutgers University Press, 1982), pp. 17–38; Gordon Wood, *Radicalism of the American Revolution,* pp. 11–23. On the larger subject of 'orders' in Western political and social discourse, see Roland Mousnier, *Social Hierarchies, 1450 to the Present* (London: Croom, Helm, 1973).

13. Daniel Dulany, *Considerations on the Propriety of Imposing Taxes in the British Colonies* (Annapolis, 1765), in *Pamphlets,* ed. Bailyn, p. 610.

14. Charles Chauncy, *A Letter to a Friend* (Boston: Greenleaf, 1774), p. 24. See also Joseph Huntington, *A Discourse, Adapted to the Present Day on the Health and Happiness or Misery and Ruin of the Body Politic, in Similitude to That of the Natural Body* (Hartford: Hunter and Goodwin, 1781), pp. 15–21. As the title suggests, the Reverend Huntington makes use of an "organic" metaphor. Such admixtures of socioconstitutional imagery and organic metaphors were common. See also Abraham Williams, "An Election Sermon" (Boston, 1762), in *American Political Writing,* ed. Hyneman and Lutz, pp. 4, 9–10, 11–12.

15. For examples of 'order', 'rank', and 'station' in mid- to late-eighteenth-century American political writings, see William Hicks, *The Nature and Extent of Parliamentary Power Considered* (Philadelphia, 1768), and Daniel Leonard's *Massachusettensis* debate with John Adams for 26 December 1775, both in *American Revolution,* ed. Jensen, pp. 169, 287. See also Jonathan Mayhew, *A Discourse concerning Unlimited Submission and Non-Resistance to the Higher Powers* (Boston, 1750), in *Pamphlets,* ed. Bailyn, p. 214; the untitled essay by U. in the *Boston Gazette,* 1 August 1763, in *American Political Writing,* ed. Hyneman and Lutz, pp. 33–36; Samuel Sherwood, *A Sermon, Containing Scriptural Instructions to Civil Rulers, and All Free-born Subjects* (New Haven: T. and S. Green, 1774), in particular the "appendix" by Ebenezer Baldwin, pp. 46, 51, 57; Samuel Williams, *The Influence of Christianity on Civil Society* (Boston: John Boyle, 1780), p. 13.

On the absence of "artificial distinctions of ranks" in the newly independent states, see David Ramsay, "An Oration on the Advantages of American Independence," *United States Magazine* 1, no. 1 (1779): 22; no. 2: 57; no. 3: 105; *Four Letters on Interesting Subjects* (Philadelphia: n.p., 1776). This latter pamphlet is examined by Carrol D. Arnold, "Early Constitutional Rhetoric in

Pennsylvania," in *American Rhetoric: Context and Criticism,* ed. Thomas W. Benson (Carbondale: Southern Illinois University Press, 1989), pp. 131–200.

16. The persistence of a lexicon of 'ranks', 'orders', and 'degrees' in rapidly changing American political and social conditions is noted by Steven Rosswurm (*Arms, Country, and Class,* p. 18). The larger question of the ability of a social lexicon to be adapted to new circumstances is discussed by Arthur L. Stinchcombe in "The Deep Structure of Moral Categories: Eighteenth Century French Stratification and the Revolution," in *Stratification and Occupation: Selected Papers* (New York: Cambridge University Press, 1986), pp. 145–73; and by Keith Wrightson in "Estates, Degrees, and Sorts in Tudor and Stuart England," *History Today* 37 (1987): 17–22. On the historical and cross-cultural presence of vertical systems of social classification, see Barry Schwartz, *Vertical Classification: A Study in Structuralism and the Sociology of Knowledge* (Chicago: University of Chicago Press, 1981).

17. On 'sorts' see Jack P. Greene, "Social Structure and Political Behavior in Revolutionary America: John Day's 'Remarks on American Affairs,' " *WMQ* 32 (1975): 482; Wrightson, "Estates, Degrees, and Sorts," pp. 20–22; Robert Malcolmson, *Life and Labour in England, 1700–1780* (New York: St. Martin's, 1981), pp. 11–17; Laura Caroline Stevenson, *Praise and Paradox: Merchants and Craftsmen in Elizabethan Popular Literature* (Cambridge: Cambridge University Press, 1984), pp. 80–89.

18. Richard Price, *Two Tracts on Civil Liberty* (London: T. Caddell, 1778), p. 27.

19. Ibid. See also the use of 'class' as synonymous with 'rank' and 'order' in Thomas Paine, *The American Crisis* (Philadelphia: M. Steiner, 1776), no. 1, p. 6; Paine, *Common Sense* (Philadelphia: R. Bell, 1776), pp. ii, 29, 40–42.

20. Penelope Corfield, "In So Many Words . . . Language and Society, 1500–1900," *History Today* 37 (1987): 16; Corfield, "From Rank to Class"; Corfield, "Class by Name and Number"; Wrightson, "Estates, Degrees, and Sorts," pp. 17–22; Wallech, "Emergence of the Modern Concept of 'Class'," pp. 1–125; Wallech, "Class versus Rank."

21. Studies of semantic change in English include Charles Barber, *Early Modern English* (London: Andre Deutch, 1976); Murray Cohen, *Sensible Words: Linguistic Practice in England, 1640–1785* (Baltimore: Johns Hopkins University Press, 1977), Geoffrey Hughes, *Words in Time: A Social History of the English Vocabulary* (Oxford: Blackwell, 1988); Susie Tucker, *Protean Shape: A Study in Eighteenth-Century Vocabulary and Usage* (London: Athlone, 1967).

22. See Livy, *The Early History of Rome* (London: Penguin, 1979), pp. 81–82.

23. Thomas Elyot, *The Dictionary* (1538; reprint, Menston, England: Scolar, 1970), n.p.

24. Thomas Cooper, *Thesaurus Linguae Romanae & Britannicae* (London: Bertheletti, 1565), n.p. John Rider's English-to-Latin dictionary, *Bibliotheca Scholastica* (1589; reprint, Menston, England: Scolar, 1970), has no entries for 'class' or its variants.

25. Sir Thomas Smith, *De Republica Anglorum: The Manner of Gouernment*

or Policie of the Realme of England (London: Gregorie Seton, 1583), pp. 18–19, 31–34. In the 1601 edition of this text, by the same publisher, Smith entitles one chapter "Of the Fourth Sort of Men who do Not Rule." David Cressy, in "Describing the Social Order of Elizabethan and Stuart England," *Literature and History* 3 (1976): 30, cites a 1583 edition of *De Republica Anglorum* that uses the spelling "classe."

On the fundamentally socioconstitutional understandings of Smith and his contemporaries about the relations of "principal citizens" to the other "sortes," see Stevenson, *Praise and Paradox,* pp. 80–89, 162–63.

26. John Florio, *A Worlde of Words* (London: Edward Blount, 1598), p. 74; John Bullokar, *An English Expositor* (1616; reprint, Menston, England: Scolar, 1967); Henry Cockeram, *The English Dictionarie* (1623; reprint, Menston, England: Scolar, 1968). See also John Florio's improved edition of his Italian-English dictionary, *Queen Anna's New World of Words* (1611; reprint, Menston, England: Scolar, 1968). For a full discussion of the metamorphosis of 'classe' in French, see Dallas L. Clouatre, "The Concept of Class in French Culture prior to the Revolution," *JHI* 45 (1984): 219–44.

27. Randle Cotgrave, *A Dictionarie of the French and English Tongues* (London: Adam Islip, 1611), n.p.

28. Thomas Blount, *Glossographia; or, the Interpretation of Hard Words* (1656; reprint, Menston, England: Scholar, 1969), n.p. Blount also ties together the derivations of 'classe' and 'classical'.

29. John Kersey, *Dictionarium Anglo-Britannicum; or, a General English Dictionary* (1708; reprint, Menston, England: Scolar, 1969), n.p. See also Kersey, *New English Dictionary* (1702; reprint, Menston, England: Scolar, 1969); Elisha Coles, *An English Dictionary* (1676; reprint, Menston, England: Scolar, 1971); Edward Phillips, *The New World of English Words* (1658; reprint, Menston, England: Scolar, 1969). Both Phillips and Coles spell the word with an *e,* while Kersey drops the final vowel.

30. Nathan Bailey, *Dictionarium Britannicum* (London: T. Cox, 1736), n.p. See also James Buchanan, *Linguae Britannicae Vera Pronunciatio* (1757; reprint, Menston, England: Scolar, 1967).

31. Samuel Johnson, *A Dictionary of the English Language* (London: W. Strahan, 1765), n.p. On Dr. Johnson's influence see David Simpson, *The Politics of American English, 1776–1850* (New York: Oxford University Press, 1986), pp. 23–36.

32. Corfield, "Class by Name and Number," pp. 39, 48–49, 55–56, 61; Corfield, "From Rank to Class," pp. 36–40. See also Wallech, "Class versus Rank," pp. 409–31.

33. Classifying and the classifications of eighteenth-century sciences of man are explored in Michael Banton, "The Classification of Races in Europe and America, 1700–1850," *International Social Science Journal* 39 (1987): 45–60; F. Kerstholt, "De traditie van klassieke klassenanalyse," *Sociologische Gids* 29 (1982): 44–47; Gianni Vaggi, "Social Classes and Income Distribution in Eighteenth Century Economics," *History of European Ideas* 9 (1988): 171–82; P. B. Wood, "The Natural History of Man in the Scottish Enlightenment," *History of Science* 28 (1990): 89–123.

34. Henry Steele Commager, *The Empire of Reason: How Europe Imagined and America Realized the Enlightenment* (London: Weidenfeld and Nicolson, 1978), pp. 40–70; Michel Foucault, *The Order of Things: An Archaeology of the Human Sciences* (New York: Random House, 1973), pp. 158–68; Gay, *Enlightenment,* 2:321–60; Gladys Bryson, *Man and Society: The Scottish Inquiry of the Eighteenth Century* (Princeton: Princeton University Press, 1945), pp. 17, 143–45, 206–18; Peter Jones, ed., *The "Science of Man" in the Scottish Enlightenment: Hume, Reid, and Their Contemporaries* (Edinburgh: Edinburgh University Press, 1989).

35. On the models and vocabularies that emerged in the sciences of man, see Stephen Gudeman, *Economics as Culture: Models and Metaphors of Livelihood* (London: Routledge and Kegan Paul, 1986), pp. 38–39, 60–88; Donald McCloskey, *The Rhetoric of Economics* (Madison: University of Wisconsin, 1985); Wallech, "Emergence of the Modern Concept of 'Class'."

On colonial Americans' perceptions of the marketplace see Janet Ann Riesman, "The Origins of American Political Economy, 1680–1781," Ph.D. diss., Brown University, 1984, pp. 140, 198, 333. See also John E. Crowley, *This Sheba, Self: The Conceptualization of Economic Life in Eighteenth Century America* (Baltimore: Johns Hopkins University Press, 1973).

36. Thomas B. Chandler, *A Friendly Address to All Reasonable Americans, on the Subject of Our Political Confusions* (New York: J. Rivington, 1774).

37. John Dickinson, *Letters from a Farmer in Pennsylvania to the Inhabitants of the British Colonies* (1768); reprint, *Memoirs of the Historical Society of Pennsylvania,* vol. 14 (Philadelphia: Historical Society of Pennsylvania, 1895), pp. 307, 349. See also John Adams, *Thoughts on Government, Applicable to the Present State* (Philadelphia: Dunlap, 1776), pp. 3–4; David Rittenhouse, "To the General Assembly of the State of Pennsylvania," 26 November 1776, in Steven Rosswurm, "Equality and Justice: Documents from Philadelphia's Popular Revolution, 1775–1780," *Pennsylvania History* 52 (1985): 256–58; Aedanus Burke, *Considerations on the Society or Order of Cincinnati* (Charleston, S.C.: A. Timothy, 1783), p. 5.

For 'orders' as referring to specific occupations see Peletiah Webster, *A Dissertation on the Political Union and Constitution of the Thirteen United States* (Philadelphia: Bradford, 1783), pp. 30–31; Benjamin Austin [Honestus], *Observations on the Pernicious Practice of the Law,* in *American Revolution,* ed. Richard B. Morris, pp. 341–45.

38. John Day, *Remarks on American Affairs* (1774); reprint, *WMQ* 32 (1975): 488–90. See also the introductory article by Jack P. Greene, "Social Structure and Political Behavior," pp. 471–84. While Greene notes that only four copies of this pamphlet were printed, its clear exposition of a taxonomy that was coming into usage makes it a suitable example for such emergent patterns in public discourse.

39. Day, *Remarks on American Affairs,* p. 488.

40. Ibid., pp. 489–90. On attitudes toward the mob in this period see, among others, Gordon Wood, "A Note on Mobs in the American Revolution," *WMQ* 23 (1966): 635–42.

41. Day, *Remarks on American Affairs,* pp. 488–90. On the range of models

in contemporary British usage, see Corfield, "Class by Name and Number," pp. 38–52.

42. See Corfield, "Class by Name and Number," p. 38; Conal Condren, "Radicals, Conservatives, and Moderates in Early American Political Thought: A Case of Sandwich Island Syndrome," *History of Political Thought* 10 (1989): 525–42.

43. My use of the terms 'model' and 'models' here and below is informed by Stephen Gudeman's *Economics as Culture.* Gudeman argues that "the word 'model' refers to a culturally constituted relationship between two entities or referents. One may be called the schema and the other the objects. The model is a projection from the domain of the schema to the domain of the object. By constituting one entity through another, a model offers a means of 'seeing' something, of knowing, interpreting, even doing something" (p. 38).

44. Studies of the Physiocrats include Elizabeth Fox-Genovese, *The Origins of Physiocracy* (Ithaca, N.Y.: Cornell University Press, 1976); Henry Higgs, *The Physiocrats* (New York: Langland, 1952); Pierre-Henri Gouette, "Evidence, ordre naturel, et science économique dans l'oeuvre de Quesnay," in *Ordre, nature, propriété,* ed. Gerard Klotz (Lyons: Presses Universitaires de Lyon, 1985), pp. 119–78; Ronald L. Meek, *The Economics of Physiocracy: Essays and Translations* (London: Allen and Unwin, 1962); Claude Morilhat, *La prise de conscience du capitalisme: Économie et philosophie chez Turgot* (Paris: Meridiens Klincksieck, 1988); Antoine Murphy, "Le developpement des idées économiques en France, 1750–1756," *Revue d'Histoire Moderne et Contemporaine* 33 (1986): 521–41; Gianni Vaggi, *The Economics of François Quesnay* (London: Macmillan, 1987). See also Hiram Caton, *Politics of Progress,* pp. 410–21; Phyllis Deane, *The Evolution of Economic Ideas* (Cambridge: Cambridge University Press, 1978); Louis Dumont, *From Mandeville to Marx: The Genesis and Triumph of Economic Ideology* (Chicago: University of Chicago Press, 1977); David McNally, *Political Economy and the Rise of Capitalism: A Reinterpretation* (Berkeley and Los Angeles: University of California Press, 1988); Claudio Napoleoni, *Smith, Ricardo, Marx* (Oxford: Blackwell, 1975), pp. 9–24.

45. François Quesnay, *The Oeconomical Table* (London: W. Owen, 1766), p. 17.

46. The intellectual and political contexts of Quesnay's classifications are examined by Michel Herland in "A propos de la définition du travail productif," *Revue Économique* 38 (1977): 109–33, with a response by M. Aglietta, "Quelques rèflexions sur la travail productif," pp. 134–45, and a rejoinder by Herland, pp. 146–49. See also Helen Boss, *Theories of Surplus and Transfer: Parasites and Producers in Economic Thought* (Boston: Unwin Hyman, 1990), pp. 30–37.

47. Meek, *Economics of Physiocracy,* p. 298; Fox-Genovese, *Origins of Physiocracy,* p. 115; Vaggi, *Economics of François Quesnay,* pp. 18, 169–77; Walter Eltis, "The Contrasting Theories of Industrialization of François Quesnay and Adam Smith," *Oxford Economic Papers* 40 (1988): 269–88.

48. Meek, *Economics of Physiocracy,* pp. 296–304; Fox-Genovese, *Origins of Physiocracy,* p. 51; Vaggi, *Economics of François Quesnay,* pp. 42–46, 169–77; Didier Deleule, "Du domestique au politique: Hume, les Physiocrates, et la

naissance du libéralisme économique," *Bulletin de la Société Française de Philosophie* 74 (1980): 81–101.

49. See Vernard Foley, "An Origin of the *Tableau Économique*," *HOPE* 5 (1973): 134; Meek, *Economics of Physiocracy*, p. 390; Boss, *Theories of Surplus and Transfer*, pp. 37–40; Murphy, "Developpement des idées économiques"; Vaggi, "Social Classes and Income Distribution." See also William Sewell, *Work and Revolution in France: The Language of Labor from the Old Regime to 1848* (New York: Cambridge University Press, 1980).

50. François Quesnay, "A Dialogue on the Work of Artisans," in Meek, *Economics of Physiocracy*, p. 203. On the terms of this dialogue see Eltis, "Contrasting Theories of Industrialization," pp. 271–72.

51. Quesnay, "Dialogue," pp. 204, 229.

52. Physiocratic assumptions that the social and natural orders could be analyzed with the same methods are discussed in Leon Dupriez, "Le concept de nature en économie politique," *Bulletin de la Classe des Lettres et des Sciences Morales et Politiques* 65 (1979): 332–35.

53. Anne-Robert-Jacques Turgot, *Turgot on Progress, Sociology, and Economics*, trans. Ronald L. Meek (Cambridge: Cambridge University Press, 1973), p. 26. Turgot's categories in the *Reflections* are discussed in Boss, *Theories of Surplus and Transfer*, pp. 38–39.

54. Anne-Robert-Jacques Turgot, *Reflections on the Formation and the Distribution of Riches* (1770; reprint, New York: A. M. Kelley, 1963), p. 54.

55. Ibid., p. 58.

56. Turgot, *Turgot on Progress*, pp. 27, 31. For a broader analysis of the French philosophes' argument that relations between the classes were essentially harmonious, see Harry C. Payne, *The Philosophes and the People* (New Haven: Yale University Press, 1976), pp. 61, 165.

57. Meek, *Economics of Physiocracy*, p. 396; Peter Groenwegen, "Turgot's Place in the History of Economic Thought: A Bicentenary Estimate," *HOPE* 15 (1983): 587–94; Morilhat, *Prise de conscience du capitalisme*, pp. 143–58, 211; Harvey Chisick, "The Ambivalence of the Idea of Equality in the French Enlightenment," *History of European Ideas* 13 (1991): 215–23.

58. On the development of what would later be known as the social sciences in the Scottish Enlightenment, see Bryson, *Man and Society;* Andrew Skinner, "Adam Smith: An Economic Interpretation of History," in *Essays on Adam Smith*, ed. Andrew Skinner and Thomas Wilson (Oxford: Clarendon, 1975), pp. 174–75; Alan Swingewood, "Origins of Sociology: The Case of the Scottish Enlightenment," *British Journal of Sociology* 21 (1970): 164–80; R. H. Campbell and Andrew Skinner, eds., *The Origins and Nature of the Scottish Enlightenment: Essays* (Edinburgh: John Donald, 1982); John Robertson, "Scottish Political Economy beyond Civic Tradition," *HOPE* 4 (1983): 451–82; Istvan Hont and Michael Ignatieff, eds., *Wealth and Virtue: The Shaping of Political Economy in the Scottish Enlightenment* (Cambridge: Cambridge University Press, 1983); Richard Bellamy, "From Feudalism to Capitalism: History and Politics in the Scottish Enlightenment," in *The Promise of History*, ed. Athanasios Moulakis (Berlin: De Gruyter, 1986), pp. 33–50; Michel Fauré, "Le Scottish Enlightenment: Naissance d'une anthropologie sociale," *Revue de Synthèse*, 4th ser., no. 4 (1986):

411–25; Sheila Dow, "The Scottish Political Economy Tradition," *Scottish Journal of Political Economy* 34 (1987): 335–48; Leonard Bauer and Herbert Matis, "From Moral to Political Economy: The Genesis of the Social Sciences," *History of European Ideas* 9 (1988): 125–43; James Farr, "Political Science and the Enlightenment of Enthusiasm," *American Political Science Review* 82 (1988): 51–69; T. W. Hutchison, *Before Adam Smith: The Emergence of Political Economy, 1662–1776* (Oxford: Blackwell, 1988), pp. 332–51; Alasdair MacIntyre, *Whose Justice? Whose Rationality?* (Notre Dame, Ind.: University of Notre Dame Press, 1988), pp. 241–325; Peter Jones, *"Science of Man"*; M. A. Stewart, ed., *Studies in the Philosophy of the Scottish Enlightenment* (Oxford: Clarendon, 1990); P. B. Wood, "Natural History of Man."

59. Among the many assessments of the extent of Hume's influence in America, especially by way of his *History of England* and his various political and economic essays, see Archie Turnbull, "Scotland and America," in *A Hotbed of Genius: The Scottish Enlightenment, 1730–1790,* ed. David Daiches, Peter Jones, and Jean Jones (Edinburgh: Edinburgh University Press, 1986), pp. 137–52; Daniel Walker Howe, "Why the Scottish Enlightenment Was Useful to the Framers of the American Constitution," *Comparative Studies in Society and History* 31 (1989): 583–84; Donald Livingston, "Hume, English Barbarism, and American Independence," in *Scotland and America in the Age of Enlightenment,* ed. Richard B. Sher and Jeffrey R. Smitten (Princeton: Princeton University Press, 1990), pp. 133–47.

60. Hume's methods for the analysis of civil society are discussed in Hume, *Writings on Economics,* ed. Eugene Rotwein (Edinburgh: Thomas Nelson, 1955), p. xxxi; David Miller, *Philosophy and Ideology in Hume's Political Thought* (Oxford: Clarendon, 1981), pp. 124–41; Jeffrey Young, "David Hume and Adam Smith on Value Premises in Economics," *HOPE* 22 (1990): 643–58; Alan Peacock, "Foreword to David Hume's *Political Discourses,*" in *The Scottish Contribution to Modern Economic Thought,* ed. Douglas Mair (Aberdeen: Aberdeen University Press, 1990), pp. 233–48; Richard H. Dees, "Hume and the Contexts of Politics," *Journal of the History of Philosophy* 30 (1992): 219–42.

61. David Hume, "On Commerce," in *Writings on Economics,* pp. 5–6.

62. Ibid., pp. 6–7; David Miller, *Philosophy and Ideology,* pp. 132–33; Miller, "Hume and Possessive Individualism," *History of Political Thought* 1 (1980): 261–78; MacIntyre, *Whose Justice?,* pp. 308–9; Deleule, "Du domestique au politique."

63. Hume, "Of Interest," in *Writings on Economics,* pp. 50–54; David Miller, *Philosophy and Ideology,* pp. 124–28, 133; Miller, "Hume and Possessive Individualism," pp. 270–72; MacIntyre, *Whose Justice?* pp. 308–9; M. M. Goldsmith, "Regulating Anew the Moral and Political Sentiments of Mankind: Bernard Mandeville and the Scottish Enlightenment," *JHI* 49 (1988): 587–601.

64. Hume, "Of Interest," pp. 50–54.

65. The larger contexts of this question are discussed in Boss, *Theories of Surplus and Transfer,* pp. 15–62.

66. The importance of social hierarchy in Hume's political writings is stressed in David Miller, *Philosophy and Ideology,* pp. 132–35, 141; Miller,

"Hume and Possessive Individualism," pp. 270–72. The use of 'republic' here and above is in the rather expansive, eighteenth-century manner of Hume, Montesquieu, et alia. David Hume was by no means a democrat or an egalitarian. He favored a "well-tempered" aristocracy and the benefits of a constitutional monarchy.

67. On the relation of Hume's analyses of economic, social, and political conditions, that is to say his understanding of 'civil society', see Bryson, *Man and Society,* pp. 107, 148–57; Anthony Flew, *David Hume: Philosopher of Moral Science* (Oxford: Blackwell, 1986); Hutchison, *Before Adam Smith,* pp. 199–214; David Miller, *Philosophy and Ideology.* On Hume and his contemporaries see W. B. Todd, ed., *Hume and the Enlightenment* (Edinburgh: Edinburgh University Press, 1974); G. P. Morice, ed., *David Hume: Bicentenary Papers* (Edinburgh: Edinburgh University Press, 1977); Duncan Forbes, "Sceptical Whiggism, Commerce, and Liberty," in *Essays on Adam Smith,* ed. Skinner and Wilson, pp. 180–93; Farr, "Political Science," pp. 52–55.

68. The influence of Ferguson in America is discussed in Daniel Walker Howe, "European Sources of Political Ideas in Jeffersonian America," in *The Promise of American History: Progress and Prospects,* ed. Stanley I. Kutler and Stanley N. Katz (Baltimore: Johns Hopkins University Press, 1982), p. 41; Daniel Walker Howe, "Why the Scottish Enlightenment Was Useful"; Gary McDowell, "Commerce, Virtue, and Politics: Adam Ferguson's Constitutionalism," *Review of Politics* 45 (1983): 536–52; Ronald Hamowy, "Progress and Commerce in Anglo-American Thought: The Social Philosophy of Adam Ferguson," *Interpretation* 14 (1986): 61–87.

Among the Americans familiar with Ferguson's *History of Civil Society* was John Witherspoon, who used the text at Nassau Hall, and Witherspoon's pupil, James Madison (McDowell, "Commerce, Virtue, and Politics," p. 538).

69. Scholarship on Ferguson includes David Kettler, *The Social and Political Thought of Adam Ferguson* (Columbus: Ohio State University Press, 1965); Hermann Strasser, *The Normative Structure of Sociology: Conservative and Emancipatory Themes in Social Thought* (London: Routledge and Kegan Paul, 1976), pp. 44–63; McDowell, "Commerce, Virtue, and Politics"; Marco Geuna, "Adam Ferguson ed il problema della divisione del lavoro: L'analisi delle 'nazioni commerciali' nell' *Essay on the History of Civil Society,*" *Annali della Fondazione Luigi Einaudi* 18 (1984): 243–71; John D. Brewer, "Adam Ferguson and the Theme of Exploitation," *British Journal of Sociology* 37 (1986): 461–78; Hamowy, "Progress and Commerce"; Richard B. Sher, "Professors of Virtue: The Social History of the Edinburgh Moral Philosophy Chair in the Eighteenth Century," in *The Scottish Enlightenment,* ed. M. A. Stewart, pp. 87–126; Swingewood, "Origins of Sociology"; Farr, "Political Science"; Robert Bierstedt, "Sociological Thought in the Eighteenth Century," in *History of Sociological Analysis,* ed. Bottomore and Nisbet, pp. 29–30.

70. Adam Ferguson, *An Essay on the History of Civil Society* (Basel: Tourneissen, 1789), p. 96.

71. Eighteenth-century conceptions of equality are discussed in Chisick, "Ambivalence of the Idea of Equality."

72. Ferguson's analyses of the social orders of commercial societies are

discussed in Kettler, *Social and Political Thought,* p. 280; McDowell, "Commerce, Virtue, and Politics," pp. 540–41; Hamowy, "Progress and Commerce," pp. 66–73, 81–82; Hamowy, *The Scottish Enlightenment and the Theory of Spontaneous Order* (Carbondale: Southern Illinois University Press, 1987), pp. 27–29; Geuna, "Adam Ferguson," pp. 254–56, 259–62. See also Norbert Waszek, "The Division of Labor: From the Scottish Enlightenment to Hegel," *Owl of Minerva* 15 (1983): 52–64.

The similarity between classifications of the natural and the social orders in the work of Ferguson and his fellow Scots is stressed by P. B. Wood, "Natural History of Man," p. 114.

73. Hermann Strasser has suggested that, because of Ferguson's emphasis on the clash of social groupings in the formation of political structures, he "may very well be called the single most important precursor of the theory of class conflict" (*Normative Structures of Sociology,* pp. 55–56).

74. Ferguson's assumptions about social conflict and his concerns for commercial republics are discussed in McDowell, "Commerce, Virtue, and Politics," pp. 540–43; Hamowy, "Progress and Commerce," pp. 71–73, 81–83; Strasser, *Normative Structures of Sociology,* pp. 52–56.

75. Ferguson's studies and uses of the histories of Greece and Rome are examined by Michael Kugler, "Adam Ferguson and Classical Antiquity," Ph.D. diss., University of Chicago, 1993. My understanding of Ferguson has been greatly enriched by many conversations with Mr. Kugler.

76. Ferguson's arguments that a "reinvigorated political order" could check the forces of luxury and corruption are stressed by McDowell, "Commerce, Virtue, and Politics," pp. 541–45; and by Hamowy, "Progress and Commerce," pp. 82–86.

77. Sir James Steuart, *An Inquiry into the Principles of Political Economy,* ed. Andrew Skinner (1767; reprint, Chicago: University of Chicago Press, 1966), p. 21. On Steuart see Skinner's "Analytic Introduction" and "Sir James Steuart: Economic Theory and Policy," in *Scottish Contribution,* ed. Mair, pp. 174–96; Walter Eltis, "Sir James Steuart's Corporate State," in *Scottish Contribution,* ed. Mair, pp. 197–219; Samar R. Sen, *The Economics of Sir James Steuart* (London: London School of Economics, 1957); Hutchison, *Before Adam Smith,* pp. 335–51; Albert O. Hirschman, *The Passions and the Interests: Political Arguments for Capitalism before Its Triumph* (Princeton: Princeton University Press, 1977), pp. 81–87.

78. Steuart's emphases on classes as the primary units of analysis are examined in Gary Anderson and Robert D. Tollison, "Sir James Steuart as the Apotheosis of Mercantilism and His Relation to Adam Smith," *Southern Economic Journal* 51 (1984): 456–59. The central role to be played by the "statesman" is discussed in Skinner, "Economic Theory and Policy," pp. 183–87; Eltis, "Corporate State," pp. 198–203.

79. Steuart, *Principles of Political Economy,* p. 88.

80. Ibid., pp. 67–68; Skinner, introduction to Steuart, *Principles of Political Economy,* pp. lxxix–lxx. Corfield argues that by the 1760s variants of the term 'working class' were beginning to appear in British public discourse ("From Rank to Class," p. 40).

81. Steuart, *Principles of Political Economy,* p. 310.

82. Ibid., p. 20; Skinner, introduction, p. lxxi. The range of Steuart's proposals for state intervention in and supervision of the economy is discussed in Skinner, "Economic Theory," pp. 183–92; Eltis, "Corporate State," pp. 197–216; Sen, *Economics of Sir James Steuart.*

In addition to the above treatments, the degree of Steuart's differences with his more "liberal" contemporaries is discussed in Ronald L. Meek, "The Rehabilitation of Sir James Steuart," in *Scottish Contribution,* ed. Mair, pp. 220–32.

83. The scholarship on Adam Smith and the *Wealth of Nations* includes Skinner and Wilson, eds., *Essays on Adam Smith;* Donald Winch, *Adam Smith's Politics: An Essay in Historiographic Revision* (Cambridge: Cambridge University Press, 1978); Winch, "Adam Smith: Scottish Moral Philosopher as Political Economist," *Historical Journal* 35 (1992): 91–114; Véronique Rostas, "Adam Smith et le mouvement des lumières écossais," *Histoire, économie, et société* 2 (1983): 337–47; Edward J. Harpham, "Liberalism, Civic Humanism, and the Case of Adam Smith," *American Political Science Review* 78 (1984): 764–74; Richard Teichgraeber, *"Free Trade" and Moral Philosophy: Rethinking the Sources of Adam Smith's Wealth of Nations* (Durham, N.C.: Duke University Press, 1986); Jerry Evensky, "The Evolution of Adam Smith's Views on Political Economy," *HOPE* 21 (1989): 123–45; Patricia Werhane, *Adam Smith and His Legacy for Modern Capitalism* (New York: Oxford University Press, 1991); Dow, "Scottish Political Economy Tradition"; McNally, *Political Economy and the Rise of Capitalism,* pp. 152–208.

84. On Smith's argument for a harmony of interests in society, see E. G. West, "Adam Smith and Alienation," and Robert Heilbroner, "The Paradox of Progress: Decline and Decay in the *Wealth of Nations,*" in *Essays on Adam Smith,* ed. Skinner and Wilson, pp. 543–46, 533; A. W. Coats, "Adam Smith's Conception of Self-Interest in Economic and Political Affairs," *HOPE* 7 (1975): 132–36; David P. O'Brien, *The Classical Economists* (Oxford: Clarendon, 1978), pp. 24–30; Hamowy, *Scottish Enlightenment,* pp. 13–21; J. Ronnie Davis, "Adam Smith on the Providential Reconciliation of Individual and Social Interests," *HOPE* 22 (1990): 341–53; Werhane, *Adam Smith and His Legacy,* p. 92. O'Brien especially emphasizes the transmission of a "nondeterministic" theory of harmony from the natural law tradition to political economy.

85. Adam Smith, *An Inquiry into the Nature and Causes of the Wealth of Nations* (1776), ed. R. H. Campbell, Andrew Skinner, and W. B. Todd (Indianapolis: Liberty Classics, 1981), p. 265.

86. Adam Smith, "Of the Division of Labour," in *Wealth of Nations,* pp. 13–24 (hereafter pages given in text). See also David A. Reisman, *Adam Smith's Sociological Economics* (London: Croom, Helm, 1976), pp. 126–29; Salim Rashid, "Adam Smith and the Division of Labour: A Historical View," *Scottish Journal of Political Economy* 33 (1986): 292–97; Waszek, "Division of Labor."

87. Smith's use of 'interest' is discussed in Bauer and Matis, "From Moral to Political Economy," pp. 129–31.

88. See H. T. Dickinson, *Liberty and Property.*

89. On the contradictions implicit in Smith's analysis of class relations, see Michael Perelman, *Classical Political Economy: Primitive Accumulation and the Social Division of Labor* (Totowa, N.J.: Rowman and Allenheld, 1984), pp. 163–66. Smith's objections to merchants and manufacturers is explored in Perelman, "Adam Smith and Dependent Social Relations," *HOPE* 21 (1989): 503–20; Evensky, "Evolution of Adam Smith's Views," pp. 123–45; D. C. Coleman, "Adam Smith, Businessmen, and the Mercantile System in England," *History of European Ideas* 9 (1988): 161–70. Coleman argues that, while Smith assumed that merchants and manufacturers would engage in self-serving conspiracies in the public arena, he fully approved of their profitable and productive activities elsewhere.

90. The points of difference and similarity between Smith's and Quesnay's systems are discussed in Eltis, "Contrasting Theories of Industrialization."

91. On these criteria and their consequences see Helen Boss, "Division of Labour and Unproductive Labour in a System of Natural Liberty: Adam Smith's Dilemma," *Historical Reflections/Réflexions Historiques* 15 (1988): 417–42.

92. The grounds for Smith's distinctions are discussed in Perelman, "Adam Smith and Dependent Social Relations."

93. On the policy implications of classification see Hiram Caton, "The Pre-Industrial Economics of Adam Smith," *JEH* 45 (1985): 844; David P. O'Brien, *Classical Economists,* p. 23.

94. The purposes and the audiences of Smith's political economy are discussed in Werhane, *Adam Smith and His Legacy,* pp. 120, 132, 180; Winch, "Adam Smith," pp. 109–11; Evensky, "Evolution of Adam Smith's Views," pp. 126, 141; Harpham, "Liberalism, Civic Humanism," pp. 768–72; Nathan Rosenberg, "Adam Smith and the Stock of Moral Capital," *HOPE* 22 (1990): 1–18; Robert E. Praschi, "The Ethics of Growth in Adam Smith's *Wealth of Nations,*" *HOPE* 23 (1991): 337–52.

95. On the prescriptive dimensions of Scottish political science and political economy, see Donald Winch, "Science and the Legislator: Adam Smith and After," *Economic Journal* 93 (1983): 501–20; Young, "David Hume and Adam Smith," pp. 645–46, 654–56. See also Albert O. Hirschman, "Rival Interpretations of Market Society: Civilizing, Destructive, or Feeble?" *Journal of Economic Literature* 20 (1982): 1463–84.

96. On the reception of Smith in Britain see Kirk Willis, "The Role in Parliament of the Economic Ideas of Adam Smith, 1776–1800," *HOPE* 11 (1979): 505–44. For America see William D. Grampp, "Adam Smith and the American Revolutionists," *HOPE* 11 (1979): 179–91; Perelman, *Classical Political Economy,* pp. 146–48; Andrew Skinner, "Adam Smith and America: The Political Economy of Conflict," in *Scotland and America,* ed. Sher and Smitten, pp. 148–62.

Chapter 2

1. On the changes in the terms of American political discourse, see Cynthia S. Jordan, "Old Words in New Circumstances: Language and Leadership in

Post-Revolutionary America," *American Quarterly* 40 (1988): 491–513; J. G. A. Pocock, "States, Republics, and Empires: The American Founding in Early Modern Perspective," *Social Science Quarterly* 68 (1987): 703–23; Simpson, *Politics of American English,* pp. 24, 40–57; Willi Paul Adams, *The First American Constitutions* (Chapel Hill: University of North Carolina Press, 1980), pp. 99–117. On parallel changes in British public discourse see Corfield, "From Rank to Class," pp. 38–42; Corfield, "Class by Name and Number," pp. 47–49, 60–61; Tucker, *Protean Shape,* pp. 91–103, 113. The connections among political, conceptual, and linguistic changes in France have been the subject of far more study than events in the Anglo-American world. See among others Lynn Hunt, *Politics, Culture, and Class,* pp. 19–51; Carol Blum, *Rousseau and the Republic of Virtue: The Language of Politics in the French Revolution* (Ithaca, N.Y.: Cornell University Press, 1986); Sewell, *Work and Revolution in France,* pp. 62–142; Stinchcombe, "Deep Structure of Moral Categories," pp. 145–73; John Morris Robert, "'Liberté,' 'Egalité,' 'Fraternité': The Hypothesis of Masonic Origins," in *Historische Semantik und Begriffsgeschichte,* ed. Koselleck, pp. 314–26; Koselleck, "Time and Revolutionary Language," pp. 117–27. Robert cautions scholars against "dogmatic assertions about the chronological precedence" of terms, especially during periods of revolutionary change (p. 314).

Neo-Progressive interpretations of the American Revolution include Marc Egnal, *A Mighty Empire: The Origins of the American Revolution* (Ithaca, N.Y.: Cornell University Press, 1988); Gary Nash, *Urban Crucible;* Rosswurm, *Arms, Country, and Class.*

2. The profound and perhaps "radical" outcomes of the Revolution are the subject of Gordon Wood, *Radicalism of the American Revolution,* esp. part 2, "Republicanism," pp. 95–225.

3. David Ramsay, "An Oration on the Advantages of American Independence," *United States Magazine* 1 (1779): 105. See as well William Vans Murray, "Political Sketches," *American Museum,* no. 3 (1787): 237. On Ramsay see Eve Kornfeld, "From Republicanism to Liberalism: The Intellectual Journey of David Ramsay," *Journal of the Early Republic* 9 (1989): 289–314.

On the question of who constituted Ramsay's and other writers' audiences, see David Paul Nord, "A Republican Literature: Magazine Reading and Readers in the Late Eighteenth Century," in *Reading in America: Literature and Social History,* ed. Cathy Davidson (Baltimore: Johns Hopkins University Press, 1989), pp. 114–40. Nord argues that urban readerships were not limited to members of the elite, but included the "common sort" as well.

4. For the most thorough discussion of the debates over the state and federal constitutions, see Gordon Wood, *The Creation of the American Republic, 1776–1787* (Chapel Hill: University of North Carolina Press, 1969), esp. chap. 6; see also John Zvesper, *Political Philosophy and Rhetoric: A Study of the Origins of American Party Politics* (Cambridge: Cambridge University Press, 1977); Willi Paul Adams, *First American Constitutions;* Lienesch, *New Order of the Ages.* On different models of and vocabularies for civil society, see Pocock, "States, Republics, and Empires," pp. 709–13; Russell Hanson, *The Democratic Imagination in America: Conversations with Our Past* (Princeton: Princeton Uni-

versity Press, 1985), pp. 54–91; David F. Ericson, "American Republicanism, 1787–1833: The Federal Farmer and Daniel Webster," Ph.D. diss., University of Chicago, 1987; Leslie Wharton, *Polity and the Public Good: Conflicting Theories of Republican Government in the New Nation* (Ann Arbor: UMI Research Press, 1980); Forrest McDonald, *Novus Ordo Seclorum: The Intellectual Origins of the Constitution* (Lawrence: University Press of Kansas, 1985); Robert Middlekauf, "The Assumptions of the Founders in 1787," *Social Science Quarterly* 88 (1987): 656–68; J. David Greenstone, "Against Simplicity: The Cultural Dimensions of the Constitution," *University of Chicago Law Review* 55 (1988): 428–49.

5. Free Republican, "Free Republican, No. 5," *Boston Magazine* 1 (1784): 420–22. The Free Republican used, as would be expected, 'class' and 'order' as synonyms: "Hence, from the moral system of things, as far as it can be traced by observation, two distinct and different orders of man seem incident to every society" (p. 420).

6. Free Republican, "Free Republican, No. 6," *Boston Magazine* 1 (1784): 547–48; "A Letter Supposed to Have Been Written by a Gentleman in This State, to His Friend in England," *Boston Magazine* 2 (1785): 403. On Servius Tullius's divisions as discussed by Livy, see chapter 1. See also Noah Webster's arguments that the lack of "perpetual distinctions of property" in the new nation checked the rise of "one class of men above another" (*Sketches of American Policy* [Hartford: Hudson and Goodwin, 1785], p. 39).

7. The historical and theoretical presumptions about conflict in republics are discussed in Michael Lienesch, "Historical Theory and Political Reform: Two Perspectives on Confederation Politics," *Review of Politics* 45 (1983): 94–115; Lienesch, *New Order of the Ages*, pp. 68–73.

8. Besides Wood's *Creation of the American Republic*, see Herbert J. Storing, *What the Anti-Federalists Were For*, vol. 1 of *The Complete Anti-Federalist*, ed. Herbert J. Storing (Chicago: University of Chicago Press, 1981). On the contours of debates over 'property' see Donald K. Pickens and G. L. Seligman, "'Unworthy Motives': Property, the Historian, and the Federal Convention: A Historiographic Speculation," *Social Science Quarterly* 88 (1987): 847–58; E. James Ferguson, "Political Economy, Political Liberty, and the Formation of the Constitution," *WMQ* 40 (1983): 389–412.

9. John Mercer, "Essays by a Farmer," no. 2 (1788), in *Complete Anti-Federalist*, ed. Storing, 5:20. See also Mercer's analysis of the "orders" of the "yeomanry" and the "gentry" in essay no. 5 (1788), p. 43.

10. Federal Farmer, "Letters from the Federal Farmer to the Republican," in *The Antifederalist Papers*, ed. Morton Borden (Lansing: Michigan State University Press, 1965), p. 159. On the Federal Farmer's sociopolitical theory see David F. Ericson, "American Republicanism," pp. 133–35.

11. Federal Farmer, "Letters," in *Antifederalist Papers*, ed. Borden, p. 160. On the disputed authorship see Gordon Wood, "The Authorship of the *Letters from the Federal Farmer*," *WMQ* 31 (1974): 299–308; Robert H. Webking, "Melancton Smith and the *Letters from a Federal Farmer*," *WMQ* 44 (1987): 510–28; John Kaminski and Gaspare Saladino, eds., *The Documentary History of the*

Ratification of the Constitution (Madison: State Historical Society of Wisconsin, 1983), 14:15–16. Though once attributed to Richard Henry Lee of Virginia, the authorship of these essays is now in doubt.

12. Federal Farmer, "Letters," in *Complete Anti-Federalist,* ed. Storing, 2: 287–88.

13. Federal Farmer, "Letters," in *Documentary History,* ed. Kaminski and Saladino, 14:31, 26, 22, 50. The Farmer's arguments in favor of a "proportional representation" of classes are discussed in David F. Ericson, "American Republicanism," pp. 133–35, 170–77.

14. The uncertain authorship of the Brutus essays is discussed in *Documentary History,* ed. Kaminski and Saladino, 13:411–12. As were the Federal Farmer's "Letters," these essays were widely circulated during the period.

15. Brutus, "Essays of Brutus," in *Complete Anti-Federalist,* ed. Storing, 2: 380–81 (hereafter pages given in text).

16. Other examples of this line of argumentation include "The Address and Reasons of Dissent of the Minority of the Convention of the State of Pennsylvania to Their Constituents," 18 December 1787, in *The Antifederalists,* ed. Cecilia Kenyon (New York: Bobbs-Merrill, 1966), p. 48; Benjamin Woolman, "The Letters of Philadelphiensis," no. 9 (1788), in *Antifederalists,* ed. Kenyon, p. 84; "Essays by the 'Impartial Examiner,'" no. 3 (1788), in *Complete Anti-Federalist,* ed. Storing, 5:14; "A Federal Republican," in *Documentary History,* ed. Kaminski and Saladino, 14:260.

17. Samuel Chase, "Notes of Speeches Delivered to the Maryland Ratifying Convention," in *Complete Anti-Federalist,* ed. Storing, 5:89–90.

18. Ibid., p. 89.

19. Melancton Smith, "Speeches Delivered in the Course of Debate by the Convention of the State of New York on the Adoption of the Federal Constitution," in *Antifederalists,* ed. Kenyon, p. 383 (hereafter pages given in text). In addition to Storing and Kenyon on the Anti-Federalists, see Michael Lienesch, "In Defense of the Anti-Federalists," *History of Political Thought* 4 (1983): 65–88.

20. The contexts of Smith's arguments are discussed in Cecil L. Eubanks, "New York: Federalism and the Political Economy of the Union," in *Ratifying the Constitution,* ed. Michael Gillespie and Michael Lienesch (Lawrence: University Press of Kansas, 1989), pp. 300–340.

21. In an analysis of Anti-Federalism reminiscent of the work of Charles Beard, Saul Cornell stresses the "striking class-conscious rhetoric" and the "class critique" of Pennsylvania Anti-Federalist rioters ("Aristocracy Assailed: The Ideology of Backcountry Anti-Federalism," *JAH* 76 [1990]: 1148–72).

22. Brutus, "Essays," in *Documentary History,* ed. Kaminski and Saladino, 14:31.

23. The class analyses and classifications of the Anti-Federalists have been discussed by Cornell, "Aristocracy Assailed," pp. 1153–68; Eubanks, "New York"; Wilson Carey McWilliams, "Afterword," in *Ratifying the Constitution,* ed. Gillespie and Lienesch, pp. 391–400; John P. Diggins, *The Lost Soul of American Politics: Virtue, Self-Interest, and the Foundations of Liberalism* (Chicago:

University of Chicago Press, 1986), pp. 100–105; Lienesch, "Historical Theory and Political Reform," pp. 100–110; Lienesch, *New Order of the Ages,* p. 132.

Anti-Federalist attitudes toward commercial policy, especially toward foreign trade, are examined in John E. Crowley, "Commerce and the Philadelphia Constitution: Neo-Mercantilism in Federalist and Anti-Federalist Political Economy, *History of Political Thought* 13 (1992): 73–98. There Crowley argues persuasively that the Anti-Federalists were far from being "agrarian localists" who were hostile toward commerce (pp. 88–93).

24. Brutus, "Essays," in *Documentary History,* ed. Kaminski and Saladino, 15:515.

25. The most thorough study of the various traditions at work in the debates over the Constitution is McDonald, *Novus Ordo Seclorum.* See also Morton White, *Philosophy, the Federalist, and the Constitution* (New York: Oxford University Press, 1987); Isaac Kramnick, "'The Great National Discussion': The Discourse of Politics in 1787," *WMQ* 45 (1988): 3–32; Lienesch, *New Order of the Ages;* Daniel Walker Howe, "Why the Scottish Enlightenment Was Useful."

26. Alexander Hamilton, "Federalist No. 35," in *Documentary History,* ed. Kaminski and Saladino, 15:270 (hereafter pages given in text). See also the objections raised against the Federal Farmer in Noah Webster's review in the *American Magazine* 1 (1787): 442.

27. On the range of the texts and traditions that Hamilton brought to bear in his writings, see Judith N. Shklar, "Alexander Hamilton and the Language of Politics," in *Languages of Political Theory,* ed. Pagden, pp. 339–55; Jacob E. Cooke, *Alexander Hamilton* (New York: Scribner's, 1982), pp. 59, 99; Bruce Miroff, "Alexander Hamilton: The Aristocrat as Visionary," *International Political Science Review* 9 (1988): 43–54; Perelman, *Classical Political Economy,* pp. 146–48. See also Daniel Walker Howe, "Why the Scottish Enlightenment Was Useful."

28. James Madison, "Federalist No. 51," in *Documentary History,* ed. Kaminski and Saladino, 14:45.

29. Ibid., 45–46. The connections between Madsion and the moral philosophers of the Scottish Enlightenment are discussed in Douglas Adair, "'That Politics May Be Reduced to a Science': David Hume, James Madison, and the Tenth Federalist," *Huntington Library Quarterly* 20 (1957): 343–60; Roy Branson, "James Madison and the Scottish Enlightenment," *JHI* 40 (1979): 235–50; James Coniff, "The Enlightenment and American Political Thought: A Study of the Origins of Madison's Federalist Number 10," *Political Theory* 8 (1980): 381–402; Robert A. Rutland, *James Madison: The Founding Father* (New York: Macmillan, 1987), pp. 23–35; Jack N. Rakove, "The Madisonian Moment," *University of Chicago Law Review* 52 (1988): 473–505; Daniel Walker Howe, "Why the Scottish Enlightenment Was Useful." For a discussion on the role of Hume's ideas in these arguments, see Douglas Adair, "The Intellectual Origins of Jeffersonian Democracy: Republicanism, the Class Struggle, and the Virtuous Farmer," Ph.D. diss., Yale University, 1943. Parts of Adair's analysis are challenged by Edmund Morgan, "Safety in Numbers: Madison,

Hume, and the Tenth Federalist," *Huntington Library Quarterly* 49 (1986): 95–112.

30. James Madison, "Federalist No. 10," in *Documentary History,* ed. Kaminski and Saladino, 14:177.

31. Ibid. As Kaminski and Saladino note in their introductory apparatus to Publius's essays, contemporary audiences did not see this essay as especially significant (*Documentary History,* 13:486–94). The process of granting privilege to this number of the *Federalist* has been part of twentieth-century American historiography and political theory. See also Alan Gibson, "Impartial Representation and the Extended Republic: Towards a Comprehensive and Balanced Reading of the Tenth 'Federalist,'" *History of Political Thought* 12 (1991): 263–304.

In contrast to those scholars who stress the importance of the Scottish sciences of society are those who emphasize the influence of classical and modern political philosophy, especially the tradition of John Locke, on Madison and his contemporaries. See David F. Epstein, *The Political Theory of the Federalist* (Chicago: University of Chicago Press, 1984); Pangle, *Spirit of Modern Republicanism;* Paul A. Rahe, *Republics Ancient and Modern: Classical Republicanism and the American Revolution* (Chapel Hill: University of North Carolina Press, 1992), esp. pp. 573–616. See also Charles Kessler, "Federalist Ten and the American Founding," in *Saving the Revolution: The Federalist Papers and the American Founding,* ed. Charles Kessler (New York: Free Press, 1987), pp. 13–39. Coniff, "Enlightenment and American Political Thought," is balanced and thoughtful on the question of which writers were "influential" in Madison's *Federalist* essays.

32. On Madison's use of territory to trump history see Gibson, "Impartial Representation"; Morgan, "Safety in Numbers."

33. James Madison to Thomas Jefferson, 24 October, 1 November, in *Documentary History,* ed. Kaminski and Saladino, 13:447–48.

34. Additional examples of this extensive use of 'class' in the socioeconomic sense of occupations and interests can be found in *Documentary History,* ed. Kaminski and Saladino: David Humphreys to George Washington, 28 September 1787, 13:261; Alexander Hamilton, "Federalist No. 12," 14:240; A Federal Republican, "A Review of the Constitution," 14:260; Centinel IV, *Philadelphia Independent Gazetteer,* 14:320–21; Tench Coxe, "An American," 15:167; Hamilton, "Federalist No. 29," 15:320; David Ramsay to Benjamin Lincoln, 29 January 1788, 15:487. More evidence for the presence of a socioeconomic understanding of class in the political lexicon of these years can be found in Jonathan Elliot, ed., *The Debates in the Several States on the Adoption of the Federal Constitution,* 5 vols. (1836; reprint, Philadelphia: J. B. Lippincott, 1863). See, for example, James Bowdoin's remarks at the Massachusetts ratification debates, 1:82; Alexander Hamilton and Charles Pinckney at the Philadelphia convention, 1:421–22, 443–44; Alexander Hamilton, Melancton Smith, and Chancellor Livingston at the New York ratification convention, 2:235, 245–48, 276–78; James Wilson at the Pennsylvania convention, 2:523; George Mason and Edmund Pendleton at the Virginia convention, 3:262–66, 294–95; Charles Pinckney at the South Carolina conven-

tion, 4:320–23. 'Class' and its standard synonyms were regularly employed by many of the speakers. Although the deliberations of the body that drafted the Constitution were not made public until the nineteenth century, James Madison's *Notes of the Debates in the Federal Convention of 1787* (Athens: Ohio University Press, 1966) contains a considerable amount of evidence on the rhetorical practices and the social lexicons of the founders. Madison's *Debates in the Federal Convention* include references by Elbridge Gerry to the "superior" and "lowest classes of Society" (p. 40), and to the "landed" and the "commercial" interests (p. 84); George Mason's observations on the "diversity of interests" that compose every society (p. 429); Alexander Hamilton on the natural division into "interests" in "every community where industy is encouraged" (p. 135); Charles Pinckney's division of the people of the United States into "three classes . . . Professional men . . . Commercial men . . . the landed interest" (pp. 185–86); Madison's observation that "[i]n all civilized Countries the people fall into different classes having a real or supposed difference of interests" (p. 196). As is the case with the sources in the Elliot collection, Madison's *Debates in the Federal Convention* are indicative of the range of terms available and employed.

35. Alexander Hamilton, in *Debates in the Several States,* ed. Elliot, 2:256. Melancton Smith was not persuaded by Hamilton's dismissal of 'aristocracy': "the dispute was not of words, but of things" (p. 260). But in the opinion of Robert Livingston, "[t]he truth is in republican governments, we know of no such ideal distinctions. We are all equally aristocrats. Offices, emoluments, honors, are open to us all" (p. 278). On the Anti-Federalist concerns see Cornell, "Aristocracy Assailed," pp. 1157–59.

36. Charles Pinckney in *Debates in the Several States,* ed. Elliot, 4:320–22.

37. Ibid., 4:322. See also Edmund Pendleton's response to Patrick Henry at the Virginia convention, *Debates in the Several States,* ed. Elliot, 3:294–95; Murray, "Political Sketches," pp. 236–37; An American Citizen [Tench Coxe], "On the Federal Government," in *Documentary History,* ed. Kaminski and Saladino, 13:432: "No qualification in monied or landed property is required by the proposed plan; nor does it admit any preference from the preposterous distinctions of birth and rank." The broader conceptual contexts for these arguments are discussed in Pocock, "States, Republics, and Empires," pp. 713–19.

38. Along with this socioeconomic sense of occupation and/or interest, 'class' was also extensively used by Federalists and Anti-Federalists alike in referring to more general groups and 'sets' of men. See the following examples of 'class' in this more expansive sense in *Documentary History: New York Journal,* 19 July 1787, 13:165; George Washington to James Madison, 31 March 1787, 13:171; David Humphreys to Alexander Hamilton, 1 September 1787, 13:176; *Pennsylvania Gazette,* 22 August 1787, 13:189; Curtius, "Address to All Federalists," *New York Daily Advertiser,* 29 September 1787, 13:270; Alexander Hamilton, "Federalist No. 1," 13:494–95; Brutus, "Essays," 13: 525; Federal Farmer, "Letters," 14:49; A Landholder, *Connecticut Courant,* 12 November 1787, 14:93; James Madison to Thomas Jefferson, 9 December

1787, 14:396; The Landholder, *Connecticut Courant* 24 December 1787, 15:75, 78; Noah Webster, "America," 15:199; Madison, "Federalist No. 38," 15:356; Madison, "Federalist No. 39," 15:381; Aristides, "Remarks on the Proposed Plan," 15:530; Mercy Otis Warren, "Observations on the Constitution," 16:276.

39. Evidence of the continued use of 'ranks', 'orders', 'estates', and so forth can be found in *Documentary History,* ed. Kaminski and Saladino. See, for example, *New York Journal,* 12 July 1787, 13:165; An American, *Massachusetts Centinel,* 4 August 1787, 13:184–85; Samuel Bryan, "Centinel 1," 13:331, where he discusses the "real distinctions of rank and interest" in England and John Adams's arguments for orders in *Defence of the Constitutions;* A Son of Liberty, *New York Journal,* 8 November 1787, 13:481–83; George Lee Tuberville to Arthur Lee, 28 October 1787, 13:505; *Boston Gazette,* 29 October 1787, 13:511; John Jay, "Federalist No. 2," 13:518; Timoleon, *New York Journal,* 13:573, quoting from Blackstone's *Commentaries;* Luther Martin, "Speech at the Maryland Convention," 14:290, referring to the "estates" of the British legislature; James Kent to Nathaniel Lawrence, 8 December 1787, 14:389; "Philadelphiensis VII," *Philadelphia Independent Gazetteer* 15:339–40. See also Elliott's *Debates in the Several States:* Gouverneur Morris at the Philadelphia convention, 1:459–60; Charles Turner at the Massachusetts ratification convention, 2:31, 171; William Widgery at the same, 2:105; Oliver Ellsworth at the Connecticut convention, 2:194; John Williams at the New York convention, 2:242; George Mason at the Virginia convention, 3:266; Zacariah Johnson at the same, 3:647. A parodic use of a language of "proper degrees and subordinations" can be found in Aristocratis, *The Government of Nature Delineated* (Carlisle, Pa.: Kline and Reynolds, 1788).

40. On the social classifications in use in the late 1780s, see Murray Dry, "Anti-Federalism in the *Federalist:* A Founding Dialogue on the Constitution, Republican Government, and Federalism," in *Saving the Revolution,* ed. Kessler, pp. 40–60; Eubanks, "New York," pp. 300–340; Robert Ferguson, "Ideology and the Framing of the Constitution," *Early American Literature* 22 (1987): 157–65; Cathy Matson and Peter Onuf, *A Union of Interests: Political and Economic Thought in Revolutionary America* (Lawrence: University Press of Kansas, 1990).

On discrepancies between the terms of political discourse and the realities of politics, see Bryan Magee, "The Language of Politics," *Encounter* 66 (1986): 20–26; Diggins, *Lost Soul of American Politics,* pp. 100–114.

41. James Madison, "A Republican Distribution of Citizens," *American Museum* 11 (1792): 109. Madison had originally published this essay in the *National Gazette* on 5 March of the same year. See also the contrasts between artificial and natural political and social arrangements in "Address of the Republican Society of Philadelphia," *American Museum* 5 (1789): 389; Murray, "Political Sketches"; Roger Coram, *Political Inquiries* (Wilmington, Del.: Andrews and Brynberg, 1791), pp. 81–97; Joel Barlow, *Advice to the Priviledged Orders* (New York: Childs and Swaine, 1792), pp. 60–69.

42. On Madison's criticisms of Hamilton's economic policies in this essay,

see Pangle, *Spirit of Modern Republicanism,* pp. 100–101. See also James R. Gibson, *Americans versus Malthus: The Population Debate in the Early Republic* (New York: Garland, 1989), pp. 27–30.

43. Alexander Hamilton, *Report on Manufactures,* in *The Reports of Alexander Hamilton,* ed. Jacob E. Cooke (New York: Harper and Row, 1964) (pages given in text refer to this edition). On Hamilton and the *Report* see Cooke, *Alexander Hamilton,* pp. 99–105; see also Wharton, *Polity and the Public Good,* pp. 74–80; Drew McCoy, *The Elusive Republic: Political Economy in Jeffersonian America* (Chapel Hill: University of North Carolina Press, 1980), pp. 140–52; Miroff, "Alexander Hamilton," pp. 45–54; Rahe, *Republics Ancient and Modern,* pp. 651–86.

44. Wharton, *Polity and the Public Good,* p. 80.

45. Tench Coxe, *A View of the United States of America* (Philadelphia: William Hall, 1794), pp. 21, 355. On Coxe and *A View* see Jacob E. Cooke, *Tench Coxe and the Early Republic* (Chapel Hill: University of North Carolina Press, 1978), pp. 207–9; McCoy, *Elusive Republic,* pp. 151–52, 225–26.

46. Tench Coxe, *Observations on the Agriculture, Manufactures, and Commerce of the United States* (New York: Childs and Swain, 1789), pp. 77–79. Similar classifications and analyses were made by Loammi Baldwin in his *Thoughts on the Study of Political Economy* (Cambridge, Mass.: Hilliard and Metcalf, 1809).

47. On the Federalists see David Hackett Fischer, *The Revolution of American Conservatism: The Federalist Party in the Era of Jeffersonian Democracy* (New York: Harper and Row, 1965); Linda K. Kerber, *Federalists in Dissent: Imagery and Ideology in Jeffersonian America* (Ithaca, N.Y.: Cornell University Press, 1970).

48. Samuel Whittlesey Dana, *Essay on Political Society* (Whitehall, Pa.: William Young, 1800), p. 33 (hereafter pages given in text).

49. See also Fischer, *Revolution of American Conservatism,* pp. 285–86.

50. See the entry "Samuel Whittlesey Dana" in *Dictionary of American Biography* (New York: Scribner's, 1956), 3:61–62 (hereafter cited as *DAB*).

51. George Logan, "Five Letters Addressed to the Yeomanry of the United States," *American Museum* 12 (1792): 161 (hereafter pages given in text).

52. On Logan see Frederick B. Tolles, *George Logan of Philadelphia* (New York: Oxford University Press, 1953), pp. 76–79; McCoy, *Elusive Republic,* pp. 223–24; Zvesper, *Political Philosophy and Rhetoric,* pp. 121–24; Lance Banning, *The Jeffersonian Persuasion: Evolution of a Party Ideology* (Ithaca, N.Y.: Cornell University Press, 1978), pp. 186–92.

53. James Lyon, "To Aristocrats Generally," *National Magazine* 1 (1799): 14–15.

54. Ibid., 14–16. On the range of positions among the partisans of Jefferson, see Lance Banning, "Jeffersonian Ideology Revisited: Liberal and Classical Ideas in the New American Republic," *WMQ* 43 (1986): 3–19; and the reply by Joyce Appleby, "Republicanism in Old and New Contexts," *WMQ* 43 (1986): 20–34. See also Richard K. Matthews, *The Radical Politics of Thomas Jefferson: A Revisionist View* (Lawrence: University Press of Kansas, 1984); David M. Post, "Jeffersonian Revisions of Locke: Education, Property Rights, and Liberty," *JHI* 47 (1986): 147–57; Clifton Luttrell, "Thomas Jefferson on Money and Banking," *HOPE* 7 (1975): 156–73. On other critics of Hamilton

see Ruth Bogin, "'Measures So Glareingly Unjust': A Response to Hamilton's Funding Plan by William Manning," *WMQ* 46 (1989): 315–32.

55. Thomas Cooper, *Political Arithmetic* (Philadelphia, 1798), pp. 5–6, 13–14. On Cooper see Dumas Malone, *The Public Life of Thomas Cooper, 1783–1839* (1926; reprint, Columbia: University of South Carolina Press, 1961); McCoy, *Elusive Republic,* pp. 176–77, 215–16, 246–47; William C. Whitten, "The Economic Ideas of Thomas Cooper," *Essays in Economics* 20 (1969): 44–82; Isaac Kramnick, "Eighteenth Century Science and Radical Social Theory: The Case of Joseph Priestley's Scientific Liberalism," *Journal of British Studies* 25 (1986): 1–30; Seymour S. Cohen, "Two Refugee Chemists in the United States, 1794," *Proceedings of the American Philosophical Society* 126 (1982): 301–15.

Cooper's significance in the world of eighteenth-century radical writing and revolutionary politics is emphasized by Kramnick; by Richard J. Twomey, "Jacobins and Jeffersonians: Anglo-American Radicalism in the United States, 1790–1920," Ph.D. diss., Northern Illinois University, 1974, pp. 51–52, 148–67; and by Michael Durey, "Thomas Paine's Apostles: Radical Emigres and the Triumph of Jeffersonian Republicanism," *WMQ* 44 (1987): 661–88. Both Twomey and Durey emphasize the importance of the work and categories of Adam Smith in this "radical" discourse. This is a tradition that should be carefully distinguished from later anticapitalist variants of Anglo-American radicalism.

56. Cooper, *Political Arithmetic,* pp. 4, 13. See also the similar analyis of class relations in "To Farmers, Mechanics, and Other Industrious Citizens of America," *Time Piece,* 14 May 1798. This New York journal was edited by Philip Freneau and John Daly Burk, both supporters of Thomas Jefferson.

57. "Lessons from History," *Port Folio* 2 (1802): 339. On Dennie see Joseph J. Ellis, *After the Revolution: Profiles of Early American Culture* (New York: Norton, 1979); James F. Featherston, "Joseph Dennie," in *American Magazine Journalists, 1741–1850,* ed. Sam G. Riley (Detroit: Gale, 1989), pp. 76–85; A. W. Cafarelli, "Joseph Dennie," in *American Writers of the Early Republic,* ed. Emory Elliott (Detroit: Gale, 1985), pp. 114–17; Gary Coll, "Joseph Dennie," in *American Newspaper Journalists, 1690–1872,* ed. Perry J. Ashley (Detroit: Gale, 1985), pp. 151–59.

58. "Lessons from History," p. 340.

59. See H. T. Dickinson, *Liberty and Property;* Donald Stewart, *The Opposition Press of the Federalist Period* (Albany: State University of New York Press, 1969), esp. pp. 371–418.

60. Aurelius, "The Progress of Democracy, No. 4," *Port Folio* 3 (1803): 74.

61. Oliver Oldschool, "Prospectus," *Port Folio* 1 (1801): ii. On similar lines of arguments in Great Britain see Trevor McGovern, "Conservative Ideology in Britain in the 1790s," *History* 73 (1988): 238–47.

62. On Burke's social and political thought see Conor Cruise O'Brien, *The Great Melody: A Thematic Biography and Commented Anthology of Edmund Burke* (London: Sinclair-Stevenson, 1992); Daniel E. Ritchie, ed., *Edmund Burke: Appraisals and Applications* (New Brunswick, N.J.: Transaction Press, 1990); Francis Canavan, *Edmund Burke: Prescription and Practice* (Durham, N.C.: Car-

olina Academic Press, 1987); Michael Freeman, *Edmund Burke and the Critique of Radicalism* (Oxford: Blackwell, 1980).

63. Edmund Burke, "Classification of Citizens," *Port Folio,* n.s., 3 (1807): 135.

64. See John R. Howe, Jr., "Republican Thought and the Political Violence of the 1790s," *American Quarterly* 19 (1967): 147–50.

65. Observer, "The Observer, No. 1," *Port Folio,* n.n.s., 9 (1812): 59. On Biddle see Thomas Payne Govan, *Nicholas Biddle: Nationalist and Public Banker* (Chicago: University of Chicago Press, 1959). The anonymous Observer and the editor Biddle were most probably one and the same.

66. Observer, "Observer, No. 1," p. 59.

67. For a contemporary analysis of the philosophical and methodological problems involved in classification, see Stefan Themerson, "What's Wrong with Thinking in Terms of Classes?" *Etc.: A Review of General Semantics* 44 (1987): 49–56. On eighteenth-century assumptions see Richard J. Petersen, "Scottish Common Sense in America, 1786–1850," Ph.D. diss., American University, 1963.

68. John Taylor, *Construction Construed, and Constitutions Vindicated* (Richmond: Shepherd and Pollard, 1820), p. 208. Thomas Cooper had made a similar complaint about the fate of "the familiar phrases of the common language" in *Political Essays* (Northumberland, Pa.: A. Kennedy, 1799), pp. 19–20.

69. On late-eighteenth- and early-nineteenth-century assumptions about political language, see Julie Tetel Andresen, *Linguistics in America, 1769–1924: A Critical History* (London: Routledge, 1990), pp. 22–67; David Simpson, *Politics of American English,* pp. 40–57; Stephen K. Land, *The Philosophy of Language in Britain* (New York: AMS Press, 1986), pp. 31–77, 193–235; Tucker, *Protean Shape,* p. 113; V. P. Bynack, "Noah Webster's Linguistic Thought and the Idea of an American National Culture," *JHI* 45 (1984): 99–114.

70. On Taylor see Robert E. Shalhope, *John Taylor of Caroline: Pastoral Republican* (Columbia: University of South Carolina Press, 1980); Paul Conkin, *Prophets of Prosperity: America's First Political Economists* (Bloomington: Indiana University Press, 1980), pp. 43–76; Duncan MacLeod, "The Political Economy of John Taylor of Caroline," *Journal of American Studies* 14 (1980): 387–405; Andrew W. Foshee, "Jeffersonian Political Economy and the Classical Republican Tradition: Jefferson, Taylor, and the Agrarian Republic," *HOPE* 17 (1985): 523–50; Gillis J. Harp, "Taylor, Calhoun, and the Decline of a Political Theory of Disharmony," *JHI* 46 (1985): 107–20; David N. Mayer, ed., "Of Principles and Men: The Correspondence of John Taylor of Caroline with Wilson Cary Nicholas, 1806–1808," *Virginia Magazine of History and Biography* 96 (1988): 345–88. See also Mark Donald Walhout, "Hermeneutical Patriotism: Interpretation and Culture in Antebellum America," Ph.D. diss., Northwestern University, 1985, pp. 75–81.

71. John Taylor, *An Inquiry into the Principles and Policies of the Government of the United States* (1814), ed. Loren Baritz (Indianapolis: Bobbs-Merrill, 1969), p. 115. John Adams's *Defence of the Constitutions of Government of the*

United States of America was first published in London by W. Strahan in 1787 and 1788.

72. Taylor's understanding of the political grounding of harmony and conflict is discussed in Harp, "Taylor, Calhoun, and the Decline," pp. 109–20.

73. John Adams, "Letters to John Taylor of Caroline, Virginia, in Reply to His Strictures on Some Parts of the *Defence of the American Constitutions*," in *The Works of John Adams,* ed. Charles Francis Adams (Boston: Little, Brown, 1851), 6:443–552. On the Adams-Taylor correspondence see Joseph J. Ellis, *Passionate Sage: The Character and Legacy of John Adams* (New York: Norton, 1993), pp. 145–73.

74. John Adams, "Letters to John Taylor," pp. 451–52, 455–56. Relevant works on Adams include Ellis, *Passionate Sage;* Giuseppe Butta, "Republicanism and Individualism in John Adams," *Studia Nordamericana* 4 (1987): 137–55; Bruce Miroff, "John Adams: Merit, Fame, and Political Leadership," *Journal of Politics* 48 (1986): 116.

75. John Adams, "Letters to John Taylor," p. 496.

76. Ibid., pp. 455, 465, 496, 509; Adams, *Works,* 10:94–96, 413.

77. John Taylor, *Construction Construed,* p. 209. On Taylor's concept of 'labour' see Shalhope, *John Taylor of Caroline,* pp. 133–35.

78. On the variety and implications of Taylor's uses of the term 'capitalist', see Conkin, *Prophets of Prosperity,* pp. 60–61. How to interpret Taylor's and other Jeffersonians' attitudes toward capitalism has been a matter of some disagreement. Steven Watts, in *The Republic Reborn: War and the Making of Liberal America, 1790–1820* (Baltimore: Johns Hopkins University Press, 1987), p. 16, sees Taylor as a critic of liberal capitalism. James Oakes, in "From Republicanism to Liberalism: Ideological Change and the Crisis of the Old South," *American Quarterly* 37 (1985): 554, finds "hostility to capitalism" in the assumptions and legacy of Jeffersonian republicanism. Joseph R. Stromberg, however, in "Country Ideology, Republicanism, and Libertarianism: The Thought of John Taylor of Caroline," *Journal of Libertarian Studies* 7 (1982): 39, 41–44, interprets Taylor's attacks on subsidized capital as an endorsement of the free market. Richard Matthews, in *Radical Politics of Thomas Jefferson,* p. 14, argues that the "very terms of the debate . . . procapitalist versus anticapitalist, or procommerce versus anticommerce" fail to do justice to the complexity of Jefferson's economic positions. I find much merit in Matthews's position. See also Jeffrey Isaac, "Republicanism versus Liberalism? A Reconsideration," *HOPE* 9 (1988): 349–77.

79. On the use of this "common" dichotomy among the poor and the middling classes, see Ruth Bogin, "Petitioning and the New Moral Economy of Post-Revolutionary America," *WMQ* 45 (1988): 391–425.

80. John Taylor, *Tyranny Unmasked* (Washington, D.C.: Davis and Force, 1822), pp. 214–15.

81. Ibid., p. 132.

82. Thomas Jefferson, introduction to Destutt de Tracy, *A Treatise on Political Economy* (Georgetown, D.C.: Joseph Milligan, 1817), p. vii. Jefferson did part of the translation of this previously unpublished work by the French ideologue de Tracy. The classes in the text are those of Adam Smith and

company. See Gilbert Chinard, *Jefferson et les idéologues* (New York: Arno, 1979).

83. Lee Soltow notes in the records of the first federal direct tax of 1798, Oliver Wolcott's division of the population into nine occupational classes (*Distribution of Wealth and Income in the United States in 1798* [Pittsburgh: University of Pittsburgh Press, 1989], p. 96).

84. Along with John Taylor's Jeffersonian analysis, see William Duane on the "farmers and industrious classes" and the "simple, honest, laboring classes of men" in *Politics for American Farmers* (Washington, D.C.: R. C. Weightman, 1807), pp. 15, 17, 81, 94. Additional usages of 'class' as a general term and as a signifier for specific socioeconomic groupings by national political figures such as George Washington, John Adams, and James Madison can be found in James Richardson, ed., *A Compilation of the Messages and Papers of the Presidents, 1789–1908* (Washington, D.C.: Bureau of National Literature and Art, 1909), 1:85, 180, 299, 524. See also the references to occupation/wealth classes and interests in Thomas Hart Benton, *Abridgement of the Debates of Congress, from 1789 to 1856* (New York: D. Appleton, 1857), 1:27, 31, 40, 57, 72, 181, 187, 188, 226, 272, 306, 555, 2:180–81, 3:338, 4:541, 549, 6:636–37, 7:280. Other political uses directed to large audiences can be found in Noble Cunningham, ed., *Circular Letters of Congressmen to Their Constituents, 1789–1829* (Chapel Hill: University of North Carolina Press, 1978), 1:309, 2:635, 778, 823, 3:1033, 1076, 1110, 1244, 1549; and Philip Foner, ed., *The Democratic-Republican Societies, 1790–1800: A Documentary Sourcebook* (Westport, Conn.: Greenwood, 1976), pp. 77, 100, 108, 121, 145, 162, 163, 172.

Chapter 3

1. "Thomas Cooper's *Lectures on the Elements of Political Economy,*" *North American Review* 25 (1827): 415.

2. The larger intellectual contexts of this debate are discussed in Hirschman, "Rival Interpretations of Market Society."

3. On the roles played by political economists in antebellum cultural and political life, see William J. Barber, ed., *Breaking the Academic Mould: Economists and American Higher Learning in the Nineteenth Century* (Middletown, Conn.: Wesleyan University Press, 1988); Conkin, *Prophets of Prosperity;* Joseph Dorfman, *The Economic Mind in American Civilization* (1946–49; reprint, New York: A. M. Kelley, 1966); Gary W. Hull, "The Prospect for Man in Early American Economic Thought, 1800–1850," Ph.D. diss., University of Maryland, 1969; Allen Kaufman, *Capitalism, Slavery, and Republican Values: Antebellum Political Economists* (Austin: University of Texas Press, 1982); João F. Normano, *The Spirit of American Economics* (New York: John Day, 1943); Michael J. L. O'Connor, *Origins of Academic Economics in the United States* (New York: Columbia University Press, 1944). See also Daniel Horowitz, "Historians and Economists: Perspectives on the Development of American Economic Thought," *HOPE* 6 (1974): 454–62.

On antebellum political science see Bernard Crick, *The American Science of Politics: Its Origins and Condition* (Berkeley and Los Angeles: University of California Press, 1959); Anna Haddow, *Political Science in American Colleges and Universities, 1636–1900* (New York: Appleton-Century, 1939); Hanson, *Democratic Imagination in America;* Daniel Rodgers, *Contested Truths: Keywords in American Politics since Independence* (New York: Basic Books, 1987); Jon Roper, *Democracy and Its Critics: Anglo-American Democratic Thought in the Nineteenth Century* (London: Unwin Hyman, 1989); Louis Hartz, *The Necessity of Choice: Nineteenth Century Political Thought* (London: Transaction, 1990); Joseph Dorfman and Rexford G. Tugwell, *Early American Policy: Six Columbia Contributors* (New York: Columbia University Press, 1960).

4. The phenomenon of the 'naturalization' of a concept is discussed by the sociolinguist Roger Fowler in *Linguistic Criticism,* pp. 17–19. On the interaction of naturalization, social and cultural power, and systems of classification, see Bourdieu, *Distinction,* pp. 466–85; Bourdieu, *Language and Symbolic Power;* John B. Thompson, *Studies in the Theory of Ideology,* pp. 121–26.

5. The importance of the reviews as vehicles for political and intellectual change is discussed in Biancamaria Fontana, *Rethinking the Politics of Commercial Society: The Edinburgh Review, 1802–1832* (Cambridge: Cambridge University Press, 1985).

6. In their studies of political economy in nineteenth-century Britain, both Phyllis Deane and David P. O'Brien have emphasized the particular institutional configurations that contributed to the significant influence of the political economists on the making of public policy. See Deane, *Evolution of Economic Ideas,* pp. 73–75; O'Brien, *Classical Economists,* pp. 12–16. See also Frank Whitson Fetter, *The Economist in Parliament, 1780–1868* (Durham, N.C.: Duke University Press, 1980); Donald Winch, "The Emergence of Economics as a Science, 1750–1870," in *The Fontana Economic History of Europe,* ed. Carlo Cipolla, vol. 3, *The Industrial Revolution* (London: Fontana, 1973), pp. 529–47; M. Norton Wise and Crosbie Smith, "Work and Waste: Political Economy and Natural Philosophy in Nineteenth Century Britain," *History of Science* 27 (1989): 263–301, 391–449; 28 (1990): 221–61; Hiram Caton, *Politics of Progress,* pp. 523–30.

On political economists on the Continent see Alain Alcouffe, "The Institutionalization of Political Economy in French Universities, 1819–1896" *HOPE* 21 (1989): 313–44; Keith Tribe, *Governing the Economy: The Reformation of German Economic Discourse, 1750–1840* (Cambridge: Cambridge University Press, 1988).

7. Edward Everett, "Louis Say's *Political Economy,*" *North American Review* 17 (1823): 425. The complex relationships between the national and international contexts of American cultural and intellectual life are discussed by David Hollinger, *In the American Province* (Bloomington: Indiana University Press, 1986). On the institutional settings of these antebellum Americans see Barber, *Breaking the Academic Mould;* Conkin, *Prophets of Prosperity;* Donald Meyer, *The Instructed Conscience: The Shaping of the American National Ethic* (Philadelphia: University of Pennsylvania Press, 1972), pp. 99–107; Wilson Smith, *Professors and Public Ethics: Studies of Northern Moral Philosophers before the Civil War* (Ithaca, N.Y.: Cornell University Press, 1956).

The larger questions of the composition of the reading audiences for these writers are considered in Richard D. Brown, *Knowledge Is Power,* pp. 131–59,

218–44; Ronald J. Zboray, "Antebellum Reading and the Ironies of Technological Innovation," in *Reading in America,* ed. Davidson, pp. 180–200; Zboray, *A Fictive People: Antebellum Reading Development and the American Reading Public* (New York: Oxford University Press, 1993); Jon P. Klancher, *The Making of English Reading Audiences, 1790–1832* (Madison: University of Wisconsin Press, 1987).

8. On the attitudes of American intellectuals toward European authorities and sources in the moral and social sciences, see Elizabeth Flower and Murray G. Murphey, *A History of Philosophy in America* (New York: G. P. Putnam's Sons, 1977), 1:343–53.

9. Boss, *Theories of Surplus and Transfer,* esp. pp. 63–88. See also Fyodor I. Kushnirsky and William J. Smith, "Productive and Unproductive Labour: Smith, Marx, and the Soviets," in *Perspectives on the History of Economic Thought,* ed. Donald A. Walker (Aldershot, England: Edward Elgar, 1989), 1:82–103.

10. Jean-Baptiste Say, *A Catechism of Political Economy* (1821; reprint, New York: A. M. Kelley, 1967), pp. 41–43, 31; Say, *Treatise on Political Economy* (Boston: Well and Lilly, 1821). On Say's notion of 'utility' see Boss, *Theories of Surplus and Transfer,* pp. 67–72. On his role as an ideologue and as a liberal see Alcouffe, "Institutionalization of Political Economy"; Thomas E. Kaiser, "Politics and Political Economy in the Thought of the Ideologues," *HOPE* 12 (1980): 141–60; Mark Weinburg, "The Social Analysis of Three Early Nineteenth Century French Liberals: Say, Comte, and Dunoyer," *Journal of Libertarian Studies* 2 (1978): 45–63. On the extensive influence and use of Smith's and Say's works, see O'Connor, *Origins of Academic Economics,* pp. 113–24, 224.

11. Daniel Raymond, *Thoughts on Political Economy* (Baltimore: F. Lucas, 1820), pp. 73–74 (hereafter pages given in text). The final edition of 1840 was entitled *The Elements of Constitutional Law and Political Economy.* On the history of the text and its reception see O'Connor, *Origins of Academic Economics,* pp. 32–36.

Raymond's career and writings are discussed in Frank Petrella, "Daniel Raymond, Adam Smith, and the Classical Growth Theory: An Inquiry into the Nature and Causes of the Wealth of America," *HOPE* 19 (1987): 239–59; Conkin, *Prophets of Prosperity,* pp. 77–107; Dorfman, *Economic Mind,* 2:566–74; Hull, "Prospect for Man," pp. 47–87; Kaufman, *Capitalism, Slavery, and Republican Values,* pp. 37–81.

12. These conventional understandings of language are considered in Andresen, *Linguistics in America,* pp. 22–67; James Berlin, *Writing Instruction in Nineteenth Century American Colleges* (Carbondale: Southern Illinois University Press, 1984). The relations between language and political economy in antebellum America are examined by Paul Royster, "Political Economy in American Literature: The Rhetoric of Emerson and Melville," Ph.D. diss., Columbia University, 1984, pp. 25–51. See also Kurt Heinzelman, *The Economics of the Imagination* (Amherst: University of Massachusetts Press, 1980), esp. pp. 70–109; Paul Friedrich, "Language, Ideology, and Political Economy," *American Anthropologist* 91 (1989): 295–314; Judith Irvine-Brandeis, "When Talk Isn't Cheap: Language and Political Economy," *American Ethnologist* 16 (1989): 248–66.

13. The juxtaposition of a popular precapitalist or anticapitalist "moral economy" to political economy as part and process of the "market revolution" has become an important rhetorical device in neo-Progressive historiography. See, for example, Bogin, "Petitioning and the New Moral Economy"; Schultz, "Thoughts among the People"; Harry Watson, *Liberty and Power: The Politics of Jacksonian America* (New York: Hill and Wang, 1990). This juxtaposition derives, in part, from the work of E. P. Thompson. See his *Making of the English Working Class* (New York: Knopf, 1966). But the tendency to contrast too sharply a traditional moral economy with liberal political economy has been criticized by Istvan Hont and Michael Ignatieff, "Needs and Justice in the Wealth of Nations," in *Wealth and Virtue,* ed. Hont and Ignatieff, p. 15. Their criticism can be applied to American sources and scholarship as well.

14. Raymond's criticism of primogeniture and entail was in keeping with those of Adam Smith and the "classical" political economists. See William L. Miller, "Primogeniture, Entails, and Endowments in English Classical Economics," *HOPE* 12 (1980): 558–81.

15. Daniel Raymond, *The Missouri Question* (Baltimore: Schaeffer and Maund, 1819). Raymond's critique of slavery is discussed in James R. Gibson, *Americans versus Malthus,* pp. 137–41; Hull, "Prospect for Man," pp. 49–50.

16. The relations between the political economies of Raymond and Smith are discussed in Petrella, "Daniel Raymond, Adam Smith." As Petrella demonstrates, scholarly depictions of Daniel Raymond as a critic of "commercial society" are extremely hard to defend (p. 249).

17. See the unsigned review of *Thoughts on Political Economy, North American Review* 12 (1821): 443–65. The journal, which subsequently moved to a protectionist position, then supported free trade and took exception with Raymond's views on the tariff, as well as his rejection of Smith's classifications. See also David Stirrat's simplification of Raymond's *Thoughts* for a more general audience, *A Treatise on Political Economy* (Baltimore: D. Stirrat, 1824).

18. On Mathew Carey as a political economist and publisher see James Green, *Mathew Carey: Publisher and Patriot* (Philadelphia: Library Co. of Philadelphia, 1985); James N. Green, "Mathew Carey," in *American Magazine Journalists,* ed. Riley, pp. 50–66; Edward C. Carter, "The Birth of a Political Economist: Mathew Carey and the Re-charter Fight of 1810–1811," *Pennsylvania History* 33 (1966): 274–88; James R. Gibson, *Americans versus Malthus,* pp. 263–319; Dorfman, *Economic Mind,* 2:576–77, 603–7; Kenneth W. Rowe, "Mathew Carey: A Study in American Economic Development," Ph.D. diss., Johns Hopkins University, 1932. See also Martin J. Burke, "The Politics and Poetics of Nationalist Historiography: Mathew Carey and the *Vindiciae Hibernicae,*" in *The Politics of Literature and the Literature of Politics,* ed. Joep Leerssen (Amsterdam: Rodopi, 1994).

19. Isaac C. Bates, "Extract from an Address Delivered to the Hampshire, Franklin, and Hampden Agricultural Society . . . on October 10, 1823," *Political Economist,* no. 4 (1824): 61. On Bates see *Lamb's Biographical Dictionary of the United States* (Boston: James H. Lamb, 1900), 1:222–23.

20. Another critical and widely circulated source for protectionist arguments was the *Weekly Register* of Hezekiah Niles. It is also a valuable source for evidence of the widespread use of the term 'class' with the modifiers

'working', 'laboring', 'middle', 'productive', 'unproductive', 'consuming', 'poorest', etc., in dozens of letters, essays, petitions, addresses, memorials, lectures, speeches, reports, and editorials printed or reprinted from around the country. See, for example, "Home Market and Internal Wealth," 19 October 1816, p. 268; "Domestic Manufactures," 25 January 1817, p. 368; "Statesmen and Politicians: Political Economy, No. 1," 7 June 1817, p. 226; "Political Economy, No. 3," 5 July 1817, p. 291; "National Interests," 17 April 1819, p. 135; "Our Manufactories," 19 June 1819, p. 274; "Want of Employment," 24 July 1819, p. 356; "Labor: Its Products and Checks," 7 August 1819, pp. 385–87; "National Interests," 14 August 1819, pp. 410–13; "National Interests," 9 October 1819, p. 91; "Agriculture versus Manufactures," 22 January 1820, p. 354; "Desultory Remarks," 16 December 1820, pp. 40–42; "Application of Principles," 31 March 1821, pp. 65–66; "Desultory Remarks," 28 April 1821, pp. 135–36; "Things as They Are," 9 June 1821, p. 227; "Agriculture versus Manufactures: A Letter by John Taylor of Caroline," 21 July 1821, pp. 332–34; "Product of Labor and Value of Human Life," 6 April 1822, pp. 83–87; "National Affairs," 23 November 1822, p. 185; "Editorial Remarks," 19 March 1825, p. 33; "Miscellaneous," 7 May 1825, p. 145; "Wages in Factories," 8 October 1825, p. 83; "Commerce," 14 January 1826, p. 306; "Labor, Subsistence, and Scientific Power," 23 September 1826, pp. 50–51; "Labor, Subsistence, Etc.," 21 October 1826, p. 114; "The Agriculture of the United States," 24 March 1827, p. 55; "A Snug Manufacturing Village," 19 May 1827, p. 194; "Agriculture and Manufactures—and Commerce," 23 February 1828, pp. 431–33; "Manufactures," 16 May 1829, p. 177; "Pressure on the Manufacturers," 27 June 1829, pp. 281–82; "Great Britain," 11 July 1829, p. 316; "Lectures on the Restrictive System," 17 October 1829, p. 114; "The Working Men," 22 May 1830, p. 231; "To the Friends of the American System," 19 March 1831, pp. 45–46; "Politics for Working Men," 9 July 1831, pp. 321–22; "Wages," 14 January 1832, pp. 353–54.

Niles' Weekly Register was unique among antebellum periodicals in that it was intended for a national, not a local, readership; it was nonpartisan; and it carried no advertising. The *Weekly Register* was a repository for all important documents in circulation; it was intended to be the nation's journal of record from 1811 through the 1840s. It is by far the best repository of the language, both technical and ordinary, of the era. On Niles see Ronald T. Farrar, "Hezekiah Niles," in *American Newspaper Journalists,* ed. Ashley, pp. 325–29; Jeffrey B. Morris, "'No Other Herald': Niles' Register and the Supreme Court," *Yearbook of the Supreme Court Historical Society* (1978): 51–60; Richard G. Stone, *Hezekiah Niles as an Economist* (Baltimore: Johns Hopkins University Press, 1933); James R. Gibson, *Americans versus Malthus,* pp. 292–305.

21. On John McVickar see Franek Rozwadowski, "From Recitation Room to Research Seminar: Political Economy at Columbia University," in *Breaking the Academic Mould,* ed. Barber, pp. 169–85; Dorfman and Tugwell, *Early American Policy,* pp. 99–154; Conkin, *Prophets of Prosperity,* pp. 111–15; Meyer, *Instructed Conscience,* p. 105; Wilson Smith, *Professors and Public Ethics,* pp. 10, 22; Haddow, *Political Science,* pp. 52–53. In keeping with the denominational profile of the college, McVickar was an Episcopal minister. Among

the many courses he taught were Intellectual Philosophy and Evidences of Christianity.

22. The phrase 'instruct the conscience' is Donald Meyer's. See *Instructed Conscience,* pp. xi–xiv. The phrase 'professors of virtue' is Richard Sher's. See Sher, "Professors of Virtue: The Social History of the Edinburgh Moral Philosophy Chair in the Eighteenth Century," in *Studies in the Philosophy of the Scottish Enlightenment,* ed. M. A. Stewart (Oxford: Clarendon Press, 1990), pp. 87–126.

23. John McVickar, *Outlines of Political Economy* (New York: Wilder and Campbell, 1825), pp. 186, 162, 50; McVickar, *First Lessons in Political Economy* (Boston: H. Gray, 1835). On McVickar's career see Joseph Dorfman's introduction, "On the Naturalization of Ricardian Economics in the United States," to the reprinted *Outlines* (New York: A. M. Kelley, 1966); Dorfman and Tugwell, *Early American Policy,* pp. 131–34; Rozwadowski, "From Recitation Room to Research Seminar," pp. 180–81; O'Connor, *Origins of Academic Economics,* pp. 135–39.

24. John Ramsay McCulloch in McVickar, *Outlines of Political Economy,* p. 50. Discussions of the theories and policies of the classical economists McCulloch and Ricardo can be found in Frank Fetter, "The Rise and Decline of Ricardian Economics" *HOPE* 1 (1969): 67–84; T. W. Hutchison, *On Revolutions and Progress in Economic Knowledge* (Cambridge: Cambridge University Press, 1978), pp. 40–45; Rajani Kanth, *Political Economy and Laissez-Faire: Economics and Ideology in the Ricardian Era* (Totowa, N.J.: Rowman and Littlefield, 1986); David P. O'Brien, *Classical Economists,* pp. 90–146; Giancarlo de Vivo, "Ricardo and His Disciples: Orthodoxy and Socialism," *History of European Ideas* 9 (1988): 183–89.

25. Hutchison, *Revolutions and Progress,* pp. 40–41, 230–31. See also de Vivo, "Ricardo and His Disciples"; William D. Grampp, "Classical Economy and Its Moral Critics," *HOPE* 5 (1973): 359–78.

26. McVickar, *Outlines of Political Economy,* pp. 161–64, 166 n, 180. On Ricardo's and McCulloch's categories and their consequences, see Robert Chernomas, "Productive and Unproductive Labor and the Rate of Profit in Malthus, Ricardo, and Marx," *Journal of the History of Economic Thought,* 12 (1990): 81–95; Boss, *Theories of Surplus and Transfer,* pp. 76–78, 81–82, 87–90, 95.

27. McVickar, *Outlines of Political Economy,* p. 178.

28. McVickar's axiomatic style of teaching and reasoning is discussed in Dorfman and Tugwell, *Early American Policy,* p. 116. On the "axiological" features of moral philosophy see Meyer, *Instructed Conscience,* pp. xii, 23–31. The argument that Ricardian political economy was not a form of apologetics but of advocacy for change is made by Hutchison, *Revolutions and Progress,* pp. 230–31; Kanth, *Political Economy and Laissez-Faire,* pp. 178–83.

29. John McVickar, *Hints on Banking: In a Letter to a Gentleman in Albany* (New York: Vanderpool and Cole, 1827). See Dorfman and Tugwell, *Early American Policy,* p. 134.

30. McVickar dedicated *Outlines of Political Economy* to the New York landowner James Wadsworth, who had first suggested that he produce a textbook.

He wrote the *Hints on Banking* at the behest of Isaac Bronson, a New York banking reformer and financier. See Rozwadowski, "From Recitation Room to Research Seminar," p. 179.

31. Thomas Cooper, *Lectures on the Elements of Political Economy* (Columbia, S.C.: D. E. Sweeny, 1826), p. 26. The scholarship on Cooper's careers in the nineteenth century includes Michael D. Bordo and William H. Phillips, "The Development of Political Economy at South Carolina College," in *Breaking the Academic Mould,* ed. Barber, pp. 44–58; Stephen Newman, "Thomas Cooper, 1759–1839: The Political Odyssey of a Bourgeois Ideologue," *Southern Studies* 24 (1985): 295–305; Whitten, "Economic Ideas of Thomas Cooper," pp. 44–82; Conkin, *Prophets of Prosperity,* pp. 141–52; Hull, "Prospect for Man," pp. 199–238; Kaufman, *Capitalism, Slavery, and Republican Values,* pp. 121–26; Malone, *Public Life of Thomas Cooper,* pp. 303–5; O'Connor, *Origins of Academic Economics,* pp. 48–56.

Cooper's place in the intellectual and political life of the antebellum South is discussed in Sarah A. Payne, *The Contribution of Southern Political Economists to the Development of American Political Philosophy* (New York: American Press, 1966), pp. 92–94; Michael O'Brien, ed., *All Clever Men, Who Make Their Way: Critical Discourse in the Old South* (Fayetteville: University of Arkansas Press, 1982), pp. 1–25.

32. On Cooper and slavery see Bordo and Phillips, "Development of Political Economy"; Newman, "Thomas Cooper." During his editorship of the *Emporium of Arts and Sciences* Cooper was in favor of some bounties and duties. In 1823 he authored a pamphlet, *On the Proposed Alteration of the Tariff,* that placed him in the front rank of southern free-trade advocates. Cooper's apparent inconsistency was criticized by Mathew Carey and Hezekiah Niles. See Whitten, "Economic Ideas of Thomas Cooper."

33. Cooper, *Lectures,* pp. 34–35. The importance of these works as sites of conceptual debate, as well as the "vehicles for transmitting information to wider audiences," is discussed by Daniel Horowitz, "Textbook Models of American Economic Growth, 1837–1911," *HOPE* 7 (1975): 227–28.

34. Cooper, *Lectures,* pp. 99–105, 107. The "Poet" is Horace, and the phrase is from the *Epistolarum* 1.2.27: "Nos numerus sumus et fruges consumere nati" (We are the many [the multitude, the common herd] born to eat the earth's fruits). Horace was explaining to his young friend Lollius that they were not like the heroes of the ancient tales but more akin to minor characters and members of the crowd. Lollius should accept his place and train himself in virtue. The phrase was a commonly used learned and literary device.

35. Thomas Cooper, *Lectures on the Elements of Political Economy,* 2nd ed. (London: R. Hunter, 1831), pp. 349–53, 355–57; Cooper, *A Manual of Political Economy* (Washington, D.C.: Duff Green, 1833), pp. 17–18; see also Cooper, "Agrarian and Educational Systems," *Southern Review* 6 (1830): 1–31. His books and pamphlets were widely read on both sides of the Atlantic. See Newman, "Thomas Cooper," p. 302; Whitten, "Economic Ideas of Thomas Cooper," pp. 81–82.

36. Cooper, *Manual of Political Economy,* pp. 29, 37.

37. Cooper, *Lectures,* 2nd ed., pp. 351–53.

38. Ibid., pp. 348–66. On Cooper's policies and politics see Whitten, "Economic Ideas of Thomas Cooper," pp. 46–51; Hull, "Prospect for Man," pp. 208–14, 219–38; O'Connor, *Origins of Academic Economics,* pp. 55–62. The dimensions of Cooper's radicalism are discussed in Newman, "Thomas Cooper," pp. 294–98. Late-eighteenth- and nineteenth-century radical currents are studied in Twomey, "Jacobins and Jeffersonians"; Isaac Kramnick, *Bourgeois Radicalism* (Ithaca, N.Y.: Cornell University Press, 1990). Among these radicals Kramnick numbers Thomas Paine.

39. Cooper, *Lectures,* p. 104.

40. "Political Economy: Rent," review of *Lectures on the Elements of Political Economy* by Thomas Cooper, *Southern Review* 1 (1826): 194.

41. Ibid. See also the review of John Ramsay McCulloch's *Principles of Political Economy, North American Review* 25 (1827): 126, in which the reviewer describes the "three great classes" of landholders, capitalists, and laborers as "a distinction, which, however, is rather formal than substantial." But compare William Jennison's classifications in *An Outline of Political Economy* (Philadelphia: W. Jennison, 1828), pp. 62–63. Here they have substance.

42. On the workingmen's parties see Edward Pessen, *Most Uncommon Jacksonians: The Radical Leaders of the Early Labor Movement* (Albany: State University of New York Press, 1967); Wilentz, *Chants Democratic;* Walter Hugins, *Jacksonian Democracy and the Working Class: A Study of the New York Workingmen's Movement, 1829–1837* (Stanford: Stanford University Press, 1960). The languages of class employed by the Workingmen et alia are discussed in chapter 4.

43. Edward Everett, *A Lecture on the Working Men's Party* (Boston: Gray and Bowen, 1830), pp. 7–8, 21–25. See also his 1838 address, "Accumulation, Property, Capital, and Credit, in *Orations and Speeches on Various Occasions* (Boston: Little, Brown, 1850), pp. 288–312. On Everett see *DAB,* 6:223–26; Ronald F. Reid, *Edward Everett: Unionist Orator* (New York: Greenwood, 1990); Paul A. Varg, *Edward Everett: The Intellectual in the Turmoil of Politics* (Selinsgrove, Pa.: Susquehanna University Press, 1992).

44. James T. Austin, "Classes of American Society," *Christian Examiner* 9 (1830): 252. On Austin see *DAB,* 1:433–34.

45. Emory Washburn, "The Laboring Classes in Europe," *North American Review* 41 (1835): 349. On Washburn see *DAB,* 19:499–500.

46. James H. Lanman, "Social Disorganization," *American Monthly Magazine* 7 (1836): 577–90. On Lanman see *Lamb's Biographical Dictionary,* 4:630.

47. Lanman, "Social Disorganization," pp. 578, 587.

48. Condy Raguet, "Political Economy," *Banner of the Constitution* 2 (1831): 111. On Raguet see Thomas L. Martin, "Neglected Aspects of the Economic Thought and Method of Condy Raguet," *HOPE* 19 (1987): 401–13; James R. Gibson, *Americans versus Malthus,* pp. 278–94; Conkin, *Prophets of Prosperity,* pp. 215–21; Dorfman, *Economic Mind,* 2:602–12; Zalia Camuera, "Condy Raguet: His Life, Work, and Education," Ph.D. diss., University of Pennsylvania, 1988.

49. William Duane, "To the Working Men," *Aurora* 1, no. 2 (1834): 9. On

Duane see William Sloane, "William Duane," in *American Newspaper Journalists,* ed. Ashley, pp. 168–74.

50. Other examples along these lines may be found in *Niles' Weekly Register.* See the editorial "The Working Men," 22 May 1830, pp. 231–32; "Politics for Working Men," 9 July 1831, pp. 321–23. "Mechanic's Association," 23 October 1830, p. 139, cites Daniel Webster's definition of 'working-men', which includes those who work "in the field, the shops of the artificer, the compting-house, or the professions."

While the "harmony of interest" position was a favorite of the Whigs, both they and the Democrats styled themselves the party of the "workingmen." See John Ashworth, *Agrarians and Aristocrats: Party Political Ideology in the United States, 1837–1856* (London: Royal Historical Society, 1983); Jean H. Baker, "From Belief into Culture: Republicanism in the Antebellum North," *American Quarterly* 37 (1985): 532–50; Thomas Brown, *Politics and Statesmanship: Essays on the American Whig Party* (New York: Columbia University Press, 1985); Daniel Walker Howe, *The Political Culture of the American Whigs* (Chicago: University of Chicago Press, 1979); Marvin Meyers, *The Jacksonian Persuasion: Politics and Belief* (Stanford: Stanford University Press, 1957); Edward K. Spann, *Ideals and Politics: New York Intellectuals and Liberal Democracy, 1820–1880* (Albany: State University of New York Press, 1972); Rush Welter, *The Mind of America, 1820–1860* (New York: Columbia University Press, 1975).

51. The issue of what could or could not be said in antebellum American political discourse is discussed in Diggins, *Lost Soul of American Politics,* pp. 105–14. Diggins ably analyzes the problems of class in eighteenth- and nineteenth-century American politics, and raises interesting and provocative questions about the limits of language and of linguistic analyses.

52. Alexander H. Everett, review of *Definitions in Political Economy* by Thomas R. Malthus, *North American Review* 28 (1829): 379. Alexander Everett was the brother of Edward. See *DAB,* 6:222–23.

Chapter 4

1. Historians' use of colligatory concepts is discussed in C. Behan McCullagh, "Colligation and Classification in History," *History and Theory* 18 (1978): 267–84. In a study of politics and language in nineteenth-century England, Gareth Stedman Jones cautions about the use of the category 'industrial revolution' as a phenomenon to which actors responded: "such an approach presupposes the observation of a social fact whose definition was common to contemporaries and later historians" (*Languages of Class,* p. 171). His admonition is applicable to the category 'market revolution' as well. On the scope of these changes see Thomas Cochran, *Frontiers of Change: Early Industrialism in America* (New York: Oxford University Press, 1981); Roger Ransom, "Class and Inequality: Measuring the Impact of Industrial Capitalism in North America," *Historical Methods* 16 (1983): 157–61.

The colligatory term 'market revolution' has become important in the historiography of the late-eighteenth through the mid–nineteenth century, especially in neo-Progressive interpretations of social and political change. See, for example, Bernstein and Wilentz, "Marketing, Commerce, and Capitalism in Rural Massachusetts"; Sean Wilentz, "Society, Politics, and the Market Revolution," in *The New American History,* ed. Eric Foner, pp. 51–72. What the specific economic contours of this revolution were, particularly for artisanal wages and rural commodity prices, is a matter of some debate among economic historians. See Rothenburg, "Markets, Values, and Capitalism," pp. 176–78; Winifred B. Rothenburg, "The Emergence of Farm Labor Markets and the Transformation of the Rural Economy: Massachusetts, 1750–1855," *JEH* 48 (1988): 537–61; Lee Soltow, "Wealth Inequality in the United States in 1798 and 1860," *Review of Economics and Statistics* 46 (1984): 444–51; Donald R. Adams, "Prices and Wages in Antebellum America: The West Virginia Experience," *JEH* 52 (1992): 206–16; Robert A. Margo and Georgia C. Villaflor, "The Growth of Wages in Antebellum America: New Evidence," *JEH* 47 (1987): 873–97. The neo-Progressive presumption that the forces of the 'market' and of 'community' were in conflict is questioned by John Majewski, Christopher Baer, and Daniel B. Klein, "Responding to Relative Decline: The Plank Road Boom of Antebellum New York," *JEH* 53 (1993): 106–20.

2. The international context of these interpretations is examined in Hirschman, "Rival Interpretations of Market Society."

3. The various uses of the terms 'social science' and 'science of society' by early nineteenth-century radicals and reformers are discussed in Fred R. Shapiro, "A Note on the Term 'Social Science'," *Journal of the History of Behavioral Sciences* 20 (1984): 20–22; Gregory Claeys, "'Individualism', 'Socialism', and 'Social Science': Further Notes on a Process of Conceptual Formation, 1800–1850," *JHI* 47 (1986): 81–93.

4. On social conflicts and contests over classification see Klancher, *Making of English Reading Audiences,* pp. 7–8, 25–28; Bourdieu, *Distinction.*

5. On Maclure, Owen, and New Harmony see Arthur Bestor, *Backwoods Utopias: The Sectarian Origins and the Owenite Phase of Communitarian Socialism in America, 1666–1829,* 2nd ed. (Philadelphia: University of Pennsylvania Press, 1970), pp. 146–59, 253–71; Roger D. Branigan, "Robert Owen's New Harmony: An American Heritage," in *Robert Owen's American Legacy,* ed. Donald E. Pitzer (Indianapolis: Indiana Historical Society, 1972), pp. 14–24; Donald F. Carmony and Josephine M. Elliott, "New Harmony, Indiana: Robert Owen's Seedbed for Utopia," *Indiana Magazine of History* 76 (1980): 161–261; Oakley Johnson, *Robert Owen in the United States* (New York: Humanities Press, 1970), pp. 1–20; David Harris, *Socialist Origins in the United States: American Forerunners of Marx, 1817–1832* (Assen, The Netherlands: Van Gorcum, 1966), pp. 54–81; John F. C. Harrison, *Quest for the New Moral World: Robert Owen and the Owenites in Britain and America* (New York; Scribner's, 1969), pp. 36–41; Claeys, *Citizens and Saints.* On Maclure's career in general see J. Percy Moore, "William Maclure, Scientist and Humanitarian," *Proceedings of the American Philosophical Society* 91 (1947): 234–49; Dennis R. Dean, "New Light on William Maclure," *Annals of Science* 46 (1989): 549–74; Simon Baatz, "Philadelphia Patronage: The Institutional Structure of Natural History in the New Republic," *Journal of the Early Republic* 8 (1988): 111–38; Charlotte Porter, *The Eagle's Nest: Natural History and American Ideas, 1812–1842* (University: University of Alabama Press, 1986).

6. William Maclure, *Opinions on Various Subjects: Dedicated to the Industrious Producers,* 3 vols. (1831; reprint, New York: A. M. Kelley, 1971); Maclure, "Division of Society," in *Opinions,* 2:442. All Maclure works below appear in *Opinions.*

7. Maclure, "Division of Society," 2:442; Maclure, "On the Effects of Representative Government," 1:1; Maclure, "Code Napoleon: Origins of the Working Men's Party," 2:50; Maclure, "Commerce, Fleets, and Armies," 1: 357–58; Maclure, "Misconstruction of the Meaning of Political Economy," 2:390–91; Maclure, "Systems of Ricardo and Malthus," 2:491–92; Maclure, "Interests of the Working Men," 2:3–4. Along with the work of Adam Smith, Maclure was favorably impressed by the writings of Turgot ("Commerce, Fleets, and Armies," 1:357–58).

8. Maclure, "Effects of Representative Government," 1:1; Maclure, "Producers and Consumers," 2:19. As was the case for many who participated in this tradition, Maclure was not consistent in his evaluation of the merchants. In "Producers and Consumers" he placed them among the consumers, while in "Producers and Non-producers" (2:363) he considered merchants to be engaged in the "useful and mechanic arts."

9. Maclure, "Money Obtained by Non-Producers under False Pretences," 1:126–27; Maclure, "Producers and Non-Producers," 2:362–63.

10. Maclure, "Effects of Representative Government," 1:1–2; Maclure, "Producers and Consumers," 2:19–21; Maclure, "Interests of the Working Men," 2:3–4; Maclure, "Trades Unions," 2:414.

11. Maclure, "Effects of Representative Government," 1:2–3. Of the two nations, Maclure felt that the French had a more favorable distribution of property and a preferable system of direct taxation.

12. Ibid., p. 3. In the course of his travels in Europe, Maclure spent an extended period in Stockholm.

13. Maclure, "Code Napoleon," 2:50; Maclure, "Trades Unions," 2:411–13; Maclure, "Interests of the Working Men," 2:3–6; Maclure, "The Strong Propensity of Nature to Equalize Property," 1:32–33.

14. Maclure, "Code Napoleon," 2:50; John Gray, *A Lecture on Human Happiness* (1825; reprint, London: London School of Economics, 1931). On the relationship between John Gray and Adam Smith see J. E. King, "Utopian or Scientific: A Reconsideration of the Ricardian Socialists," *HOPE* 15 (1983): 345–73.

15. Maclure, "Effects of Representative Government," 1:4. On Maclure's educational schemes, in particular his support of Pestalozzian methods and his preference for such "useful" subjects as mathematics and the natural sciences, see Arthur Bestor, ed., *Education and Reform at New Harmony: Correspondence of William Maclure and Marie Duclos Fretageot, 1820–1833* (Indianapolis: Indiana Historical Society, 1948); Paul Bernard, "Irreconcilable Opinions: The Social and Educational Theories of Robert Owen and William Maclure," *Journal of the Early Republic* 8 (1988): 21–44; David Harris, *Socialist Origins,* pp. 66–81; John F. C. Harrison, *Quest for the New Moral World,* pp. 38–40; Porter, *Eagle's Nest,* pp. 56–57, 93–94, 101–3.

16. Maclure, "Strong Propensity of Nature," 1:32.

17. Maclure, "Trades Unions," 2:414; Maclure, "Effects of Representative Government," 1:1; Maclure, "Interests of the Working Men," 2:4–6. Maclure's ideal model was an egalitarian, democratic New England township transposed to the agricultural expanses of the Mississippi valley. See Bestor, *Backwoods Utopias,* p. 18; David Harris, *Socialist Origins,* pp. 80–81. On the goals of the Owenites see John F. C. Harrison, "Owenite Communitarianism in Britain and America," *Communal Societies* 4 (1984): 244; Anthony F. C. Wallace, *Rockdale: The Growth of an American Village in the Early Industrial Revolution* (New York: Norton, 1980), pp. 263–69, 280–84.

18. Frances Wright D'Arusmont, "On the Existing Evils, and Their Remedy," in *A Course of Popular Lectures* (New York: Free Enquirer, 1829), pp. 150–51; Wright D'Arusmont, "Address to Young Mechanics," pp. 3, 4, 6, in *A Course of Popular Lectures,* 4th ed. (New York: Free Enquirer, 1831). On Wright see Celia M. Eckhardt, *Fanny Wright: Rebel in America* (Cambridge: Harvard University Press, 1984); Alice J. G. Perkins and Theresa Wolfson, *Frances Wright, Free Enquirer: The Study of a Temperament* (Philadelphia: Porcupine, 1972); Eva C. Topping, "Fanny Wright: Petticoat Lecturer," *Cincinnati Historical Society Bulletin* 36 (1978): 43–56; Earl Conn, "Frances Wright," in *American Magazine Journalists,* ed. Riley, pp. 357–62; Carol Kolmerten, *Women in Utopia: The Ideology of Gender in the American Owenite Communities* (Bloomington: Indiana University Press, 1990); Barbara Taylor, *Eve and the New Jerusalem: Socialism and Feminism in the Nineteenth Century* (New York: Pantheon, 1983); Leslie Goldstein, "Europe Looks at American Women, 1820–1840," *Social Research* 54 (1987): 519–42.

19. Wright D'Arusmont, "Address to Young Mechanics," pp. 3–4.

20. Ibid., p. 5; Wright D'Arusmont, "Address on the State of the Public Mind and the Measures Which It Calls For," and "Parting Address," both in *Course of Public Lectures,* 4th ed., pp. 11–13, 16.

21. Wright D'Arusmont, "Address to Young Mechanics," pp. 3–4; Wright D'Arusmont, "State of the Public Mind," pp. 10–13, 15.

22. Frances Wright D'Arusmont, "The People at War," *Free Enquirer,* 27 November 1830, p. 39.

23. On the terminology of late-eighteenth- and early-nineteenth-century British radical political discourse, see Patricia Hollis, ed., *Class and Conflict in Nineteenth-Century England, 1815–1860* (London: Routledge and Kegan Paul, 1973), pp. 79–90; Gareth Stedman Jones, *Languages of Class,* pp. 103, 112, 142–43. See also Gertrude Himmelfarb, *The Idea of Poverty: England in the Early Industrial Age* (New York: Knopf, 1984), pp. 231–35. On Robert Owen's emphasis on peaceful social change see John F. C. Harrison, *Quest for the New Moral World,* pp. 80–81.

24. Wright D'Arusmont, "Address to Young Mechanics," pp. 4, 5. On groupings within the New York Workingmen's party, or parties, see Hugins, *Jacksonian Democracy and the Working Class* pp. 12–16; Pessen, *Most Uncommon Jacksonians,* p. 19; Wilentz, *Chants Democratic,* pp. 201–11.

25. Wright D'Arusmont, "Existing Evils," pp. 156, 162–70; Wright D'Arusmont, "Parting Address," pp. 16–18. On Wright's educational ideas see Eckhardt, *Fanny Wright,* pp. 105–96, 203, 206, 217–19; Perkins and Wolfson,

Frances Wright, pp. 250–55. On the place of institutions in Owen's thought see John F. C. Harrison, *Quest for the New Moral World,* pp. 79–80.

On the importance of education see C. K. McFarland and Robert L. Thistlewaite, "Labor Press Demands Equal Education in the Age of Jackson," *Journalism Quarterly* 65 (1988): 600–608.

26. Frances Wright D'Arusmont, "Address III, Delivered at the Opening of the Hall of Science, New York," in *Course of Popular Lectures* (London: James Watson, 1834), pp. 152–53. On the American Owenites' criticisms of social arrangements and proposals for reform, see also the writings of Paul Brown, esp. *The Radical and Advocate of Equality* (Albany: Stone and Munsell, 1834). Brown, too, stressed the centrality of educational reform, but unlike either Maclure or Wright he followed the logic of the communitarian dimensions of Owen's ideas and insisted on the complete community of property.

27. Langton Byllesby, *Observations on the Sources and Effects of Unequal Wealth* (1826; reprint, New York: Russell and Russell, 1961), pp. 22–28. On Byllesby see Conkin, *Prophets of Prosperity,* pp. 234–36; Dorfman, *Economic Mind,* 2: 638–41; David Harris, *Socialist Origins,* pp. 34–53. See also Joseph Dorfman's introduction, "L. Byllesby and His Plan for Economic Reconstruction," in Byllesby, *Unequal Wealth,* pp. 5–17.

28. Byllesby, *Unequal Wealth,* pp. 22, 34–42, 53–58, 74–80, 120–24.

29. Ibid., pp. 60–63, 64–67, 102, 126–27.

30. Ibid., pp. 102–4, 136–57, 157–66, 169–95, 25.

31. Ibid., pp. 102–5, 155–157. Just how radical Byllesby's text was has been a matter of some scholarly disagreement. Compare the analysis of *Unequal Wealth* as a "stinging diatribe against capitalist development," offered by Wilentz (in *Chants Democratic,* pp. 164–67), to Dorfman's remarks about Byllesby's ability to "combine business promotion with a radical idiom," and Dorfman's characterization of Byllesby's "associations" as foreshadowings of the modern corporation (*Economic Mind,* 2:641; introduction to Byllesby, *Unequal Wealth,* pp. 16–17). Friedrich Lenger has noted that, while "producers' cooperatives were viewed as the means to end the dependency of self-employed artisans on parasitic middlemen," they were "by no means part of far-reaching early socialist schemes" ("Beyond Exceptionalism: Notes on the Artisanal Phase of the Labour Movement in France, England, Germany, and the United States," *International Review of Social History* 36 [1991]: 18). Lenger's comments on cooperatives are useful in contextualizing the "radicalism" of Byllesby and company.

32. Thomas Skidmore, *The Rights of Man to Property!* (New York: A. Ming, 1829), p. 1. Skidmore cites, as does Byllesby, Thomas Jefferson but is critical of his failure to specify 'property' in the Declaration of Independence (pp. 58–64).

On Skidmore see Mark Lause's introduction and annotation of Amos Gilbert, *A Sketch of the Life of Thomas Skidmore* (Chicago: Kerr, 1984); Conkin, *Prophets of Prosperity,* pp. 237–39; Dorfman, *Economic Mind,* 2:641–45; David Harris, *Socialist Origins,* pp. 91–139; Pessen, *Most Uncommon Jacksonians,* pp. 58–66, 176–78. See also the analysis of Skidmore by Wilentz in *Chants Demo-*

cratic, pp. 182–88, and compare it to that of Dorfman, "The Jackson Wage-Earner Thesis," in the appendix to *Economic Mind,* vol. 2.

My understanding of Skidmore has benefited from conversations with Professor Kiril Andersen, who translated *Rights of Man to Property!* into Russian.

33. Michael Levy has described Skidmore's proposals as a form of radical, "confiscatory" liberalism rather than as a form of early socialism, since they continue to presume the presence of a capitalist market ("Liberal Equality and Inherited Wealth," *Political Theory* 11 [1983]: 545–64). See also John W. Seaman, "Thomas Paine: Ransom, Civil Peace, and the Natural Right to Welfare," *Political Theory* 16 (1988): 120–42.

34. Skidmore, *Rights of Man to Property!* pp. 146, 159–63, 276, 342, 369. On the intersection between the discourses of class and gender, see Carol Lasser, "Gender, Ideology, and Class in the Early Republic," *Journal of the Early Republic* 10 (1990): 331–37.

35. Skidmore, *Rights of Man to Property!* pp. 7, 23–28, 58–64, 369, 384–85. On the criticism of Skidmore see, for example, Thomas Cooper, "Agrarian and Educational Systems," review of *Rights of Man to Property!* by Skidmore, *Observations on the Sources and Effects of Unequal Wealth* by Byllesby, and *Popular Political Economy* by Thomas Hodgskin, *Southern Review* 6 (1830): 1–31. On "agrarian" thought in antebellum America see Conkin, *Prophets of Prosperity,* pp. 222–58.

36. Skidmore, *Rights of Man to Property!* pp. 1, 10–11; Skidmore, "Report of the Committee of Fifty," *Working Man's Advocate,* 31 October 1829, p. 1. On Skidmore and the Workingmen's party see Pessen, *Most Uncommon Jacksonians,* pp. 58–64; Wilentz, *Chants Democratic,* pp. 191–203.

37. George Henry Evans, "Prospectus," *Working Man's Advocate,* 31 October 1829, p. 3. On the programs of the parties see Pessen, *Most Uncommon Jacksonians,* pp. 20–23; Ronald P. Formisano, *The Transformation of Political Culture: Massachusetts Parties, 1790s–1840s* (New York: Oxford University Press, 1983), pp. 222–44; Dirk Hoerder, "Some Connections between Craft Consciousness and Political Thought among Mechanics, 1820s–1840s," *Amerikastudien* 30 (1985): 327–51. On Evans see Pessen, *Most Uncommon Jacksonians,* pp. 71–75; Conkin, *Prophets of Prosperity,* pp. 243–52. On the role of the press in both the workingmen's and trade union movements, see C. K. McFarland and Robert L. Thistlewaite, "Twenty Years of a Successful Labor Paper: *The Working Man's Advocate,* 1829–1849," *Journalism Quarterly* 60 (1983): 35–40; Maurice F. Neufeld, "Realms of Thought and Organized Labor in the Age of Jackson," *Labor History* 10 (1969): 5–43; Alexander Saxton, "Problems of Class and Race in the Origins of the Mass Circulation Press," *American Quarterly* 36 (1984): 214–15, 234; Pessen, *Most Uncommon Jacksonians,* pp. 7, 11–13, 22. Along with his own journal, Evans cited and reprinted widely from both the commercial press and other journals friendly to the cause, such as Heighton's *Mechanic's Free Press,* the *Village Chronicle* of Newark, and the *Spirit of the Age* of Rochester.

38. William Heighton, *An Address to the Members of Trade Societies, and to the Working Classes Generally* (Philadelphia: W. Heighton, 1827), pp. 2, 25, 39–40.

Heighton was citing Judge Joseph Story's use of Bacon. On William Heighton see Philip Foner, *William Heighton: Pioneer Labor Leader of Jacksonian Philadelphia* (New York: International Publishers, 1991).

39. Seth Luther, *An Address to the Working-Men of New England on the State of Education and on the Condition of the Producing Classes in Europe and America* (Boston: S. Luther, 1832), p. 5. On Luther see Louis Hartz, "Seth Luther: Working Class Rebel," *New England Quarterly* 13 (1940): 401–18. For examples of the 'productive'/'nonproductive' categories, see articles from the *Working Man's Advocate:* 31 October 1829, p. 3; "Toasts Drank at the Philadelphia Typographical Society Meeting," 28 November 1829, p. 4; "Lecture at Canton, Ohio, Mechanic's Society," 9 January 1830, p. 4; "Address of a General Meeting of New York Mechanics," 16 January 1830, p. 1; "Exclusive Party," 9 April 1830, p. 2; "Proceedings of the New England Convention of Farmers, Mechanics, and Other Working Men," 20 October 1832, p. 4. See also Heighton, *Members of Trade Societies,* pp. 2, 6, 8; Luther, *Working-Men of New England,* pp. 5–6, 32; Ely Moore, *Address Delivered before the General Trades' Union of the City of New York . . . 1833* (New York: J. Ormond, 1833), pp. 9, 31. On classes useful and otherwise see articles from the *Working Man's Advocate:* "Meeting of the Mechanics and Other Working Men," 31 October 1829, p. 2; "The Mechanics," 11 December 1829, p. 4; "Unequal Taxation," 27 March 1830, p. 1; "Fourth of July: Philadelphia Working Men's Celebration, Toasts," 7 July 1831, p. 4. On vertical gradations both bi- and tripartite see articles from the *Working Man's Advocate:* "Working Man's Meeting," 31 October 1829, p. 2; "The Working Men" and "An Address to Those Who Live by Their Own Industry," 13 March 1830, p. 1; "The Feudal System of Modern Times," 2 May 1835, p. 1. See as well Heighton, *Members of Trade Societies,* p. 2; Luther, *Working-Men of New England,* pp. 7–8, 15–16, 32–35. On the rich or aristocrats versus the poor see articles from the *Working Man's Advocate:* "Working Man's Meeting," 31 October 1829, p. 2; "Loose Thoughts No. 2," 28 November 1829, p. 1; "Communications," 27 February 1830, p. 2; "Report of the Woodstock, Vermont, Working Men's Meeting," 31 July 1830, p. 4; on the laboring or working classes see "Loose Thoughts No. 1," 14 November 1829, p. 1; "Lien Law," 12 December 1829, p. 1; "What Is a Working-Man," 3 April 1830, p. 2; "Working Men of Boston," 28 August 1830, p. 1. For an example of the variety of terms used in one text, in this instance from Philadelphia, see "Preamble of the Mechanics' Union of Trade Associations," in *A Documentary History of American Industrial Society,* ed. John R. Commons (Cleveland: A. H. Clark, 1910–11), 5:84–90. On the broad distinction made by the workers of New York, see Douglas T. Miller, *Jacksonian Aristocracy: Class and Democracy in New York, 1830–1860* (New York: Oxford University Press, 1967), pp. 29–30.

40. George Henry Evans, "Exclusive Party," *Working Man's Advocate,* 4 September 1830, p. 2.

41. See "Minutes of the February 24, 1836, Meeting of the New York General Trades Union," in *Documentary History,* ed. Commons, 5:292: "Our object in the formation of trades unions was not to trample upon the rights of the employer, was not to create a feeling of enmity against the non-

producers, was not, as it is often charged, to tear down the whole social system; it was merely to advance the moral and pecuniary interests of the oppressed mechanic." For additional evidence of instances of this rhetoric see, in addition to such sources as the *Working Man's Advocate,* the citations from the *Man* and the *National Trades' Union,* especially those relating to proceedings of the National Trades' Union conventions of 1834 and 1835, in *Documentary History,* ed. Commons, 6:39–42, 179, 205–9, 211–16, 240–41. See also the pamphlets and printed addresses by leaders such as Luther, *Working-Men of New England;* John Finch, *Rise and Progress of the General Trades Union of the City of New York and Its Vicinity* (New York: J. Ormond, 1833); Moore, *General Trades' Union.* Luther pointed to the present "state of society," which deterred the laboring and producing classes from enjoying equal benefits; it was an opinion shared by Finch, who urged the "operative classes" to assert themselves by way of the ballot and "combination." For both, the current conflicts would be displaced only when the interests of all classes were truly served (Luther, *Working-Men of New England,* pp. 6–8, 14–16; Finch, *Rise and Progress,* pp. 10–11, 12–14). From the 1840s see the selections reprinted fron the *Awl* and the *Mechanic's Mirror* in *Documentary History,* ed. Commons, 8:233–61. "We do not war against wealth," Robert MacFarlane maintained at a meeting of New York Mechanics in 1847, " . . . we believe in the rights of labor, and the rights of capital, and we wish the protection of both" (p. 260).

42. Stephen Simpson, *The Working Man's Manual: A New Theory of Political Economy* (Philadelphia: Th. Bonsal, 1831), pp. 4, 7, 14, 23, 27, 45, 77. On Simpson see Pessen, *Most Uncommon Jacksonians,* pp. 75–78, 105–9; Dorfman, *Economic Mind,* 2:645–48; Conkin, *Prophets of Prosperity,* pp. 239–40. See also Schultz, "Thoughts among the People," pp. 383–85.

43. Stephen Simpson, *Working Man's Manual,* pp. 11–13, 18, 20, 30, 45, 47, 69, 83.

44. Ibid., pp. 46, 59, 65, 76–77, 81. For a comparison of the position that the "constructs, concepts, and analytical tools" of political economy could be used in defense of the interests of the British working classes, see Noel W. Thompson, *The People's Science: The Popular Political Economy of Exploitation and Crisis, 1816–1834* (Cambridge: Cambridge University Press, 1984), pp. 12–13.

45. Stephen Simpson, *Working Man's Manual,* pp. 69–71.

46. Ibid., pp. 52, 66–71, 76, 86–88, 127, 133–34, 230.

47. On Simpson's political career after 1830, see Dorfman, *Economic Mind,* 2:647–48. On the connections between the arguments of the workingmen's parties and trade unions and the broader "public domain of thought," see Neufeld, "Realms of Thought and Organized Labor," pp. 5–7. For other instances of such appeals to the "laboring classes" see William H. Hale, *Useful Knowledge for the Producers of Wealth* (New York: G. H. Evans, 1833); Theophilus Fisk, *Labor the Only True Source of Wealth* (Charleston, S.C.: Office of the Examiner, 1837).

48. John L. O'Sullivan, "The Democratic Principle," *Democratic Review* 1 (October 1837): 5, 11. Although this opening piece is unsigned, Joseph Blau

has suggested that it was probably written by O'Sullivan, the journal's editor. See Joseph Blau, ed., *Social Theories of Jacksonian Democracy: Representative Writings of the Period 1825–1850* (New York: Hafner, 1947), p. 21. See also the analysis of the unwarranted "opposition of mutually dependent classes" made in an essay, "Democracy," *Democratic Review* 7 (March 1840): 227.

49. On the political rhetoric of the Jacksonians and the various uses of class therein, see Christine Oravec, "The Democratic Critics: An Alternate American Rhetorical Tradition in the Nineteenth Century," *Rhetorica* 4 (1988): 395–421; Perry Goldman, "Political Rhetoric in the Age of Jackson," *Tennessee Historical Quarterly* 29 (1970–71): 360–71; Meyers, *Jacksonian Persuasion*, pp. 20–24, 68–70, 174–77, 200–205, 211–19; Spann, *Ideas and Politics*, pp. 64–78, 142–54; Douglas T. Miller, *Jacksonian Aristocracy;* M. J. Heale, *The Presidential Quest: Candidates and Images in American Political Culture, 1787–1852* (London: Longman, 1982), pp. 104–5; Lawrence Kohl, *The Politics of Individualism: Parties and the American Character in the Jacksonian Era* (New York: Oxford University Press, 1989), pp. 45, 202–3, 214–20. See also William Leggett, *Democratick Editorials: Essays in Jacksonian Political Economy*, ed. Lawrence White (Indianapolis: Liberty Press, 1984).

50. The rapid changes in American society and organized politics are discussed in Charles G. Sellers, *The Market Revolution: Jacksonian America, 1815–1846* (New York: Oxford University Press, 1991); Watson, *Liberty and Power;* Daniel Feller, "Politics and Society: Toward a Jacksonian Synthesis," *Journal of the Early Republic* 10 (1990): 135–61; Marc W. Kruman, "The Second Party System and the Transformation of Revolutionary Republicanism," *Journal of the Early Republic* 12 (1992): 509–38; Major Wilson, "Republicanism and the Idea of Party in the Jacksonian Period," *Journal of the Early Republic* 8 (1989): 419–42.

Change and continuity in the discourse of the Jacksonians are considered in John Ashworth, "The Democratic Republicans before the Civil War: Political Ideology and Economic Change," *Journal of American Studies* 20 (1986): 375–90; Jean H. Baker, "From Belief into Culture," pp. 532–50; Bruce Collins, "The Ideology of the Antebellum Northern Democrats," *Journal of American Studies* 11 (1977): 103–21; Steven J. Ross, "The Transformation of Republican Ideology," *Journal of the Early Republic* 10 (1990): 323–30; Lawrence White, "William Leggett: Jacksonian Editorialist as Classical Liberal Political Economist," *HOPE* 18 (1986): 307–24.

51. The partisan and public policy dimensions of the "Bank War" and the tariff controversy are examined in Edwin J. Perkins, "Lost Opportunities for Compromise in the Bank War: A Reassessment of Jackson's Veto Message," *Business History Review* 61 (1987): 531–50; Jeffrey R. Hummel, "The Jacksonians, Banking, and Economic Theory: A Reinterpretation," *Journal of Libertarian Studies* 2 (1978): 151–65; John M. McFaul, *The Politics of Jacksonian Finance* (Ithaca, N.Y.: Cornell University Press, 1972); James Roger Sharp, *The Jacksonians versus the Banks: Politics in the States after the Panic of 1837* (New York: Columbia University Press, 1970); Thomas Payne Govan, "Fundamental Issues of the Bank War," *Pennsylvania Magazine of History and Biography* 82 (1958): 305–15; Bray Hammond, *Banks and Politics in America: From the Revo-*

lution to the Civil War (Princeton: Princeton University Press, 1957), pp. 358–405.

52. Andrew Jackson, "Veto Message: Bank of the United States, July 10, 1832," in *Messages and Papers of the Presidents,* ed. Richardson, 2:578–90.

53. George McDuffie, "Tariff Bill, April 18, 1828," in *Debates of Congress,* ed. Benton, 10:98–99. See also McDuffie's remarks, "Tariff Bill, April 16, 1824," 8:27–33; "Bank of the United States, February 27, 1832," 11:610; both in *Debates of Congress.* On McDuffie see Edwin L. Green, *George McDuffie* (Columbia, S.C.: State Co., 1936). McDuffie was a vociferous opponent of the protective tariff, but a strong supporter of the Bank.

54. Andrew Jackson, "Veto Message: Subscription of Stock in the Maysville, Washington . . . Turnpike Road Co., May 27, 1830," and "Farewell Address, March 4, 1837," in *Messages and Papers of the Presidents,* ed. Richardson, 3:1052, 4:1518–24.

55. Samuel J. Tilden, "Currency, Prices, and Wages: A Speech Delivered in New Lebanon, N.Y., October 3, 1840," in *The Writings and Speeches of Samuel J. Tilden,* ed. John Bigelow (New York: Harper and Brothers, 1885), 1:150–64; see also Tilden, "Divorce of Bank and State: An Address to the Farmers, Mechanics, and Workingmen of the State of New York, Delivered in Tammany Hall, February 26, 1838," in *Writings and Speeches,* 1:82–86. On Tilden see Alexander Flick, *Samuel Jones Tilden: A Study in Political Sagacity* (Port Washington, N.Y.: Kennikat, 1963).

56. To what degree the Jacksonians were advocates or enemies of laissez-faire capitalism has been a recurring point of debate in American historiography. Compare Sellers, *Market Revolution,* and Watson, *Liberty and Power,* to Lawrence White, "William Leggett," Hummel, "Jacksonians, Banking, and Economic Theory," McFaul, *Politics of Jacksonian Finance,* Sharp, *Jacksonians versus the Banks,* and Hammond, *Banks and Politics.* Much of this debate revolves around the employment of anachronistic or historicized senses of 'capitalism'.

See also the speeches and writings of John C. Calhoun, although his analyses should not be conflated with those of Jackson's supporters. For example, see "Speech on the Proposition of Mr. Webster to Re-Charter the Bank of the United States, March 21, 1834," 2:344–49; "Speech on the Independent Treasury Bill, February 15, 1838," 3:240; "Senate Select Committee: Report on the Extent of Executive Patronage, February 9, 1835," 5:175; all in Calhoun, *Works*, ed. Richard K. Cralle (New York: D. Appleton, 1854). Calhoun's analysis of American society is examined in Harp, "Taylor, Calhoun, and the Decline," pp. 107–20.

57. William Gouge, *A Short History of Paper Money and Banking in the United States* (Philadelphia: T. W. Ustick, 1833). On William Gouge and his widely read text see Joseph Dorfman's introduction to the reprint (New York: A. M. Kelley, 1968).

58. On William Leggett see Lawrence White, "William Leggett," and his introduction to Leggett, *Democratick Editorials;* Spann, *Ideals and Politics.* See also Oravec, "Democratic Critics," pp. 395–421.

59. Leggett, *Democratick Editorials,* pp. 55, 128, 172, 196, 244. Leggett's

"political class analysis" is examined in Lawrence White, "William Leggett," pp. 318–19.

60. Leggett also expressed admiration for the works of Dugald Stewart and Jeremy Bentham, and for the politics of Thomas Jefferson. He cited as well the *Thoughts on Political Economy* of Daniel Raymond, although his arguments and Raymond's were quite different (*Democratick Editorials,* pp. 36–38, 195; Lawrence White, "William Leggett," pp. 309–10).

61. Leggett, *Democratick Editorials,* pp. 32–38, 124, 128, 172, 283–300, 365. Leggett was also in favor of the abolition of slavery, a minority position among Jacksonian Democrats. The case for Leggett as an "original thinker" and an "unrivalled advocate of laissez-faire" is made in Lawrence White, "William Leggett."

62. Andrew Jackson, "Farewell Address," 4:1524; Jackson, "Veto Message: Bank of the United States," 3:1140–41; both in *Messages and Papers of the Presidents,* ed. Richardson; James K. Polk, "Inaugural Address," in *Messages and Papers of the Presidents,* ed. Richardson (1897 ed.), 5:2226. The message against the bank was prepared by Amos Kendall, Roger B. Taney, and Andrew Donelson. See Hammond, *Banks and Politics,* p. 405.

On who was and was not included within this egalitarian embrace, see Rowland Berthoff, "Conventional Mentality: Free Blacks, Women, and Business Corporations as Unequal Persons, 1820–1870," *JAH* (1989): 753–84; Alexander Saxton, *The Rise and Fall of the White Republic: Class Politics and Mass Culture in Nineteenth Century America* (New York: Verso, 1990). The larger contexts of conceptions of equality are explored in Richard J. Ellis, "Rival Versions of Equality in American Political Culture," *Review of Politics* 54 (1992): 253–80; Ellis, "Radical Lockeanism in American Political Culture," *Western Political Quarterly* 45 (1992): 825–50.

63. Andrew Jackson, "First Annual Message," 3:1013; Jackson, "Veto Message: Bank of the United States," 3:1140–41; Jackson, "Second Inaugural Address," 3:1224; Jackson, "Seventh Annual Message," 4:1381; Jackson, "Farewell Address," 4:1524; James K. Polk, "Inaugural Address," 5:2226; Polk, "Second Annual Address," 6:2349; all in *Messages and Papers of the Presidents,* ed. Richardson (1897 ed.). See also the unsigned *Address to the Workingmen of the United States* (Washington, D.C.: n.p., 1840); Samuel Tilden, "Divorce of Bank and State," in *Writings and Speeches,* 1:85; Tilden, "Currency, Prices, and Wages," in *Writings and Speeches,* 1:15.

64. Other examples of the Democrats' lexicon and analyses of class in Benton's *Debates of Congress* include Thomas Hart Benton, "Bank of the United States, February 2, 1831," 11:148–61; Felix Grundy, "Tariff-Reduction of Duties, February 15, 1832," 11:398–99; Littleton Tazewell, "Tariff-Reduction of Duties, March 22, 1832," 11:434–35; Jesse Speight, "Tariff, June 27, 1832," 11:741; Robert John Walker, "The Public Lands, January 14, 1837," 13:110; Ambrose Sevier, "Permanent Prospective Pre-Emption Law, January 14, 1841," 14:211–12. In *Messages and Papers of the Presidents,* ed. Richardson (1897 ed.) see Martin Van Buren, "Special Session Message, September 4, 1837," 4:1551–61; Van Buren, "Third Annual Message, December 2, 1839," 4:1771; Van Buren, "Fourth Annual Message, December

5, 1840," 5:1828–29; James K. Polk, "Inaugural Address, March 4, 1845," 5:2226–29; Polk, "First Annual Message, December 2, 1845," 5:2254–55; Polk, "Second Annual Message, December 8, 1846," 6:2349; Polk, "Fourth Annual Message, December 5, 1848," 6:2504–7; James Buchanan, "Second Annual Message, December 6, 1858," 7:3051; Buchanan, "Veto Message: Homestead Bill, June 22, 1860," 7:3142. See also Buchanan's "Speech on the New Tariff Bill," 1:61–62; "Remarks in the House of Representatives on the Duties on Wool and Woolens, January 22, 1827," 1:236; "Duties on Wool . . . , February 7, 1827," 1:240–41; "Speech on the Tariff Bill, April 1–2, 1828," 1:333–45; "Address on the Establishment of Common Schools, Delivered at Dickinson College, June 1828," 1:373–78; "Speech in the Senate on the Independent Treasury Bill, January 22, 1840," 4:148–73; "Remarks regarding the Treasury Bill, March 3, 1840," 4:194–203; "Remarks on the Tariff, August 27, 1842," 5:395–96; "Remarks on the Bankrupt Bill, February 25, 1843," 5:429; all in *The Works of James Buchanan,* ed. John B. Moore (Philadelphia: J. B. Lippincott, 1908).

65. Orestes Brownson, "The Laboring Classes," review of *Chartism* by Thomas Carlyle, *Boston Quarterly Review* 3 (July 1840): 358–95. On the publishing history and the controversy surrounding the essay, see Martin K. Doudna, introduction to *The Laboring Classes (1840), with Brownson's Defence of the Article on the Laboring Classes,* ed. Martin K. Doudna (Delmar, N.Y.: Scholar's Facsimiles, 1978), pp. v–xxii. See also James P. Hannigan, "Orestes Brownson and the Election of 1840," *Records of the American Catholic Historical Society of Philadelphia* 73 (1962): 45–50. On Brownson's variegated career see Arthur Schlesinger, Jr., *Orestes A. Brownson: A Pilgrim's Progress* (New York: Octagon, 1963); Leonard Gilhooley, *Contradiction and Dilemma: Orestes Brownson and the American Idea* (New York: Fordham University Press, 1972); Gilhooley, ed., *No Divided Allegiance: Essays in Brownson's Thought* (New York: Fordham University Press, 1980); Roger Lips, "Orestes Brownson," in *American Literary Critics and Scholars, 1800–1850,* ed. John W. Rathbun and Monica M. Grecu (Detroit: Gale, 1987), pp. 168–71; Gregory S. Butler, *In Search of the American Spirit: The Political Thought of Orestes Brownson* (Carbondale: Southern Illinois University Press, 1992).

66. In so describing the merchant, Brownson noted that, while he did not wish to "belie our acquaintance with political economy" by arguing against the social and economic utility of that class, such "non-workingmen" did in actuality receive disproportionate shares of the wealth produced. In Brownson's reformed system, their rewards would be only those fair and equal ones due them (p. 367).

67. The often complicated history of comparisons between wage workers and chattel slaves is examined in Marcus Cunliffe, *Chattel Slavery and Wage Slavey: The Anglo-American Context, 1830–1860* (Athens: University of Georgia Press, 1979). See also Jonathan Glickstein, *Concepts of Free Labor in Antebellum America* (New Haven: Yale University Press, 1991).

68. Brownson's critique of inherited wealth is discussed in Levy, "Liberal Equality and Inherited Wealth," pp. 551–53.

69. For examples of the Whig response to Brownson see "Critical Notices,"

review of "The Laboring Classes," *New York Review* 7 (October 1840): 514–52; and two of the Junius pamphlets of Calvin Colton, *American Jacobinism* (New York: n.p., 1840) and *Sequel to the Crisis of the Country* (New York: Egbert Benson, 1840). The anonymous *New York Review* commentator questions the meaningfulness and narrowness of Brownson's definition of 'laboring class', since it removes from that class even the "poor ditcher" if he owns his spade or the cobbler if he owns his awl. He doubts as well the reliabilty of Brownson's prediction of social strife: "the approaching conflict between the employer and the employed, or, to use Mr. Brownson's language, between 'the oppressor and the oppressed,' seems to have greatly disturbed the imagination of the author" (p. 517). See also "The Rich against the Poor," *Methodist Quarterly Review,* 1 (January 1841): 92–122; Elisha Bartlett, *A Vindication of the Character and Condition of the Females Employed in the Lowell Mills . . .* (Lowell: L. Huntress, 1841). For a discussion of other responses to Brownson, both pro and con, see Doudna's introduction to *The Laboring Classes,* pp. vi–xiv; Arthur Schlesinger, Jr., *The Age of Jackson* (Boston: Little, Brown, 1953), pp. 299–304; Schlesinger, *Orestes A. Brownson,* pp. 100–111.

70. Brownson's conjoining of religious and social criticism is examined in Patrick Carey, "Christian Socialism in the Early Brownson," *Records of the American Catholic Historical Society of Philadelphia* 99 (1988): 17–39.

71. On St. Simon, see Brownson's review of *Society, Manners, and Politics in the United States* by Michel Chevalier, *Boston Quarterly Review* 3 (April 1840): 217–20. See also Brownson's surveys of the range of answers given to the question of how to improve social conditions, in "Brook Farm," *Democratic Review* 11 (November 1842): 481–86.

72. For a more self-consciously partisan appeal to the "real producers" to support the Locofoco party, see Orestes Brownson, "An Address to the Workingmen of Charlestown, Massachusetts, to Their Brethren throughout the Commonwealth and the Union, 1840," *Boston Quarterly Review* 4 (January 1841): 112–27.

73. Arthur Bestor has noted Albert Brisbane's use of 'proletaries' as a term for the "wages classes" in 1845 ("The Evolution of the Socialist Vocabulary," *JHI* 9 [1948]: 264). The term 'proletarians' appears in John Campbell, *A Theory of Equality* (Philadelphia: J. B. Perry, 1848), p. 75. On the appearance of 'prolétariat' in French public discourse in the 1830s and 1840s, see Daniel Lindenberg, "Prolétariat," in *Nouvelle histoire des idées politiques,* ed. Pascal Orly (Paris: Hachette, 1987), pp. 260–64.

74. For other instances of these conventions see Campbell, *Theory of Equality;* John Pickering, *The Working Man's Political Economy* (Cincinnati: Th. Varney, 1847). See also George Henry Evans's renewed *Working Man's Advocate,* 1841–45; for example, Louis Masquerier, "Declaration of Independence, of the Producing from the Non-Producing Class," 28 September 1844, p. 4, where Masquerier declares "that they [the producing class] should take measures to make all producers as well as consumers; that all division of society into high, middle, and lower classes cease; and that the most republican party should assume the name of Producer and call the aristocratic Non-Producer";

"Address of Mechanics and Laborers at the Boston Convention," 2 November 1844, pp. 1–2; "National Industrial Convention," 18 October 1845, p. 2. See as well the unsigned pieces in the *Democratic Review,* for example, "True Theory and Philosophy of Our System of Government," 15 (September 1844): 230–32; "Capital and Labor," 25 (November 1849): 387–89.

On the permeability of definitions of 'working class' see Hugins, *Jacksonian Democracy and the Working Class,* pp. 220–21.

75. On Brownson's guardedly positive assessment of at least the social criticisms made by American Fourierists, see his article "Albert Brisbane," *Democratic Review* 11 (September 1842): 303–4. On Brownson's critiques of Fourier's religious theories see *Brownson's Quarterly Review* 1 (October 1844): 450–87. In light of Brownson's rapidly changing opinions it is important to note that his attitudes toward politics, religion, and social organization became decidedly more conservative through the 1840s and onward. See, for example, his essay "Origins and Ground of Government," *Democratic Review* 13 (August 1843): 129–37. On Brownson's intellectual and spiritual transition in the 1840s, see Gilhooley, *Contradiction and Dilemma,* pp. 93–107. See also David W. Lovell, "Early French Socialism and Class Struggle," *HOPE* 9 (1988): 327–48; Paul Claval, *Les mythes fondateurs des sciences sociales* (Paris: Presses Universitaires de France, 1980), pp. 95–100.

76. Albert Brisbane, *Social Destiny of Man; or, Association and Reorganization of Industry* (Philadelphia: C. F. Stollmeyer, 1840); Brisbane, *A Concise Exposition of the Doctrine of Association* (New York: J. S. Redfield, 1843), p. 7; Brisbane, "On Association and Attractive Industry," *Democratic Review* 10 (January, February, April, June 1842).

On Charles Fourier see Jonathan Beecher, *Charles Fourier: The Visionary and His World* (Berkeley: University of California Press, 1986); Paul E. Corcoran, "Early French Socialism Reconsidered: The Propaganda of Fourier and Cabet," *History of European Ideas* 7 (1986): 469–88. On the varieties of American Fourierism see Carl J. Guarneri, *The Utopian Alternative: Fourierism in Nineteenth Century America* (Ithaca, N.Y.: Cornell University Press, 1991); Guarneri, "Importing Fourierism to America," *JHI* 43 (1982): 581–94. See also Richard N. Pettit, Jr., "Albert Brisbane: Apostle of Fourierism in the United States, 1834–1840," Ph.D. diss., Miami University, 1982, pp. 35–99; Edward K. Spann, *Brotherly Tomorrows: Movements for a Cooperative Society in America, 1820–1920* (New York: Columbia University Press, 1989), pp. 67–142; John R. Wennerstern, "Albert Brisbane," in *Antebellum Writers in New York and the South,* ed. Joel Myerson (Detroit: Gale, 1979), pp. 25–27.

77. Brisbane, *Social Destiny of Man,* pp. 63, 109–12; Brisbane, *Doctrine of Association,* pp. 7–8, 36; Brisbane, "Association and Attractive Industry," pp. 32–40. Brisbane claimed to base his estimate of the number in the "hired classes" by taking an average from the respective nations (*Social Destiny of Man,* p. 63).

78. Brisbane, *Social Destiny of Man,* pp. 66–67, 74; Brisbane, *Doctrine of Association,* pp. 13, 36. Brisbane reasoned that portions of the otherwise productive classes involved in manufacturing, commerce, and transportation

were "non-producing classes in the present social order," due to wasted effort and poor quality of product. These ills were symptomatic of the false economy of competition (*Social Destiny of Man,* p. 66).

79. Brisbane, *Doctrine of Association,* p. 7; Brisbane, "Association and Attractive Industry," *Democratic Review* 10 (1842): 321–31. On the Associationists and American politics see Guarneri, *Utopian Alternative.*

80. Brisbane, *Social Destiny of Man,* pp. 12, 29, 63, 74; Brisbane, *Doctrine of Association,* pp. 7–8, 36; Brisbane, "Association and Attractive Industry," *Democratic Review* 10 (1842): 331–33. See also Brisbane's introductory essay, "Fundamental Principles of Fourier's System of Social Organization," in *Social Destiny of Man: With a Treatise on the Function of the Human Passions* (New York: Robert M. DeWitt, 1857), pp. 90–91, 140. See also "The American Associationists," *Democratic Review* 18 (February 1846): 142–44; Brisbane's correspondence with H. L. Ellsworth of the U.S. Patent Office in regard to the Georgia railroad Brisbane intended to build according to Fourierist principles, reprinted in *Niles National Register,* 25 March 1843, p. 56. On the Associationists and private property see William B. Scott, *In Pursuit of Happiness: American Conceptions of Property from the Seventeenth to the Twentieth Century* (Bloomington: Indiana University Press, 1977), pp. 81–83.

81. On the troubles that beset the phalanxes and a record of their existence, see Robert S. Fogarty, *Dictionary of American Communal and Utopian History* (Westport, Conn.: Greenwood Press, 1980). For Parke Godwin's exposition of Associationism see his *Popular View of the Doctrines of Charles Fourier* (New York: J. S. Redfield, 1844). On Godwin see Spann, *Ideals and Politics,* pp. 142–54; John R. Wennersten, "Parke Godwin," in *Antebellum Writers,* ed. Myerson, pp. 120–23; Sterling F. Delano, "Parke Godwin," in *American Literary Critics and Scholars,* ed. Rathbun and Grecu, pp. 82–86. Godwin also served as editor of the *Harbinger.* On that journal as a promoter of Associationist social theories and its relation to the wider currents of reform in the 1840s, see Sterling F. Delano, *The Harbinger and New England Transcendentalism* (London: Associated Universities Presses, 1983), pp. 15–50, 148–50. From Horace Greeley's works see his *Hints toward Reforms* (New York: Harper and Bros., 1850). For other examples of Associationist writing see the unsigned review of Brisbane's *Social Destiny of Man, Democratic Review* 8 (November 1840): 435–54; see also the unsigned essay "What Is the Reason?" *Democratic Review* 16 (January 1845): 17–30. On the broader influence of Brisbane and Associationist ideas, see Pettit, "Albert Brisbane," pp. 99–100, 320–21.

82. Brisbane, *Social Destiny of Man,* pp. 12, 74; Brisbane, *Doctrine of Association,* pp. 8, 36; Brisbane, "Fourier's System," pp. 77, 90–91; Godwin, *Popular View,* pp. 69, 110–13. On Associationism's status as a science Godwin observed that "we wish to rest the claims of the social science of Fourier upon precisely the same grounds on which Herschel rested the science of astronomy. Fourier and his principles are entitled to rank as a science, being capable of that rigorous demonstration which only willful prejudice rejects" (*Popular View,* p. 5).

83. Godwin, *Popular View,* pp. 59, 69, 76, 85, 110–13, 116–17. On the Associationist critique of political economy see also "What Is the Reason?"

pp. 29–30. On the larger question of harmonic models in such schools of thought, see Barbara Goodwin, *Social Science and Utopia: Nineteenth-Century Models of Social Harmony* (Sussex, England: Harvester, 1978).

84. For examples of such disagreements over the true relations between capital and labor, and the importance of politics, see the citations from the *Working Man's Advocate* and the *Phalanx* in *Documentary History,* ed. Commons, 7:325–30. For examples of where practical goals outweighed tactical differences, see "Resolutions of the First Convention of the New England Working Men's Association" (NEWMA), held in Boston, October 1844, and "Preamble and Resolutions," March 1845 convention of same association held in Lowell, in *Documentary History,* ed. Commons, 8:96–104. The NEWMA was an association that advocated a ten-hour workday.

85. Leggett, *Democratick Editorials,* p. 48.

Chapter 5

1. On antebellum assumptions and arguments about rhetorical and cultural power, see Kenneth Cmiel, *Democratic Eloquence: the Fight over Popular Speech in Nineteenth Century America* (New York: William Morrow, 1990). See also Meyer, *Instructed Conscience;* Wilson Smith, *Professors and Public Ethics;* Richard D. Brown, *Knowledge Is Power.*

2. On the ideologies of individualism in antebellum political culture, see Kohl, *Politics of Individualism.*

3. Francis Wayland, *The Elements of Political Economy* (New York: Leavitt, Lord and Co., 1837), pp. 3–31, 45 (hereafter pages given in text). On Wayland see William J. Barber, "Political Economy from the Top Down: Brown University," in *Breaking the Academic Mould,* ed. Barber, pp. 72–94; Edward H. Madden, "Francis Wayland and the Scottish Tradition," *Transactions of the Charles S. Peirce Society* 21 (1985): 301–26; Wilson Smith, *Professors and Public Ethics,* pp. 20, 128–46; Conkin, *Prophets of Prosperity,* pp. 116–23; Dorfman, *Economic Mind,* 2:758–70; Meyer, *Instructed Conscience,* pp. 101–2.

The widespread use and influence of Wayland's two major texts are discussed in Crick, *American Science of Politics,* p. 12; O'Connor, *Origins of Academic Economics,* pp. 172–90. The *Elements of Political Economy* sold over 200,000 copies in the sixty years it was in print. See Madden, "Francis Wayland," p. 301; Joseph L. Blau, introduction to the reprint of the *Elements of Political Economy* (Cambridge: Harvard University Press, 1963).

4. Henry Vethake, *Principles of Political Economy* (Philadelphia: P. H. Nicklin, 1838), pp. vii, 38 (hereafter pages given in text). On Vethake see Dorfman and Tugwell, *Early American Policy,* pp. 155–204; Steven A. Sass, "An Uneasy Relationship: The Business Community and Academic Economists at the University of Pennsylvania," in *Breaking the Academic Mould,* ed. Barber, pp. 225–26; Conkin, *Prophets of Prosperity,* pp. 123–34; Hull, "Prospect for Man," pp. 174–97; O'Connor, *Origins of Academic Economics,* pp. 191–204; Meyer, *Instructed Conscience,* p. 103.

5. Vethake also discussed the "different senses attached to the same words and phrases" in *An Introductory Lecture on Political Economy* (New York: J. K. Moore, 1833), p. 24.

6. Bourdieu, *Distinction*, pp. 479–81. See also Pierre Bourdieu, "The Economics of Linguistic Exchanges," *Social Science Information* 16 (1977): 645–68. On the question of "who are the 'working-men' in the United States," see also Theodore Sedgwick, *Public and Private Economy* (New York: Harper, 1836), 1:219–30; An American, *An Essay upon the Principles of Political Economy: Designed as a Manual for Practical Men* (New York: Th. Foster, 1837); James W. Alexander, *The Working-Man* (Philadelphia: H. Perkins, 1839).

7. Alonzo Potter, *Political Economy: Its Objects, Uses, and Principles, Considered with Reference to the Condition of the American People* (New York: Harper, 1841), p. 301 (hereafter pages given in text). On Potter see Dorfman, *Economic Mind*, 2:826–33; Meyer, *Instructed Conscience*, pp. 102–3; Wilson Smith, *Professors and Public Ethics*, pp. 5–10.

8. George Poulett Scrope, *Principles of Political Economy, Deducted from the Natural Laws of Social Welfare, as Applied to the Present State of Great Britain* (London: Longman, 1833). On Scrope see Rodney P. Sturges, *A Bibliography of George Poulett Scrope: Geologist, Economist, and Local Historian* (Boston: Baker Library, 1984); Mark Blaug, ed., *George Scrope* (Aldershot, England: Edward Elgar, 1991); Fetter, "Rise and Decline of Ricardian Economics"; Wallech, "Emergence of the Modern Concept of 'Class'," pp. 383–95.

9. Potter also made this argument in a review of *Essay on the Rate of Wages* by Henry Carey and "Address to the General Trades' Union of New York" by Ely Moore, *New York Review* 2 (1838): 5–48.

10. Henry C. Carey, *Essay on the Rate of Wages* (Philadelphia: Carey, Lea and Blanchard, 1835); Carey, *Principles of Political Economy*, 3 vols. (Philadelphia: Carey, Lea and Blanchard, 1837–40). On 'mutual dependence' see *Political Economy*, 1:142–43.

Studies on Henry Carey include Rodney J. Morrison, *Henry C. Carey and American Economic Development*, Transactions of the American Philosophical Society, vol. 76, part 3 (Philadelphia: American Philosophical Society, 1986); Morrison, "Henry C. Carey and American Economic Development," *Explorations in Entrepreneurial History* 5 (1968): 132–44; Abraham Kaplan, *Henry Charles Carey: A Study in American Economic Thought* (Baltimore: Johns Hopkins University Press, 1931); Conkin, *Prophets of Prosperity*, pp. 261–79; Dorfman, *Economic Mind*, 2:789–805; Daniel Walker Howe, *Political Culture of the American Whigs*, pp. 109–22.

On the range of Carey's influence see Walter T. K. Nugent, "Tocqueville, Marx, and American Class Structure," *Social Science History* 12 (1988): 327–48; Michael Perelman, "Political Economy and the Press: Karl Marx and Henry Carey at the *New York Tribune*," in *Marx's Crises Theory: Scarcity, Labor, and Finance* (New York: Praeger, 1989), pp. 10–26; de Vivo, "Ricardo and His Disciples," p. 185; Allen Oakley, *Marx's Critique of Political Economy: Intellectual Sources and Evolution* (London: Routledge and Kegan Paul, 1984). Marx devoted considerable attention to the study and the refutation of Carey's work.

11. Henry C. Carey, *Essay on the Rate of Wages*, p. 15 (hereafter pages given in text).

12. Henry C. Carey, *Political Economy*, 1:3–6.

13. William Dolby, "Abuses of Classification," *Merchant's Magazine* 6 (1842): 43.

14. George W. Burnap, "The Social Influences of Trade and the Dangers and Duties of the Mercantile Class," *Merchant's Magazine* 4 (1841): 418. On Burnap see *DAB,* 3:292.

15. George W. Burnap, "The Sources of National Wealth," *Southern Quarterly Review* 3 (1843): 363.

16. Ibid., p. 364.

17. A similar estimation of the effects of proper and improper social knowledge was made by Richard Sulley, "The True Theory of Capital and Labor," *Merchant's Magazine* 20 (1849): 370–75. Sulley argued that "the existence of society itself is in peril" because this subject has not been "sufficiently understood." Such a dearth of information had encouraged the "present unfounded prejudice" against capital, which he found in wide circulation.

18. Francis Bowen, "Mill's *Political Economy,*" review of *The Principles of Political Economy* by John Stuart Mill, *North American Review* 67 (1848): 370–411; Bowen, "Phillips' Protection and Free Trade," review of *Propositions concerning Protection and Free Trade* by Willard Phillips, *North American Review* 72 (1851): 396–415; Bowen, "Newman's Lectures," review of *Lectures on Political Economy* by Francis W. Newman, *North American Review* 74 (1852): 221–22.

Studies of Francis Bowen's career and writings include Byrd L. Jones, "A Quest for National Leadership: Institutionalization of Economics at Harvard," in *Breaking the Academic Mould,* ed. Barber, pp. 96–100; Monica M. Grecu, "Francis Bowen," in *American Literary Critics and Scholars,* ed. Rathbun and Grecu, pp. 20–25; Daniel Walker Howe, *The Unitarian Conscience: Harvard Moral Philosophy, 1805–1861* (Cambridge: Harvard University Press, 1970), pp. 226–31, 309–10; Bruce Kuklick, *The Rise of American Philosophy: Cambridge, Massachusetts, 1860–1930* (New Haven: Yale University Press, 1977), pp. 28–45; Meyer, *Instructed Conscience,* p. 148; Haddow, *Political Science,* pp. 116–17, 126; Wilson Smith, *Professors and Public Ethics,* pp. 5–11, 40 n; Dorfman, *Economic Mind,* 2:835–44.

19. Bowen, "Philips' Protection and Free Trade," pp. 405, 415.

20. Bowen, "Newman's Lectures," pp. 221–22.

21. Francis Bowen, *The Principles of Political Economy Applied to the Condition, the Resources, and the Institutions of the American People* (Boston: Little, Brown, 1856).

22. Ibid., pp. 18, 239–40; Bowen, "Mill's *Political Economy,*" pp. 370–71.

23. In *Studies in the Theory of Ideology,* John B. Thompson argues that ideology should be analyzed not as a source of collectively shared values—be they pluralistically agreed upon or hegemonically imposed—but as a way in which "meaning is mobilized for the maintenance of relations of domination." For Thompson, classification is a critical locus for the relations of ideology and language: "By limiting the area of concern, classification serves as an instrument for the control of information and experience" (pp. 5–9, 62–63, 81–83, 121–22). The term 'ideologia americana' is borrowed from Pocock, "Between Gog and Magog."

24. Calvin Colton, *Public Economy for the United States* (New York: A. S. Barnes, 1848), p. 289. On Colton see Conkin, *Prophets of Prosperity,* pp. 188–99; Kaufman, *Capitalism, Slavery, and Republican Values,* pp. 43–46, 158–59; Dorfman, *Economic Mind,* 2:777–79.

For examples of the American-European comparison see Josiah Bigelow, *A Review of Seth Luther's Address to the Working Men of New England* (Cambridge, Mass.: E. W. Metcalf, 1832); John Inman, "Who Are the People?" *Democratic Review* 10 (1842): 345; Junius Smith, "Reasons Why the Aspect of Society in England and the United States Must Be Radically and Permanently Different," *Democratic Review* 19 (1848): 25–28; Nathan Appleton, "Labor: Its Relations in the United States and Europe, Compared," *Merchant's Magazine* 11 (1844): 217–21; Ephraim George Squier, *The Working Man's Miscellany: Lectures on the Condition and the True Interests of the Laboring Classes of America* (Albany: New York Mechanic and Cultivator, 1843). The rhetorical uses of Europe in the discourse of American politics are explored in Henry May, "Europe and the American Mind," *History of European Ideas* 5 (1984): 137–48.

25. See also Calvin Colton's ten pamphlets, published together as *The Junius Tracts* (New York: Greeley and McElrath, 1844), especially "Labor and Capital," tract 7, pp. 2–15. The widespread Whig subscription to a "harmony of interests" analysis of society is discussed in Thomas Brown, *Politics and Statesmanship;* Brown, "The Massachusetts Whigs and Industrialism," *Historical Journal of Massachusetts* 14 (1986): 25–42; Brown, "The Southern Whigs and Economic Development," *Southern Studies* 20 (1981): 20–38; David F. Ericson, *The Shaping of American Liberalism* (Chicago: University of Chicago Press, 1993); Formisano, *Transformation of Political Culture;* Daniel Walker Howe, *Political Culture of the American Whigs.*

26. Daniel Webster, "Address to a Mass Meeting of Whigs at Saratoga, New York, August 19, 1840," 3:24–25; Webster, "Convention of the Whigs of Essex County Massachusetts, Held at Andover, November 9, 1843," 3:177; Webster, "Public Dinner for Mr. Webster, Philadelphia, December 2, 1846," 4:51; all in *The Writings and Speeches of Daniel Webster* (Boston: Little, Brown, 1903); Webster, "Debate on the Tariff, House of Representatives, April 2, 1824," in *Debates in Congress,* ed. Benton, 7:712–17. See also "Address to the Citizens of Pittsburg, July 8, 1833," where Webster explained that "nine-tenths of the whole people belong to the laborious, industrious, and productive classes" (*Writings and Speeches,* 2:148–49). See also in Webster's *Writings and Speeches* "Speech at Reception in New York City at Niblo's Saloon, March 15, 1837," 2:227; "Speech at Convention of Whigs of Chester and Montgomery Counties, at Valley Forge, Pa., October 3, 1844," 3:287–88; "Speech at Faneuil Hall, Boston, October 24, 1848," 4:164–65; "Lecture before the Society for the Diffusion of Useful Knowledge, Boston, November 11, 1837," 13:67–76; "Speech at the State Agricultural Fair, Rochester, New York, September 20, 1843," 13:184–85; "Speech at Whig Meeting on Boston Common, September 25, 1844," 13:263–64; "Speech at a Whig Gathering in New York City, October 9, 1844," 13:274. Webster's political theory is examined in David F. Ericson, *Shaping of American Liberalism.*

27. Daniel Webster, "Debate on the Tariff, House of Representatives, April 2, 1824," in *Debates in Congress,* ed. Benton, 7:712–17. For additional examples of expansive and harmonious conceptions of classes in Whig political discourse, see Hugh Swinton Legaré, "Speech on the Sub-Treasury Bill, House of Representatives, October 13, 1837," 13:534–37; Joseph Trumbull, "Bankrupt Law, House of Representatives, August 11, 1841," 14:339; both in *Debates in Congress.*

See also Francis Lieber, *Essays on Property and Labor as Connected with the Natural Law and the Constitution of Society* (New York: Harper and Bros., 1841), where Lieber argues that "to draw a distinct line fit to divide society into two antagonistic parts, between the poorest woodsman, whose only capital consists of his clothes, a frying-pan, and an axe and knife, on the one hand, and the richest manufacturer . . . on the other, is very hard" (p. 208).

28. Colton, *Public Economy,* p. 29. See also "System of Positive Philosophy," *Democratic Review* 20 (1847): 148–50; "On the Importance of the Social Sciences in the Present Day," *Southern Literary Messenger* 15 (1849): 77–80. On the influence of Comte see Richmond L. Hawkins, *Auguste Comte and the United States* (New York: Kraus, 1966); Hawkins, *Positivism in the United States* (Cambridge: Harvard University Press, 1938); Terence R. Wright, *The Religion of Humanity: The Impact of Comtean Positivism on Victorian Britain* (Cambridge: Cambridge University Press, 1986).

29. Henry C. Carey, *Principles of Social Science* (Philadelphia: Lippincott, 1858–59), 1:v–vi, 21–28, 3:113. On Carey and Comte see Arnold W. Green, *Henry Charles Carey: Nineteenth Century Sociologist* (Philadelphia: University of Pennsylvania Press, 1951).

30. Henry C. Carey, *Principles of Social Science,* 2:291, 1:29–31, 224–30, 260.

31. Ibid., 1:445–47, 224, 468. On the political and ideological importance of the protective tariff for the Republicans, see James L. Hutson, "A Political Response to Industrialism: The Republican Embrace of Protectionist Labor Doctrine," *JAH* 70 (1983): 35–57. Carey, as Hutson notes, played a central role in shaping this mainstay of Republican policy.

32. On the Carey "school" see Sass, "Uneasy Relationship," pp. 226–29; Morrison, *Henry C. Carey,* pp. 81–82; Dorfman, *Economic Mind,* 2:789–826.

33. Thomas Prentice Kettell, "Review, Historical and Critical, of the Different Systems of Social Philosophy," *Merchant's Magazine* 41, no. 4 (1859): 402–7; no. 5: 536–41; no. 6: 672–73; vol. 42, no. 1 (1860): 42; no. 5: 541–52; vol. 43, no. 5 (1860): 532–37; vol. 44, no. 3 (1861): 277–85. On Kettell see Dorfman, *Economic Mind,* 2:632.

34. Kettell, "Review, Historical and Critical," *Merchant's Magazine* 41, no. 6 (1859): 672–73. On the origins of the term 'sociology' see Shapiro, "Note on the Term 'Social Science'," pp. 20–22; Claeys, "'Individualism', 'Socialism', and 'Social Science'."

35. Kettell, "Review, Historical and Critical," *Merchant's Magazine* 41, no. 6 (1859): 672–73.

36. Ibid., *Merchant's Magazine* 42, no. 5 (1860): 541.

37. Ibid., *Merchant's Magazine* 42, no. 1 (1860): 42; no. 5: 541–42.

38. Ibid., *Merchant's Magazine* 41, no. 5 (1859): 536–41; vol. 44, no. 3 (1861): 277–85.

39. See, for example, James A. McMaster, "Societary Theories," *American Whig Review* 7 (1848): 632–34; "Socialists, Communists, and Red Republicans," *American Review* 10 (1849): 402–17; Richard Hildreth, *Theory of Politics: An Inquiry into the Foundations of Governments and the Causes and Progress of Political Revolutions* (1854; reprint, New York: B. Franklin, 1971); "Review of *The History of the Working Classes,* by Robert DuVar," *Southern Literary Messenger* 21 (1855): 193–206. On the larger contexts of liberal responses to socialism, see Eugene Kamenka and F. B. Smith, eds., *Intellectuals and Revolution: Socialism and the Experience of 1848* (New York: St. Martin's, 1979).

40. This point is particularly well developed in Hutson, "Political Response to Industrialism."

Chapter 6

1. M. Schele De Vere, *Americanisms: The English of the New World* (New York: Scribner, 1872), p. 227.

2. Wendell Phillips, "The Eight Hour Movement: An Address at Faneuil Hall, November 2, 1865," in *Speeches, Lectures, and Letters,* 2nd series (Boston: Lee and Shepard, 1892), p. 138. On Phillips see James B. Stewart, *Wendell Phillips: Liberty's Hero* (Baton Rouge: Louisiana State University Press, 1986).

3. The extent of the audience and the roles played by the academic and amateur moral scientists in late-nineteenth-century America are discussed by Dorothy Ross, *The Emergence of Social Science* (Cambridge: Cambridge University Press, 1990); Horowitz, "Textbook Models of American Economic Growth"; Dorfman, *Economic Mind,* 3:49–82; Haddow, *Political Science,* pp. 222–49; O'Connor, *Origins of Academic Economics,* pp. 260–88.

See also R. Jackson Wilson, *In Quest of Community: Social Philosophy in the United States, 1860–1920* (New York: John Wiley, 1968); Walter T. K. Nugent, *Money and American Society, 1865–1880* (New York: Free Press, 1968), pp. 21–55; Irwin Unger, *The Greenback Era: A Social and Political History of American Finance, 1865–1879* (Princeton: Princeton University Press, 1964), pp. 13–40; Sidney Fine, *Laissez Faire and the General Welfare State: A Study of Conflict in American Thought, 1865–1901* (Ann Arbor: University of Michigan Press, 1956), pp. 47–95; Mary O. Furner, *Advocacy and Objectivity: A Crisis in the Professionalization of American Social Science* (Lexington: University of Kentucky Press, 1975), pp. 35–58; Irwin Yellowitz, ed., *The Position of the Worker in American Society, 1865–1896* (Englewood Cliffs, N.J.: Prentice Hall, 1969), pp. 1–50.

4. Amasa Walker, *The Science of Wealth: A Manual of Political Economy* (Boston: Little and Brown, 1866), pp. 5–7, 21. On Walker and his widely read text see *Breaking the Academic Mould,* ed. Barber, pp. 13, 87, 143, 152, 297, 300–301; Dorfman, *Economic Mind,* 2:749–52, 3:49–56, 81–82; O'Connor, *Origins of Academic Economics,* pp. 263–64. Although he assigns to political economy a place alongside inductive physical sciences such as chemistry and

astronomy, Walker admits that, due to prejudice and ignorance, "it is the only science that cannot obtain a candid and impartial examination from the mass of mankind" (*Science of Wealth,* p. 5).

5. Amasa Walker, *Science of Wealth,* pp. 6–7. Along these lines see also Charles F. Dunbar, "Economic Science in America, 1776–1876," *North American Review* 122 (1876): 124–54. In considering the discipline's problems with misconceptions and "equivocal use," Dunbar admitted that "its vocabulary is drawn from the language of popular discourse" (p. 148). See also Bonamy Price, "Is Political Economy a Science?" *North American Review* 129 (1879): 570–86. Price noted that Adam Smith, for one, discussed economic questions in "the language of the common world" (p. 571).

6. Amasa Walker, *Science of Wealth,* pp. 18–22. See also Walker, "Labor and Capital in Manufactures," *Scribner's Monthly* 4 (1872): 460–65; Walker, "The Union of Capital and Labor," *Bankers' Magazine* 27 (1873): 802–7. Walker first presented his arguments on capital and labor to the public during the 1850s in a series of essays for the *Merchant's Magazine.* See, for example, "Political Economy: Wages," 31 (1854): 178; "Political Economy," 36 (1857): 277.

7. Amasa Walker, *Science of Wealth,* pp. 71–76.

8. Arthur Latham Perry, *Elements of Political Economy* (New York: Scribner, 1866), pp. 89, 107, 120, 132–33, 141–43. On Perry and *Elements of Political Economy* see *Breaking the Academic Mould,* ed. Barber, pp. 13, 69, 87, 149; O'Connor, *Origins of Academic Economics,* pp. 265–66; Dorfman, *Economic Mind,* 3:56–63, 80–81. Also in line with Walker, Perry credited *Harmonies économiques* by the French political economist Claude-Frédéric Bastiat for the theoretical basis of his position on societal harmony (Perry, *Elements of Political Economy,* pp. 20–21; Walker, *Science of Wealth,* p. viii).

9. Albert S. Bolles, *Chapters in Political Economy* (New York: D. Appleton, 1874), pp. 15–17, 20, 40. Bolles cites Perry's *Elements of Political Economy* as an authoritative example. See also Bolles's essays for the *Bankers' Magazine:* "Some Economic Conditions of the Future," 26 (1872): 923–27; "The Field and Importance of Political Economy," 28 (1874): 761–70; "The Labor Question," 28 (1874): 841–60; "Political Economy," 29 (1878): 528–43. On Bolles see the *National Cyclopedia of American Biography* (New York: J. T. White and Co., 1893), 30:270. Bolles later became editor of *Bankers' Magazine* and taught at a number of institutions, including the Wharton School. For other instances of these lines of reasoning as presented by authors in favor of free trade, see John Bascom, *Political Economy: Designed as a Text-book for Colleges* (Andover, Mass.: W. Draper, 1874), pp. 59–64, 143–44; James T. Champlin, *Lessons on Political Economy* (New York: A. S. Barnes, 1868), pp. 43, 61.

10. Henry C. Carey, *Capital and Labor* (Philadelphia: Collins, 1873), pp. 6–7. On the protectionists and the Careyites see Morrison, *Henry C. Carey,* pp. 81–89; Sass, "Uneasy Relationship," pp. 226–29; Dorfman, *Economic Mind,* 3:27, 80–82; Nugent, *Money and American Society,* pp. 24–25, 30–31, 129–31. See also L. L. Bernard and Jessie Bernard, *Origins of American Sociology* (New York: Russell and Russell, 1965), pp. 389–457. For the extent of

Carey and the Careyites' influence in the 1860s and 1870s, in particular their "soft-money" position on the currency question, see Unger, *Greenback Era,* pp. 50–60.

11. Robert Ellis Thompson, *Social Science and the National Economy* (Philadelphia: Porter and Coates, 1875), pp. 146, 150. On Thompson see Sass, "Uneasy Relationship," pp. 226–29; Bernard and Bernard, *Origins of American Sociology,* pp. 424–28; Dorfman, *Economic Mind,* 3:80.

12. Robert Ellis Thompson, *Social Science and the National Economy,* pp. 30, 40, 130–33, 146–50. The policy that would best guarantee American social harmony was for Thompson the protective tariff. He also suggests the arbitration of labor disputes, and profit-sharing plans, and was willing to consider cooperative ventures, although he found both "theoretical" and "practical" limits in the latter (pp. 150–52, 256). See also Thompson's contributions to the *Penn Monthly,* including his series "The Communisms of the Old World," vol. 5, no. 1 (1874): 12–28; no. 3: 196–98; no. 4: 278–91; Thompson, "Carey and Ricardo in Europe," *Penn Monthly* 8 (1877): 548–77.

Similar analyses of the state of American class relations by members of the Carey school are found in William Elder, *Questions of the Day: Economic and Social* (Philadelphia: H. C. Baird, 1871), pp. 98, 290–94, 326–29; Elder, *Conversations on the Principal Subjects of Political Economy* (Philadelphia: H. C. Baird, 1882), pp. 146–47; Erasmus Peshine Smith, *A Manual of Political Economy* (Philadelphia: H. C. Baird, 1872), p. 113; William Dexter Wilson, *First Principles of Political Economy* (Ithaca, N.Y.: Finch and Apgar, 1875), pp. 343–48.

13. Albert S. Bolles, *The Conflict between Labor and Capital* (Philadelphia: Lippincott, 1876), p. 75.

14. Ibid., pp. vii, 17–24, 79.

15. Ibid., pp. vii, 1, 27, 74–75. Although Francis Bowen disagreed with Bolles over the tariff, see as well Bowen's corresponding analysis of the "misunderstanding and antagonism" between capital, labor, and the respective classes in his *American Political Economy* (New York: Scribner, 1870), pp. 14, 41–42, 116–17, 177–78. In this text Bowen also reiterated the definition of 'middle class' that he had first made in 1856 in *Principles of Political Economy.* They included "what on the continent would be called the bourgeoisie: the merchants, manufacturers, small tradesmen, the master mechanics" (p. 106). For other examples of the rejection of "mutual misunderstanding," see Lyman H. Atwater, "Political Economy: A Science of What?" *Princeton Review* 5 (May 1880): 439; David A. Wasson, "The Modern Types of Oppression," *North American Review* 119 (October 1874): 279; David A. Wells, "The Production and Distribution of Wealth," *Journal of Social Science* 8 (May 1876): 20; John B. Jervis, *The Question of Labour and Capital* (New York: G. P. Putnam's Sons, 1877); the unsigned essay "The Struggles of Labor and Capital," *Bankers' Magazine* 33 (August 1878): 85; Edward Atkinson, *Labor and Capital Allies Not Enemies* (New York: Harper, 1879); Joseph Thompson, *The Workman: His False Friends and His True Friends* (New York: American Tract Society, 1879).

16. For an analysis of the labor-reform movement and the trade union officials, clergymen, reformers, and "pamphleteers" involved in it, see David

Montgomery, *Beyond Equality: Labor and the Radical Republicans, 1862–1872* (New York: Knopf, 1967), pp. 135–96, 462–69; Montgomery, *The Fall of the House of Labor: The Workplace, the State, and American Labor Activism, 1865–1925* (New York: Cambridge University Press, 1987). Especially in the latter, Montgomery stresses the power of the "spoken and printed word" in creating and disseminating a "widely shared analysis of society" (pp. 1–2). See also Gerald N. Grob, *Workers and Utopia: A Study of Ideological Conflict in the American Labor Movement, 1865–1900* (Evanston, Ill.: Northwestern University Press, 1961), pp. 11–59; Unger, *Greenback Era,* pp. 180–94. Compare Reddy, *Money and Liberty in Modern Europe.*

A very informative comparative analysis of the American situation may be found in Sima Lieberman, "The American Labor Movement in the Light of European Thought," in *Labor Movements and Labor Thought: France, Germany, and the United States* (New York: Praeger, 1986), pp. 230–64.

17. William H. Sylvis, "Address to the Buffalo Convention, January 1864," in *The Life, Speeches, Labors, and Essays of William H. Sylvis,* ed. James C. Sylvis (Philadelphia: Claxton, Remsen, and Haffelfinger, 1872), pp. 97–98 (all Sylvis's works cited here are in this collection). In the course of emphasizing the importance of the laboring classes to the social and economic "wealth of the nation," Sylvis cited the work of Adam Smith for support. On Sylvis, the IMIU, and the NLU, see Jonathan Grossman, *William Sylvis, Pioneer of American Labor: A Study of the Labor Movement during the Era of the Civil War* (New York: Columbia University Press, 1945); Montgomery, *Beyond Equality,* pp. 223–29; Grob, *Workers and Utopia,* pp. 11–33. On the tendency of Sylvis and the IMIU to "look upon their employers as enemies," see *Documentary History,* ed. Commons, 9:89–93. On the social positions of "economical" writers see "The Working-Man's View of Capital," *Nation* 8 (1869): 85. There the unsigned contributor notes that these writers are "middle"- and "upper"-class men.

18. Sylvis, "Address to the Buffalo Convention," pp. 97, 99–102, 104–5. In denying the "existence of an identity of interests between capital and labor," Sylvis distinguished between his use of the former term as interchangeable with 'capitalist', and its use as a synonym for money. He did not wish to imply a lack of identity with the latter (p. 100). In his assessment of the wages issue, Sylvis assumed that the share alloted to the laboring classes would steadily decrease, and that in the "never-ending conflict between the two classes," capital will always be the aggressor (p. 101). For other applications of Seward's "irrepressible conflict" imagery to the labor question, see the unsigned essay "Capital and Labor," *Old Guard* 5 (1867): 119–21; Ben E. Green, *The Irrepressible Conflict between Labor and Capital* (Philadelphia: Claxton, Remsen, and Haffelfinger, 1872).

19. Sylvis, "Address to the Buffalo Convention," pp. 105–6; Sylvis, "Address to the Chicago Convention, January 1865," pp. 130–32. For other examples of Sylvis's stress on the "never-ending conflict," see "Address to the Boston Convention, January 1867," p. 181; "Address to the Workingmen's Assembly at Birmingham, Pennsylvania, September 1865," p. 225; "To Your Tents," pp. 439–40.

See also Sylvis's and the NLU's response to a request from Karl Marx and the International Workingmen's Association, in *Documentary History,* ed. Commons, 9:340–41, in which Sylvis notes that "a little blood letting is sometimes necessary in desperate cases." For criticisms of Sylvis's often inflammatory language, as well as his intentions, see Charles F. Dunbar, "International Association of Working Men," *Old and New* 5 (1872): 318.

20. Sylvis, "Address to the Chicago Convention," pp. 130–31, 159–60. Given the occasional nature of the piece, Sylvis did not here acknowledge other sources, but in a number of passages his phrasing is exactly that of Simpson's. Compare pages 157 and 159 to Stephen Simpson, *Working Man's Manual,* pp. 66, 45–46. On Simpson and this work see chapter 4 above. Although both of these workingmen's advocates were residents of Philadelphia, a direct influence cannot be attributed in this instance; but Sylvis's usage strongly suggests familiarity with Simpson's work, and thus at least an intertextual connection.

21. Sylvis, "Address to the Buffalo Convention," p. 114; Sylvis, "Address to the Chicago Convention," p. 168; Sylvis, "Address to the National Convention," p. 114; Sylvis, "Address to the Boston Convention," pp. 188, 193–98; Sylvis, "Address to the Workingmen's Assembly," pp. 265–75.

See also Sylvis, "Platform of Principles of the National Labor Union," pp. 285–90. In this document, the "producing" and the "non-producing classes" were rather scientifically classified according to the unreformed canons of Smithian political economy, with the latter including bankers, insurers, middlemen, etc. In addition to cooperative endeavors in manufacturing, Sylvis advocated consumer cooperatives along the lines of the British Rochdale system. On Sylvis's and the NLU's arguments for the socially transformative powers of cooperation, see Grob, *Workers and Utopia,* pp. 19–21; Grossman, *William Sylvis,* pp. 189–219; Montgomery, *Beyond Equality,* pp. 176–79.

22. Andrew C. Cameron et al., "Address . . . to the Workingmen of the United States," in *Documentary History,* ed. Commons, 9:152. David Montgomery calls this piece "a synopsis of the labor-reform aspirations of the day" (*Beyond Equality,* pp. 180). The program of the NLU as presented in this address included the eight-hour day, cooperatives, an end to racial discrimination in trade unions, an attack on the "agency of interest laws and banking systems," and a National Labor party. It was opposed to "injudicious and ill-advised" strikes, except as a last resort, and preferred to replace the prevailing "antagonism and jealousy" between employer and employee with "a bond of sympathy" (9:132–38, 141–68).

23. Cameron et al., "Address . . . to the Workingmen," pp. 159, 164, 165–67. On Andrew C. Cameron see Montgomery, *Beyond Equality,* p. 463. For a further exposition of Cameron's confidence in the "spirit" of American republican institutions, see his comments on the 1869 Basel congress of the International Workingmen's Association, to which he was the NLU delegate. Cameron felt that its resolutions against the ownership and inheritance of private property—resolutions owing to Marx—were not applicable to American conditions, given the different "texture of society" here. See "The Delegate to Basle," in *Documentary History,* ed. Commons, 9:341–50.

24. Cameron et al., "Address . . . to the Workingmen"; NLU, "Declaration of Principles" (1867); both in *Documentary History,* ed. Commons, 9:141–68, 176–83; NLU, *Address of the National Labor Union to the People of the United States* (Washington, D.C.: McGill and Witherow, 1870); Ira Steward, *The Eight Hour Movement* (Boston: Labor Reform Association, 1865), p. 23. This last piece shows the increasing importance of the currency-credit issue, or 'greenbackism', in labor-reform circles. See also "Labor Reform Platform of 1872," in *National Party Platforms, 1840–1964,* ed. Kirk H. Porter and Donald B. Johnson (Urbana: University of Illinois Press, 1966), pp. 43–44. On this issue see Montgomery, *Beyond Equality,* pp. 425–47; Unger, *Greenback Era,* pp. 94–114. On Steward see Montgomery, *Beyond Equality,* pp. 249–60; David Roediger, "Ira Steward and the Anti-Slavery Origins of American Eight Hour Theory," *Labor History* 27 (1986): 410–26.

For other instances of this general rhetorical stance taken by labor reformers, albeit with differing emphases on how severe the current conflict might be and how it would best be rectified, see Lucius Hine, *Hine's Political and Social Economy* (Cincinnati: L. Hine, 1861); Frederic Hinckley, *The Philosophy of the Labor Movement* (Boston: G. H. Ellis, 1874); A Merchant, "Labor and Capital," *Radical* 10 (1872): 96–104; Lewis Masquerier, *Sociology; or, the Reconstruction of Society, Government, and Property* (New York: L. Masquerier, 1877); Wendell Phillips, "The Outlook," *North American Review* 127 (1878): 97–116; Marvin Warren, *American Labor: Its Great Wrongs, and How It Can Redress Them* (St. Joseph, Mo.: Steam Printing Co., 1877); Hendrick B. Wright, *A Practical Treatise on Labor* (New York: G. W. Carleton, 1871). See also Adolfe A. Granier De Cassagnac, *History of the Working and Burgher Classes,* trans. Ben E. Green (1838; reprint, Philadelphia: Claxton, Remsen, and Haffelfinger, 1871). In his dedication to the "working and burgher classes" Green includes not only laborers, mechanics, husbandmen, and merchants, but lawyers, physicians, ministers, and all others in the "learned professions" within these classes (p. v). On the call for a "scientific reconciliation" of the classes, see also David Herreshoff, *The Origins of American Marxism, from the Transcendentalists to De Leon* (New York: Monad Press, 1973), pp. 84–85, 91.

25. Cameron, "Delegate to Basle," pp. 342–45; Edwin M. Chamberlin, *The Sovereigns of Industry* (Boston: Lee and Shepard, 1875), pp. 4, 41, 68. Chamberlin had campaigned for the Massachusetts governorship in 1869 as the Labor Reform candidate. On Chamberlin see Donald D. Egbert and Stow Persons, eds., *Socialism and American Life* (Princeton: Princeton University Press, 1952), 2:298; Montgomery, *Beyond Equality,* pp. 369–70.

26. Chamberlin, *Sovereigns of Industry,* pp. 6, 32–33, 57–58, 68–69, 81, 84.

27. Ibid., pp. 4, 57–58, 68–69, 72–74, 79–81, 122, 157. Chamberlin also advocated a system of cooperation in which the possession and exchange of money would be replaced by the direct exchange of labor and materials: "in the future the capitalist will release himself from a similar position [of being dominated] in regard to labor, only so far as he becomes a laborer himself" (p. 58). Chamberlin's proposals here resemble those of the American anarchist and radical individualist Josiah Warren, the influence of whose works he acknowledged. With his recommendation for nationalization, Chamberlin

moved well past the Sovereigns' goals of cooperation and banking/currency reforms. While the latter called on the working classes to "study the various questions of political economy and social science," they did not necessarily expect or endorse all of Chamberlin's answers. See their "Preamble" and "Report on the Committee on Principles" in Chamberlin, *Sovereigns of Industry,* pp. 145, 154, 157–58.

28. Chamberlin, *Sovereigns of Industry,* pp. 4, 29, 41, 68, 83, 95, 165. Although Chamberlin noted that the "schemes" of Robert Owen, Pierre-Joseph Proudhon, Charles Fourier, and Josiah Warren would "accomplish all that the workingmen could ask," he did not directly identify himself or his ideas as socialist (pp. 164–65). Other calls for the political mobilization of the working/producing classes include One of the Many, *The Coming Crisis* (San Francisco: A. L. Bancroft, 1879). On the intersections of labor radicalism and political mobilization, see Richard Schneriov, "Political Cultures and the Role of the State in Labor's Republic," *Labor History* 32 (1991): 376–400; Seymour Martin Lipset, "Radicalism or Reformism: The Sources of Working Class Politics," *American Political Science Review* 77 (1983): 1–18.

29. Chamberlin, *Sovereigns of Industry,* pp. 4, 160, 164. On the Sovereigns and the varieties of "agitation by the working classes," see also Richard J. Hinton, "Trades Unions and Cooperation," *Old and New* 11 (1875): 69–73. Among the other radical advocates of the common ownership of means of transportation and communication was Victoria C. Woodhull. See her 1873 address at New York's Cooper Institute, *Reformation or Revolution, Which?* (New York: Woodhull and Claflin, 1873); and her 1876 Boston Theatre address, *The Review of the Century* (London: Women's Co-operative Printing Union, 1893). In both addresses Woodhull classifies the American population in terms of 'producers' and 'nonproducers'.

30. Ezra Hervey Heywood, "The Great Strike," *Radical Review* 1 (1877): 553–54, 557, 565. On Heywood see Martin Blatt, *Free Love and Anarchism: The Biography of Ezra Heywood* (Urbana: University of Illinois Press, 1989); Alden Whitman, ed., *American Reformers* (New York: Wilson, 1985), pp. 428–29; Montgomery, *Beyond Equality,* pp. 411–12. Heywood was also a prominent advocate of "marriage reform" and of equality between the sexes.

For other, less tolerant, evaluations of the Great Strike see Edwin L. Godkin, "The Late Riots," *Nation* 24 (1877): 68. Godkin observes that the recent events had shaken fifty years of a prevailing faith that in the United States, at least, labor and capital could "live together in political harmony," and that there was "no proletariat and no dangerous class" in the republic. See also the unsigned piece "The Month," *Penn Monthly* 8 (August 1877): 574–75, which notes the "embitterment" of the working classes' "opinions" due to depression, lowered wages, and unemployment in the preceeding years. See also An Anglo-American, *The Labor Problem in the United States* (New York: Atheneum, 1878).

31. Heywood, "Great Strike," pp. 554–57, 565–66, 576. In addition to labor reform, Heywood finds other examples of the "assertion of the rights of 1776" in the works of Josiah Warren and Pierre-Joseph Proudhon and, despite their manifest differences with the above, in the works of Adam Smith

and John Stuart Mill (p. 575). See also his essay *Yours or Mine* (Boston: Weekly American Workman, 1869).

On the reactions to the railway strike of 1877 see David Roediger, "Not Only the Ruling Class to Overcome, but Also the So-Called Mob: Class, Skill, and Community in the St. Louis General Strike of 1877," *Journal of Social History* 19 (1985): 213–39.

32. Heywood, "Great Strike," p. 556. See also Stephen Pearl Andrews, "The Labor Dollar," *Radical Review* 1 (1877): 287–97. Andrews contrasted the "current political economy" with a "radical political economy." The first studied the laws of the production and distribution of wealth as they now were, while the second proposed laws for things as they should be (p. 291). See also Woodhull, *Review of the Century*.

33. Jesse H. Jones, "The Labor Problem: A Statement of the Question from the Labor-Reform Side," *International Review* 9 (1880): 53. In an introductory statement (p. 50), the *Review*'s editor noted that, while Jones's "doctrines" regarding the "so-called laboring class" were "erroneous," the question was so important that it warranted exposure.

34. Jesse H. Jones, "Labor Problem," pp. 53–54, 56, 67. On Jones see Howard Quint, *The Forging of American Socialism: Origins of the Modern Movement* (Indianapolis: Bobbs-Merrill, 1953), pp. 105–6, 110; Henry May, *Protestant Churches and Industrial America* (1949; reprint, New York: Octagon Books, 1963), pp. 74–79; Montgomery, *Beyond Equality*, p. 210.

35. Jesse H. Jones, "Labor Problem," pp. 53–58, 61, 64–68. In his exposition of the "organization" of society, Jones also contended that "society is an organism," humans are its "living parts," and the "relations in which they stand form the structure into which it is shaped." With this construal of "relations" he then notes the "contradiction" between injurious social relations, such as slavery and wage labor, and the good people who may be involved in them, such as slaveholders and managers. Jones holds that a man's function in this system of relations, not his character, is to be faulted (p. 55). Jones's equation of slavery and wage labor and his calls for the abolition of the latter are indicative of the continuities between the rhetoric of New England antislavery and of New England labor reform.

36. Jesse H. Jones, "Labor Problem," pp. 61, 64–68. Though he did not advert to it in this essay, Jones favored the nationalization of most capital assets and the abolition of profits, rents, and interest as measures to eliminate both of the classes. As a Christian Socialist, however, he assigned final agency in this social reconstruction not to any particular class, but to "the Most High" (p. 59).

37. Jesse H. Jones, "Labor Problem," pp. 53, 56, 67. On the 'proletarians' of the city see also Henry George, *Progress and Poverty* (1879; reprint, New York: Robert Schalekenbach, 1934), p. 302. George's text includes dichotomies between working and "propertied" classes, "producers" and "nonproducers," laborers and capitalists, and lower and upper classes. George's remedies for the "working classes," however, did not include socialism, nor did he assume that capital and labor were necessarily in conflict (pp. 320–21, 393, 452–53).

38. Jesse H. Jones, "Labor Problem," p. 56; "General Rules of the Association of the United Workers of America, 1874," in *Documentary History,* ed. Commons, 9:377; John Francis Bray, Joseph A. Labadie, and Judson Grenell, *Tracts of the Socialistic Labor Party* (Detroit: Socialistic Tract Association, 1879–80).

On both these socialisms in the United States during this period, see Mark Lause, "The American Radicals and Organized Marxism: The Initial Experience,"*Labor History* 33 (1992): 55–80; Carol Poore, "The Role of German Immigrants in the American Socialist Movement, 1877–1886," *Jahrbuch des Institute für Deutsche Geschichte* 12 (1983): 255–84; Quint, *Forging of American Socialism,* pp. 3–36; Herreshoff, *Origins of American Marxism,* pp. 74–104. On Bray see Ray Boston, *British Chartists in America* (Manchester: Manchester University Press, 1971), pp. 61–63, 67–70, 89. On Labadie see Quint, *Forging of American Socialism,* pp. 139–40. For other instances of the dispersal of such socialist analyses in English, see the 1873 address by the Boston section no. 1 of the International Workingmen's Association, in *Socialistic, Communistic, Mutualistic, and Financial Fragments,* ed. William Batchelder Greene (Boston: Lee and Shepard, 1875), pp. 230–60. See also Robert A. Gorman, *Yankee Red: Nonorthodox Marxism in Liberal America* (New York: Praeger, 1979), pp. 2–7; Lieberman, *Labor Movements and Labor Thoughts,* pp. 233–38; Kenneth Fones-Wolf, "Boston Eight-Hour Men, New York Marxists, and the Emergence of the International Labor Union," *Historical Journal of Massachusetts* 9 (1981): 47–59.

39. Bray, Labadie, and Grenell, "What Is Socialism," tract 1, pp. 1–4; "Government," tract 2, p. 3; "What Socialism Means," tract 3, pp. 2–3; "Who Should Be Socialists?" tract 4, pp. 2–4; "What Socialism Offers," tract 5, p. 1; "A Just Criticism," tract 6, p. 1; all in *Tracts of the Socialistic Labor Party.*

See also Socialistic Labor Party, *Platform, Constitution, and Resolutions* (Detroit: National Executive Committee of the Socialistic Labor Party, 1880), pp. 1–3, 10. The party advocated less-sweeping measures, such as eight-hour-workday legislation, reform of the taxation on land, currency reform, a "ministry of labor" and bureau of labor statistics, and the revocation of land grants to railroads. Many of these measures were common to the broader movement of labor reform. On the preference for evolution over revolution among American socialists, see Mark A. Pittenger, *American Socialists and Evolutionary Thought, 1870–1920* (Madison: University of Wisconsin Press, 1993).

40. Bray, Labadie, and Grenell, "Government," tract 2, p. 1; Socialistic Labor Party, *Platform, Constitution, and Resolutions,* pp. 9–10. Among the other journals that the SLP noted as having discussed the socialist movement in an "earnest," albeit "unfavorable," way were the *International Review,* the *Nineteenth Century,* and the *Boston Investigator.*

41. "Labor Congresses at Home and Abroad," *Merchant's Magazine* 59 (1868): 292. In this unsigned piece the contributor takes issue with the proponents of the "so-called 'working classes,' " a title that is "a misnomer in itself," since it excludes merchants, lawyers, doctors, etc. See also the Republican party platform for 1872 and 1876 in *National Party Platforms,* ed. Porter and Johnson, pp. 46–48, 53–55.

42. Edwin L. Godkin, "Co-operation," *North American Review* 106 (1868): 154–56, 158, 170. On Godkin, particularly his economic and social views, see William M. Armstrong, *E. L. Godkin: A Biography* (Albany: State University of New York Press, 1978), pp. 9–11, 67, 93–94, 112–19, 204, 231; Edward Caudill, "E. L. Godkin and the Science of Society," *Journalism Quarterly* 66 (1989): 57–64; Terry Hynes, "E. L. Godkin," in *American Magazine Journalists,* ed. Riley, pp. 160–73; Frank Tariello, Jr., *The Reconstruction of American Political Ideology, 1865–1917* (Charlottesville: University Press of Virginia, 1982), pp. 34–56. On Godkin and labor reform see Montgomery, *Beyond Equality.*

43. Godkin, "Co-operation," pp. 152, 155–56, 172–75; Godkin, "The Labor Crisis," *Nation* 4 (1867): 335; see also Godkin, "Why Political Economy Has Not Been Cultivated in America," *Nation* 5 (1867): 255–56.

44. Godkin, "Co-operation," pp. 152, 155–56, 159–63, 169–70, 174–75; Godkin, "Labor Crisis," p. 335; Godkin, "The Working-Men's Congresses," *Nation* 7 (1868): 245; Godkin, "The Working-Man's View of Capital," *Nation* 8 (1869): 85–86; Godkin, "Latest Phase of the Labor Trouble," *Nation* 8 (1869): 249–50; "The Workingmen's Ideal Society," *Nation* 9 (1869): 286; Godkin, "The Future of Capital," *Nation* 12 (1871): 429–30.

45. Simon Newcomb, "The Labor Question," *North American Review* 111 (1870): 122–23, 124, 126–28, 140–41. On Newcomb see William J. Barber, "Political Economy in the Flagship of Postgraduate Studies: The Johns Hopkins University," in *Breaking the Academic Mould,* ed. Barber, pp. 209–20; Barber, "Should the American Economic Association Have Toasted Simon Newcomb at Its 100th Birthday Party?" *Journal of Economic Perspectives* 1 (1987): 179–83; Dorfman, *Economic Mind,* 3:83–87. See Albert Moyer, *A Scientist's Voice in American Culture: Simon Newcomb and the Rhetoric of Scientific Method* (Berkeley: University of California Press, 1992).

46. Newcomb, "Labor Question," p. 122.

47. Ibid., pp. 123–24, 126–28, 133–34, 140–45, 149. See also Frederick Lockley, "The Labor Reform Party," *Western Monthly* 4 (1870): 356–57, wherein Lockley notes that the great "agricultural class," which for him made up one-third of the population, was not represented by the NLU, nor were the one-half of workers in the "mechanical trades" who were not members of trades unions.

48. Newcomb, "Labor Question," pp. 124, 150–55. For similar analyses in the "prominent publications" see Charles C. P. Clark, "Work, Wages, and Combination," *Putnam's Magazine* 13 (1869): 141–48; S. G. Fisher, "The Eight Hour Movement," *Nation* 1 (1865): 517; Hamilton A. Hill, "The Relations of the Businessmen of the United States to the National Legislation," *Journal of Social Science* 3 (1871): 148–49; J. B. Hodgskin, "The Eight Hour Movement," *Nation* 10 (1870): 399; Arthur G. Sedgwick, "What Labor Reform Means," *Nation* 9 (1869): 454; "Labor Congresses at Home and Abroad," *Merchant's Magazine* 59 (1868): 292–95; "General Intelligence: Home," *Journal of Social Science* 3 (1870): 207–8; "Certain Dangerous Tendencies in American Life," *Atlantic Monthly* 42 (1878): 393–97.

49. Horace Greeley, *Essays Designed to Elucidate the Science of Political Economy* (Boston: Fields, Osgood, 1870), p. 160. On Greeley and the *Science of*

Political Economy see Suzanne Schultz, *Horace Greeley: A Bio-Bibliography* (New York: Greenwood, 1992); Erik S. Lunde, *Horace Greeley* (Boston: Twayne, 1981), pp. 98–99; Glyndon G. Van Deunsen, *Horace Greeley: Nineteenth Century Crusader* (Philadelphia: University of Pennsylvania Press, 1953), pp. 379–80. The science of political economy, as interpreted by Greeley, mandated a protective tariff, a conclusion at odds with the free-trade principles of Newcomb, Godkin, et alia.

50. Greeley, *Science of Political Economy,* pp. 159–60.

51. Ibid., pp. 41, 43, 83–86, 89, 159. As examples of the cooperative spirit Greeley notes the British Rochdale enterprises and the "shares" distributed to the crews of whaling ships.

52. Samuel Johnson, "Labor Parties and Labor Reform," *Radical* 9 (1871): 243–47. This essay was subsequently issued as a pamphlet. On the Reverend Johnson see Roger C. Mueller, ed., *Selected Writings of Samuel Johnson* (Delmar, N.Y.: Scholar's Facsimiles, 1977); Mueller, *Samuel Johnson, American Transcendentalist: A Short Biography* (Salem: Essex Institute, 1979). On Johnson and the labor reformers see Montgomery, *Beyond Equality,* pp. 336–37.

53. Samuel Johnson, "Labor Parties and Labor Reform," pp. 243, 244–45, 246–48. Johnson also introduced a higher authority into this discussion by observing that "God hath joined labor and capital, and that no man or party has authority to put them asunder, or to declare them foes" (p. 247).

54. Ibid., pp. 242–43, 245, 248, 251–52.

55. Ibid., p. 247.

56. Ibid., p. 243. For other instances of this type of argument see Carl Benson, "The Labor Question," *Galaxy* 15 (1873): 312–18; Charles C. P. Clark, "Work, Wages, and Combination," p. 142; Dunbar, "International Association of Working Men," pp. 318–21; Edwin L. Godkin, "'The Commune' and the Labor Question," *Nation* 12 (1871): 333–34; Godkin, "Some of the Remedies for Socialism," *International Review* 6 (June 1879): 676–94; Godkin, "The Cormorants and the Commune," *Nation* 31 (1880): 181; Lockley, "Labor Reform Party," pp. 356–64; David A. Wasson, "The International," *Journal of Social Science* 5 (1873): 109–21; Wasson, "Modern Types of Oppression," pp. 253–85. Wasson, in this last piece, compares the International Workingmen's Association slogan of "Down with the middle classe!" to the labor reformers' cry that "he who works for wages is a slave" (p. 275). See also the unsigned essays "The Internationale," *Lippincott's Magazine* 8 (1871): 466–74; "Capital, Labor, and Wages," *Republic* 2 (1874): 114–19; "The Communistic Movement," *Nation* 26 (1878): 302.

See also Henry Ammon James, *Communism in America* (New York: H. Holt, 1879); An Anglo-American, *Labor Problem in the United States;* Jervis, *Question of Labour and Capital;* Joseph Thompson, *Workman.*

57. Other examples of this general argument include Ernest Gryzanovski, "The International Workingmen's Association," *North American Review* 113 (1872): 309–76. There Gryzanovski, a doctor of medicine in Florence and correspondent to the *North American Review,* stresses the difference between the "working classe" of Europe and the "workingmen constituting no class at all" in the United States. When the latter listen to the former "declare war

against the capitalists," they have "difficulty in understanding the theoretical antagonism between labor and capital, which has never been brought home . . . in the tangible shape of stereotyped class distinctions" (p. 357).

See also Erastus H. Bigelow, "The Relations of Labor and Capital," *Atlantic Monthly* 42 (1879): 475–86. Bigelow argues that "in this country the social pyramid rises in such just proportions that there is no marked line which separates the laborer from the capitalist" (p. 486).

58. Noah Webster, Chauncy Goodrich, and Noah Porter, *An American Dictionary of the English Language* (Springfield, Mass.: G. and C. Merriam, 1880), p. 1585. On 'working class' see their 1865 edition of *An American Dictionary* (Springfield, Mass.: G. and C. Merriam), p. 1525. This edition has three examples of the entry 'class': "the different classes of society; the educated class; the lower class" (p. 236). Joseph E. Worchester, *A Dictionary of the English Language* (Boston: Brewer and Tileson, 1869), has as examples of 'class' "the trading class, the laboring class . . . high, low, or middle class" (p. 249).

59. For discussions of the limitation of the term 'workingmen' to manual laborers in "popular" language, see Frederick J. Kingsbury, "The Eight-Hour Delusion," *Nation* 3 (1866): 412; Isaac Butts, "Capital and Labor," *North American Review* 116 (1873): 56; "The Working Man and the Panic," *Nation* 17 (1873): 284.

Epilogue

1. U. S. Congress, House, "Investigation by a Select Committee of the House of Representatives relative to the Causes of the General Depression in Labor and Business," in *Miscellaneous Documents of the House of Representatives for the Third Session, Forty-fifth Congress, 1878–1879,* vol. 3, doc. 29 (Washington, D.C.: Government Printing Office, 1879), pp. 181–208. The members of the committee included Abram S. Hewitt of New York, J. M. Thompson of Pennsylvania, W. W. Rice of Massachusetts, and Thomas A. Boyd of Illinois. Sumner gave his testimony on 22 August 1878. Additional hearings were held in Scranton and Washington.

2. Ibid., pp. 191, 204–5. On Hewitt see Allan Nevins, *Abram S. Hewitt* (New York: Octagon Books, 1967).

3. House, "Investigation," pp. 18, 27, 46, 76–77, 120, 180, 554. See in particular the testimonies of Isaac Bennett, pp. 25–29; Adolph Douai, a Marxist socialist, pp. 29–41; Hugh McGregor, a New York City jeweler, who called for a bureau of labor that would "classify the people according to their occupations," pp. 8–9; Robert H. Bartholomee, chairman of the SLP of America, pp. 17–25; Robert W. Hume, pp. 76–77; George McNeill of Somerville, Mass., who argued that "we will be able to demonstrate that the old political economists were false, and we will evolve soon a social science that will give us light on these questions," p. 120; William G. Smart, a stonecutter from Boston, pp. 180–81.

4. Ibid., pp. 76, 154–55, 181–208. See in particular the testimonies of Joseph Bishop, pp. 487–89; William Godwin Moody, the Boston printer, pp. 154–55; John O. Edwards, an unemployed iron worker from Allegheny City, Pa., pp. 475–76; Miles F. Humphreys of Pittsburgh, a puddler, p. 510. See

also the published testimony of J. H. Walker, a mechanic from Worcester, Mass., *Common Sense Views on Political Economy, Capital, Labor, Socialism* (Worcester: American News, 1878).

5. U. S. Congress, Senate, *Report of the Committee of the Senate upon the Relations between Labor and Capital, and the Testimony Taken by the Committee* (Washington, D.C.: Government Printing Office, 1885), 1:5, 36, 49, 51, 241–42, 255–56, 322, 358, 376, 383, 561, 578–79, 601, 664, 758, 954, 2:76, 216, 438, 586, 696, 795, 802, 3:403, 4:381; Robert Layton and Hugh Blair, 1:1–5; John Campbell, a telegraph operator, Knight of Labor, and member of the Brotherhood of Telegraphers, and Senator Blair, 1:106. See also Charles Lenz of the SLP and Senator James George of Mississippi, 1:255–56; P. J. McGuire of the Carpenters' Union and Senator Wilkinson Call of Florida, 1:350; John Morrison, a machinist from New York City and a supporter of Lassalle and Marx, and Senator George, 1:758–59; Thomas McGuire, a New York City teamster, and Senator Call, 1:779; Richard J. Hinton, the New York journalist, and Senator Call, 2:439; Adolf Douai of the SLP and Senator Call, 2:719; Edward King of New York's Central Labor Union and Senator Blair, 2:886–88; John Keogh of Fall River, Mass., a self-employed printer, and Senator Blair, 3:488.

6. In the Senate *Report* the rhetoric of reconcilable class conflict was employed by Robert Layton, 1:16; Frank Foster of the International Typographical Union, 1:88; John McClelland of the Knights of Labor, 1:218; Henry George, 1:467–507; P. H. McLogan of the Chicago Federation of Trades Unions, 1:576–79; John Swinton, an editor of the *New York Sun,* 1:1095–1112; E. C. Alphonse, a "workman" from Orange, N.J., 2:391; Isaac Sturgeon of St. Louis, 2:395; Rev. R. H. Newton of All Souls Protestant Episcopal Church in Garden City, N.Y., 2:553–77.

Analyses that assumed that a more fundamental, "ever-recurring" class antagonism was characteristic of American capitalism included those of P. J. McGuire, 1:322–55, 812–13; Samuel Gompers, 1:567; John Morrison, 1: 759–64; Adolf Douai, 2:702–43.

Class harmony was emphasized by Senator Blair, 1:62; Jay Gould, the New York investor, 1:1088; Colonel Dexter Hawkins of New York, 2:152; William Lawrence, president of the Association of American Economists, 2:216; A Pittsburgh Lawyer, 2:334–62; Erastus Goodwin, a farmer from Falls Village, Conn., 2:688–94; John M. Gregory of Chicago, a member of the Civil Service Commission, 2:784–802; Walter Barnett of New York City, a cigar manufacturer, 2:840; Timothy Wright of New York City, a "student of political economy and social science," 2:856; Danford Knowlton, a "mercantile gentleman" from New York, 2:1072.

Responses to these hearings include Matthew Trumbull, *Signing the Document: The Laokoon of Labor, Chopping Sand, and Other Essays* (Chicago: Radical Review, 1884).

7. For examples of the rhetorical and conceptual salience of class antagonism see *Labor: Its Rights and Wrongs* (Washington, D.C.: Labor Publishing Co., 1886), a volume of sources and commentaries compiled by the Knights

of Labor; S. M. Jelley, ed., *The Voice of Labor* (Chicago: A. B. Gehman, 1887); Clare Lacombe, *The History of a Peaceful Revolution* (Boston: Knights of Labor, 1886); William H. Lyon, *The People's Problem and Its Solution* (Sioux Falls, Dakota: W. Lyon, 1886); George McNeill, ed., *The Labor Movement: The Problem of Today* (New York: A. M. Bridgman, 1887); William Godwin Moody, *Land and Labor in the United States* (New York: Scribner's, 1883).

See also the platforms of the Democratic and Greenback parties for 1880; the Anti-Monopoly party for 1884; the United Labor party for 1888; the Democratic, People's, and Socialistic Labor parties for 1892; and the Democrats and the Socialistic Labor parties for 1896; all in *National Party Platforms*, ed. Porter and Johnson, pp. 56–58, 64–66, 84–85, 86–90, 95–96, 109–11.

Usages of 'class' were as open to debate among these critics as among other communities of discourse. See, for example, Terrence V. Powderly, "A Few Practical Hints," *Journal of United Labor* 1 (1880): 21. In a critical evaluation of trade unions, the Knights of Labor's Powderly announced, "I hate that word 'class' and would drive it from the English language if I could."

8. On the usages of 'class' by late-nineteenth-century critics of the social order, see Leon Fink, *Workingmen's Democracy: The Knights of Labor and American Politics* (Urbana: University of Illinois Press, 1983), pp. 3–6, 220; Jonathan Garlock, "A Structural Analysis of the Knights of Labor: A Prolegomenon to the History of the Producing Classes," Ph.D. diss., University of Rochester, 1974, pp. 1, 58; Steven J. Ross, "The Culture of Political Economy: Henry George and the American Working Class," *South California Quarterly* 65 (1983): 148, 152, 154–55; Scott G. McNall, *The Road to Rebellion: Class Formation and Kansas Populism, 1865–1900* (Chicago: University of Chicago Press, 1988), pp. 142–84; John L. Thomas, *Alternative America: Henry George, Edward Bellamy, Henry Demarest Lloyd, and the Adversary Tradition* (Cambridge, Mass.: Belknap, 1983); David Green, *Shaping Political Consciousness: The Language of Politics in America from McKinley to Reagan* (Ithaca, N.Y.: Cornell University Press, 1987); Clark D. Halker, *For Democracy, Workers, and God: Labor Song-Poems and Labor Protest, 1865–1895* (Urbana: University of Illinois Press, 1991).

For the variations of 'class' in twentieth-century American discourse, see Anderson, "Language of Class in Twentieth Century America," pp. 349–75; Fussell, *Class*, pp. 15–27, Werner S. Landecker, *Class Crystallization* (New Brunswick, N.J.: Rutgers University Press, 1981), pp. 5–6; Marwick, *Class;* Mary R. Jackman and Robert W. Jackman, *Class Awareness in the United States* (Berkeley and Los Angeles: University of California Press, 1983).

9. Examples of the continued salience of the model of social harmony include Charles Oliver Brown, *Talks on the Labor Troubles* (Chicago: F. A. Revell, 1886); James A. Waterworth, "The Conflict Historically Considered," in *The Labor Problem: Plain Questions and Practical Answers*, ed. William E. Barnes (New York: Harper, 1886), pp. 2–51; John Milton Gregory, *A New Political Economy* (Chicago: American Book, 1882); Jonathan Baxter Harrison, *Certain Dangerous Tendencies in American Life, and Other Papers* (Boston: Houghton, Osgood, 1880); John J. Lalor, ed., *Cyclopaedia of Political Science,*

Political Economy, and of the Political History of the United States (Chicago: Rand, McNally, 1882–84); Simon Newcomb, *A Plain Man's Talk on the Labor Question* (New York: Harper, 1886).

10. See, for example, the Republican platforms for 1884, 1892, and 1900 in *National Party Platforms,* ed. Porter and Johnson, pp. 72–74, 93–95, 121–24; the following addresses, all in *Messages and Papers of the Presidents,* ed. Richardson: Benjamin Harrison, "Inaugural Address, March 4, 1889," 9:8; Harrison, "Third Annual Message, December 9, 1891," 9:194; Harrison, "Fourth Annual Message, December 6, 1892," 9:311; William McKinley, "Inaugural Address, March 4, 1897," 10:41. See also Jeffrey Nelson, "The Rhetoric of the 1896 Republican National Convention at St. Louis," *Missouri Historical Review* 77 (1983): 395–409.

11. William Graham Sumner, *What Social Classes Owe to Each Other,* pp. 22, 40, 58, 73–75, 101. Bruce Curtis has called Sumner's view on class relations one of "antagonistical co-operation" (*William Graham Sumner,* pp. 83, 95, 99, 124).

Along with these syncretizing arguments of Sumner, see the works of John Stahl Patterson, especially *Conflict in Nature and in Life* (New York: D. Appleton, 1883) and *Reforms: Their Difficulties and Possibilities* (New York: D. Appleton, 1884).

12. The changes in the idioms of the political discourse of American liberalism in the late nineteenth century are discussed in Tariello, *Reconstruction of American Political Ideology;* Rodgers, *Contested Truths;* Roper, *Democracy and Its Critics.* Comparable changes in the social sciences are studied in Bannister, *Sociology and Scientism;* Dorothy Ross, "Socialism and American Liberalism: Academic Social Thought in the 1880s," *Perspectives in American History* 11 (1977–78): 7–79.

13. John Bates Clark, "The Nature and Progress of True Socialism," *New Englander* 38 (1879): 568–69. In addition to this piece of Clark's see Clark, "Unrecognized Forces in Political Economy," *New Englander* 36 (1877): 710–35; Clark, "How to Deal with Communism," *New Englander* 37 (1878): 533–42; Richard T. Ely, *The Labor Movement in America* (1886; reprint, New York: Arno, 1969); Ely, *Recent American Socialism* (Baltimore: Johns Hopkins University Press, 1885); Henry Carter Adams, "The Position of Socialism in the Development of Political Economy," *Penn Monthly* 10 (1879): 285–94; Adams, *Outline of Lectures upon Political Economy* (Baltimore: n.p., 1881); Lester Frank Ward, "Politico-social Functions," *Penn Monthly* 12 (1881): 321–36; Ward, *Dynamic Sociology* (1883; reprint, New York: Johnson, 1968).

On John Bates Clark see *Breaking the Academic Mould,* ed. Barber, pp. 199–201, 221–24, 303; Joel Jalladeau, "The Methodological Conversion of John Bates Clark," *HOPE* 7 (1975): 209–26; John F. Henry, "John Bates Clark and the Marginal Product: An Historical Inquiry into the Origins of Value-Free Economic Theory," *HOPE* 15 (1983): 375–89; Dorfman, *Economic Mind,* 3: 188–205. On Richard T. Ely see *Breaking the Academic Mould,* ed. Barber, pp. 209–25, 325–38; Benjamin G. Rader, *The Academic Mind and Reform: The Influence of Richard T. Ely in American Life* (Lexington: University of Kentucky Press, 1966). On Henry Carter Adams see Dorfman, *Economic Mind,* 3:

164–74. On Lester Frank Ward see Page, *Class and American Sociology,* pp. 29–72.

On the organizational and methodological changes in American social sciences in the late nineteenth century, see Furner, *Advocacy and Objectivity;* Thomas Haskell, *The Emergence of Professional Social Science: The American Social Science Association and the Nineteenth-Century Crisis of Authority* (Urbana: University of Illinois Press, 1977); C. D. W. Goodwin, "Marginalism Moves to the New World," *HOPE* 4 (1973): 551–70; Dorothy Ross, "Socialism and American Liberalism."

For definitional changes see Francis Amasa Walker, *The Wages Question: A Treatise on Wages and the Wages Class* (New York: Henry Holt, 1876), pp. 8–10, 206–23, 226–42; Fine, *Laissez Faire,* pp. 198–251.

14. Sumner, *What Social Classes Owe to Each Other,* p. 25.

15. Richard Grant White, "Class Distinctions in America," *North American Review* 137 (1883): 232. See also White, *Words and Their Uses Past and Present: A Study of the English Language* (Boston: Houghton Mifflin, 1870); White, *Every-Day English* (Boston: Houghton Mifflin, 1881). On White see Glenn M. Johnson, "Richard Grant White," in *American Literary Critics and Scholars,* ed. Rathbun and Grecu, pp. 82–86.

BIBLIOGRAPHY

Primary Sources: Periodicals

American Laborer, 1842–43.
American Magazine, 1787–88.
American Magazine and General Repository, 1769.
American Magazine and Monthly Chronicle, 1757–58.
American Monthly Magazine, 1836.
American Museum, 1787–92.
American Register, 1806–10.
American Whig Review, 1845–52.
Atlantic Monthly, 1857–80.
The Aurora, 1834–35.
Bankers' Magazine, 1848–78.
Banner of the Constitution, 1829–32.
Boston Magazine, 1783–86.
Boston Quarterly Review, 1840–41.
Brownson's Quarterly Review, 1844.
Christian Examiner, 1830.
Columbian Magazine, 1786–93.
De Bow's Review, 1846–80.
Democratic Review, 1837–59.
The Galaxy, 1869–74.
International Review, 1877–80.
Journal of Social Science, 1869–80.
Journal of Speculative Philosophy, 1878.
Journal of the Franklin Institute, 1834.
Journal of United Labor, 1880.
Lakeside Monthly, 1870.
Library Journal, 1880.
Lippincott's Magazine, 1868–1878.
Literary and Scientific Repository, 1820–22.
Literary Register, 1828–29.
Massachusetts Magazine, 1789–93.
Mechanic Apprentice, 1845–46.
Merchant's Magazine and Commercial Review, 1839–70.
Methodist Quarterly Review, 1841.
The Nation, 1865–80.
National Magazine, 1799–1802.
New American Magazine, 1758–60.
New Englander, 1849–50.
New York Review, 1837–40.
Niles' Weekly Register, 1811–49.
North American Review, 1815–83.
Old and New, 1871–75.
Old Guard, 1862–70.
The Patriot, 1801–2.
Penn Monthly, 1870–82.
Pennsylvania Magazine, 1775–76.
The Political Censor, 1796–97.
Political Economist, 1824.
Popular Science Monthly, 1876–80.
Port Folio, 1801–27.
Princeton Review, 1880.
The Radical, 1865–72.
Radical Review, 1877.
Republic, 1874–76.
The Republican Magazine, 1798.

Royal American Magazine, 1774–75.
The Rush Light, 1800.
Scribner's Monthly, 1870–80.
Southern Literary Messenger, 1842–60.
Southern Magazine, 1868–75.
Southern Quarterly Review, 1842–57.
Southern Review, 1828–32.
U.S. Literary Gazette, 1825.
United States Magazine, 1779.
United States Magazine, 1823.
Weekly Inspector, 1806–7.
Western Journal and Civilian, 1848–56.
The Western Monthly, 1870.
Western Monthly Review, 1827–29.
The Working Man's Advocate, 1829–45.

Primary Sources: Books and Pamphlets

Adams, Henry Carter. *Outline of Lectures upon Political Economy.* Baltimore: n.p., 1881.

Adams, John. *Defence of the Constitutions of Government of the United States of America.* Vol. 4 of *The Works of John Adams.* Boston: Little, Brown, 1851.

———. *Thoughts on Government, Applicable to the Present State.* Philadelphia: Dunlap, 1776.

———. *The Works of John Adams.* Ed. Charles Francis Adams. 10 vols. Boston: Little, Brown, 1851.

Address to the Workingmen of the United States. Washington, D.C.: n.p., 1840.

Alexander, Caleb. *The Columbian Dictionary of the English Language.* Boston: Thomas and Andrews, 1800.

Alexander, James W. *The American Mechanic.* Philadelphia: H. Perkins, 1839.

———. *The Working-Man.* Philadelphia: H. Perkins, 1839.

An American. *An Essay upon the Principles of Political Economy: Designed as a Manual for Practical Men.* New York: Th. Foster, 1837.

American Federation of Labor. *Proceedings of the American Federation of Labor, 1881–1888.* Bloomington: American Federation of Labor, 1906.

Andrews, Stephen Pearl. *The Science of Society.* New York: Fowler and Wells, 1852.

An Anglo-American. *The Labor Problem in the United States.* New York: Atheneum, 1878.

Appleton, Nathan. *Labor: Its Relations in Europe and the United States Compared.* Boston: Eastburn's, 1844.

Aristocratis. *The Government of Nature Delineated.* Carlisle, Pa.: Kline and Reynolds, 1788.

Aristotle. *Politiques; or, Discourses of Government.* Trans. Loys Leroy. London: Adam Islip, 1598.

Atkinson, Edward. *Labor and Capital Allies Not Enemies.* New York: Harper, 1879.

Ayer, J. C. *Some of the Usages and Abuses in the Management of Our Manufacturing Corporations.* Lowell: C. H. Langely, 1863.

Backus, Isaac. *Government and Liberty Described, and Ecclesiastical Tyranny Exposed.* Boston: Powers and Willis, 1778.

Bailey, Nathan. *Dictionarium Britannicum.* London: T. Cox, 1736.

Bailey, Nathan, and Joseph Nicol Scott. *A New Universal Etymological English Dictionary*. London: T. Osborne, 1764.

Baldwin, Loammi. *Thoughts on the Study of Political Economy*. Cambridge, Mass.: Hilliard and Metcalf, 1809.

Ballou, Adin. *Practical Christian Socialism*. New York: Fowlers and Wells, 1854.

Barlow, Joel. *Advice to the Priviledged Orders*. New York: Childs and Swaine, 1792.

Barnes, David M. *The Draft Riots in New York, July 1863*. New York: Baker and Godwin, 1863.

Barnes, William E., ed. *The Labor Problem: Plain Questions and Practical Answers*. New York: Harper, 1886.

Bartlett, Elisha. *A Vindication of the Character and Condition of the Females Employed in the Lowell Mills* . . . Lowell: L. Huntress, 1841.

Barton, William. *The True Interest of the United States, and Particularly of Pennsylvania, Considered*. Philadelphia: Charles Cist, 1786.

Bascom, John. *Political Economy: Designed as a Text-book for Colleges*. Andover, Mass.: W. Draper, 1874.

Beecher, Henry Ward. *Patriotic Addresses*. New York: Ford, Howard, and Hubert, 1890.

Bigelow, Josiah. *A Review of Seth Luther's Address to the Working Men of New England*. Cambridge, Mass.: E. W. Metcalf, 1832.

Bishop, James L. *A History of American Manufactures from 1608 to 1860*. Philadelphia: E. Young, 1864.

Blanchard, Calvin. *The Essence of Science; or, the Catechism of Positive Sociology and Physical Mentality*. New York: C. Blanchard, 1859.

Blodget, Lorin. *The Commercial and Financial Strength of the United States*. Philadelphia: King and Baird, 1864.

Blount, Thomas. *Glossographia; or, the Interpretation of Hard Words*. 1656. Reprint. Menston, England: Scolar, 1969.

Bolles, Albert S. *Chapters in Political Economy*. New York: D. Appleton, 1874.

———. *The Conflict between Labor and Capital*. Philadelphia: Lippincott, 1876.

Bolton, Edmund Maria. *The Cities Advocate, in This Case or Question of Honor and Armes: Whether Apprenticeship Extinguisheth Gentry?* London: William Lee, 1629.

Boucher, Jonathan. *A Letter from a Virginian, to the Members of Congress*. New York: n.p., 1774.

Bowen, Francis. *American Political Economy*. New York: Scribner, 1870.

———. *The Principles of Political Economy Applied to the Condition, the Resources, and the Institutions of the American People*. Boston: Little, Brown, 1856.

Boyer, Abel. *The Royal Dictionary*. London: J. and J. Knapton, 1748.

Braxton, Carter. *An Address to the Convention of the Colony of Ancient Domain of Virginia*. Philadelphia: Dunlap, 1776.

Bray, John Francis. *American Destiny: What Shall It Be, Republican or Cossack?* New York: Columbian Association, 1864.

Bray, John Francis, Joseph A. Labadie, and Judson Grenell. *Tracts of the Socialistic Labor Party*. Detroit: Socialistic Tract Association, 1879–80.

Brisbane, Albert. *A Concise Exposition of the Doctrine of Association*. New York: J. S. Redfield, 1843.

———. *A General Introduction to Social Science*. New York: C. P. Somerby, 1876.

———. *Social Destiny of Man; or, Association and Reorganization of Industry*. Philadelphia: C. F. Stollmeyer, 1840.

Brown, Charles Oliver. *Talks on the Labor Troubles*. Chicago: F. A. Revell, 1886.

Brown, Paul. *The Radical and Advocate of Equality*. Albany: Stone and Munsell, 1834.

Brown, William Laurence. *An Essay on the Natural Equality of Men*. Philadelphia: Woodward for Ormond, 1793.

Brownson, Orestes. *The Laboring Classes (1840), with Brownson's Defence of the Article on the Laboring Classes*. Ed. Martin K. Doudna. Delmar, N.Y.: Scholar's Facsimiles, 1978.

Buchanan, James. *Linguae Britannicae Vera Pronunciatio*. 1757. Reprint. Menston, England: Scolar, 1967.

Buchanan, James. *The Works of James Buchanan*. Ed. John B. Moore. Philadelphia: J. B. Lippincott, 1908.

Bullokar, John. *An English Expositor*. 1616. Reprint. Menston, England: Scolar, 1967.

Burke, Aedanus. *Considerations on the Society or Order of Cincinnati*. Charleston, S.C.: A. Timothy, 1783.

Burke, Edmund. "Classification of Citizens." *Port Folio*, n.s., 3 (1807): 135.

Burn, John. *A Pronouncing Dictionary of the English Language*. 1786. Reprint. Menston, England: Scolar, 1969.

Burns, James D. *Three Years among the Working-Classes in the United States during the War*. London: Smith, Elder, 1865.

Byllesby, Langton. *Observations on the Sources and Effects of Unequal Wealth*. 1826. Reprint. New York: Russell and Russell, 1961.

Calhoun, John C. *A Disquisition on Government and a Discourse on the Constitution and Government of the United States*. 1851. Reprint. New York: Russell and Russell, 1968.

———. *Works*. Ed. Richard K. Cralle. 6 vols. New York: D. Appleton, 1854.

Callender, James T. *The Prospects before Us*. Richmond: Jones, Pleasants, and Lyon, 1800.

Calvert, George H. *Introduction to Social Science*. New York: Redfield, 1856.

Campbell, John. *A Theory of Equality*. Philadelphia: J. B. Perry, 1848.

Candidus. *Plain Truth*. Philadelphia: R. Bell, 1776.

Cardozo, Jacob Newton. *Notes on Political Economy*. Charleston, S.C.: A. E. Miller, 1826.

Carey, Henry C. *Capital and Labor*. Philadelphia: Collins, 1873.

———. *Essay on the Rate of Wages*. Philadelphia: Carey, Lea and Blanchard, 1835.

———. *Miscellaneous Works*. Philadelphia: H. C. Baird, 1872.

———. *Of the Rate of Interest and of Its Influence on the Relations of Capital and Labor*. Philadelphia: Collins, 1873.
———. *The Past, the Present, and the Future*. Philadelphia: Carey and Hart, 1848.
———. *Principles of Political Economy*. 3 vols. Philadelphia: Carey, Lea and Blanchard, 1837–40.
———. *Principles of Social Science*. Philadelphia: Lippincott, 1858–59.
———. *Review of the Decade 1857–1867*. Philadelphia: Collins, 1867.
———. *Shall We Have Peace? Peace Financial and Peace Political?* Philadelphia: Collins, 1869.
———. *The Slave Trade, Domestic and Foreign*. Philadelphia: A. Hart, 1853.
Carey, Mathew. *Essays on the Public Charities of Philadelphia*. Philadelphia: Clark and Raser, 1830.
———. *Information to Europeans Who Are Disposed to Migrate*. Philadelphia: Carey and Stuart, 1790.
Carr, Ezra S. *The Patrons of Husbandry on the Pacific Coast*. San Francisco: A. L. Bancroft, 1875.
Cawdrey, Robert. *A Table Alphabeticall: Of Hard Usual English Words*. 1604. Reprint. Gainesville, Fla.: Scholars' Facsimiles, 1966.
Chamberlin, Edwin M. *The Sovereigns of Industry*. Boston: Lee and Shepard, 1875.
Champlin, James T. *Lessons on Political Economy*. New York: A. S. Barnes, 1868.
Chandler, Thomas B. *The American Querist*. New York: J. Rivington, 1774.
———. *A Friendly Address to All Reasonable Americans, on the Subject of Our Political Confusions*. New York: J. Rivington, 1774.
Channing, William E. *The Present Age*. Manchester, N.H.: Abel Heywood, 1841.
Chauncy, Charles. *A Letter to a Friend*. Boston: Greenleaf, 1774.
Chipman, Nathaniel. *Sketches of the Principles of Government*. Rutland, Vt.: Lyon, 1793.
Choate, Rufus. *Addresses and Orations*. Boston: Little, Brown, 1878.
Clark, Charles C. P. "Work, Wages, and Combination." *Putnam's Magazine* 13 (1869): 141–48.
Clark, Jonas. *A Sermon Preached before His Excellency John Hancock . . . May 30, 1781*. Boston: J. Gill, 1781.
Clay, Henry. *The Works of Henry Clay*. Ed. Calvin Colton. 6 vols. New York: A. S. Barnes and Burr, 1857.
Cockeram, Henry. *The English Dictionarie*. 1623. Reprint. Menston, England: Scolar, 1968.
Coles, Elisha. *An English Dictionary*. 1676. Reprint. Menston, England: Scolar, 1971.
Colton, Calvin. *American Jacobinism*. New York: n.p., 1840.
———. *The Junius Tracts*. New York: Greeley and McElrath, 1844.
———. *Public Economy for the United States*. New York: A. S. Barnes, 1848.
———. *Sequel to the Crisis of the Country*. New York: Egbert Benson, 1840.
Congdon, Charles T. *Tribune Essays*. New York: J. S. Redfield, 1869.

Cook, Charles H. W. *The True Solution of the Labor Question.* New York: New York Labor Library, 1886.

Cook, Joseph. *Labor: With Preludes on Current Events.* Boston: Houghton, Osgood, 1880.

———. *Socialism: With Preludes on Current Events.* Boston: Houghton, Mifflin, 1880.

Cooper, James Fenimore. *Notions of the Americans.* 1828. Reprint. New York: Ungar, 1963.

Cooper, Thomas. *Thesaurus Linguae Romanae & Britannicae.* London: Berthelетti, 1565.

Cooper, Thomas. *Lectures on the Elements of Political Economy.* Columbia, S.C.: D. E. Sweeny, 1826.

———. *Lectures on the Elements of Political Economy.* 2nd ed. London: R. Hunter, 1831.

———. *A Manual of Political Economy.* Washington, D.C.: Duff Green, 1833.

———. *Political Arithmetic.* Philadelphia: n.p., 1798.

———. *Political Essays.* Northumberland, Pa.: A. Kennedy, 1799.

Coram, Robert. *Political Inquiries.* Wilmington, Del.: Andrews and Brynberg, 1791.

Cotgrave, Randle. *A Dictionarie of the French and English Tongues.* London: Adam Islip, 1611.

Coxe, Tench. *Observations on the Agriculture, Manufactures, and Commerce of the United States.* New York: Childs and Swain, 1789.

———. *Reflexions on the State of the Union.* Philadelphia: M. Carey, 1792.

———. *A View of the United States of America.* Philadelphia: William Hall, 1794.

Cushing, Caleb. *Summary of the Practical Principles of Political Economy.* Cambridge, Mass.: Hilliard and Metcalf, 1826.

Dacus, J. A. *Annals of the Great Strikes in the United States.* St. Louis: Scammel, 1877.

Dana, Samuel Whittlesey. *Essay on Political Society.* Whitehall, Pa.: William Young, 1800.

Day, John. *Remarks on American Affairs.* 1774. Reprint. *WMQ* 32 (1975): 487–94.

De Bow, James. *Eighty Years' Progress of the United States.* New York: L. Stebbins, 1861.

———. *The Industrial Resources, etc. of the Southern and Western States.* New Orleans: De Bow's Review, 1852.

———. *The Interest in Slavery of the Southern Non-Slaveholders.* Charleston, S.C.: Evans and Cogswell, 1860.

A Definition of Parties. Philadelphia: Bailey, 1794.

De Vere, M. Schele. *Americanisms: The English of the New World.* New York: Scribner, 1872.

Devyr, Thomas Ainge. *The Odd Book of the Nineteenth Century.* Greenpoint, N.Y.: T. Devyr, 1882.

Dewey, Orville. *Moral Views of Commerce, Society, and Politics.* New York: David Felt, 1838.

Dickinson, John. *An Essay on the Constitutional Power of Great Britain over the Colonies in America.* Philadelphia: W. and T. Bradford, 1774.

———. *Letters from a Farmer in Pennsylvania to the Inhabitants of the British Colonies.* 1768. Reprint. *Memoirs of the Historical Society of Pennsylvania,* vol. 14. Philadelphia: Historical Society of Pennsylvania, 1895.

Douglass, Frederick. *The Frederick Douglass Papers.* Ed. John W. Blassingame. New Haven: Yale University Press, 1982.

Dowler, Bennet. *Researches on the Vital Dynamics of Civil Government.* New Orleans: Weld, 1849.

Drayton, William. *Letters of a Freeman.* London: n.p., 1771.

———. *The Speech of William Drayton . . . Delivered on the 20th of January, 1778 in the General Assembly . . . upon the Articles of Confederation.* Charleston, S.C.: David Bruce, 1778.

Duane, William. *Politics for American Farmers.* Washington, D.C.: R. C. Weightman, 1807.

Elder, William. *Conversations on the Principal Subjects of Political Economy.* Philadelphia: H. C. Baird, 1882.

———. *Questions of the Day: Economic and Social.* Philadelphia: H. C. Baird, 1871.

Elwyn, Alfred L. *Glossary of Supposed Americanisms.* Philadelphia: J. B. Lippincott, 1859.

Ely, Richard T. *The Labor Movement in America.* 1886. Reprint. New York: Arno, 1969.

———. *Recent American Socialism.* Baltimore: Johns Hopkins University, 1885.

Elyot, Thomas. *The Dictionary.* 1538. Reprint. Menston, England: Scolar, 1970.

Emerson, Ralph Waldo. *The Complete Writings of Ralph Waldo Emerson.* New York: William H. Wise, 1875.

An Essay upon Government: Adopted by the Americans. Philadelphia: n.p., 1775.

Everett, Alexander. *New Ideas on Population.* Boston: O. Everett, 1826.

Everett, Edward. *A Lecture on the Working Men's Party.* Boston: Gray and Bowen, 1830.

———. "Louis Say's *Political Economy.*" *North American Review* 17 (1823): 425.

———. *Orations and Speeches on Various Occasions.* Vol. 2. Boston: Little, Brown, 1850.

A Fellow Citizen. *The Political Establishments of the United States of America.* Philadelphia: R. Bell, 1784.

Fenning, Daniel. *The New and Complete Spelling Dictionary.* London: S. Crowder, 1773.

———. *The Royal English Dictionary.* London: Baldwin, Hawes and Co., 1768.

Fenno, John Ward. *Desultory Reflections on the New Political Aspects.* New York: Waite and Fenno, 1800.

Ferguson, Adam. *An Essay on the History of Civil Society.* Basel: Tourneissen, 1789.

Finch, John. *Rise and Progress of the General Trades Union of the City of New York and Its Vicinity.* New York: J. Ormond, 1833.

Fisher, William. *An Examination of the New System of Society by Robert Owen.* Philadelphia: J. Mortimer, 1826.

Fisk, Theophilus. *Labor the Only True Source of Wealth.* Charleston, S.C.: Office of the Examiner, 1837.

Fitzhugh, George. *Cannibals All!* Richmond: A. Morris, 1857.

———. *Sociology for the South.* Richmond: A. Morris, 1854.

Florio, John. *Queen Anna's New World of Words.* 1611. Reprint. Menston, England: Scolar, 1968.

———. *A Worlde of Words.* London: Edward Blount, 1598.

Forrest, Michael. *The Political Reformer; or, a Proposed Plan of Reformations.* Philadelphia: Woodward, 1797.

Foster, Dan. *A Short Essay on Civil Government.* Hartford: Eben. Watson, 1775.

Foucaud, Edward. *The Book of Illustrious Mechanics of Europe and America.* Trans. John Frost. New York: D. Appleton, 1846.

Four Letters on Interesting Subjects. Philadelphia: n.p., 1776.

Franklin, Benjamin. *The Way to Wealth.* Philadelphia: Daniel Humphreys, 1785.

Gallatin, Albert. *Views of the Public Debt, Receipts, and Expenditures of the United States.* New York: Davis, 1800.

Galloway, Joseph. *A Candid Examination of the Mutual Claims of Great Britain, and the Colonies.* New York: James Rivington, 1775.

———. *Galloway's American Tracts.* London: G. Wilkie, R. Faulder, 1788.

Gazophylacium Anglicanum. 1689. Reprint. Menston, England: Scolar, 1969.

Gentz, Friedrich von. *The Origin and Principles of the American Revolution Compared with the Origin and Principles of the French Revolution.* Philadelphia: Maxwell, 1800.

George, Henry. *Progress and Poverty.* 1879. Reprint. New York: Robert Schalekenbach, 1934.

Girard, Gabriel. *A New Guide to Eloquence.* 1762. Reprint. Menston, England: Scolar, 1970.

Godwin, Parke. *A Popular View of the Doctrines of Charles Fourier.* New York: J. S. Redfield, 1844.

Gordon, William. *A Discourse Preached December 15th, 1774, Being the Day Recommended by the Provincial Congress; and Afterwards at the Boston Lecture.* Boston: T. Leverett, 1775.

Gouge, William. *A Short History of Paper Money and Banking in the United States.* Philadelphia: T. W. Ustick, 1833.

Granier De Cassagnac, Adolfe. *History of the Working and Burgher Classes.* Trans. Ben E. Green. 1838. Reprint. Philadelphia: Claxton, Remsen, and Haffelfinger, 1871.

Gray, John. *A Lecture on Human Happiness.* 1825. Reprint. London: London School of Economics, 1931.

Greeley, Horace. *Essays Designed to Elucidate the Science of Political Economy.* Boston: Fields, Osgood, 1870.

———. *Hints toward Reforms.* New York: Harper and Bros., 1850.

Green, Ben. E. *The Irrepressible Conflict between Labor and Capital.* Philadelphia: Claxton, Remsen, and Haffelfinger, 1872.

Green, Jacob. *Observations on the Reconciliation of Great Britain and the Colonies.* Philadelphia: R. Bell, 1776.

Greene, William Batchelder, ed. *Socialistic, Communistic, Mutualistic, and Financial Fragments.* Boston: Lee and Shepard, 1875.

Gregory, John Milton. *A New Political Economy.* Chicago: American Book, 1882.

Hale, William H. *Useful Knowledge for the Producers of Wealth.* New York: G. H. Evans, 1833.

Hales, John. *A Compendious or Briefe Examination of Certayne Ordinary Complaints of Divers of Our Country Men in These Our Dayes.* London: W. S. Gentleman, 1581.

Hamilton, Alexander. *The Argument of the Secretary of the Treasury upon the Constitutionality of a National Bank.* Philadelphia: United States Treasury Office, 1791.

———. *A Letter from Phocion to the Considerate Citizens of New York.* New York: Loudon, 1784.

———. *The Reports of Alexander Hamilton.* Ed. Jacob E. Cooke. New York: Harper and Row, 1964.

Hamilton, Alexander, John Jay, and James Madison. *The Federalist Papers.* 1788. Reprint. New York: Modern Library, 1937.

Hamilton, Robert S. *Present Status of the Philosophy of Society.* New York: C. S. Westcott, 1866.

Harrington, James. *The Common-Wealth of Oceana.* London: Livewell Chapman, 1656.

Harrison, Jonathan Baxter. *Certain Dangerous Tendencies in American Life, and Other Papers.* Boston: Houghton, Osgood, 1880.

Hartlib, Samuel. *The Parliament's Reformation.* London: T. Bates, 1646.

Hazen, Edward. *The Panorama of Professions and Trades; or, Every Man's Book.* Philadelphia: U. Hunt and Son, 1836.

Heighton, William. *An Address to the Members of Trade Societies, and to the Working Classes Generally.* Philadelphia: W. Heighton, 1827.

Henry, Caleb S. *Considerations of Some of the Elements and Conditions of Social Welfare and Human Progress.* New York: D. Appleton, 1861.

Heywood, Ezra Hervey. *Yours or Mine.* Boston: Weekly American Workman, 1869.

Hildreth, Richard. *Theory of Politics: An Inquiry into the Foundations of Governments and the Causes and Progress of Political Revolutions.* 1854. Reprint. New York: B. Franklin, 1971.

Hinckley, Frederic. *The Philosophy of the Labor Movement.* Boston: G. H. Ellis, 1874.

Hine, Lucius. *Hine's Political and Social Economy.* Cincinnati: L. Hine, 1861.

Hollis, Thomas. *The True Sentiments of America.* London: I. Almon, 1768.

Howe, Julia Ward. *Modern Society.* Boston: Roberts Bros., 1880.

Hughes, Henry. *Treatise on Sociology, Theoretical and Practical.* 1854. Reprint. New York: Negro Universities Press, 1968.

Hume, David. *Political Essays.* Ed. Charles Hendel. New York: Liberal Arts Press, 1953.

———. *Writings on Economics.* Ed. Eugene Rotwein. Edinburgh: Thomas Nelson, 1955.

Hundley, Daniel R. *Social Relations in Our Southern States.* New York: H. B. Price, 1860.

Hunt, Isaac. *The Political Family.* Philadelphia: James Humphreys, 1775.

Huntington, Eliphalet. *The Freeman's Directory.* Hartford: Green and Watson, 1768.

Huntington, Joseph. *A Discourse, Adapted to the Present Day on the Health and Happiness or Misery and Ruin of the Body Politic, in Similitude to That of the Natural Body.* Hartford: Hunter and Goodwin, 1781.

Inglis, Charles. *The True Interest of America Impartially Stated, in Certain Strictures on a Pamphlet, Intitled "Common Sense."* Philadelphia: James Humphreys, 1776.

James, Henry Ammon. *Communism in America.* New York: H. Holt, 1879.

Jefferson, Thomas. *Notes on the State of Virginia.* London: John Stockdale, 1787.

———. Introduction to Destutt de Tracy, *A Treatise on Political Economy.* Georgetown, D.C.: Joseph Milligan, 1817.

Jelley, S. M. ed. *The Voice of Labor.* Chicago: A. B. Gehman, 1887.

Jennison, William. *An Outline of Political Economy.* Philadelphia: W. Jennison, 1828.

Jervis, John B. *The Question of Labour and Capital.* New York: G. P. Putnam's Sons, 1877.

Johnson, Samuel. *A Dictionary of the English Language.* London: W. Strahan, 1765.

Kellogg, Edward. *Labor and Other Capital: The Rights of Each Secured.* New York: E. Kellogg, 1849.

Kersey, John. *Dictionarium Anglo-Britannicum; or, a General English Dictionary.* 1708. Reprint. Menston, England: Scolar, 1969.

———. *New English Dictionary.* 1702. Reprint. Menston, England: Scolar, 1969.

Kersey, John, and Edward Phillips. *The New World of Words; or, Universal English Dictionary.* London: J. Phillips, 1706.

Knights of Labor. *Preamble and Declaration of Principles.* N.p., n.d.

———, comp. *Labor: Its Rights and Wrongs.* Washington, D.C.: Labor Publishing Co., 1886.

Lacombe, Clare. *The History of a Peaceful Revolution.* Boston: Knights of Labor, 1886.

Lalor, John J., ed. *Cyclopaedia of Political Science, Political Economy, and of the Political History of the United States.* Chicago: Rand, McNally, 1882–84.

Lawrence, William B. *Two Lectures on Political Economy.* New York: G. and H. Carvill, 1832.

Ledyard, Isaac. *Mentor's Reply to Phocion's Letter.* New York: Shepard Kollock, 1784.

Lee, Charles. *Strictures on a Pamphlet, Entitled "A Friendly Address to All Reasonable Americans."* Philadelphia: William and Thomas Bradford, 1774.

Leggett, William. *Democratick Editorials: Essays in Jacksonian Political Economy.* Ed. Lawrence White. Indianapolis: Liberty Press, 1984.

Lieber, Francis. *Essays on Property and Labour as Connected with Natural Law and the Constitution of Society.* New York: Harper and Bros., 1841.

———. *On Civil Liberty and Self-Government.* 1877. Reprint. New York: Da Capo, 1972.

List, Friedrich. *Outlines of American Political Economy.* Philadelphia: S. Parker, 1827.

Livy. *The Early History of Rome.* Trans. Aubrey de Selincourt. London: Penguin, 1979.

Locke, John. *Two Treatises of Government.* Edited and introduced by Peter Laslett. Cambridge: Cambridge University Press, 1963.

Logan, George. *An Address on the Natural and Social Order of the World, as Intended to Produce Universal Good.* Philadelphia: Benjamin Franklin Bache, 1798.

———. *A Letter to the Citizens of Pennsylvania, on the Necessity of Promoting Agriculture, Manufactures, and the Useful Arts.* Philadelphia: Patterson and Cochran, 1800.

Luther, Seth. *An Address to the Working-Men of New England on the State of Education and on the Condition of the Producing Classes in Europe and America.* Boston: S. Luther, 1832.

Lyon, William H. *The People's Problem and Its Solution.* Sioux Falls, Dakota: W. Lyon, 1886.

McHenry, James. *A Brief Exposition, of the Leading Principles of a Bank.* Baltimore: Edwards and Allen, 1795.

Maclure, William. *Opinions on Various Subjects: Dedicated to the Industrious Producers.* 1831. Reprint. New York: A. M. Kelley, 1971.

McNeill, George, ed. *The Labor Movement: The Problem of Today.* New York: A. M. Bridgman, 1887.

McVickar, John. *First Lessons in Political Economy.* Boston: H. Gray, 1835.

———. *Hints on Banking: In a Letter to a Gentleman in Albany.* New York: Vanderpool and Cole, 1827.

———. *Outlines of Political Economy.* New York: Wilder and Campbell, 1825.

Marcet, Jane. *John Hopkin's Notions of Political Economy.* Boston: Allen and Ticknor, 1833.

Martineau, Harriet. *Illustrations of Political Economy.* London: Routledge, 1859.

Marx, Karl. *A Contribution to the Critique of Political Economy.* Introduced by Maurice Dobb. Moscow: Progress, 1970.

Marx, Karl, and Frederick Engels. *Marx and Engels on the United States.* Compiled by Nelly Rumyansteva. Moscow: Progress, 1979.

Masquerier, Lewis. *Sociology; or, the Reconstruction of Society, Government, and Property.* New York: L. Masquerier, 1877.

Massachusettensis. *Strictures and Observations upon the Three Executive Departments of the Government of the United States.* N.p., 1792.

Mein, John. *Sagittarius's Letters and Political Speculations.* Boston: n.p., 1775.

Melville, George. *The Poor Whites of the South.* Washington, D.C.: Buell and Blanchard, 1856.

A Member of the Society. *A Reply to a Pamphlet, Entitled "Considerations on the Society or Order of Cincinnati."* Annapolis: Frederick Green, 1783.

Mill, John Stuart. *The Logic of the Moral Sciences.* 1872. Reprint. La Salle, Ill.: Open Court, 1988.

Millar, John. *The Origin of the Distinction of Ranks.* London: J. Murray, 1781.

Moody, William Godwin. *Land and Labor in the United States.* New York: Scribner's, 1883.

———. *Our Labor Difficulties: The Cause, and the Way Out.* Boston: A. Williams, 1878.

Moore, Ely. *Address Delivered before the General Trades' Union of the City of New York . . . 1833.* New York: J. Ormond, 1833.

Moylan, Stephen. *Observations on a Late Pamphlet Entitled "Considerations on the Society or Order of the Cincinnati."* Philadelphia: Robert Bell, 1783.

Nash, Joseph. *The Relations between Capital and Labor in the United States.* Boston: Lee and Shepard, 1878.

National Convention for the Protection of American Interests. *Proceedings of the Convention.* New York: Greeley and McElrath, 1842.

National Labor Union. *Address of the National Labor Union to the People of the United States.* Washington, D.C.: McGill and Witherow, 1870.

Newcomb, Simon. *A Plain Man's Talk on the Labor Question.* New York: Harper, 1886.

Norton, Charles Eliot. *Considerations on Some Recent Social Theories.* Boston: Little, Brown, 1853.

An Old Whig. *From the Independent Gazetteer.* Philadelphia: E. Oswald, 1787.

One of the Many. *The Coming Crisis.* San Francisco: A. L. Bancroft, 1879.

Opdyke, George. *A Treatise on Political Economy.* New York: Putnam, 1851.

Owen, Robert. *A Development of the Principles and Plans on Which to Establish Self-Supporting Home Colonies.* London: Home Colonization Society, 1841.

———. *A Discourse on a New System of Society.* Washington, D.C.: Gales and Seaton, 1825.

———. *The Revolution in the Mind and Practice of the Human Race.* London: E. Wilson, 1849.

Owen, Robert Dale. *Labor: Its History and Prospects.* Cincinnati: Herald of Truth, 1848.

Paine, Thomas. *The American Crisis.* Philadelphia: M. Steiner, 1776.

———. *Common Sense.* Philadelphia: R. Bell, 1776.

———. *Dissertation on the First-Principles of Government.* Carlisle, Pa.: Steel, 1796.

———. *Letter Addressed to the Addressers, on the Late Proclamation.* New York: Thomas Greenleaf, 1793.

———. *Rights of Man: Part the First.* New York: Berry, Rogers and Berry, 1792.

———. *Rights of Man: Part the Second.* New York: Gaine, 1792.

Parker, Theodore. *Social Classes in a Republic.* Boston: American Unitarian Association, 1907.

Patterson, John Stahl. *Class Interests: Their Relations to Each Other and to Government.* New York: D. Appleton, 1886.

———. *Conflict in Nature and in Life*. New York: D. Appleton, 1883.
———. *Reforms: Their Difficulties and Possibilities*. New York: D. Appleton, 1884.
Peck, John. *Facts and Calculations respecting the Population and Territory of the United States of America*. Boston: J. Russell, 1799.
Perry, Arthur Latham. *Elements of Political Economy*. New York: Scribner, 1866.
Petit, Charles. *An Impartial Review of the Rise and Progress of the Controversy*. Philadelphia: Ormrod, 1800.
Philadelphia Society for the Promotion of National Industry. *Addresses*. Philadelphia: J. Maxwell, 1820.
Phillips, Edward. *The New World of English Words*. 1658. Reprint. Menston, England: Scolar, 1969.
Phillips, Wendell. *Speeches, Lectures, and Letters*. Boston: Lee and Shepard, 1892.
Philodemus. *Conciliatory Hints, Attempting, by a Fair State of Matters, to Remove Party Prejudices*. Charleston, S.C.: A. Timothy, 1784.
Pickering, John. *A Vocabulary; or, a Collection of Words and Phrases . . . Peculiar to the United States*. Boston: Cummings and Hilliard, 1816.
Pickering, John. *The Working Man's Political Economy*. Cincinnati: Th. Varney, 1847.
Piozzi, Hester Lynch. *British Synonymy*. 1794. Reprint. Menston, England: Scolar, 1968.
Potter, Alonzo. *Political Economy: Its Objects, Uses, and Principles: Considered with Reference to the Condition of the American People*. New York: Harper, 1841.
Price, Richard. *Observations on the Importance of the American Revolution*. Boston: Powars and Willis, 1784.
———. *Two Tracts on Civil Liberty*. London: T. Caddell, 1778.
Proceedings of the National Convention of Business Men. Philadelphia: Haswell, Barrington, Haswell, 1837.
Putnam, Oliver. *Tracts on Sundry Topics of Political Economy*. Boston: Russell, Odiorne, 1834.
A Querist. *Queries to the Whigs of Maryland*. Baltimore: M. K. Goddard, 1779.
Quesnay, François. *The Oeconomical Table*. London: W. Owen, 1766.
Rae, John. *Statement of Some New Principles on the Subject of Political Economy*. Boston: Hilliard and Gray, 1834.
Ramsay, David. "An Oration on the Advantages of American Independence." *United States Magazine* 1, no. 1 (1779): 22; no. 2: 57; no. 3: 105.
Raymond, Daniel. *The Missouri Question*. Baltimore: Schaeffer and Maund, 1819.
———. *Thoughts on Political Economy*. Baltimore: F. Lucas, 1820.
Ricardo, David. *Principles of Political Economy*. 1821. Reprint. London: J. M. Dent, 1960.
Rider, John. *Bibliotheca Scholastica*. 1589. Reprint. Menston, England: Scolar, 1970.
Robinson, Henry. *The Office of Addresses and Encounters*. London: Matthew Simmons, 1650.

Rousseau, Jean-Jacques. *A Dissertation on Political Economy.* Albany: Barber and Southwick, 1797.

———. *A Treatise on the Social Compact.* Albany: Barber and Southwick, 1797.

Ruffin, Edmund. *The Political Economy of Slavery.* Washington, D.C.: L. Towers, 1857.

Say, Jean-Baptiste. *A Catechism of Political Economy.* 1821. Reprint. New York: A. M. Kelley, 1967.

———. *Letters to Thomas Robert Malthus on Political Economy and Stagnation of Commerce.* 1821. Reprint. London: G. Harding's, 1936.

———. *Treatise on Political Economy.* Boston: Well and Lilly, 1821.

Scrope, George Poulett. *Principles of Political Economy, Deducted from the Natural Laws of Social Welfare, as Applied to the Present State of Great Britain.* London: Longman, 1833.

Seaman, Ezra. *Essay on the Progress of Nations.* Detroit: M. Geiger, 1846.

Sedgwick, Theodore. *Public and Private Economy.* New York: Harper, 1836.

Sheridan, Thomas. *A General Dictionary of the English Language.* 1780. Reprint. Menston, England: Scolar, 1967.

Sherman, Roger. *Remarks on a Pamphlet, Entitled "A Dissertation on the Political Union . . . "* New Haven: T. and S. Green, 1784.

Sherwood, Samuel. *A Sermon, Containing Scriptural Instructions to Civil Rulers, and All Free-born Subjects.* New Haven: T. and S. Green, 1774.

Simpson, Stephen. *The Working Man's Manual: A New Theory of Political Economy.* Philadelphia: Th. Bonsal, 1831.

Skidmore, Thomas. *The Rights of Man to Property!* New York: A. Ming, 1829.

Smith, Adam. *An Inquiry into the Nature and Causes of the Wealth of Nations.* 1776. Ed. R. H. Campbell, Andrew Skinner, and W. B. Todd. Indianapolis: Liberty Classics, 1981.

Smith, Erasmus Peshine. *A Manual of Political Economy.* Philadelphia: H. C. Baird, 1872.

Smith, Sir Thomas. *De Republica Anglorum: The Manner of Government or Policie of the Realme of England.* London: Gregorie Seton, 1583.

Socialistic Labor Party. *Platform, Constitution, and Resolutions.* Detroit: National Executive Committee of the Socialistic Labor Party, 1880.

Spence, Thomas. *The Grand Repository of the English Language.* 1775. Reprint. Menston, England: Scolar, 1969.

Spencer, Herbert. *Social Statics.* London: J. Chapman, 1851.

Spooner, Lysander. *Poverty: Its Illegal Causes and Legal Cure.* Boston: B. Marsh, 1846.

Squier, Ephraim George. *The Working Man's Miscellany: Lectures on the Condition and the True Interests of the Laboring Classes of America.* Albany: New York Mechanic and Cultivator, 1843.

Steuart, Sir James. *An Inquiry into the Principles of Political Economy.* Ed. Andrew Skinner. Chicago: University of Chicago Press, 1966.

Steward, Ira. *The Eight Hour Movement.* Boston: Labor Reform Association, 1865.

Stirrat, David. *A Treatise on Political Economy.* Baltimore: D. Stirrat, 1824.

Strong, Josiah. *Our Country: Its Possible Future and Its Present Crisis.* New York: Baker and Taylor, 1885.

Sullivan, James. *Observations upon the Government of the United States.* Boston: Hall, 1791.

———. *The Path to Riches.* Boston: P. Edes, 1792.

Sullivan, William. *The Political Class Book.* Boston: Hendee, Jenks, and Palmer, 1845.

Sumner, Charles. *The Works.* Boston: Lee and Shepard, 1875–80.

Sumner, William Graham. *What Social Classes Owe to Each Other.* 1883. Reprint. Caldwell, Idaho: Caxton, 1954.

Swan, James. *National Arithmetick.* Boston: Adams and Nourse, 1786.

Sylvis, James C., ed. *The Life, Speeches, Labors, and Essays of William H. Sylvis.* Philadelphia: Claxton, Remsen, and Haffelfinger, 1872.

Taylor, John. *Construction Construed, and Constitutions Vindicated.* Richmond: Shepherd and Pollard, 1820.

———. *An Inquiry into the Principles and Policies of the Government of the United States.* 1814. Reprint. Ed. Loren Baritz. Indianapolis: Bobbs-Merrill, 1969.

———. *An Inquiry into the Principles and Tendency of Certain Public Measures.* Philadelphia: Thomas Dobson, 1794.

———. *Tyranny Unmasked.* Washington, D.C.: Davis and Force, 1822.

Thomas, Charles Grandison. *Hereditary Property Justified.* Cambridge, Mass.: Metcalf, Torry, Ballou, 1841.

Thompson, Joseph. *The Workman: His False Friends and His True Friends.* New York: American Tract Society, 1879.

Thompson, Robert Ellis. *Social Science and the National Economy.* Philadelphia: Porter and Coates, 1875.

Tilden, Samuel J. *The Writings and Speeches of Samuel J. Tilden.* Ed. John Bigelow. 2 vols. New York: Harper and Bros., 1885.

Trumbull, Matthew. *Signing the Document: The Laokoon of Labor, Chopping Sand, and Other Essays.* Chicago: Radical Review, 1884.

Tucker, George. *The Laws of Wages, Profits, and Rents Investigated.* Philadelphia: E. L. Carey and A. Hart, 1837.

———. *Political Economy for the People.* Philadelphia: C. Sherman and Son, 1859.

———. *Progress of the United States in Population and Wealth in Fifty Years.* New York: Hunt's Merchants' Magazine, 1843.

Turgot, Anne-Robert-Jacques. *Reflections on the Formation and Distribution of Riches.* 1770. Reprint. New York: A. M. Kelley, 1963.

———. *Turgot on Progress, Sociology, and Economics.* Trans. Ronald L. Meek. Cambridge: Cambridge University Press, 1973.

Tyng, Stephen. *Twenty-First Anniversary Address before the American Institute of the City of New York.* New York: Van Norden and Amerman, 1848.

United States Congress. House of Representatives. "Investigation by a Select Committee of the House of Representatives relative to the Causes of the General Depression in Labor and Business." In *Miscellaneous Documents of the House of Representatives for the Third Session, Forty-fifth Congress, 1878–*

1879. Vol. 3, doc. 29. Washington, D.C.: Government Printing Office, 1879.

United States Congress. Senate. *Report of the Committee of the Senate upon the Relations between Labor and Capital, and the Testimony Taken by the Committee.* Washington, D.C.: Government Printing Office, 1885.

Vale, Gilbert. *Manual of Political Economy.* New York: Beacon, 1841.

Vaughan, William. *The Catechism of Man.* Philadelphia: Humphrey, 1794.

Vethake, Henry. *An Introductory Lecture on Political Economy.* 1831. Reprint. New York: J. K. Moore, 1833.

———. *Principles of Political Economy.* Philadelphia: P. H. Nicklin, 1838.

Walker, Amasa. *The Science of Wealth: A Manual of Political Economy.* Boston: Little and Brown, 1866.

Walker, Francis Amasa. *The Wages Question: A Treatise on Wages and the Wages Class.* New York: Henry Holt, 1876.

Walker, J. H. *Common Sense Views on Political Economy, Capital, Labor, Socialism.* Worcester: American News, 1878.

Walker, John. *A Critical Dictionary and Exposition of the English Language.* New York: Stansbury, Ronalds, Osborn, Hopkins, 1807.

———. *A Critical Pronouncing Dictionary.* 1791. Reprint. Menston, England: Scolar, 1968.

Ward, Lester Frank. *Dynamic Sociology.* 1883. Reprint. New York: Johnson, 1968.

Ware, Nathaniel. *Notes on Political Economy.* New York: Leavitt and Trow, 1844.

Warren, Josiah. *Equitable Commerce.* New Harmony, Ind.: J. Warren, 1846.

———. *The Quarterly Letter.* Cliftondale, Mass.: J. Warren, 1867.

———. *True Civilization an Immediate Necessity.* Boston: J. Warren, 1863.

Warren, Marvin. *American Labor: Its Great Wrongs, and How It Can Redress Them.* St. Joseph, Mo.: Steam Printing Co., 1877.

Wayland, Francis. *A Discourse Delivered in the First Baptist Church, Providence, R.I., on the Day of Public Thanksgiving, July 21, 1842.* Providence: H. H. Brown, 1842.

———. *The Elements of Moral Science.* Boston: Gould, Kendall and Lincoln, 1836.

———. *The Elements of Political Economy.* New York: Leavitt, Lord and Co., 1837.

Webster, Daniel. *The Writings and Speeches of Daniel Webster.* 18 vols. Boston: Little, Brown, 1903.

Webster, Noah. *An American Dictionary of the English Language.* New York: S. Converse, 1829.

———. *A Compendious Dictionary of the English Language.* New Haven: Sidney's, 1806.

———. *Dissertations on the English Language with Notes Historical and Critical.* 1789. Reprint. Menston, England: Scolar, 1967.

———. *Sketches of American Policy.* Hartford: Hudson and Goodwin, 1785.

———. *Ten Letters to Dr. Joseph Priestly.* New Haven: Read and Morse, 1800.

Webster, Noah, and Chauncy Goodrich. *An American Dictionary of the English Language*. Rev. ed. New York: Harper, 1847.

Webster, Noah, Chauncy Goodrich, and Noah Porter. *An American Dictionary of the English Language*. New ed. Springfield, Mass.: C. and G. Merriam, 1865.

———. *An American Dictionary of the English Language*. New ed. with Supplement. Springfield, Mass.: C. and G. Merriam, 1880.

Webster, Pelatiah. *An Address to the Stockholders of the Bank of North America: On the Subject of the Old and New Bank*. Philadelphia: Cruikshank, 1791.

———. *A Dissertation on the Political Union and Constitution of the Thirteen United States*. Philadelphia: Bradford, 1783.

———. *An Essay on Free Trade and Finance*. Philadelphia: Bradford, 1779.

Webster, William G. *An Elementary Dictionary*. New York: G. Cooledge, 1844.

Weld, Theodore. *Report on Manual Labor in Literary Institutions*. New York: S. W. Benedict, 1833.

White, Richard Grant. *Every-Day English*. Boston: Houghton Mifflin, 1881.

———. *Words and Their Uses Past and Present: A Study of the English Language*. Boston: Houghton Mifflin, 1870.

Wigglesworth, Edward. *Calculations on American Population*. Boston: John Boyle, 1775.

Williams, Samuel. *The Influence of Christianity on Civil Society*. Boston: John Boyle, 1780.

Wilmer, James Jones. *An Address to the Citizens of the United States*. Baltimore: Pechin, 1796.

Wilson, William Dexter. *First Principles of Political Economy*. Ithaca, N.Y.: Finch and Apgar, 1875.

Winchester, Elhanan. *A Plain Political Cathechism*. Greenfield, Mass.: Dickman, 1796.

Woodhull, Victoria C. *Reformation or Revolution, Which?* New York: Woodhull and Claflin, 1873.

———. *The Review of a Century*. London: Women's Co-operative Printing Union, 1893.

Woolman, John. *Considerations on the True Harmony of Mankind*. Philadelphia: Crukshank, 1770.

Worchester, Joseph E. *A Comprehensive Pronouncing and Explanatory Dictionary*. Boston: Jenks and Palmer, 1845.

———. *A Dictionary of the English Language*. Boston: Brewster and Tileson, 1869.

Wren, Roger. *Sentiments of the Humours and Amusements of the Times*. Boston: n.p., 1763.

Wright, Hendrick B. *A Practical Treatise on Labor*. New York: G. W. Carleton, 1871.

Wright, Robert Joseph. *Principia; or, Basis of Social Science*. Philadelphia: J. B. Lippincott, 1875.

Wright D'Arusmont, Frances. *A Course of Popular Lectures*. New York: Free Enquirer, 1829.

———. *A Course of Popular Lectures.* 4th ed. New York: Free Enquirer, 1831.
———. *Course of Popular Lectures.* London: James Watson, 1834.
———. *Life, Letters, and Lectures.* New York: Arno, 1972.
———. "The People at War." *Free Enquirer,* 27 November 1830, p. 39.

Primary Sources: Collections

Bailyn, Bernard, ed. *Pamphlets of the American Revolution, 1750–1776.* Cambridge, Mass.: Belknap, 1965.

Benton, Thomas Hart, ed. *Abridgement of the Debates of Congress, from 1789 to 1856.* 16 vols. New York: D. Appleton, 1857.

Bestor, Arthur, ed. *Education and Reform at New Harmony: Correspondence of William Maclure and Marie Duclos Fretageot, 1820–1833.* Indianapolis: Indiana Historical Society, 1948.

Blau, Joseph L., ed. *Social Theories of Jacksonian Democracy: Representative Writings of the Period 1825–1850.* New York: Hafner, 1947.

Borden, Morton, ed. *The Antifederalist Papers.* Lansing: Michigan State University Press, 1965.

Commons, John R., ed. *A Documentary History of American Industrial Society.* 10 vols. Cleveland: A. H. Clark, 1910–11.

Cunningham, Noble, ed. *Circular Letters of Congressmen to Their Constituents, 1789–1829.* Chapel Hill: University of North Carolina Press, 1978.

Elliot, Jonathan, ed. *The Debates in the Several States on the Adoption of the Federal Constitution.* 2nd ed. 1836. Reprint. Philadelphia: J. B. Lippincott, 1863.

Foner, Philip, ed. *The Democratic-Republican Societies, 1790–1800: A Documentary Sourcebook.* Westport, Conn.: Greenwood, 1976.

Ford, Paul, ed. *Pamphlets on the Constitution of the United States.* Brooklyn: Paul Ford, 1888.

Hyneman, Charles S., and Donald S. Lutz, eds. *American Political Writing during the Founding Era.* Indianapolis: Liberty, 1983.

Jensen, Merrill, ed. *Tracts of the American Revolution, 1763–1776.* Indianapolis: Bobbs-Merrill, 1967.

Kaminski, John, and Gaspare Saladino, eds. *The Documentary History of the Ratification of the Constitution.* Madison: State Historical Society of Wisconsin, 1983.

Kenyon, Cecilia, ed. *The Antifederalists.* New York: Bobbs-Merrill, 1966.

Madison, James. *Notes of the Debates in the Federal Convention of 1787.* Introduction by Adrienne Koch. Athens: Ohio University Press, 1966.

Miller, Marion Mills, ed. *Great Debates in American History.* Vols. 5, 10, 11. New York: Current Literature, 1913.

Morgan, Edmund S., ed. *Prologue to Revolution: Sources and Documents on the Stamp Act Crisis, 1764–1766.* Chapel Hill: University of North Carolina Press, 1959.

Morris, Richard B., ed. *The American Revolution, 1763–1783.* New York: Harper and Row, 1970.

Niles, Hezekiah, ed. *Principles and Acts of the Revolution in America.* Baltimore: W. O. Niles, 1822.

Porter, Kirk H., and Donald B. Johnson, eds. *National Party Platforms, 1840–1964*. Urbana: University of Illinois Press, 1966.

Reid, Ronald F., ed. *Three Centuries of American Rhetorical Discourse: An Anthology*. Prospect Heights, Ill.: Waveland, 1988.

Richardson, James, ed. *A Compilation of the Messages and Papers of the Presidents, 1789–1908*. Washington, D.C.: Bureau of National Literature and Art, 1909.

Sandoz, Ellis, ed. *Political Sermons of the American Founding Era, 1730–1805*. Indianapolis: Liberty, 1991.

Storing, Herbert J., ed. *The Complete Anti-Federalist*. Chicago: University of Chicago Press, 1981.

Veysey, Laurence, ed. *The Perfectionists: Radical Social Thought in the North, 1815–1860*. New York: J. Wiley and Sons, 1973.

Yellowitz, Irwin, ed. *The Position of the Worker in American Society, 1865–1896*. Englewood Cliffs, N.J.: Prentice Hall, 1969.

Secondary Sources

Aarsleff, Hans. *From Locke to Saussure: Essays on the Study of Language and Intellectual History*. Minneapolis: University of Minnesota Press, 1982.

———. *The Study of Language in England, 1780–1860*. Westport, Conn.: Greenwood, 1979.

Adair, Douglas. "The Intellectual Origins of Jeffersonian Democracy: Republicanism, the Class Struggle, and the Virtuous Farmer." Ph.D. diss., Yale University, 1943.

———. "'That Politics May Be Reduced to a Science': David Hume, James Madison, and the Tenth Federalist." *Huntington Library Quarterly* 20 (1957): 343–60.

Adams, Donald R. "Prices and Wages in Antebellum America: The West Virginia Experience." *JEH* 52 (1992): 206–16.

Adams, Willi Paul. *The First American Constitutions*. Trans. Rita and Robert Kimber. Chapel Hill: University of North Carolina Press, 1980.

Alcouffe, Alain. "The Institutionalization of Political Economy in French Universities, 1819–1896." *HOPE* 21 (1989): 313–44.

Allen, Irving Lewis. *The Language of Ethnic Conflict: Social Organization and Lexical Culture*. New York: Columbia University Press, 1983.

Anderson, Gary, and Robert D. Tollison. "Sir James Steuart as the Apotheosis of Mercantilism and His Relation to Adam Smith." *Southern Economic Journal* 51 (1984): 456–59.

Anderson, Margo J. *The American Census: A Social History*. New Haven: Yale University Press, 1988.

———. "The Language of Class in Twentieth Century America." *Social Science History* 12 (1988): 349–75.

Andresen, Julie Tetel. *Linguistics in America, 1769–1924: A Critical History*. London: Routledge, 1990.

Angus, Ian, and Lenore Langsdorf. *The Critical Turn: Rhetoric and Philosophy in Postmodern Discourse*. Carbondale: Southern Illinois University Press, 1993.

Appleby, Joyce. *Capitalism and a New Social Order: The Republican Vision of the 1790s.* New York: New York University Press, 1984.

———. *Economic Thought and Ideology in Seventeenth Century England.* Princeton: Princeton University Press, 1978.

———. *Liberalism and Republicanism in the Historical Imagination.* Cambridge: Harvard University Press, 1992.

———. "Republicanism as Ideology." *American Quarterly* 37 (1985): 461–73.

———. "Republicanism in Old and New Contexts." *WMQ* 43 (1986): 20–34.

———. "The Social Origins of American Revolutionary Ideology." *JAH* 64 (1978): 935–59.

Armstrong, William M. *E. L. Godkin: A Biography.* Albany: State University of New York Press, 1978.

Arnold, Carrol D. "Early Constitutional Rhetoric in Pennsylvania." In *American Rhetoric: Context and Criticism,* ed. Thomas W. Benson. Carbondale: Southern Illinois University Press, 1989.

Aron, Raymond. *Main Currents in Sociological Thought.* Trans. Richard Howard and Helen Weaver. New York: Basic Books, 1965.

———. "Two Definitions of Class." In *Social Inequality,* ed. Andre Beteille. Baltimore: Penguin Books, 1969.

Aronowitz, Stanley. *The Crisis in Historical Materialism: Class, Politics, and Culture in Marxist Theory.* New York: Praeger, 1981.

Ashworth, John. *Agrarians and Aristocrats: Party Political Ideology in the United States, 1837–1856.* London: Royal Historical Society, 1983.

———. "The Democratic Republicans before the Civil War: Political Ideology and Economic Change." *Journal of American Studies* 20 (1986): 375–90.

Baatz, Simon. "Philadelphia Patronage: The Institutional Structure of Natural History in the New Republic." *Journal of the Early Republic* 8 (1988): 111–38.

Babcock, Robert H. "The Decline of Artisan Republicanism in Portland, Maine, 1825–1850." *New England Quarterly* 63 (1990): 3–34.

Backhouse, Roger. *Economists and the Economy: The Evolution of Economic Ideas, 1600 to the Present Day.* Oxford: Blackwell, 1988.

Bailey, Fred. "Class Contrasts in Old South Tennessee." *Tennessee Historical Quarterly* 45 (1986): 273–86.

———. "Tennessee's Antebellum Society from the Bottom Up." *Southern Studies* 22 (1983): 260–73.

Bailyn, Bernard. "Common Sense." In *Fundamental Testaments of the American Revolution.* Washington, D.C.: Library of Congress, 1973.

———. *The Ideological Origins of the American Revolution.* Cambridge, Mass.: Belknap, 1967.

———. "Political Experience and Enlightenment Ideas in Eighteenth-Century America." *American Historical Review* 67 (1962): 339–51.

Bailyn, Bernard, and John B. Hench, eds. *The Press and the American Revolution.* Boston: Northeastern University Press, 1981.

Baker, Jean H. *Affairs of Party: The Political Culture of Northern Democrats in the Mid-Nineteenth Century.* Ithaca, N.Y.: Cornell University Press, 1983.

———. "From Belief into Culture: Republicanism in the Antebellum North." *American Quarterly* 37 (1985): 532–50.

Baker, Robert P. "Labor History, Social Science, and the Concept of the Working Class." *Labor History* 14 (1973): 98–105.

Ball, Terrence. *Transforming Political Discourse: Political Theory and Critical Conceptual History*. Oxford: Blackwell, 1988.

Ball, Terrence, James Farr, and Russell Hanson, eds. *Political Innovation and Conceptual Change*. Cambridge: Cambridge University Press, 1989.

Ball, Terrence, and J. G. A. Pocock, eds. *Conceptual Change and the Constitution*. Lawrence: University Press of Kansas, 1988.

Banning, Lance. "Jeffersonian Ideology Revisited: Liberal and Classical Ideas in the New American Republic" *WMQ* 43 (1986): 3–19.

———. *The Jeffersonian Persuasion: Evolution of a Party Ideology*. Ithaca, N.Y.: Cornell University Press, 1978.

Bannister, Robert C. *Sociology and Scientism: The American Quest for Objectivity, 1880–1940*. Chapel Hill: University of North Carolina Press, 1987.

———. "William Graham Sumner's Social Darwinism: A Reconsideration." *HOPE* 5 (1973): 89–109.

Banton, Michael. "The Classification of Races in Europe and America, 1700–1850." *International Social Science Journal* 39 (1987): 45–60.

Barber, Charles. *Early Modern English*. London: Andre Deutch, 1976.

Barber, William J. "Should the American Economic Association Have Toasted Simon Newcomb at Its 100th Birthday Party?" *Journal of Economic Perspectives* 1 (1987): 179–83.

———, ed. *Breaking the Academic Mould: Economists and American Higher Learning in the Nineteenth Century*. Middletown, Conn.: Wesleyan University Press, 1988.

Barnow, Jeffrey. "American Independence: Revolution of the Republican Ideal." In *The American Revolution in Eighteenth Century Culture*, ed. Paul J. Korshin. New York: AMS Press, 1986.

Bartolomeo, Joseph. "Public Debate and the Social Bases of Politics: Philadelphia, 1844." Ph.D. diss., University of Pennsylvania, 1977.

Bauer, Leonard, and Herbert Matis. "From Moral to Political Economy: The Genesis of the Social Sciences." *History of European Ideas* 9 (1988): 125–43.

Bauman, Zygmunt. "Class, Social." In *The Social Science Encyclopedia*, ed. Adam Kuper and Jessica Kuper. London: Routledge and Kegan Paul, 1985.

———. *Memories of Class: The Pre-history and After-Life of Class*. London: Routledge and Kegan Paul, 1983.

Baumol, William J. "On Method in United States Economics a Century Earlier." *American Economic Review* 75 (1985): 1–12.

Beecher, Jonathan. *Charles Fourier: The Visionary and His World*. Berkeley: University of California Press, 1986.

Beeman, Richard, Stephen Botein, and Edward C. Carter, II, eds. *Beyond Confederation: Origins of the Constitution and American National Identity*. Chapel Hill: University of North Carolina Press, 1987.

Bell, Daniel. "The Once and Future Marx." *American Journal of Sociology* 83 (1977): 187–97.

Bendix, Reinhard, ed. *Class, Status, and Power*. London: Routledge and Kegan Paul, 1967.

Benson, Leslie. *Proletarians and Parties: Five Essays on Social Class*. London: Tavistock, 1978.

Berkhofer, Robert F. *Beyond the Great Story: History as Text and Discourse*. Cambridge: Harvard University Press, 1995.

Berlin, James. *Writing Instruction in Nineteenth Century American Colleges*. Carbondale: Southern Illinois University Press, 1984.

Berman, David. "Irish Philosophy and the American Enlightenment during the Eighteenth Century." *Eire—Ireland* 24 (1989): 28–39.

Bernard, L. L., and Jessie Bernard. *Origins of American Sociology*. New York: Russell and Russell, 1965.

Bernard, Paul. "Irreconcilable Opinions: The Social and Educational Theories of Robert Owen and William Maclure." *Journal of the Early Republic* 8 (1988): 21–44.

Bernstein, Michael A., and Sean Wilentz. "Marketing, Commerce, and Capitalism in Rural Massachusetts." *JEH* 44 (1984): 171–73.

Berthoff, Rowland. "Conventional Mentality: Free Blacks, Women, and Business Corporations as Unequal Persons, 1820–1870." *JAH* 75 (1989): 753–84.

———. "The Working Class." In *The Reconstruction of American History*, ed. John Higham. London: Hutchinson, 1962.

Bestor, Arthur. *Backwoods Utopias: The Sectarian Origins and the Owenite Phase of Communitarian Socialism in America, 1666–1829*. 2nd ed. Philadelphia: University of Pennsylvania Press, 1970.

———. "The Evolution of the Socialist Vocabulary." *JHI* 9 (1948): 259–302.

Black, Max. *Models and Metaphors: Studies in Language and Philosophy*. Ithaca, N.Y.: Cornell University Press, 1962.

———. *Philosophy and the Historical Understanding*. New York: Schocken, 1964.

———, ed. *The Importance of Language*. Ithaca, N.Y.: Cornell University Press, 1969.

Black, R. D. Collinson, ed. *Ideas in Economics*. London: Macmillan, 1986.

Blatt, Martin. *Free Love and Anarchism: The Biography of Ezra Heywood*. Urbana: University of Illinois Press, 1989.

Blaug, Mark. *Economic History and the History of Economics*. New York: New York University Press, 1986.

———. *Economic Theory in Retrospect*. 4th ed. Cambridge: Cambridge University Press, 1985.

———, ed. *George Scrope*. Aldershot, England: Edward Elgar, 1991.

Blum, Carol. *Rousseau and the Republic of Virtue: The Language of Politics in the French Revolution*. Ithaca, N.Y.: Cornell University Press, 1986.

Boase, Paul, ed. *The Rhetoric of Protest and Reform, 1878–1898*. Athens: Ohio University Press, 1980.

Bogin, Ruth. "'Measures So Glareingly Unjust': A Response to Hamilton's Funding Plan by William Manning." *WMQ* (1989): 315–32.

———. "Petitioning and the New Moral Economy of Post-Revolutionary America." *WMQ* 45 (1988): 391–425.

Boss, Helen. "Division of Labour and Unproductive Labour in a System of Natural Liberty: Adam Smith's Dilemma." *Historical Reflections/Réflexions Historiques* 15 (1988): 417–42.

———. *Theories of Surplus and Transfer: Parasites and Producers in Economic Thought.* Boston: Unwin Hyman, 1990.

Boston, Ray. *British Chartists in America.* Manchester: Manchester University Press, 1971.

Bottomore, Tom. *Classes in Modern Society.* New York: Vantage Books, 1966.

———. "Class Structure and Social Consciousness." In *Aspects of History and Class Consciousness,* ed. Istvan Meszaros. London: Routledge and Kegan Paul, 1971.

———. *Critics of Society: Radical Thought in North America.* New York: Pantheon, 1968.

Bottomore, Tom, and Robert Nisbet, eds. *A History of Sociological Analysis.* New York: Basic Books, 1978.

Bourdieu, Pierre. *Distinction: A Social Critique of the Judgment of Taste.* Trans. Richard Nice. Cambridge: Harvard University Press, 1984.

———. "The Economics of Linguistic Exchanges." *Social Science Information* 16 (1977): 645–68.

———. *In Other Words: Towards a Reflexive Sociology.* Stanford: Stanford University Press, 1990.

———. *Language and Symbolic Power.* Ed. and introduced by John B. Thompson. Trans. Gino Raymond and Matthew Adamson. Cambridge: Harvard University Press, 1991.

Branigan, Roger D. "Robert Owen's New Harmony: An American Heritage." In *Robert Owen's American Legacy,* ed. Donald E. Pitzer. Indianapolis: Indiana Historical Society, 1972.

Branson, Roy. "James Madison and the Scottish Enlightenment." *JHI* 40 (1979): 235–50.

Briggs, Asa. "The Language of 'Class' in Early Nineteenth Century England." In *Essays in Labour History,* ed. Asa Briggs and John Saville. London: Macmillan, 1960.

———. "The Language of 'Mass' and 'Masses' in Nineteenth Century England." In *Ideology and the Labour Movement: Essays Presented to John Saville,* ed. David E. Martin and David Rubenstein. Totowa, N.J.: Rowman and Littlefield, 1979.

Brody, David. *Workers in Industrial America: Essays on the Twentieth Century Struggle.* New York: Oxford University Press, 1980.

Brown, Henry Phelps. *Egalitarianism and the Generation of Inequality.* Oxford: Clarendon, 1988.

Brown, Richard D. *Knowledge Is Power: The Diffusion of Information in Early America, 1700–1865.* New York: Oxford University Press, 1989.

Brown, Richard Harvey. *Social Science as Civic Discourse: Essays on the Invention, Legitimation, and Uses of Social Theory.* Chicago: University of Chicago Press, 1989.

———. *Society as Text: Essays on Rhetoric, Reason, and Reality*. Chicago: University of Chicago Press, 1987.

Brown, Thomas. "The Massachusetts Whigs and Industrialism." *Historical Journal of Massachusetts* 14 (1986): 25–42.

———. *Politics and Statesmanship: Essays on the American Whig Party*. New York: Columbia University Press, 1985.

———. "The Southern Whigs and Economic Development." *Southern Studies* 20 (1981): 20–38.

Bryson, Gladys. *Man and Society: The Scottish Inquiry of the Eighteenth Century*. Princeton: Princeton University Press, 1945.

Buel, Richard, Jr. *Securing the Revolution: Ideology in American Politics, 1789–1815*. Ithaca, N.Y.: Cornell University Press, 1972.

Burawoy, Michael. "Karl Marx and the Satanic Mills: Factory Politics under Early Capitalism in England, the United States, and Russia." *American Journal of Sociology* 90 (1984): 247–82.

Burke, Kenneth. *A Rhetoric of Motives*. New York: Brazillier, 1955.

Burke, Peter. *History and Social Theory*. Ithaca, N.Y.: Cornell University Press, 1992.

Burton, Frank, and Pat Carlen. *Official Discourse: On Discourse Analysis, Government Publications, Ideology, and the State*. London: Routledge and Kegan Paul, 1979.

Busse, Dietrich. *Historische Semantik: Analyse eines Programme* . Stuttgart: Klett-Cotta, 1987.

Busse, Winfried, and Jürgen Trabant, eds. *Les Idéologues: Sémiotique, théories, et politiques linguistiques pendant la Révolution française*. Amsterdam: John Benjamins, 1986.

Calhoun, Craig. *The Question of Class Struggle: Social Foundations of Popular Radicalism during the Industrial Revolution*. Chicago: University of Chicago Press, 1982.

Calvert, Peter. *The Concept of Class: An Historical Introduction*. London: Hutchinson, 1982.

Campbell, R. H., and Andrew Skinner, eds. *The Origins and Nature of the Scottish Enlightenment: Essays*. Edinburgh: John Donald, 1982.

Care, Norman S. "On Fixing Social Concepts." *Ethics* 84 (1973): 10–21.

Carey, Patrick. "Christian Socialism in the Early Brownson." *Records of the American Catholic Historical Society of Philadelphia* 99 (1988): 17–39.

Carmony, Donald F., and Josephine M. Elliott. "New Harmony, Indiana: Robert Owen's Seedbed for Utopia." *Indiana Magazine of History* 76 (1980): 161–261.

Carter, Edward C. "The Birth of a Political Economist: Mathew Carey and the Re-charter Fight of 1810–1811." *Pennsylvania History* 33 (1966): 274–88.

Caton, Hiram. *The Politics of Progress: The Origins and Development of the Commercial Republic, 1600–1835*. Gainesville: University of Florida Press, 1988.

———. "The Pre-Industrial Economics of Adam Smith." *JEH* 45 (1985): 833–53.

Caudill, Edward. "E. L. Godkin and the Science of Society." *Journalism Quarterly* 66 (1989): 57–64.

Centers, Peter. *The Psychology of Social Classes: A Study of Class Consciousness.* 1949. Reprint. New York: Russell and Russell, 1961.

Chernomas, Robert. "Productive and Unproductive Labor and the Rate of Profit in Malthus, Ricardo, and Marx." *Journal of the History of Economic Thought* 12 (1990): 81–95.

Chisick, Harvey. "The Ambivalence of the Idea of Equality in the French Enlightenment." *History of European Ideas* 13 (1991): 215–23.

Claeys, Gregory. *Citizens and Saints: Politics and Anti-Politics in Early British Socialism.* Cambridge: Cambridge University Press, 1989.

———. "'Individualism', 'Socialism', and 'Social Science': Further Notes on a Process of Conceptual Formation, 1800–1850." *JHI* 47 (1986): 81–93.

Claval, Paul. *Les mythes fondateurs des sciences sociales.* Paris: Presses Universitaires de France, 1980.

Clouatre, Dallas L. "The Concept of Class in French Culture prior to the Revolution." *JHI* 45 (1984): 219–44.

Cmiel, Kenneth. *Democratic Eloquence: The Fight over Popular Speech in Nineteenth Century America.* New York: William Morrow, 1990.

Coats, A. W. "Adam Smith's Conception of Self-Interest in Economic and Political Affairs." *HOPE* 7 (1975): 132–36.

———. "The Classical Economists and the Labourer." In *Land, Labour, and Population in the Industrial Revolution: Essays Presented to J. D. Chambers,* ed. E. L. Jones and G. E. Mingay. New York: Barnes and Noble, 1968.

Cochran, Thomas. *Frontiers of Change: Early Industrialism in America.* New York: Oxford University Press, 1981.

Cohen, Murray. *Sensible Words: Linguistic Practice in England, 1640–1785.* Baltimore: Johns Hopkins University Press, 1977.

Cohen, Seymour S. "Two Refugee Chemists in the United States, 1794." *Proceedings of the American Philosophical Society* 126 (1982): 301–15.

Colley, Linda. "Whose Nation? Class and National Consciousness in Britain, 1750–1830." *Past and Present* 113 (1986): 97–117.

Collins, Bruce. "The Ideology of the Antebellum Northern Democrats." *Journal of American Studies* 11 (1977): 103–21.

Commager, Henry Steele. *The Empire of Reason: How Europe Imagined and America Realized the Enlightenment.* London: Weidenfeld and Nicolson, 1978.

Condren, Conal. "Radicals, Conservatives, and Moderates in Early Modern Political Thought: A Case of Sandwich Island Syndrome." *History of Political Thought* 10 (1989): 525–42.

Coniff, James. "The Enlightenment and American Political Thought: A Study of the Origins of Madison's Federalist Number 10." *Political Theory* 8 (1980): 381–402.

Conk, Margo A. *The United States Census and Labor Force Change: A History of Occupation Statistics, 1870–1940.* Ann Arbor: UMI Research Press, 1980.

Conkin, Paul. *Prophets of Prosperity: America's First Political Economists.* Bloomington: Indiana University Press, 1980.

———. *Self-Evident Truths: Being a Discourse on the Origins and Development of the First Principles of American Government: Popular Sovereignty, Natural Rights, and Balance and Separation of Powers.* Bloomington: Indiana University Press, 1974.

Connolly, William E. *Politics and Ambiguity.* Madison: University of Wisconsin Press, 1987.

———. *The Terms of Political Discourse.* Lexington, Mass.: D. C. Heath, 1974.

Connolly, William E., and Glen Gordon, eds. *Social Structure and Political Theory.* Lexington, Mass.: D. C. Heath, 1974.

Conze, Werner. "Histoire des notions dans le domaine socio-politique." In *Problèmes de stratification sociale,* ed. Roland Mousnier. Paris: Presses Universitaires de France, 1968.

Cooke, Jacob E. *Alexander Hamilton.* New York: Scribner's, 1982.

———. *Tench Coxe and the Early Republic.* Chapel Hill: University of North Carolina Press, 1978.

Corcoran, Paul E. "Early French Socialism Reconsidered: The Propaganda of Fourier and Cabet." *History of European Ideas* 7 (1986): 469–88.

———. *Political Language and Rhetoric.* St. Lucia: University of Queensland Press, 1979.

Corfield, Penelope. "Class by Name and Number in Eighteenth Century Britain." *History* 72 (1987): 38–61.

———. "From Rank to Class: Innovation in Georgian England." *History Today* 37 (1987): 36–42.

———. "In So Many Words . . . Language and Society, 1500–1900." *History Today* 37 (1987): 16.

Cornell, Saul. "Aristocracy Assailed: The Ideology of Backcountry Anti-Federalism." *JAH* 76 (1990): 1148–72.

Coser, Lewis. "Class." In *Dictionary of the History of Ideas,* ed. Philip Wiener, 1:441–49. New York: Scribner's, 1968.

Coxon, Anthony P. M., P. M. Davies, and C. L. Jones. *Class and Hierarchy: The Social Meaning of Occupations.* London: Macmillan, 1979.

———. *Images of Social Stratification: Occupational Structures and Class.* London: Sage, 1986.

Cressy, David. "Describing the Social Order of Elizabethan and Stuart England." *Literature and History* 3 (1976): 29–44.

Crick, Bernard. *The American Science of Politics: Its Origins and Conditions.* Berkeley and Los Angeles: University of California Press, 1959.

Crossick, Geoffrey. "Classes and Masses in Victorian England." *History Today* 37 (1987): 29–35.

Crowley, John E. "Commerce and the Philadelphia Constitution: Neo-Mercantilism in Federalist and Anti-Federalist Political Economy." *History of Political Thought* 13 (1992): 73–98.

———. *This Sheba, Self: The Conceptualization of Economic Life in Eighteenth Century America.* Baltimore: Johns Hopkins University Press, 1973.

Cunliffe, Marcus. *Chattel Slavery and Wage Slavey: The Anglo-American Context, 1830–1860.* Athens: University of Georgia Press, 1979.

Curtis, Bruce. *William Graham Sumner.* Boston: Twayne, 1981.

———. "William Graham Sumner on the Concentration of Wealth." *JAH* 55 (1969): 823–32.

Dahrendorf, Ralf. *Classes and Class Conflict in Industrial Society*. Stanford: Stanford University Press, 1959.

———. *Essays in the Theory of Society*. London: Routledge and Kegan Paul, 1968.

Dallmayr, Fred R. *Language and Politics: Why Does Language Matter to Political Philosophy?* Notre Dame, Ind.: University of Notre Dame Press, 1984.

———. *Margins of Political Discourse*. Albany: State University of New York Press, 1989.

Daniels, Bruce C. "Defining Economic Classes in Colonial Massachusetts, 1700–1776." *Proceedings of the American Antiquarian Society* 83 (1977): 251–60.

———. "Defining Economic Classes in Colonial New Hampshire, 1700–1770." *Historical New Hampshire* 28 (1973): 53–62.

Davidson, Cathy, ed. *Reading in America: Literature and Social History*. Baltimore: Johns Hopkins University Press, 1989.

Davis, Howard. *Beyond Class Images: Explorations in the Structure of Social Consciousness*. London: Croom, Helm, 1979.

Davis, J. Ronnie. "Adam Smith on the Providential Reconciliation of Individual and Social Interests." *HOPE* 22 (1990): 341–53.

Davis, Susan. "Strike Parades and the Politics of Representing Class in Antebellum Philadelphia." *Drama Review* 29 (1985): 106–16.

Dawley, Alan. *Class and Community: The Industrial Revolution in Lynn*. Cambridge: Harvard University Press, 1976.

Deane, Phyllis. *The Evolution of Economic Ideas*. Cambridge: Cambridge University Press, 1978.

Deleule, Didier. "Du domestique au politique: Hume, les Physiocrates, et la naissance du libéralisme économique." *Bulletin de la Société Française de Philosophie* 74 (1980): 81–101.

Denning, Michael. *Mechanic Accents: Dime Novels and Working Class Culture in America*. London: Verso, 1987.

de Vivo, Giancarlo. "Ricardo and His Disciples: Orthodoxy and Socialism." *History of European Ideas* 9 (1988): 183–89.

Dickinson, H. T. *Liberty and Property: Political Ideology in Eighteenth-Century Britain*. New York: Holmes and Meier, 1977.

Diggins, John P. *The Lost Soul of American Politics: Virtue, Self Interest, and the Foundations of Liberalism*. Chicago: University of Chicago Press, 1986.

Dobb, Maurice. *Theories of Value and Distribution since Adam Smith: Ideology and Economic Theory*. Cambridge: Cambridge University Press, 1973.

Doerflinger, Thomas M. *A Vigorous Spirit of Enterprise: Merchants and Economic Development in Revolutionary Philadelphia*. Chapel Hill: University of North Carolina Press, 1986.

Dorfman, Joseph. *The Economic Mind in American Civilization*. 3 vols. 1946–49. Reprint. New York: A. M. Kelley, 1966.

Dorfman, Joseph, and Rexford G. Tugwell. *Early American Policy: Six Columbia Contributors*. New York: Columbia University Press, 1960.

Douglas, Mary. "Institutions Do the Classifying." In *How Institutions Think*. Syracuse: Syracuse University Press, 1986.

Dow, Sheila. "The Scottish Political Economy Tradition." *Scottish Journal of Political Economy* 34 (1987): 335–48.

Dumont, Louis. *From Mandeville to Marx: The Genesis and Triumph of Economic Ideology*. Chicago: University of Chicago Press, 1977.

———. *Homo Hierarchicus: An Essay on the Caste System.* Trans. Mark Sainsbury. Chicago: University of Chicago Press, 1970.

Dupriez, Leon. "Le concept de nature en économie politique." *Bulletin de la Classe des Lettres et des Sciences Morales et Politiques* 65 (1979): 332–35.

Durkheim, Emile. *The Elementary Forms of the Religious Life.* Trans. Joseph W. Swain. New York: Free Press, 1965.

Durkheim, Emile, and Marcel Mauss. *Primitive Classification.* Trans. and ed. Rodney Needham. Chicago: University of Chicago Press, 1963.

Dworetz, Stephen M. *The Unvarnished Doctrine: Locke, Liberalism, and the American Revolution.* Durham, N.C.: Duke University Press, 1990.

Eckhardt, Celia M. *Fanny Wright: Rebel in America.* Cambridge: Harvard University Press, 1984.

Edelman, Murray. *Constructing the Political Spectacle.* Chicago: University of Chicago Press, 1988.

———. *Political Language: Words That Succeed and Policies That Fail.* New York: Academic Press, 1977.

Egnal, Marc. *A Mighty Empire: The Origins of the American Revolution.* Ithaca, N.Y.: Cornell University Press, 1988.

Egnal, Marc, and Joseph E. Ernst. "An Economic Interpretation of the American Revolution." *WMQ* 29 (1972): 3–32.

Eichar, Douglas. *Occupation and Class Consciousness in America.* New York: Greenwood, 1989.

Ellis, Joseph J. *After the Revolution: Profiles of Early American Culture.* New York: Norton, 1979.

———. "Culture and Capitalism in Pre-Revolutionary America." *American Quarterly* 31 (1979): 169–86.

———. *Passionate Sage: The Character and Legacy of John Adams.* New York: Norton, 1993.

Ellis, Richard J. "Radical Lockeanism in American Political Culture." *Western Political Quarterly* 45 (1992): 825–50.

———. "Rival Versions of Equality in American Political Culture." *Review of Politics* 54 (1992): 253–80.

Eltis, Walter. "The Contrasting Theories of Industrialization of François Quesnay and Adam Smith." *Oxford Economic Papers* 40 (1988); 269–88.

Epstein, David F. *The Political Theory of the Federalist.* Chicago: University of Chicago Press, 1984.

Ericson, David F. *The Shaping of American Liberalism.* Chicago: University of Chicago Press, 1993.

———. "American Republicanism, 1787–1833: The Federal Farmer and Daniel Webster." Ph.D. diss., University of Chicago, 1987.

Evans, Charles. *American Bibliography.* New York: Peter Smith, 1941.

Evensky, Jerry. "The Evolution of Adam Smith's Views on Political Economy." *HOPE* 21 (1989): 123–45.

Fairclough, Norman. *Language and Power.* London: Longman, 1989.

Faler, Paul. *Mechanics and Manufacturers in the Early Industrial Revolution.* Albany: State University of New York Press, 1981.

Farr, James. "Political Science and the Enlightenment of Enthusiasm." *American Political Science Review* 82 (1988): 51–69.

Feller, Daniel. "Politics and Society: Toward a Jacksonian Synthesis." *Journal of the Early Republic* 10 (1990): 135–61.

Ferguson, E. James. "Political Economy, Public Liberty, and the Formation of the Constitution." *WMQ* 40 (1983): 389–412.

Ferguson, Robert. "Ideology and the Framing of the Constitution." *Early American Literature* 22 (1987): 157–65.

Fetter, Frank Whitson. *The Economist in Parliament, 1780–1868.* Durham, N.C.: Duke University Press, 1980.

———. "The Rise and Decline of Ricardian Economics." *HOPE* 1 (1969): 67–84.

Feuer, Lewis S. "The Influence of the American Communist Colonies on Engels and Marx." *Western Political Quarterly* 19 (1966): 456–74.

———. "The North American Origin of Marx's Socialism." *Western Political Quarterly* 16 (1963): 53–67.

Fine, Sidney. *Laissez Faire and the General Welfare State: A Study of Conflict in American Thought, 1865–1901.* Ann Arbor: University of Michigan Press, 1956.

Fink, Leon. "Class Conflict and the Gilded Age: The Figure and the Phantom." *Radical History Review* 3 (1975): 56–76.

———. *Workingmen's Democracy: The Knights of Labor and American Politics.* Urbana: University of Illinois Press, 1983.

Fischer, David Hackett. *The Revolution of American Conservatism: The Federalist Party in the Era of Jeffersonian Democracy.* New York: Harper and Row, 1965.

Flew, Anthony. *David Hume: Philosopher of Moral Science.* Oxford: Blackwell, 1986.

Foley, Vernard. "An Origin of the *Tableau Économique.*" *HOPE* 5 (1973): 134.

———. *The Social Physics of Adam Smith.* West Lafayette, Ind.: Purdue University Press, 1976.

Foner, Eric. *Free Soil, Free Labor, Free Men: The Ideology of the Republican Party before the Civil War.* New York: Oxford University Press, 1970.

———. *Politics and Ideology in the Age of the Civil War.* New York: Oxford University Press, 1980.

———, ed. *The New American History.* Philadelphia: Temple University Press, 1990.

Foner, Philip S. "Marx's *Capital* in the United States." *Science and Society* 31 (1967): 461–66.

———. *William Heighton: Pioneer Labor Leader of Jacksonian Philadelphia.* New York: International Publishers, 1991.

Fones-Wolf, Kenneth. "Boston Eight-Hour Men, New York Marxists, and the Emergence of the International Labor Union." *Historical Journal of Massachusetts* 9 (1981): 47–59.

Fontana, Biancamaria. *Rethinking the Politics of Commercial Society: The Edin-*

burgh Review, 1802–1832. Cambridge: Cambridge University Press, 1985.

Ford, Lacy K. "Republican Ideology in a Slave Society: The Political Economy of John C. Calhoun." *Journal of Southern History* 54 (1988): 405–24.

Formisano, Ronald. *The Transformation of Political Culture: Massachusetts Parties, 1790s–1840s.* New York: Oxford University Press, 1983.

Foshee, Andrew W. "Jeffersonian Political Economy and the Classical Republican Tradition: Jefferson, Taylor, and the Agrarian Republic." *HOPE* 17 (1985): 523–50.

Foucault, Michel. *Language, Counter-Memory, Practice: Selected Essays and Interviews.* Ed. Donald F. Bouchard. Trans. Donald F. Bouchard and Sherry Simon. Ithaca, N.Y.: Cornell University Press, 1977.

———. *The Order of Things: An Archaeology of the Human Sciences.* New York: Random House, 1973.

Fowler, Roger. *Linguistic Criticism.* New York: Oxford University Press, 1986.

———. *Literature as Social Discourse: The Practice of Linguistic Criticism.* Bloomington: Indiana University Press, 1981.

Fowler, Roger, Bob Hodge, Gunther Kress, and Tony Trew. *Language and Control.* London: Routledge and Kegan Paul, 1979.

Fox-Genovese, Elizabeth. *The Origins of Physiocracy.* Ithaca, N.Y.: Cornell University Press, 1976.

Frisch, Michael, and Daniel Walkowitz, eds. *Working-Class America: Essays on Labor, Community, and American Society.* Urbana: University of Illinois Press, 1983.

Furbank, P. N. *Unholy Pleasure; or, the Idea of Social Class.* Oxford: Oxford University Press, 1985.

Furner, Mary O. *Advocacy and Objectivity: A Crisis in the Professionalization of American Social Science.* Lexington: University of Kentucky Press, 1975.

Fussell, Paul. *Class: A Guide through the American Status System.* New York: Summit, 1983.

Gadamer, Hans-Georg. "The History of Concepts and the Language of Philosophy." *International Studies in Philosophy* 18 (1986): 1–16.

Gallie, William B. *Philosophy and the Historical Understanding.* New York: Schocken, 1964.

Garver, Eugene. "Rhetoric and Essentially Contested Arguments." *Philosophy and Rhetoric* 11 (1978): 156–72.

Gay, Peter. *The Enlightenment: An Interpretation.* 2 vols. New York: Knopf, 1969.

Gellner, Ernest. "Rhetoric and Essentially Contested Concepts." *Philosophy and Rhetoric* 11 (1978): 156–72.

Genovese, Eugene D. *The Political Economy of Slavery: Studies in the Economy and Society of the Slave South.* New York: Random House, 1961.

———. *The World the Slaveholders Made: Two Essays in Interpretation.* New York: Pantheon, 1969.

Gibbons, Michael T., ed. *Interpreting Politics.* New York: New York University Press, 1987.

Gibson, Alan. "Impartial Representation and the Extended Republic: Towards a Comprehensive and Balanced Reading of the Tenth 'Federalist.'" *History of Political Thought* 12 (1991): 263–304.

Gibson, James R. *Americans versus Malthus: The Population Debate in the Early Republic.* New York: Garland, 1989.

Giddens, Anthony. *The Class Structure of the Advanced Societies.* New York: Harper and Row, 1975.

Giddens, Anthony, and Gavin Mackenzie, eds. *Social Class and the Division of Labour: Essays in Honour of Ilya Neustadt.* Cambridge: Cambridge University Press, 1982.

Gilhooley, Leonard. *Contradiction and Dilemma: Orestes Brownson and the American Idea.* New York: Fordham University Press, 1972.

———, ed. *No Divided Allegiance: Essays in Brownson's Thought.* New York: Fordham University Press, 1980.

Gillespie, Michael, and Michael Lienesch, eds. *Ratifying the Constitution.* Lawrence: University Press of Kansas, 1989.

Glickstein, Jonathan. *Concepts of Free Labor in Antebellum America.* New Haven: Yale University Press, 1991.

Goldman, Perry. "Political Rhetoric in the Age of Jackson." *Tennessee Historical Quarterly* 29 (1970–71): 360–71.

Goldstein, Leslie. "Europe Looks at American Women, 1820–1840." *Social Research* 54 (1987): 519–42.

Goodwin, Barbara. *Social Science and Utopia: Nineteenth-Century Models of Social Harmony.* Sussex, England: Harvester, 1978.

Goodwin, C. D. W. "Marginalism Moves to the New World." *HOPE* 4 (1973): 551–70.

Gordon, Milton M. *Human Nature, Class, and Ethnicity.* New York: Oxford University Press, 1978.

———. *Social Class in American Sociology.* Durham, N.C.: Duke University Press, 1958.

Gorman, Robert A. *Yankee Red: Nonorthodox Marxism in Liberal America.* New York: Praeger, 1979.

Gough, Robert J. "Towards a Theory of Class and Social Conflict." Ph.D. diss., University of Pennsylvania, 1977.

Govan, Thomas Payne. *Nicholas Biddle: Nationalist and Public Banker.* Chicago: University of Chicago Press, 1959.

Grace, George W. *The Linguistic Construction of Reality.* London: Croom, Helm, 1987.

Gracia, Jorge J. E. "Texts and Their Interpretation." *Review of Metaphysics* 43 (1990): 495–542.

Graham, Keith. "Class: A Simple View." *Inquiry* 32 (1989): 419–36.

Grampp, William D. "Adam Smith and the American Revolutionists." *HOPE* 11 (1979): 179–91.

———. "Classical Economy and Its Moral Critics." *HOPE* 5 (1973): 359–78.

Gray, John. "On Liberty, Liberalism, and Essential Contestability." *British Journal of Political Science* 8 (1978): 385–402.

Green, David. *Shaping Political Consciousness: The Language of Politics in America from McKinley to Reagan.* Ithaca, N.Y.: Cornell University Press, 1987.

Green, James. *Mathew Carey: Publisher and Patriot.* Philadelphia: Library Co. of Philadelphia, 1985.

Greene, Jack P. "Social Structure and Political Behavior in Revolutionary America: John Day's 'Remarks on American Affairs.'" *WMQ* 32 (1975): 471–84.

Greene, Jack P., and J. R. Pole, eds. *Colonial British America: Essays in the New History of the Early Modern Era.* Baltimore: Johns Hopkins University Press, 1984.

Greenstone, J. David. "Against Simplicity: The Cultural Dimensions of the Constitution." *University of Chicago Law Review* 55 (1988): 428–49.

Grob, Gerald N. *Workers and Utopia: A Study of Ideological Conflict in the American Labor Movement, 1865–1900.* Evanston, Ill.: Northwestern University Press, 1961.

Grossman, Jonathan. *William Sylvis, Pioneer of American Labor: A Study of the Labor Movement during the Era of the Civil War.* New York: Columbia University Press, 1945.

Guarneri, Carl J. "Importing Fourierism to America." *JHI* 43 (1982): 581–94.

———. *The Utopian Alternative: Fourierism in Nineteenth Century America.* Ithaca, N.Y.: Cornell University Press, 1991.

———. "Utopian Socialism and American Ideas: The Origin and Doctrine of American Fourierism, 1832–1848." Ph.D. diss., Johns Hopkins University, 1979.

Gudeman, Stephen. *Economics as Culture: Models and Metaphors of Livelihood.* London: Routledge and Kegan Paul, 1986.

Haddow, Anna. *Political Science in American Colleges and Universities, 1636–1900.* New York: D. Appleton–Century, 1939.

Halker, Clark D. *For Democracy, Workers, and God: Labor Song-Poems and Labor Protest, 1865–1895.* Urbana: University of Illinois Press, 1991.

Halliday, Michael A. K. *Language as Social Semiotic: The Social Interpretation of Language and Meaning.* London: University Park Press, 1978.

Hammond, Bray. *Banks and Politics in America: From the Revolution to the Civil War.* Princeton: Princeton University Press, 1957.

Hamowy, Ronald. "*Cato's Letters,* John Locke, and the Republican Paradigm." *History of Political Thought* 11 (1990): 273–94.

———. "Progress and Commerce in Anglo-American Thought: The Social Philosophy of Adam Ferguson." *Interpretation* 14 (1986): 61–87.

———. *The Scottish Enlightenment and the Theory of Spontaneous Order.* Carbondale: Southern Illinois University Press, 1987.

Hanson, Russell. *The Democratic Imagination in America: Conversations with Our Past.* Princeton: Princeton University Press, 1985.

Harp, Gillis J. "Taylor, Calhoun, and the Decline of a Political Theory of Disharmony." *JHI* 46 (1985): 107–20.

Harris, David. *Socialist Origins in the United States: American Forerunners of Marx, 1817–1832.* Assen, The Netherlands: Van Gorcum, 1966.

Harris, Wendell V. *Interpretive Acts: In Search of Meaning.* Oxford: Clarendon, 1988.

Harrison, John F. C. "Owenite Communitarianism in Britain and America." *Communal Societies* 4 (1984): 243–48.

———. *Quest for the New Moral World: Robert Owen and the Owenites in Britain and America.* New York: Scribner's, 1969.

Hartz, Louis. *The Necessity of Choice: Nineteenth Century Political Thought.* London: Transaction, 1990.

———. "Seth Luther: Working Class Rebel." *New England Quarterly* 13 (1940): 401–18.

Haskell, Thomas. *The Emergence of Professional Social Science: The American Social Science Association and the Nineteenth-Century Crisis of Authority.* Urbana: University of Illinois Press, 1977.

Hawkins, Richmond L. *Auguste Comte and the United States.* New York: Kraus, 1966.

Heale, M. J. *The Presidential Quest: Candidates and Images in American Political Culture, 1787–1852.* London: Longman, 1982.

Henderson, James P. "An English Communist: Mr. Bray and His Remarkable Work." *HOPE* 17 (1985): 73–96.

Henry, John F. "John Bates Clark and the Marginal Product: An Historical Inquiry into the Origins of Value-Free Economic Theory." *HOPE* 15 (1983): 375–89.

Herreshoff, David. *The Origins of American Marxism, from the Transcendentalists to De Leon.* New York: Monad Press, 1973.

Hill, Christopher. "Political Discourse in Early Seventeenth Century England." In *Politics and People in Revolutionary England,* ed. Colin Jones. Oxford: Blackwell, 1986.

Himmelfarb, Gertrude. *The Idea of Poverty: England in the Early Industrial Age.* New York: Knopf, 1984.

Hindess, Barry. *Political Choice and Social Structure: An Analysis of Actors, Interests, and Rationality.* Aldershot, England: Edward Elgar, 1989.

———. *Politics and Class Analysis.* Oxford: Blackwell, 1987.

Hirsch, Susan. *Roots of the American Working Class: The Industrialization of Crafts in Newark, 1800–1860.* Philadelphia: University of Pennsylvania Press, 1978.

Hirschman, Albert O. *The Passions and the Interests: Political Arguments for Capitalism before Its Triumph.* Princeton: Princeton University Press, 1977.

———. "Rival Interpretations of Market Society: Civilizing, Destructive, or Feeble?" *Journal of Economic Literature* 20 (1982): 1463–84.

Hite, James C., and Ellen J. Hall. "The Reactionary Evolution of Economic Thought in Antebellum Virginia." *Virginia Magazine of History and Biography* 80 (1972): 476–88.

Hobsbawm, Eric. "Class Consciousness and History." In *Aspects of History and Class Consciousness,* ed. Istvan Meszaros. London: Routledge and Kegan Paul, 1971.

Hoerder, Dirk. "Some Connections between Craft Consciousness and Political Thought among Mechanics, 1820s–1840s." *Amerikastudien* 30 (1985): 327–51.

Hoffman, Ronald, and John McCusker, eds. *The Economy of Early America: The Revolutionary Period, 1763–1790.* Charlottesville: University Press of Virginia, 1988.

Hollis, Martin. *Models of Man: Philosophical Thoughts on Social Action.* Cambridge: Cambridge University Press, 1977.

———. "The Social Destruction of Reality." In *Rationality and Relativism,* ed. Martin Hollis and Steven Lukes. Oxford: Blackwell, 1982.

Hollis, Martin, and Edward J. Nell. *Rational Economic Man: A Philosophical Critique of Neo-Classical Economics.* Cambridge: Cambridge University Press, 1975.

Hollis, Patricia, ed. *Class and Conflict in Nineteenth-Century England, 1815–1860.* London: Routledge and Kegan Paul, 1973.

Holmberg, Georgia. "British-American Whig Political Rhetoric, 1765–1771." Ph.D. diss., University of Pittsburgh, 1979.

Holt, James. "The Trade Unions and Socialism in the United States." *Journal of American Studies* 7 (1973): 321–27.

Hont, Istvan, and Michael Ignatieff, eds. *Wealth and Virtue: The Shaping of Political Economy in the Scottish Enlightenment.* Cambridge: Cambridge University Press, 1983.

Hoornstra, Jean, and Trudy Heath, eds. *American Periodicals, 1741–1900.* Ann Arbor: UMI Research Press, 1979.

Hope, Barney Francis. "The Concept of Productive and Unproductive Labor in Classical Economics." Ph.D. diss., University of California, Riverside, 1979.

Horne, Thomas A. "Bourgeois Virtue, Property, and Moral Philosophy in America, 1750–1800." *History of Political Thought* 4 (1983): 318–40.

Horowitz, Daniel. "Historians and Economists: Perspectives on the Development of American Economic Thought." *HOPE* 6 (1974): 454–62.

———. "Textbook Models of American Economic Growth, 1837–1911." *HOPE* 7 (1975): 227–51.

Horwitz, Richard P. *Anthropology toward History: Culture and Work in a Nineteenth Century Maine Town.* Middletown, Conn.: Wesleyan University Press, 1978.

Howe, Daniel Walker. "European Sources of Political Ideas in Jeffersonian America." In *The Promise of American History: Progress and Prospects,* ed. Stanley I. Kutler and Stanley N. Katz. Baltimore: Johns Hopkins University Press, 1982.

———. *The Political Culture of the American Whigs.* Chicago: University of Chicago Press, 1979.

———. "The Political Psychology of *The Federalist.*" *WMQ* 44 (1987): 485–509.

———. *The Unitarian Conscience: Harvard Moral Philosophy, 1805–1861.* Cambridge: Harvard University Press, 1970.

———. "Why the Scottish Enlightenment Was Useful to the Framers of the American Constitution." *Comparative Studies in Society and History* 31 (1989): 573–87.

Howe, John R., Jr. "Republican Thought and the Political Violence of the 1790s." *American Quarterly* 19 (1967): 147–50.

Hudson, Peter. "Proletarian Experience, Class Interest, and Discourse: How Far Can Classical Marxism Still Be Defended?" *Politikon* 14 (1987): 16–35.

Hughes, Geoffrey. *Words in Time: A Social History of the English Vocabulary.* Oxford: Blackwell, 1988.

Hugins, Walter. *Jacksonian Democracy and the Working Class: A Study of the New York Workingmen's Movement, 1829–1837.* Stanford: Stanford University Press, 1960.

Hull, Gary. "The Prospect for Man in Early American Economic Thought, 1800–1850." Ph.D. diss., University of Maryland, 1969.

Hummel, Jeffrey R. "The Jacksonians, Banking, and Economic Theory: A Reinterpretation." *Journal of Libertarian Studies* 2 (1978): 151–65.

Hunt, Lynn. *Politics, Culture, and Class in the French Revolution.* Berkeley and Los Angeles: University of California Press, 1984.

Hutchison, T. W. *Before Adam Smith: The Emergence of Political Economy, 1662–1776.* Oxford: Blackwell, 1988.

———. *On Revolutions and Progress in Economic Knowledge.* Cambridge: Cambridge University Press, 1978.

Hutson, James L. "Facing an Angry Labor: The American Public Interprets the Shoemaker's Strike of 1860." *Civil War History* 28 (1982): 197–212.

———. *The Panic of 1857 and the Coming of the Civil War.* Baton Rouge: Louisiana State University Press, 1987.

———. "A Political Response to Industrialism: The Republican Embrace of Protectionist Labor Doctrines." *JAH* 70 (1983): 35–57.

Innes, Stephen, ed. *Work and Labor in Early America.* Chapel Hill: University of North Carolina Press, 1988.

Isaac, Jeffrey. "Republicanism versus Liberalism? A Reconsideration." *HOPE* 9 (1988): 349–77.

Jackman, Mary R., and Robert W. Jackman. *Class Awareness in the United States.* Berkeley and Los Angeles: University of California Press, 1983.

Jalladeau, Joel. "The Methodological Conversion of John Bates Clark." *HOPE* 7 (1975): 209–26.

Johnson, Oakley. *Marxism in United States History before the Russian Revolution.* New York: Humanities Press, 1974.

———. *Robert Owen in the United States.* New York: Humanities Press, 1970.

Jones, Alice Hanson. *Wealth of a Nation to Be: The American Colonies on the Eve of the Revolution.* New York: Columbia University Press, 1980.

Jones, Gareth Stedman. *Languages of Class: Studies in English Working Class History, 1832–1982.* Cambridge: Cambridge University Press, 1983.

Jones, Peter, ed. *The "Science of Man" in the Scottish Enlightenment: Hume, Reid, and Their Contemporaries.* Edinburgh: Edinburgh University Press, 1989.

Jordan, Cynthia S. "Old Words in New Circumstances: Language and Leadership in Post-Revolutionary America." *American Quarterly* 40 (1988): 491–513.

Kanth, Rajani. *Political Economy and Laissez-Faire: Economics and Ideology in the Ricardian Era.* Totowa, N.J.: Rowman and Littlefield, 1986.

Kaster, Gregory. "We Will Not Be Slaves to Avarice: The American Labor Jeremiad, 1827–1877." Ph.D. diss., Boston University, 1990.

Katz, Michael. "Occupational Classification in History." *Journal of Interdisciplinary History* 3 (1972): 63–87.

———. "Social Class in North American Urban History." *Journal of Interdisciplinary History* 11 (1981): 579–606.

Katznelson, Ira, and Aristide Zolberg, eds. *Working-Class Formation: Nineteenth-Century Patterns in Western Europe and the United States.* Princeton: Princeton University Press, 1986.

Kaufman, Allen. *Capitalism, Slavery, and Republican Values: Antebellum Political Economists.* Austin: University of Texas Press, 1982.

Kellner, Hans. *Language and Historical Representation: Getting the Story Crooked.* Madison: University of Wisconsin Press, 1989.

Kent, Christopher. "Presence and Absence: History, Theory, and the Working Class." *Victorian Studies* 29 (1986): 437–62.

Kenyon, Cecilia M. "Republicanism and Radicalism in the American Revolution." *WMQ* 39 (1962): 153–82.

Kerber, Linda K. *Federalists in Dissent: Imagery and Ideology in Jeffersonian America.* Ithaca, N.Y.: Cornell University Press, 1970.

Kerstholt, F. "De traditie van klassieke klassenanalyse." *Sociologische Gids* 29 (1982): 44–47.

Kessler, Charles, ed. *Saving the Revolution: The Federalist Papers and the American Founding.* New York: Free Press, 1987.

Kettler, David. *The Social and Political Thought of Adam Ferguson.* Columbus: Ohio State University Press, 1965.

King, J. E. "Utopian or Scientific: A Reconsideration of the Ricardian Socialists." *HOPE* 15 (1983): 345–73.

Klancher, Jon. *The Making of English Reading Audiences, 1790–1832.* Madison: University of Wisconsin Press, 1987.

Kloppenberg, James T. "The Virtues of Liberalism: Christianity, Republicanism, and Ethics in Early American Political Discourse." *JAH* 74 (1987): 9–33.

Klotz, Gerard, ed. *Ordre, nature, proprieté.* Lyons: Presses Universitaires de Lyon, 1985.

Kohl, Lawrence. *The Politics of Individualism: Parties and the American Character in the Jacksonian Era.* New York: Oxford University Press, 1989.

Kolmerten, Carol A. *Women in Utopia: The Ideology of Gender in the American Owenite Communities.* Bloomington: Indiana University Press, 1990.

Kornblith, Gary. "From Artisans to Businessmen: Master Mechanics in New England, 1789–1850." Ph.D. diss., Princeton University, 1983.

———. "Self-Made Men: The Development of Middling-Class Consciousness in New England." *Massachusetts Review* 26 (1985): 461–74.

Kornfeld, Eve. "From Republicanism to Liberalism: The Intellectual Journey of David Ramsay." *Journal of the Early Republic* 9 (1989): 289–314.

Koselleck, Reinhart. *Futures Past: On the Semantics of Historical Time*. Trans. Keith Tribe. Cambridge: MIT Press, 1985.

———. "Linguistic Change and the History of Events." *JMH* 61 (1989): 649–66.

———. "Time and Revolutionary Language." *Graduate Faculty Philosophy Journal* 9 (1983): 117–27.

———, ed. *Historische Semantik und Begriffsgeschichte*. Stuttgart: Klett-Cotta, 1979.

Kramnick, Isaac. *Bourgeois Radicalism*. Ithaca, N.Y.: Cornell University Press, 1990.

———. "Eighteenth Century Science and Radical Social Theory: The Case of Joseph Priestly's Scientific Liberalism." *Journal of British Studies* 25 (1986): 1–30.

———. "The 'Great National Discussion': The Discourse of Politics in 1787." *WMQ* 45 (1988): 3–32.

Kress, Gunther, and Robert Hodge. *Language as Ideology*. London: Routledge and Kegan Paul, 1979.

Kruman, Marc W. "The Second Party System and the Transformation of Revolutionary Republicanism." *Journal of the Early Republic* 12 (1992): 509–38.

Kuklick, Bruce. *The Rise of American Philosophy: Cambridge, Massachusetts, 1860–1930*. New Haven: Yale University Press, 1977.

Kulikoff, Allan. *The Agrarian Origins of American Capitalism*. Charlottesville: University Press of Virginia, 1992.

———. "The Transition to Capitalism in Rural America." *WMQ* 46 (1989): 120–44.

La Capra, Dominick. *Rethinking Intellectual History: Texts, Contexts, Language*. Ithaca, N.Y.: Cornell University Press, 1983.

Laslett, John H. M. *Reluctant Proletarians: A Comparative History of American Socialism*. Westport, Conn.: Greenwood, 1984.

Laslett, John H. M., and Seymour M. Lipset, eds. *Failure of a Dream? Essays in the History of American Socialism*. Berkeley and Los Angeles: University of California Press, 1984.

Laslett, Peter. *The World We Have Lost*. New York: Scribner's, 1971.

Laslett, Peter, W. G Runciman, and Quentin Skinner, eds. *Philosophy, Politics, and Society*. 4th ser. Oxford: Blackwell, 1972.

Lasser, Carol. "Gender, Ideology, and Class in the Early Republic." *Journal of the Early Republic* 10 (1990): 331–37.

Laurie, Bruce. *Working People of Philadelphia, 1800–1850*. Philadelphia: Temple University Press, 1980.

Lause, Mark. "The American Radicals and Organized Marxism: The Initial Experience." *Labor History* 33 (1992): 55–80.

———. "The 'Unwashed Infidelity': Thomas Paine and Early New York City Labor History." *Labor History* 27 (1986): 385–409.

Layder, Derek. *The Realist Image in Social Science*. New York: St. Martin's, 1990.

Lenger, Friedrich. "Beyond Exceptionalism: Notes on the Artisanal Phase of the Labour Movement in France, England, Germany, and the United States." *International Review of Social History* 36 (1991): 1–23.

Lerner, Ralph. "Commerce and Character: The Anglo-American as New Model Man." *WMQ* 36 (1979): 3–26.

Letwin, William. *The Origins of Scientific Economics: English Economic Thought, 1660–1776.* London: Methuen, 1963.

Levy, Michael. "Liberal Equality and Inherited Wealth." *Political Theory* 11 (1983): 545–64.

Lieberman, Sima. "The American Labor Movement in the Light of European Thought." In *Labor Movements and Labor Thought: France, Germany, and the United States.* New York: Praeger, 1986.

Lienesch, Michael. "Historical Theory and Political Reform: Two Perspectives on Confederation Politics." *Review of Politics* 45 (1983): 94–115.

———. "In Defense of the Anti-Federalists." *History of Political Thought* 4 (1983): 65–88.

———. *New Order of the Ages: Time, the Constitution, and the Making of Modern American Political Thought.* Princeton: Princeton University Press, 1988.

Lincoln, Bruce. *Discourse and the Construction of Society: Comparative Studies of Myth, Ritual, and Classification.* New York: Oxford University Press, 1989.

Lindenberg, Daniel. "Prolétariat." In *Nouvelle histoire des idées politiques,* ed. Pascal Orly. Paris: Hachette, 1987.

Lips, Roger. "Orestes Brownson." In *American Literary Critics and Scholars, 1800–1850,* ed. John W. Rathbun and Monica M. Grecu. Detroit: Gale, 1987.

Lipset, Seymour Martin. "Radicalism or Reformism: The Sources of Working Class Politics." *American Political Science Review* 77 (1983): 1–18.

Looby, Christopher. "The Constitution of Nature: Taxonomy as Politics in Jefferson, Peale, and Bartram." *Early American Literature* 22 (1987): 252–74.

Lovell, David W. "Early French Socialism and Class Struggle." *HOPE* 9 (1988): 327–48.

Lukes, Steven. "Class." In *The Blackwell Encyclopedia of Political Thought,* ed. David Miller. Oxford: Blackwell, 1987.

Lunde, Erik S. *Horace Greeley.* Boston: Twayne, 1981.

Luttrell, Clifton. "Thomas Jefferson on Money and Banking." *HOPE* 7 (1975): 156–73.

Lynd, Staughton. *Class Conflict, Slavery, and the United States Constitution: Ten Essays.* Indianapolis: Bobbs-Merrill, 1967.

McCloskey, Donald. *The Rhetoric of Economics.* Madison: University of Wisconsin Press, 1985.

McConachie, Bruce. "Economic Values in Popular American Melodramas, 1815–1860." Ph.D. diss., University of Wisconsin, 1977.

McCoy, Drew. *The Elusive Republic: Political Economy in Jeffersonian America.* Chapel Hill: University of North Carolina Press, 1980.

McCullagh, C. Behan. "Can Our Understanding of Old Texts Be Objective?" *History and Theory* 30 (1991): 302–23.

———. "Colligation and Classification in History." *History and Theory* 18 (1978): 267–84.

McDonald, Forrest. "A Founding Father's Library." *Literature of Liberty* 1 (1978): 4–15.

———. *Novus Ordo Seclorum: The Intellectual Origins of the Constitution.* Lawrence: University Press of Kansas, 1985.

———. "The Rhetoric of Alexander Hamilton." *Modern Age* 25 (1981): 114–24.

McDowell, Gary. "Commerce, Virtue, and Politics: Adam Ferguson's Constitutionalism." *Review of Politics* 45 (1983): 536–52.

McEndowney, Doral. "Bourgeois Radicalism: The American Libertarian Tradition." Ph.D. diss., City University of New York, 1976.

McFarland, C. K., and Robert L. Thistlewaite. "Labor Press Demands Equal Education in the Age of Jackson." *Journalism Quarterly* 65 (1988): 600–608.

———. "Twenty Years of a Successful Labor Paper: *The Working Man's Advocate,* 1829–1849." *Journalism Quarterly* 60 (1983): 35–40.

McFaul, John M. *The Politics of Jacksonian Finance.* Ithaca, N.Y.: Cornell University Press, 1972.

McGovern, Trevor. "Conservative Ideology in Britain in the 1790s." *History* 73 (1988): 238–47.

MacIntyre, Alasdair. "The Essential Contestability of Some Social Concepts." *Ethics* 84 (1973): 1–9.

———. *Whose Justice? Whose Rationality?* Notre Dame, Ind.: University of Notre Dame Press, 1988.

MacLeod, Duncan. "The Political Economy of John Taylor of Caroline." *Journal of American Studies* 14 (1980): 387–405.

McNall, Scott G. *The Road to Rebellion: Class Formation and Kansas Populism, 1865–1900.* Chicago: University of Chicago Press, 1988.

McNally, David. *Political Economy and the Rise of Capitalism: A Reinterpretation.* Berkeley and Los Angeles: University of California Press, 1988.

Madden, Edward H. "Francis Wayland and the Scottish Tradition." *Transactions of the Charles S. Peirce Society* 21 (1985): 301–26.

Magee, Bryan. "The Language of Politics." *Encounter* 66 (1986): 20–26.

Maidment, Richard, and John Zvesper, eds. *Reflections on the Constitution: The American Constitution after Two Hundred Years.* Manchester: Manchester University Press, 1989.

Mailloux, Steven. *Rhetorical Power.* Ithaca, N.Y.: Cornell University Press, 1989.

Main, Jackson Turner. *The Social Structure of Revolutionary America.* Princeton: Princeton University Press, 1965.

Majewski, John, Christopher Baer, and Daniel B. Klein. "Responding to Relative Decline: The Plank Road Boom of Antebellum New York." *JEH* 53 (1993): 106–20.

Malcolmson, Robert. *Life and Labour in England, 1700–1780.* New York: St. Martin's, 1981.

Malone, Dumas. *The Public Life of Thomas Cooper, 1783–1839.* 1926. Reprint. Columbia: University of South Carolina Press, 1961.

Malone, Dumas, Arthur Schlesinger, Jr., et al., eds. *Rhetoric and the Founders.* Lanham, Md.: University Press of America, 1987.

Margo, Robert A., and Georgia C. Villaflor. "The Growth of Wages in Antebellum America: New Evidence." *JEH* 47 (1987): 873–97.

Martin, Peter. "The Concept of Class." In *Classic Disputes in Sociology,* ed. R. J. Anderson, J. A. Hughes, and W. W. Sharrock. London: Allen and Unwin, 1987.

Martin, Thomas L. "Neglected Aspects of the Economic Thought and Method of Condy Raguet." *HOPE* 19 (1987): 401–13.

Marwick, Arthur. *Class: Image and Reality in Britain, France, and the United States of America since 1930.* New York: Oxford University Press, 1980.

Matson, Cathy, and Peter Onuf. "Toward a Republican Empire: Interest and Ideology in Revolutionary America." *American Quarterly* 37 (1985): 491–533.

———. *A Union of Interests: Political and Economic Thought in Revolutionary America.* Lawrence: University Press of Kansas, 1990.

Matthews, Richard K. *The Radical Politics of Thomas Jefferson: A Revisionist View.* Lawrence: University Press of Kansas, 1984.

May, Henry. "Europe and the American Mind." *History of European Ideas* 5 (1984): 137–48.

———. *Protestant Churches and Industrial America.* 1949. Reprint. New York: Octagon Books, 1963.

Mayer, David N., ed. "Of Principles and Men: The Correspondence of John Taylor of Caroline with Wilson Cary Nicholas, 1806–1808." *Virginia Magazine of History and Biography* 96 (1988): 345–88.

Meek, Ronald L. *Economics and Ideology and Other Essays: Studies in the Development of Economic Thought.* London: Chapman and Hall, 1967.

———. *The Economics of Physiocracy: Essays and Translations.* London: Allen and Unwin, 1962.

———. "Smith, Turgot, and the 'Four-Stages' Theory." *HOPE* 3 (1971): 9–27.

Meyer, Donald. *The Democratic Enlightenment.* New York: Putnam's, 1976.

———. *The Instructed Conscience: The Shaping of the American National Ethic.* Philadelphia: University of Pennsylvania Press, 1972.

Meyers, Marvin. *The Jacksonian Persuasion: Politics and Belief.* Stanford: Stanford University Press, 1957.

Middlekauf, Robert. "The Assumptions of the Founders in 1787." *Social Science Quarterly* 88 (1987): 656–68.

Miller, David. "Hume and Possessive Individualism." *History of Political Thought* 1 (1980): 261–78.

———. *Philosophy and Ideology in Hume's Political Thought.* Oxford: Clarendon, 1981.

Miller, Douglas T. *Jacksonian Aristocracy: Class and Democracy in New York, 1830–1860.* New York: Oxford University Press, 1967.

Miller, William L. "Primogeniture, Entails, and Endowments in English Classical Economics." *HOPE* 12 (1980): 558–81.

Miroff, Bruce. "Alexander Hamilton: The Aristocrat as Visionary." *International Political Science Review* 9 (1988): 43–54.

Montgomery, David. *Beyond Equality: Labor and the Radical Republicans, 1862–1872.* New York: Knopf, 1967.

———. *The Fall of the House of Labor: The Workplace, the State, and American Labor Activism, 1865–1925.* New York: Cambridge University Press, 1987.

———. "The Working Class of the Pre-Industrial American City." *Labor History* 9 (1968): 3–22.

Moody, J. Carroll, and Alice Kessler-Harris, eds. *Perspectives on American Labor History: The Problems of Synthesis.* De Kalb: Northern Illinois University Press, 1989.

Morgan, Edmund. *Inventing the People: The Rise of Popular Sovereignty in England and America.* New York: Norton, 1988.

———. "Safety in Numbers: Madison, Hume, and the Tenth Federalist." *Huntington Library Quarterly* 49 (1986): 95–112.

Morilhat, Claude. *La prise de conscience du capitalisme: Économie et philosophie chez Turgot.* Paris: Meridiens Klincksieck, 1988.

Morris, Jeffrey B. "'No Other Herald': Niles' Register and the Supreme Court." *Yearbook of the Supreme Court Historical Society* (1978): 51–60.

Morris, R. J. *Class and Class Consciousness in the Industrial Revolution, 1780–1850.* London: Macmillan, 1979.

Morris, Richard B. "Class Struggle and the American Revolution." *WMQ* 39 (1962): 3–29.

———. *Government and Labor in Early America.* New York: Columbia University Press, 1946.

Morrison, Rodney J. "Henry C. Carey and American Economic Development." *Explorations in Entrepreneurial History* 5 (1968): 132–44.

———. *Henry C. Carey and American Economic Development.* Transactions of the American Philosophical Society, vol. 76, part 3. Philadelphia: American Philosophical Society, 1986.

Moyer, Albert. *A Scientist's Voice in American Culture: Simon Newcomb and the Rhetoric of Scientific Method.* Berkeley: University of California Press, 1992.

Mueller, Roger C. *Samuel Johnson, American Transcendentalist: A Short Biography.* Salem: Essex Institute, 1979.

———, ed. *Selected Writings of Samuel Johnson.* Delmar, N.Y.: Scholar's Facsimiles, 1977.

Mulkay, Michael. *The Word and the World: Explorations in the Form of Sociological Analysis.* London: Allen and Unwin, 1985.

Murphy, Antoine. "Le developpement des idées économiques en France, 1750–1756." *Revue d'Histoire Moderne et Contemporaine* 33 (1986): 521–41.

Nash, Gary. *Race, Class, and Politics: Essays on Colonial and Revolutionary Society.* Urbana: University of Illinois Press, 1986.

———. *The Urban Crucible: Social Change, Political Consciousness, and the Origins of the American Revolution.* Cambridge: Harvard University Press, 1979.

———, ed. *Class and Society in Early America.* Englewood Cliffs, N.J.: Prentice Hall, 1970.

Neale, R. S. *Class and Ideology in the Nineteenth Century.* London: Routledge and Kegan Paul, 1972.

———. *Class in English History, 1680–1850.* Oxford: Blackwell, 1981.

Needham, Rodney. *Symbolic Classification.* Santa Monica, Calif.: Goodyear, 1979.

———, ed. *Right and Left: Essays on Dual Symbolic Classification.* Chicago: University of Chicago Press, 1973.

Nelson, Jeffrey. "The Rhetoric of the 1896 Republican National Convention at St. Louis." *Missouri Historical Review* 77 (1983): 395–409.

Neufeld, Maurice F. "Realms of Thought and Organized Labor in the Age of Jackson." *Labor History* 10 (1969): 5–43.

Newman, Stephen. "Thomas Cooper, 1759–1839: The Political Odyssey of a Bourgeois Ideologue." *Southern Studies* 24 (1985): 295–305.

Nisbet, Robert. "The Decline and Fall of Social Class." *Pacific Sociological Review* 2 (1959): 11–17.

Normano, João F. *The Spirit of American Economics.* New York: John Day, 1943.

Nugent, Walter T. K. *Money and American Society, 1865–1880.* New York: Free Press, 1968.

———. "Tocqueville, Marx, and American Class Structure." *Social Science History* 12 (1988): 327–48.

Oakes, James. "From Republicanism to Liberalism: Ideological Change and the Crisis of the Old South." *American Quarterly* 37 (1985): 551–71.

Oakley, Allen. *Marx's Critique of Political Economy: Intellectual Sources and Evolution.* London: Routledge and Kegan Paul, 1984.

O'Brien, Conor Cruise. *The Great Melody: A Thematic Biography and Commented Anthology of Edmund Burke.* London: Sinclair-Stevenson, 1992.

O'Brien, David P. *The Classical Economists.* Oxford: Clarendon, 1978.

O'Brien, Michael, ed. *All Clever Men, Who Make Their Way: Critical Discourse in the Old South.* Fayetteville: University of Arkansas Press, 1982.

O'Connor, Michael J. L. *Origins of Academic Economics in the United States.* New York: Columbia University Press, 1944.

Ollman, Bertell. "Marx's Use of 'Class'." *American Journal of Sociology* 73 (1968): 573–80.

Olsen, Mark, and Louis George Harvey. "Contested Methods: Daniel T. Rodger's *Contested Truths.*" *JHI* 49 (1989): 653–68.

Oravec, Christine. "The Democratic Critics: An Alternate American Rhetorical Tradition in the Nineteenth Century." *Rhetorica* 4 (1988): 395–421.

Ossowski, Stanislaw. *Class Structure in the Social Consciousness.* Trans. Sheila Patterson. New York: Free Press, 1963.

Pagden, Anthony, ed. *The Languages of Political Theory in Early-Modern Europe.* Cambridge: Cambridge University Press, 1987.

Page, Charles. *Class and American Sociology: From Ward to Ross.* 1940. Reprint. New York: Octagon, 1964.

Palmer, Bryan. *Descent into Discourse.* Philadelphia: Temple University Press, 1990.

Pangle, Thomas L. *The Spirit of Modern Republicanism: The Moral Vision of the American Founders and the Philosophy of Locke.* Chicago: University of Chicago Press, 1988.

Parkin, Frank. *Class Inequality and Political Order: Social Stratification in Capitalist and Communist Societies.* London: MacGibbon and Kee, 1971.

———. *Marxism and Class Theory: A Bourgeois Critique.* London: Tavistock, 1979.

———, ed. *The Social Analysis of Class Structure.* London: Tavistock, 1974.

Perelman, Michael. "Adam Smith and Dependent Social Relations." *HOPE* 21 (1989): 503–20.

———. *Classical Political Economy: Primitive Accumulation and the Social Division of Labor.* Totowa, N.J.: Rowman and Allanheld, 1984.

———. *Marx's Crises Theory: Scarcity, Labor, and Finance.* New York: Praeger, 1989.

Perkins, Alice J. G., and Theresa Wolfson. *Frances Wright, Free Enquirer: The Study of a Temperament.* Philadelphia: Porcupine, 1972.

Perkins, Edwin J. *The Economy of Colonial America.* 2nd ed. New York: Columbia University Press, 1988.

———. "Lost Opportunities for Compromise in the Bank War: A Reassessment of Jackson's Veto Message." *Business History Review* 61 (1987): 531–50.

Pessen, Edward. *Most Uncommon Jacksonians: The Radical Leaders of the Early Labor Movement.* Albany: State University of New York Press, 1967.

———. "Social Structure and Politics in American History." *American Historical Review* 87 (1982): 1290–1325.

———. "The Working Men's Party Revisited." *Labor History* 4 (1963): 203–26.

Petrella, Frank. "Daniel Raymond, Adam Smith, and Classical Growth Theory: An Inquiry into the Nature and Causes of the Wealth of America." *HOPE* 19 (1987): 239–59.

Pettit, Richard N., Jr. "Albert Brisbane: Apostle of Fourierism in the United States, 1834–1840." Ph.D. diss., Miami University, 1982.

Phillipson, Nicholas, and Quentin Skinner, eds. *Political Discourse in Early Modern Britain.* Cambridge: Cambridge University Press, 1993.

Pickens, Donald K., and G. L. Seligman. "'Unworthy Motives': Property, the Historian, and the Federal Convention: A Historiographic Speculation." *Social Science Quarterly* 88 (1987): 847–58.

Pittenger, Mark A. *American Socialists and Evolutionary Thought, 1870–1920.* Madison: University of Wisconsin Press, 1993.

Pocock, J. G. A. "Between Gog and Magog: The Republican Thesis and the Ideologia Americana." *JHI* 48 (1987): 325–46.

———. *The Machiavellian Moment: Florentine Political Thought and the Atlantic Republican Tradition.* Princeton: Princeton University Press, 1975.

———. *Politics, Language, and Time: Essays on Political Thought and History.* London: Methuen, 1972.

———. "The Reconstitution of Discourse: Toward the Historiography of Political Thought." *Modern Language Notes* 96 (1981): 959–80.

———. "States, Republics, and Empires: The American Founding in Early Modern Perspective." *Social Science Quarterly* 68 (1987): 703–23.

———. "Verbalizing a Political Act: Towards a Politics of Speech." *Political Theory* 1 (1973): 27–45.

Poore, Carol. "The Role of German Immigrants in the American Socialist Movement, 1877–1886." *Jahrbuch des Institute für Deutsche Geschichte* 12 (1983): 255–84.

Porter, Charlotte. *The Eagle's Nest: Natural History and American Ideas, 1812–1842.* University: University of Alabama Press, 1986.

Post, David M. "Jeffersonian Revisions of Locke: Education, Property Rights, and Liberty." *JHI* 47 (1986): 147–57.

Prude, Jonathan. *The Coming of Industrial Order: Town and Factory in Rural Massachusetts, 1810–1860.* Cambridge: Cambridge University Press, 1985.

Quint, Howard. *The Forging of American Socialism: Origins of the Modern Movement.* Indianapolis: Bobbs-Merrill, 1953.

Rader, Benjamin G. *The Academic Mind and Reform: The Influence of Richard T. Ely in American Life.* Lexington: University of Kentucky Press, 1966.

Rahe, Paul A. *Republics Ancient and Modern: Classical Republicanism and the American Revolution.* Chapel Hill: University of North Carolina Press, 1992.

Rakove, Jack N. "The Madisonian Moment." *University of Chicago Law Review* 52 (1988): 473–505.

Ransom, Roger. "Class and Inequality: Measuring the Impact of Industrial Capitalism in North America." *Historical Methods* 16 (1983): 157–61.

Rashid, Salim. "Adam Smith and the Division of Labour: A Historical View." *Scottish Journal of Political Economy* 33 (1986): 292–97.

Reddy, William. *Money and Liberty in Modern Europe: A Critique of Historical Understanding.* Cambridge: Cambridge University Press, 1987.

Reichart, Rolf, and Eberhard Schmitt, eds. *Handbuch politisch-sozialer Grundbegriffe in Frankreich, 1680–1820.* Munich: Oldenbourg, 1985.

Reid, Ronald F. *Edward Everett: Unionist Orator.* New York: Greenwood, 1990.

Resnick, Stephen A., and Richard D. Wolff. "Classes in Marxian Theory." *Review of Radical Political Economics* 13 (1982): 1–18.

———. *Knowledge and Class: A Marxian Critique of Political Economy.* Chicago: University of Chicago Press, 1987.

Richard, Carl J. "A Dialogue with the Ancients: Thomas Jefferson and Classical Philosophy and History." *Journal of the Early Republic* 9 (1989): 431–55.

Richter, Melvin. "Begriffsgeschichte and the History of Ideas." *JHI* 48 (1987): 247–63.

———. "Conceptual History (Begriffsgeschichte) and Political Theory." *Political Theory* 14 (1986): 604–37.

———. "Reconstructing the History of Political Languages: Pocock, Skinner, and the *Geschichtliche Grundbegriffe.*" *History and Theory* 39 (1990): 38–70.

———. "Understanding 'Begriffsgeschichte': A Rejoinder." *Political Theory* 17 (1989): 296–301.

Ricoeur, Paul. *Hermeneutics and the Human Sciences: Essays on Language, Action, and Interpretation.* Trans. and ed. John B. Thompson. Cambridge: Cambridge University Press, 1981.

———. *Interpretation Theory: Discourse and the Surplus of Meaning.* Fort Worth: Texas Christian University Press, 1976.

Riesman, Janet Ann. "The Origins of American Political Economy, 1680–1781." Ph.D. diss., Brown University, 1984.

Ritchie, Daniel E., ed. *Edmund Burke: Appraisals and Applications.* New Brunswick, N.J.: Transaction Press, 1990.

Ritter, Kurt, and James Andrews. *The American Ideology: Reflections of the Revolution in American Rhetoric.* Washington, D.C.: Speech Communication Association, 1978.

Rodgers, Daniel. *Contested Truths: Keywords in American Politics since Independence.* New York: Basic Books, 1987.

Roediger, David. "Ira Steward and the Anti-Slavery Origins of American Eight Hour Theory." *Labor History* 27 (1986): 410–26.

———. "Not Only the Ruling Class to Overcome, but Also the So-Called Mob: Class, Skill, and Community in the St. Louis General Strike of 1877." *Journal of Social History* 19 (1985): 213–39.

———. "What Was the Labor Movement? Organization and the St. Louis General Strike." *Mid-America* 67 (1985): 37–51.

Roper, Jon. *Democracy and Its Critics: Anglo-American Democratic Thought in the Nineteenth Century.* London: Unwin Hyman, 1989.

Ross, Dorothy. *The Emergence of Social Science.* Cambridge: Cambridge University Press, 1990.

———. "Socialism and American Liberalism: Academic Social Thought in the 1880s." *Perspectives in American History* 11 (1977–78): 7–79.

Ross, Steven J. "The Culture of Political Economy: Henry George and the American Working Class." *South California Quarterly* 65 (1983): 148–55.

———. "The Transformation of Republican Ideology." *Journal of the Early Republic* 10 (1990): 323–30.

Rosswurm, Steven. *Arms, Country, and Class: The Philadelphia Militia and the "Lower Sort" during the American Revolution.* New Brunswick, N.J.: Rutgers University Press, 1987.

———. "Equality and Justice: Documents from Philadelphia's Popular Revolution, 1775–1780." *Pennsylvania History* 52 (1985): 254–68.

Rothenburg, Winifred B. "The Emergence of Farm Labor Markets and the Transformation of the Rural Economy: Massachusetts, 1750–1855." *JEH* 48 (1988): 537–61.

Rutland, Robert A. *James Madison: The Founding Father.* New York: Macmillan, 1987.

———. "Madison's Bookish Habits." *Quarterly Journal of the Library of Congress* 37 (1980): 176–91.

Saccaro-Battisti, Giuseppa. "Changing Metaphors of Political Structures." *JHI* 44 (1983): 31–55.

Saum, Lewis O. *The Popular Mood of Pre–Civil War America.* Westport, Conn.: Greenwood, 1980.

Saxton, Alexander. "Problems of Class and Race in the Origins of the Mass Circulation Press." *American Quarterly* 36 (1984): 211–34.

———. *The Rise and Fall of the White Republic: Class Politics and Mass Culture in Nineteenth Century America.* New York: Verso, 1990.

Schlesinger, Arthur, Jr. *The Age of Jackson.* Boston: Little, Brown, 1953.

———. *Orestes A. Brownson: A Pilgrim's Progress.* New York: Octagon, 1963.

Schneriov, Richard. "Political Cultures and the Role of the State in Labor's Republic." *Labor History* 32 (1991): 376–400.

Schultz, Ronald. "Small Producer Thought in Early America." *Pennsylvania History* 54 (1987): 115–47.

———. "Thoughts among the People: Popular Thought, Radical Politics, and the Making of Philadelphia's Working Class, 1765–1828." Ph.D. diss., University of California, Los Angeles, 1985.

Schultz, Suzanne. *Horace Greeley: A Bio-Bibliography.* New York: Greenwood, 1992.

Schwartz, Barry. *Vertical Classification: A Study in Structuralism and the Sociology of Knowledge.* Chicago: University of Chicago Press, 1981.

Scott, William B. *In Pursuit of Happiness: American Conceptions of Property from the Seventeenth to the Twentieth Century.* Bloomington: Indiana University Press, 1977.

Seaman, John W. "Thomas Paine: Ransom, Civil Peace, and the Natural Right to Welfare." *Political Theory* 16 (1988): 120–42.

Searle, John. *Speech Acts: An Essay in the Philosophy of Language.* Cambridge: Cambridge University Press, 1969.

Sellers, Charles G. *The Market Revolution: Jacksonian America, 1815–1846.* New York: Oxford University Press, 1991.

Sen, Samar R. *The Economics of Sir James Steuart.* London: London School of Economics, 1957.

Sewell, William. *Work and Revolution in France: The Language of Labor from the Old Regime to 1848.* New York: Cambridge University Press, 1980.

Shalhope, Robert E. *John Taylor of Caroline: Pastoral Republican.* Columbia: University of South Carolina Press, 1980.

Shapiro, Fred R. "A Note on the Term 'Social Science'." *Journal of the History of Behavioral Sciences* 20 (1984): 20–22.

Shapiro, Michael J. *Language and Political Understanding: The Politics of Discursive Practices.* New Haven: Yale University Press, 1981.

———. *The Politics of Representation: Writing Practices in Biography, Photography, and Policy Analysis.* Madison: University of Wisconsin Press, 1988.

Sharp, James Roger. *The Jacksonians versus the Banks: Politics in the States after the Panic of 1837.* New York: Columbia University Press, 1970.

Sheehan, James. "Begriffsgeschichte: Theory and Practice." *JMH* 50 (1978): 312–19.

Shore, Laurence. *Southern Capitalists: The Ideological Leadership of an Elite, 1832–1885.* Chapel Hill: University of North Carolina Press, 1986.

Simpson, David. *The Politics of American English, 1776–1850.* New York: Oxford University Press, 1986.

Skinner, Andrew. "Adam Smith and the American Economic Community." *JHI* 37 (1976): 57–78.

Skinner, Andrew, and Thomas Wilson, eds. *Essays on Adam Smith.* Oxford: Clarendon, 1975.

Skinner, Quentin. "Language and Social Change." In *The State of the Language,* ed. Leonard Michaels and Christopher Ricks. Berkeley and Los Angeles: University of California Press, 1980.

———. "Meaning and Understanding in the History of Ideas." *History and Theory* 8 (1969): 3–53.

———. "Some Problems in the Analysis of Political Thought and Action." *Political Theory* 2 (1974): 277–303.

Smith, Wilson. *Professors and Public Ethics: Studies of Northern Moral Philosophers before the Civil War.* Ithaca, N.Y.: Cornell University Press, 1956.

Soltow, Lee. *Distribution of Wealth and Income in the United States in 1798.* Pittsburgh: University of Pittsburgh Press, 1989.

———. "Socioeconomic Classes in South Carolina and Massachusetts in the 1790s and the Observations of John Drayton." *South Carolina Historical Magazine* 81 (1980): 283–305.

———. "The Wealth, Income, and Social Class of Men in Large Northern Cities in 1860." In *The Personal Distribution of Income and Wealth,* ed. James D. Smith. New York: National Bureau of Economic Research, 1975.

———. "Wealth Inequality in the United States in 1798 and 1860." *Review of Economics and Statistics* 46 (1984): 444–51.

Spann, Edward K. *Brotherly Tomorrows: Movements for a Cooperative Society in America, 1820–1920.* New York: Columbia University Press, 1989.

———. *Ideals and Politics: New York Intellectuals and Liberal Democracy, 1820–1880.* Albany: State University of New York Press, 1972.

Steffen, Charles S. *The Mechanics of Baltimore: Workers and Politics in the Age of Revolution, 1763–1812.* Urbana: University of Illinois Press, 1984.

Steinberg, Marc. "Worthy of Hire: Discourse, Ideology, and Collective Action among English Working Class Trade Groups, 1800–1830." Ph.D. diss., University of Michigan, 1989.

Stevenson, Laura Caroline. *Praise and Paradox: Merchants and Craftsmen in Elizabethan Popular Literature.* Cambridge: Cambridge University Press, 1984.

Stewart, Donald. *The Opposition Press of the Federalist Period.* Albany: State University of New York Press, 1969.

Stewart, James B. *Wendell Phillips: Liberty's Hero.* Baton Rouge: Louisiana State University Press, 1986.

Stewart, M. A., ed. *Studies in the Philosophy of the Scottish Enlightenment.* Oxford: Clarendon, 1990.

Stinchcombe, Arthur L. "The Deep Structure of Moral Categories: Eighteenth Century French Stratification and the Revolution." In *Stratification and Occupation: Selected Papers.* New York: Cambridge University Press, 1986.

Strasser, Hermann. *The Normative Structures of Sociology: Conservative and*

Emancipatory Themes in Social Thought. London: Routledge and Kegan Paul, 1976.

Stromberg, Joseph R. "Country Ideology, Republicanism, and Libertarianism: The Thought of John Taylor of Caroline." *Journal of Libertarian Studies* 7 (1982): 35–48.

Sturges, Rodney P. *A Bibliography of George Poulett Scrope: Geologist, Economist, and Local Historian.* Boston: Baker Library, 1984.

Tariello, Frank, Jr. *The Reconstruction of American Political Ideology, 1865–1917.* Charlottesville: University Press of Virginia, 1982.

Taylor, Anne. *Visions of Harmony: A Study in Nineteenth Century Millenarianism.* Oxford: Clarendon, 1987.

Taylor, Barbara. *Eve and the New Jerusalem: Socialism and Feminism in the Nineteenth Century.* New York: Pantheon, 1983.

Taylor, Charles. "Interpretation and the Sciences of Man." *Review of Metaphysics* 25 (1971): 3–51.

Teichgraeber, Richard. *"Free Trade" and Moral Philosophy: Rethinking the Sources of Adam Smith's Wealth of Nations.* Durham, N.C.: Duke University Press, 1986.

Thomas, John L. *Alternative America: Henry George, Edward Bellamy, Henry Demarest Lloyd, and the Adversary Tradition.* Cambridge, Mass.: Belknap, 1983.

Thompson, E. P. "Eighteenth Century English Society: Class Struggle without Class?" *Social History* 3 (1978): 133–66.

———. *The Making of the English Working Class.* New York: Knopf, 1966.

Thompson, John B. *Ideology and Modern Culture: Critical Social Theory in the Era of Mass Communication.* Cambridge: Polity Press, 1990.

———. *Studies in the Theory of Ideology.* Cambridge: Polity Press, 1984.

Thompson, Noel W. *The People's Science: The Popular Political Economy of Exploitation and Crisis, 1816–1834.* Cambridge: Cambridge University Press, 1984.

Tribe, Keith. *Governing Economy: The Reformation of German Economic Discourse, 1750–1840.* Cambridge: Cambridge University Press, 1988.

———. *Land, Labour, and Economic Discourse.* London: Routledge and Kegan Paul, 1979.

Tucker, Susie. *Protean Shape: A Study in Eighteenth-Century Vocabulary and Usage.* London: Athlone, 1967.

Tully, James, ed. *Meaning and Context: Quentin Skinner and His Critics.* Princeton: Princeton University Press, 1989.

Twomey, Richard. "Jacobins and Jeffersonians: Anglo-American Radicalism in the United States, 1790–1820." Ph.D. diss., Northern Illinois University, 1974.

Unger, Irwin. *The Greenback Era: A Social and Political History of American Finance, 1865–1879.* Princeton: Princeton University Press, 1964.

Vaggi, Gianni. *The Economics of François Quesnay.* London: Macmillan, 1987.

———. "Social Classes and Income Distribution in Eighteenth Century Economics." *History of European Ideas* 9 (1988): 171–82.

Vanneman, Reeve, and Lynn Cannon. *The American Perception of Class*. Philadelphia: Temple University Press, 1984.

Varg, Paul A. *Edward Everett: The Intellectual in the Turmoil of Politics*. Selinsgrove, Pa.: Susquehanna University Press, 1992.

Veeser, H. Aram, ed. *The New Historicism*. New York: Routledge, 1989.

Veit-Brause, Irmline. "A Note on Begriffsgeschichte." *History and Theory* 20 (1981): 61–67.

Vincent, David. *Bread, Knowledge, and Freedom: A Study of Nineteenth Century Working Class Autobiography*. London: Europa, 1981.

Vinovskis, Maris A. "Searching for Classes in Urban North America." *Journal of Urban History* 11 (1985): 353–60.

Walhout, Mark Donald. "Hermeneutical Patriotism: Interpretation and Culture in Antebellum America." Ph.D. diss., Northwestern University, 1985.

Walker, Donald A., ed. *Perspectives on the History of Economic Thought*. Aldershot, England: Edward Elgar, 1989.

Walkowitz, Daniel, ed. *The Working Class in America*. Urbana: University of Illinois Press, 1981.

Wallace, Michael L. "Ideologies of Party in the Ante-Bellum Republic." Ph.D. diss., Columbia University, 1973.

Wallech, Steven. "Class versus Rank: The Transformation of Eighteenth Century English Social Terms and Theories of Production." *JHI* 47 (1986): 409–31.

———. "The Emergence of the Modern Concept of 'Class' in the English Language." Ph.D. diss., Claremont Graduate School, 1981.

Warner, William Lloyd. *Social Class in America: A Manual of Procedure for the Measurement of Social Status*. New York: Harper, 1960.

Waszek, Norbert. "The Division of Labor: From the Scottish Enlightenment to Hegel." *Owl of Minerva* 15 (1983): 51–76.

Watson, Harry. *Jacksonian Politics and Community Conflict*. Baton Rouge: Louisiana State University Press, 1981.

———. *Liberty and Power: The Politics of Jacksonian America*. New York: Hill and Wang, 1990.

Watts, Steven. *The Republic Reborn: War and the Making of Liberal America, 1790–1820*. Baltimore: Johns Hopkins University Press, 1987.

Wellenreuther, Hermann. "Labor in the Era of the American Revolution: A Discussion of Recent Concepts and Theories." *Labor History* 22 (1981): 573–600.

Welter, Rush. *The Mind of America, 1820–1860*. New York: Columbia University Press, 1975.

Wennerstern, John R. "Albert Brisbane." In *Antebellum Writers in New York and the South*, ed. Joel Myerson. Detroit: Gale, 1979.

Westerhoff, John H. *McGuffey and His Readers: Piety, Morality, and Education in Nineteenth-Century America*. Nashville: Abingdon, 1978.

Wharton, Leslie. *Polity and the Public Good: Conflicting Theories of Republican Government in the New Nation*. Ann Arbor: UMI Research Press, 1980.

White, James Boyd. *When Words Lose Their Meaning: Constitutions and Reconsti-*

tutions of Language, Character, and Community. Chicago: University of Chicago Press, 1984.

White, Lawrence. "William Leggett: Jacksonian Editorialist as Classical Liberal Political Economist." *HOPE* 18 (1986): 307–24.

White, Morton. *The Philosophy of the American Revolution.* New York: Oxford University Press, 1978.

———. *Philosophy, the Federalist, and the Constitution.* New York: Oxford University Press, 1987.

Whitten, William C. "The Economic Ideas of Thomas Cooper." *Essays in Economics* 20 (1969): 44–82.

Wiebe, Robert H. *The Opening of American Society.* New York: Knopf, 1984.

Wilentz, Sean. *Chants Democratic: New York City and the Rise of the American Working Class, 1788–1850.* New York: Oxford University Press, 1984.

———. "Class Consciousness and the American Labor Movement." *International Labor and Working Class History,* no. 26 (1984): 1–31.

———. "The Rise of the American Working Class." In *Perspectives on American Labor History: The Problems of Synthesis,* ed. J. Carroll Moody and Alice Kessler-Harris. De Kalb: Northern Illinois University Press, 1989.

Williams, Raymond. *Keywords: A Vocabulary of Culture and Society.* New York: Oxford University Press, 1976.

Willis, Kirk. "The Role in Parliament of the Economic Ideas of Adam Smith, 1776–1800." *HOPE* 11 (1979): 505–44.

Wilson, Major. "Republicanism and the Idea of Party in the Jacksonian Period." *Journal of the Early Republic* 8 (1989): 419–42.

Wilson, R. Jackson. *In Quest of Community: Social Philosophy in the United States, 1860–1920.* New York: John Wiley, 1968.

Winch, Donald. "Adam Smith: Scottish Moral Philosopher as Political Economist." *Historical Journal* 35 (1992): 91–114.

———. *Adam Smith's Politics: An Essay in Historiographic Revision.* Cambridge: Cambridge University Press, 1978.

———. "The Emergence of Economics as a Science, 1750–1870." In *The Fontana Economic History of Europe,* ed. Carlo Cipolla, vol. 3, *The Industrial Revolution.* London: Fontana, 1973.

———. "Science and the Legislator: Adam Smith and After." *Economic Journal* 93 (1983): 501–20.

Wise, M. Norton, and Crosbie Smith. "Work and Waste: Political Economy and Natural Philosophy in Nineteenth Century Britain." *History of Science* 27 (1989): 263–301, 391–449; 28 (1990): 221–61.

Wish, Judith. "From Yeoman Farmer to Industrious Producer: The Relationship between Classical Republicanism and the Development of Manufacturing in America from the Revolution to 1850." Ph.D. diss., Washington University, 1976.

Wood, Gordon. "The Authorship of *The Letters from a Federal Farmer.*" *WMQ* 31 (1974): 299–308.

———. *The Creation of the American Republic, 1776–1787.* Chapel Hill: University of North Carolina Press, 1969.

———. "A Note on Mobs in the American Revolution." *WMQ* 23 (1966): 635–42.

———. *The Radicalism of the American Revolution.* New York: Knopf, 1992.

———. "Rhetoric and Reality in the American Revolution." *WMQ* 23 (1966): 3–32.

———. "Social Radicalism and Equality in the American Revolution." In *The B. K. Smith Lectures in History, 1976.* Houston: University of St. Thomas, 1976.

Wood, P. B. "The Natural History of Man in the Scottish Enlightenment." *History of Science* 28 (1990): 89–123.

Wright, Erik Olin. *Classes.* London: Verso, 1985.

———. "Typologies, Scales, and Class Analysis." *American Sociological Review* 58 (1993): 31–34.

———. "Varieties of Marxist Interpretations of Class Structure." *Politics and Society* 9 (1980): 323–70.

Wright, Terence R. *The Religion of Humanity: The Impact of Comtean Positivism on Victorian Britain.* Cambridge: Cambridge University Press, 1986.

Wrightson, Keith. *English Society, 1580–1680.* New Brunswick, N.J.: Rutgers University Press, 1982.

———. "Estates, Degrees, and Sorts in Tudor and Stuart England." *History Today* 37 (1987): 17–22.

Xenos, Nicholas. "Classical Political Economy: The Apolitical Discourse of Civil Society." *Humanities and Society* 3 (1980): 229–42.

Young, Alfred, ed. *The American Revolution: Explorations in the History of American Radicalism.* De Kalb: Northern Illinois University Press, 1976.

Zboray, Ronald J. *A Fictive People: Antebellum Reading Development and the American Reading Public.* New York: Oxford University Press, 1993.

Zvesper, John. "The American Founders and Classical Political Thought." *History of Political Thought* 10 (1989): 700–718.

———. "The Madisonian Systems." *Western Political Quarterly* 37 (1984): 236–56.

———. *Political Philosophy and Rhetoric: A Study of the Origins of American Party Politics.* Cambridge: Cambridge University Press, 1977.

INDEX